CLASSICAL SOCIOLOGICAL THEORY: A READER

CLASSICAL SOCIOLOGICAL THEORY

A READER

Edited by Ian McIntosh

EDINBURGH UNIVERSITY PRESS

The texts are reprinted by permission of other publishers

Edinburgh University Press
22 George Square, Edinburgh

Reprinted 2000, 2002

Typeset in Garamond
by Bibliocraft, Dundee, and
printed and bound in Great Britain by
Bookcraft Ltd, Midsomer Norton, Bath

A CIP record for this book is available from the British Library

ISBN 0 7486 0873 7 (hardback)
ISBN 0 7486 0809 5 (paperback)

CONTENTS

ACKNOWLEDEMENTS

I would like to extend my thanks to the following people: Jackie Jones at Edinburgh University Press for her patience, Nicky Carr at EUP, Gail Hawkes, Emmanuelle Tulle-Winton and Janet Jamieson. Finally, thanks to Fiona Gavine.

NOTE ON THE TEXTS

For the sake of clarity and simplicity, many of the original footnotes have been omitted.

INTRODUCTION

'Marx, Weber and Durkheim. Why Bother?' Discuss.

Although the above 'exam question' is intended to be tongue-in-cheek it does tap into a serious issue that requires some attention. Perhaps it is reasonable to be sceptical as to what three long since dead men born in the nineteenth century can say to us as we fast approach the twenty-first. Obviously this book stands as ample testimony to the fact that I believe that they can still tell us a great deal. However, given that it is aimed primarily at those who may be coming to the works of Marx, Weber and Durkheim (MWD) for the first time it seems incumbent upon me to outline why I think much of value and interest can be found in their work. As part of this it may be useful initially to sketch out some context within which the writings of MWD can be located before pointing to their contemporary relevance. How I will be brief, as the main focus of this text is on the selection of readings and it is not my intention to add to the already long list of commentaries about MWD.

The Development of 'Sociological' Ideas

MWD are often held up as being the 'founding fathers' of sociology. This is something of a grand but misleading claim. All three have had a profound influence on the development of sociology, and will undoubtedly continue to do so for the foreseeable future; most introductory sociology courses, for example, devote a substantial amount of time to their work. However, concepts and ideas which could be described as 'sociological' pre-date MWD by hundreds of years and can be found, for example, in the writings and thought of the classical Greek philosophers. There are a number of individuals since that time who could sensibly be credited with 'founding' sociology, particularly those associated with the 'Enlightenment'. The 'Enlightenment' of the late seventeenth and eighteenth centuries involved a series of radical reorientations of Western thought that was in large part a consequence of the 'scientific revolution' of the late seventeenth century. René Descartes (1596–1650), Jean-Jacques Rousseau (1712–78) and Immanuel Kant (1724–1804) were among the key figures of this 'movement' which altered the way in which the social world, and the role of individuals within it, was understood and studied. The 'strong' Enlightenment vision argued that the human mind and human society were akin to nature inasmuch that they were 'rational' – they were ordered and governed by laws which could be understood through the application of a rigorous scientific approach, or, in short, the application of 'Reason'. The more optimistic Enlightenment thinkers thought that Reason could guide a process of positive change in the world and individuals could influence the course of history in the name of 'Progress'. Such 'Progress' could, it was hoped, free the individual from the yoke and shackles of traditional forms of power and authority – embodied by religion and the myriad ties of feudal obligation.

The 'social world' and 'society' increasingly came to be seen as objects of inquiry during the eighteenth century. Charles Louis de Secondat Montesquieu (1689–1755), portrayed by some as the first true sociologist, sought to uncover, via an empirically grounded and historical analysis, a definite structure and consistency to human behaviour under the apparently chaotic appearance of the social world. Montesquieu was a major influence on the glittering array of intellectuals such as David Hume (1711–76), Adam Smith (1723–90), Adam Ferguson (1723–1816), Dugald Stewart (1753–1828) and John Millar (1735–1801) who gravitated around Edinburgh and Glasgow and collectively constituted the 'Scottish Enlightenment'. From this group society, or perhaps more accurately 'civil society', in all its complexities, emerged firmly as a focus for historical and empirical inquiry. Indeed it could be argued that Ferguson's *An Essay on the History of Civil Society* (1767) and Millar's *The Origin of the Distinction of Ranks* (1779) were among the first works of sociology.

Two other figures from this period should be mentioned. Henri de Saint-Simon (1760–1825) was a crucial influence on generations of sociologists and through his investigations of the transition from a feudal society based on consumption to a modern society based on production he became the first and one of the most important analysts of 'Industrial Society'. Auguste Comte (1798–1857), who gave us the term 'sociology', a one time employee and acolyte of Saint-Simon, was important for developing the first comprehensive system of sociology. He sought to establish sociology as a positive science of society, one that could utilise the procedures of the natural sciences in order to uncover the 'universal laws' which he thought must govern social life. Such knowledge could be used, he thought, in the name of 'Progress', to improve the life of individuals and guide social change.

All of the above, and others besides, were important for laying down the intellectual and cognitive foundations upon which sociology would be constructed and they left, in different ways, their stamp on the work of MWD. But the development of sociology is not reducible solely to a number of individuals and their ideas. Many of the changes to the intellectual climate and culture of parts of Western Europe emerged from, and were the manifestations of, a series of dramatic social, political and economic upheavals. What arose out of this turmoil were in many ways the basic structures and relations of 'modern society' and this provided a powerful catalyst for the development of sociology as people grappled with the changes taking place around them.

The Birth of the 'Modern'

It is now part of the familiar history of sociology to state that it 'came of age' during two great transformations: the French Revolution (1789) and the 'Industrial

Revolution' which began in England in the eighteenth century and spread unevenly across parts of Europe. In many respects what emerged out of these transformations was 'modern society' and sociology developed as a consequence of the efforts made to try understand what constituted modern society – what was specifically 'modern' about it?

The French Revolution, and to a lesser extent the American revolution of 1776, ushered in new conceptions of politics and notions of individual rights and called into question traditional forms of power and authority such as the church, the absolutist state and feudal bondage. As Kumar suggests: 'no other event in the history of modern times has so powerfully aroused the sentiments of novelty, transformation, and the creation of a new order.'[1] The French Revolution created a climate of political change that dislocated individuals from existing social relations, often associated with the obligations of feudalism, and swept people along a path of political and social change propelled by secular ideals of liberty, equality and democracy. The legitimacy of 'traditional' lines of authority and control were, in many parts of Europe, if not broken up and dismantled, then at least placed under severe strain and scrutiny.

With the Industrial Revolution came, amongst other things, a dramatic increase in productive power with the development of mechanisation and the factory system, disruptions to the traditional organisation of labour and the widespread use of wage-labour, an intensification of the division of labour – roughly defined as the differentiation of tasks involved in the production of goods and services and the allocation of individuals or groups to them – a sometimes rapid process of urbanisation as people moved from the country to the town, the transformation of rural economies and societies into industrialised capitalist societies . . . one could go on. The point is that such changes taxed the minds of many theorists and generated not only a 'scientific' curiosity about how best to understand these developments but also a great concern for the consequences of 'traditional' society's apparently unstoppable passage along the road to modernity – although it is important not to underestimate the length of time this involved and the highly variable nature of this journey for many societies.

A number of social observers began to lament the passing of a 'traditional' form of life and, as Kumar writes, 'In a striking series of polarities the movement from the previous to the present order of society was conceptualised as a succession of two logically and sociologically contrasting states or types of society'.[2] Probably the most typical and famous of these was that of Ferdinand Tönnies (1855–1935) who drew a distinction between *Gemeinschaft* (community) and *Gesellschaft* (society or association); contrasting a social order which was rural, small-scale, communal and family based with one that was urban, industrial, impersonal and individualistic. Although these clear-cut polarities were never intended as accurate descriptions of any particular society – clearly tradition and family relations, for example, still play a key role in the life of even us late twentieth century 'moderns' – they did point to the cutting edge of change and graphically highlighted some of the major concerns of the early sociologists, concerns that have continued to play a crucial role within sociology and beyond.

This is where MWD are of such great importance. All three helped to map out the central concerns and parameters of sociology, in the process demarcating it from other intellectual disciplines such as psychology, philosophy, history and economics and posing some of the key questions of sociology. Questions such as: what is new about the world, how is modern society experienced, what is the essence of modernity, what were the conditions of its emergence, how is society possible, how is it maintained, what is going to happen to it, how can we understand the role of the individual within society? Questions such as these became the very stuff of sociology, ones that we are still endeavouring to answer and in an effort to do so we continue to utilise the approaches, insights and methods adopted by MWD and others such as Georg Simmel (1858–1918). We should not downplay the incredible diversity of what people do under the banner of sociology, but this period was crucial in carving out the core areas and concerns of sociology, marking out its parameters and delineating it, however fuzzily, from other approaches and academic disciplines.

Marx, Weber and Durkheim and Modernity

Perhaps it is their role as theorists of modernity that is the secret of the enduring influence of MWD. Unfortunately, but perhaps predictably, modernity is not an easy term to define. However it is fair to say that it refers to the constellation of characteristics typical of industrial, capitalist, and usually Western, societies, the contours of which were fashioned out of the great upheavals and transformations touched on above. It was part of the hopes of the Enlightenment that modern society, guided and aided by science, technology and Reason would represent shining examples of human 'Progress'. Unfortunately modernity appeared to have its 'dark side'. In 1835 the French politician, historian and sociologist Alexis de Tocqueville (1805–59) travelled, as did many other writers and intellectuals, to observe a rapidly expanding and crowded Manchester, the first truly industrial city and regarded as a great symbol of the modern age. Tocqueville caught the ambiguous and Janus-faced nature of modernity well when he wrote of Manchester that:

> From this foul drain the greatest stream of human industry flows out to fertilise the whole world. From this filthy sewer pure gold flows. Here humanity attains its most complete development and its most brutish; here civilisation makes its miracles, and civilised man is turned back almost into a savage.[3]

It was this negative side to modern society that became a focus for much of the work of MWD. In his celebrated study of modernity, *All That is Solid Melts Into Air*[4] Marshall Berman holds up the *Communist Manifesto* – from which Berman took his book title – as being the first great analysis of modernity. In this text, which is reproduced in large part below, Marx writes of the awesome productive power of capitalism and of how 'the bourgeoisie, during its rule of scarcely one hundred years, has created more massive and more colossal productive forces than have all preceding generations together', as it has 'pitilessly torn asunder the motley feudal ties that bound man to his natural superiors'. But the 'achievements' of capitalism and the methods of modern industry had not been achieved without a great cost. Wage-labour for Marx was a central pillar of capitalism and a social arrangement which was inherently exploitative and 'alienating', detaching the worker, in a number of ways, from the process of production. As Marx put it, in typically dramatic and damning tones, 'for exploitation, veiled by religious and political illusions, it has substituted naked, shameless, direct brutal exploitation'. However, Marx was above all a revolutionary and, unlike many other theorists, offered a 'way out': the revolutionary overthrow of capitalism and a socialist future.

Durkheim asked some basic questions about how, given the intensification of the division of labour within modern societies, it was still possible for society to be 'held' together and for individuals not to be embroiled in an anarchic free-for-all. The answer for Durkheim lay in the kind of solidarity and morality that bonded individuals together and formed a recognisable, and scientifically 'observable', social world. Durkheim drew a distinction between the 'mechanical solidarity' of 'simple' social forms and the 'organic solidarity' that was characteristic of complex societies. However the movement towards a perfectly functioning and balanced organic society was not a smooth process. Imbalances of regulation and integration within society could lead to situations of *anomie* – roughly, a state of normlessness – a social pathology which, amongst other things, could lead to an increase of the suicide rate. Durkheim was enough of an Enlightenment figure to believe that the 'science' of sociology, which he probably did more than any other to establish, could be used as a diagnostic tool to improve society and alleviate conditions of *anomie*.

Weber is regarded as the most pessimistic of the three writers, probably with good reason, for he believed that many tendencies and institutional arrangements within modern society involved grave consequences for the lives of individuals. Modern Western capitalist society was unremittingly a rational one. Rationality – for Weber, the key characteristic of modern times – pervaded all aspects of social life and was probably most evident in the bureaucratic forms of organisation that are a crucial part of modern life. Rationality, or too much of it, can have irrational consequences as ideals and values of liberty, fraternity and humanity can be suffocated under the weight of demands for efficiency and calculability, particularly within the capitalist marketplace. The modern world, thought Weber, was a disenchanted one and we were perhaps doomed to inhabit an 'iron cage' of rationality: a metaphor that is one of the most memorable and often used within sociology.

Marx, Weber and Durkheim and the Contemporary World

It seems clear, to me at least, that much of what MWD wrote still has a great contemporary relevance. Marx's analyses of the dynamics and workings of capitalism, the exploitative and alienating nature of wage-labour and the stratification of society into classes may all be controversial and continue to generate much debate and discussion but they still stand as a powerful set of arguments about, and critique of, modern society. One only has to think of the work that many people do and the conditions under which they do it, and the great concentrations of wealth and privilege and gross inequalities that are evident throughout a society such as ours, to appreciate the continued worth of many of Marx's writings.

Likewise, Weber's discussion of the pervasive nature of rationality – think, for example, of the expansion of the 'market' into the 'public sector' – and his 'ideal type' construction of bureaucratic organisations can surely still aid our understanding of the contemporary situation. After reading the selections included below taken from Weber's discussion of bureaucracy many familiar organisations (hospitals, universities etc.) may be seen in a different light. Further, Weber's analysis of 'charisma' is surely still useful for understanding recent public figures such as Mikhail Gorbachev and Margaret Thatcher. Durkheim's questions, and his attempts to answer them, about how, within an ever more complex society and intensified division of labour, 'society' still can be understood as a coherent entity and still, as it were, 'hangs' together in a meaningful sense are still central to anyone wishing to understand modern society. Have you ever wondered how such a complex society such as ours actually manages to 'work', or why it 'breaks down'?

MWD help us, in their different ways, to understand the relationship we, as individuals, have to this larger entity called society or the social world. A proper understanding of large constructions such as 'society' or 'nations' would, for those influenced by Weber, have to begin with the actions of individuals whereas after reading the work of Durkheim we may want to appreciate the *sui generis* nature of collective constructs: the 'fact' that many aspects of society are, for Durkheim, not reducible to individuals. To paraphrase Marx, people make history but not under circumstances of their own choosing, and it is this tension between individuals and society (or agency and structure to use the sociological terminology) that is a cornerstone of sociology, a proper understanding of which cannot be gained without recourse to the writings of MWD.

Most of these issues and more besides are dealt with in the selections below and they still, I would argue, have a great resonance today. This is not to say that everything that MWD wrote is still topical and up-to-the-minute; this is obviously not the case, and a number of the selections are included here primarily to illustrate the development of their thought rather than to be of direct contemporary relevance. Nor is it to argue that the world has remained exactly the same since the time of MWD it clearly has not, but then again has it changed all that much? If it has, then in what ways? Sometimes it appears that we are moving through times of unprecedented change, and many sociologists start out from this position, and at other times it is the clear lines of continuity with the past that become apparent. In either case MWD continue to be a great source of inspiration, ideas and explanation for those of us operating within sociology. If this were not the case then we could cheerfully confine them to a museum of sociological curiosities where those interested in such things can pay a visit now and again – but their ideas and programmatic statements for sociology have not yet, I would contend, passed their shelf-life.

Modern sociology everywhere reflects their influence. Weber is generally credited with being the central influence on interpretative and organisational sociology. Durkheim's influence is more pervasive and less easy to attach labels to, but his contribution to functionalism, anthropology, the sociology of crime and religion, for example, has been profound. Marx has a left an indelible mark on a vast range of academic disciplines, intellectual pursuits and political activities too numerous and extensive to be properly dealt with here. It should be noted that claiming Marx for sociology is somewhat problematic as he, as far as we can tell, never used the term sociology and certainly never thought of himself as a sociologist. Indeed one suspects that he would have been rather dismissive of such a 'bourgeois science' as sociology. But his impact on its development is such that he is routinely included amongst the classical sociologists. Indeed it would not be inaccurate to claim that much sociology in the twentieth century could be understood as a response to, and a critique of, Marxism – calling into question somewhat the radical and left-wing label that is consistently applied to sociology.

However it is time to strike a cautionary note. MWD dealt with many of the 'big' questions and were not constrained by the narrow concerns and specialisms that are a feature of academic life today. They ranged around the intellectual landscape borrowing from a range of disciplines as they saw fit, never concerned about treading on academic toes. However they were at the end of the day white middle class men of their times and this is reflected in their approaches, concerns and conclusions. All three were, to varying degrees, eurocentric and at times displayed an arrogance typical of male scholars of their own time – and of ours perhaps. Predictably they were also to a large extent 'gender blind' and all three operated within, and gazed upon, a 'masculine' world where women, if they featured at all, did so fleetingly. This is not to say that feminists, for example, have not found much of great value in their writings, particularly those of Marx, but their gender blindness, although by no means total, does have deleterious consequences for their theoretical frameworks, their methodological approaches and their ability to claim they have constructed a comprehensive account of the world. The best I can do within the context of these texts is to ask readers to bear this in mind.

How to Use This Book

The general aim of this book is to provide a convenient, useful and interesting starting point for a further exploration of the work of MWD. I have already indicated above some reasons why I believe this to be a worthwhile activity. However it is not without its pitfalls. MWD wrote a lot. The sight of the complete works of all three would be enough to demoralise even the most stout-hearted and committed students and send them running for cover. Also, as mentioned above, an awful lot of what MWD wrote is best avoided, unless you really have nothing else to do with your life or are given a long prison sentence – or, perhaps, both. The parts that are, in my opinion, worth reading are still vast and voluminous and involve a great deal of hard work to get through – it would not be the first time that I have nodded off whilst ploughing through, for example, Weber's *Economy and Society*. But it is well worth the effort, again for reasons touched on above, and at a more basic level it is surprising how often apparently 'new' sociological insights and theories have been covered and dealt with much earlier, often in a more convincing and incisive manner, by MWD. So perseverance pays off.

MWD's work, perhaps as a consequence of their output over a long period, all display contradictions, grey areas and confusions: given that they all possessed powerfully analytic and inquiring minds we can hardly expect it to be otherwise. Given this, and their aforementioned wide range of interests, attempts to squash, for instance, Weber into a box marked 'Conflict Theorist' and to attach a 'Functionalist' label to Durkheim, are at the least misleading and probably counterproductive. It is better to accept the nuances and subtleties of their writings and accommodate, and make allowances for, the contradictions and the inconsistencies, such as they are. Remember the social world is a complicated place!

Other consequences of their prodigious output are the issues of selection, interpretation and commentary. Numerous 'readers' such as this one could be culled from the works of MWD. This is not said in an effort to devalue this text – I hope that this 'reader' would rank with the best of them! – but it should alert us to the dangers of seeing certain books as 'definitive' statements or accounts of MWD. None, including this one, are; and we should bear in mind that all commentaries on MWD are other people's interpretations of certain texts and reflect their own particular interests and prejudices. This is not to say that there are no excellent and insightful commentaries about MWD (a number are suggested below) or to pretend that we will all find the time to read everything written by MWD; but it is best to be aware that all commentaries have their limitations. However this book does have the advantage of containing substantial selections of MWD's own writings and, after all, the best way really to get to grips with MWD is to read what they themselves wrote.

Before each section I have added a brief biography in order to sketch out some background and for each selection I have added a short introduction. This is done not as an attempt to 'explain' each piece but to provide some context for those who may be reading these writings for the first time, many of which are taxing enough without having to come to them completely 'cold'.

Obviously many of the selections below will be difficult to comprehend at first but this book is also intended as a resource, one that you can come back to time and again. The work of MWD is such that it justifies a constant re-reading. At the end of the day if this selection fuels a desire in some to seek out more from MWD then it can be counted a success.

Notes

1. K. Kumar, *Prophecy and Progress: The Sociology of Industrial and Post-Industrial Society* (Penguin: Harmondsworth, 1986) p.19.
2. Kumar, p.59.
3. C. Harvie, G. Martin and A. Scharf (eds), *Industrialisation and Culture* (Macmillan: London, 1970) p.42.
4. M. Berman, *All That is Solid Melts Into Air: The Experience of Modernity* (Verso: London, 1983).

GUIDE TO FURTHER READING: GENERAL

As mentioned above, the best way to understand Marx, Weber and Durkheim is, of course, to read the work of MWD themselves. However there is no point in being puritanical about this and there are a number of excellent texts which deal with all three of our authors. For a long time the best treatment of MWD within one volume was Anthony Giddens' *Capitalism and Modern Social Theory* (Cambridge University Press: London, 1971), although students often find this to be rather difficult in places. However, Giddens' long established text now, at last, has a serious rival in the form of *Understanding Classical Sociology: Marx, Weber and Durkheim* (Sage: London, 1995) by J. A. Hughes, P. Martin and W. W. Sharrock. Both of these books are highly recommended. R. A. Nisbet's book *The Sociological Tradition* (Heinemann: London, 1966) is still an excellent introduction to key sociological concepts via a discussion of MWD and others besides such as Hegel and Simmel. Krishan Kumar's classic *Prophecy and Progress* (Penguin: Harmondsworth, 1986) provides an excellent account of the 'great transformation' to 'industrial society' and the variety of ideas and theories that emerged to explain it. Similarly, Philip Abrams' *Historical Sociology* (Open Books: London, 1983) devotes much space to MWD's discussions of the development of industrialism.

David Lee and Howard Newby's well established text *The Problem of Sociology* (Hutchinson: London, 1983) contains much discussion of MWD. David Frisby and Derek Sayer's *Society* (Tavistock: London, 1986) deals with MWD in relation to the concept of 'society'. Raymond Aron's *Main Currents Within Sociological Thought*, Volumes 1 and 2 (Penguin: Harmondsworth, 1968) contains useful discussions of MWD. *Consciousness and Society: the Reorientation of European Social Thought 1890–1930* (MacGibbon and Kee: London, 1958) by H. Stuart Hughes is a beautifully written and provocative book that includes excellent appraisals of MWD. Tom Campbell's *Seven Theories of Human Society* (Oxford University Press: Oxford, 1981) is a surprisingly little used text which contains good introductions to MWD and some others. Alan Swingewood's *A Short History of Sociological Thought*, second edition, (Macmillan: London 1991) is an excellent and wide ranging introductory text. Another new text which deals with MWD is *Marx, Durkheim and Weber: Formations of Modern Social Thought* (Sage: London, 1995) by K. Morrison.

SECTION ONE
KARL MARX

KARL MARX: A BRIEF BIOGRAPHY

Karl Marx was born in 1818 in Trier, an ancient cathedral town on the River Moselle in Germany. Both Marx's parents were Jewish and most of the rabbis of Trier from the sixteenth century onwards were amongst his ancestors. Marx was brought up in a comfortable and relatively well-to-do middle-class home. In 1835 Marx, like his father before him, went to university (Bonn) to study law. At Bonn he seemed to spend most of his time, much to the chagrin of his father, drinking (he even spent a night in jail for 'disturbing the peace'), duelling, getting into debt (a tendency that never left him) and writing fairly bad romantic poetry. In 1836 Marx's father decided that he should transfer to Berlin University.

It was at Berlin that Marx came under the sway of the work of the great German philosopher Hegel. Although he quickly distanced himself from Hegel's idealist approach the emphasis within his system upon change and conflict as the driving force of history and his powerful dialectical form of thinking had an enduring influence upon Marx. After completing his doctoral thesis in 1841 (*The Difference Between the Democritean and Epicurean Philosophy of Nature*) Marx's increasingly radical views met with hostility from an increasingly reactionary Prussian state and he was denied a career in academia. Marx went to Cologne in 1842 and became editor of the *Rheinische Zeitung*. The paper was suppressed by the state and folded in 1843 and he moved to Paris. That year Marx married his long-time companion Jenny von Westphalen, daughter of the wealthy Baron von Westphalen; it was a marriage that would last until Jenny's death in 1881. Paris at this time was probably Europe's most vibrant and dynamic city and something of a hotbed of political and intellectual activity. It was here that Marx first encountered organised sections of the industrial working class and this had a great impact on him. It was in Paris also that Marx threw himself into a vast amount of reading, particularly the work of the classical political economists such as David Ricardo and Adam Smith. Long-time friend and comrade Arnold Ruge noted that Marx:

> reads a lot. He works in an extraordinarily intense way . . . but he never finishes anything – he interrupts every bit of research to plunge into a fresh ocean of books . . . He is more excited and violent than ever, especially when his work has made him ill and he has not been to bed for three or even four nights on end.[1]

At this time Marx wrote the famous '1844' or 'Paris' manuscripts (published, to something of a fanfare, in 1932) which contained an early formulation of his materialist method, his fullest discussion of alienation and an analysis of the revolutionary role of the working class. It was in Paris, in 1844, that Marx first cemented his crucial and lifelong friendship with Friedrich Engels, who at only twenty-three was already established as a brilliant radical journalist and author two years previously of the classic *The Condition of the Working Class in England.*

At the beginning of 1845 Marx was forced by the French Government to leave Paris and made his way to Brussels where he was joined by Engels who had by now become a full time 'revolutionary'. Together they wrote the *German Ideology* and became extremely politically active, establishing the Communist League in 1847 for which they produced, in 1848, the most famous of all socialist texts, *The Communist Manifesto.* 1848 was a year which witnessed a great wave of political upheaval and revolutionary activity in many parts of Europe. Predictably Marx was expelled from Belgium and went back to Paris for a time then returned to Cologne to edit the *Neue Rheinische Zeitung.* More political persecution followed and Marx finally arrived in London, via Paris again, in August 1849. In London he and Engels continued with their revolutionary activities starting up the Communist League again and editing yet another radical journal.

In 1850, and generally less politically active, Marx obtained a ticket for the reading-room of the British Museum and set off on a mammoth intellectual journey through the vast collection of books, particularly the huge economics section. This was intended to provide the research for a vast six-volume work, the *Economics,* which in the event he never finished and for which *Capital* was only a part.

That Marx achieved such an astonishing output is testimony to his enormous tenacity and capacity for work in the face of long periods of financial hardship – Engels constantly gave the Marx's money – frequent bouts of ill health and family tragedies; Marx outlived his wife and three of their children. He died in London in 1883 at the age of sixty-four leaving behind him a monumental body of work that continues to exert a major influence to this day.

Note

1. Quoted in D. McLellan, *Karl Marx: The Legacy* (BBC Books: London, 1983 p.22).

1.1 Alienated Labour

This selection, written when Marx was twenty-six, is part of Marx's famous 'Paris Manuscripts' of 1844 – not published until 1932. During this time Marx immersed himself in the writings of the great political economists such as David Ricardo (1772–1823) and Adam Smith (1723–90). Although he agreed with much of what they said, in particular that labour was the source of all wealth, he was critical of their tendency to see capitalism as a *natural* organisation of society and not, as he viewed it, as an *historically specific*, and thus not necessarily permanent, ensemble of relationships.

For Marx the ability to labour, to interact with nature and others, defined our humanness and set us apart from the instinctive 'labour' of animals. However, within capitalism the widespread use of wage-labour and the existence of private property leads to the 'alienation' of labour. The different aspects of alienation are discussed in this extract.

From: D. McLellan, *Karl Marx: Selected Writings* (Oxford University Press, 1977 pp.77–86).

We started from the presuppositions of political economy. We accepted its vocabulary and its laws. We presupposed private property, the separation of labour, capital, and land, and likewise of wages, profit, and ground rent; also division of labour; competition; the concept of exchange value, etc. Using the very words of political economy we have demonstrated that the worker is degraded to the most miserable sort of commodity; that the misery of the worker is in inverse proportion to the power and size of his production; that the necessary result of competition is the accumulation of capital in a few hands, and thus a more terrible restoration of monopoly; and that finally the distinction between capitalist and landlord, and that between peasant and industrial worker disappears and the whole of society must fall apart into the two classes of the property owners and the propertyless workers.

Political economy starts with the fact of private property, it does not explain it to us. It conceives of the material process that private property goes through in reality in general abstract formulas which then have for it a value of laws. It does not understand these laws, i.e. it does not demonstrate how they arise from the nature of private property. Political economy does not afford us any explanation of the reason for the separation of labour and capital, of capital and land. When, for example, political economy defines the relationship of wages to profit from capital, the interest of the capitalist is the ultimate court of appeal, that is, it presupposes what should be its result. In the same way competition enters the argument everywhere. It is explained by exterior circumstances. But political economy tells us nothing about how far these exterior, apparently fortuitous circumstances are merely the expression of a necessary development. We have seen how it regards exchange itself as something fortuitous. The only wheels that political economy sets in motion are greed and war among the greedy, competition.

It is just because political economy has not grasped the connections in the movement that new contradictions have arisen in its doctrines, for example, between that of monopoly and that of competition, freedom of craft and corporations, division of landed property and large estates. For competition, free trade, and the division of landed property were only seen as fortuitous circumstances created by will and force, not developed and comprehended as necessary, inevitable, and natural results of monopoly, corporations, and feudal property.

So what we have to understand now is the essential connection of private property, selfishness, the separation of labour, capital, and landed property, of exchange and competition, of the value and degradation of man, of monopoly and competition, etc. – the connection of all this alienation with the money system.

Let us not be like the political economist who, when he wishes to explain something, puts himself in an imaginary original state of affairs. Such an original stage of affairs explains nothing. He simply pushes the question back into a grey and nebulous distance. He presupposes as a fact and an event what he ought to be deducing, namely the necessary connection between the two things, for example, between the division of labour and exchange. Similarly, the theologian explains the origin of evil through the fall, i.e. he presupposes as an historical fact what he should be explaining.

We start with a contemporary fact of political economy:

The worker becomes poorer the richer is his production, the more it increases in power and scope. The worker becomes a commodity that is all the cheaper the more commodities he creates. The depreciation of the human world progresses in direct proportion to the increase in value of the world of things. Labour does not only produce commodities; it produces itself and the labourer as a commodity and that to the extent to which it produces commodities in general.

What this fact expresses is merely this: the object that labour produces, its product, confronts it as an alien being, as a power independent of the producer. The product of labour is labour that has solidified itself into an object, made itself into a thing, the objectification of labour. The realization of labour is its objectification. In political economy this realization of labour appears as a loss of reality for the worker, objectification as a loss of the object or slavery to it, and appropriation as alienation, as externalization.

The realization of labour appears as a loss of reality to an extent that the worker loses his reality by dying of starvation. Objectification appears as a loss of the object to such an extent that the worker is robbed not only of the objects necessary for his life but also of the objects of his work. Indeed, labour itself becomes an object he can only have in his power with the greatest of efforts and at irregular intervals. The appropriation of the object appears as alienation to such an extent that the more objects the worker produces, the less he can possess and the more he falls under the domination of his product, capital.

All these consequences follow from the fact that the worker relates to the product of his labour as to an alien object. For it is evident from this presupposition that the more the worker externalizes himself in his work, the more powerful becomes the alien, objective world that he creates opposite himself, the poorer he becomes himself in his inner life and the less he can call his own. It is just the same in religion. The more man puts into God, the less he retains in himself. The worker puts his life into the object and this means that it no longer belongs to him but to the object. So the greater this activity, the more the worker is without an object. What the product of his labour is, that he is not. So the greater this product the less he is himself. The externalization of the worker in his product implies not only that his labour becomes an object, an exterior existence but also that it exists outside him, independent and alien, and becomes a self-sufficient power opposite him, that the life that he has lent to the object affronts him, hostile and alien.

Let us now deal in more detail with objectification, the production of the worker, and the alienation, the loss of the object, his product, which is involved in it.

The worker can create nothing without nature, the sensuous exterior world. It is the matter in which his labour realizes itself, in which it is active, out of which and through which it produces.

But as nature affords the means of life for labour in the sense that labour cannot live without objects on which it exercises itself, so it affords a means of life in the narrower sense, namely the means for the physical subsistence of the worker himself.

Thus the more the worker appropriates the exterior world of sensuous nature by his labour, the more he doubly deprives himself of the means of subsistence, firstly since the exterior sensuous world increasingly ceases to be an object belonging to his work, a means of subsistence for his labour; secondly, since it increasingly ceases to be a means of subsistence in the direct sense, a means for the physical subsistence of the worker.

Thus in these two ways the worker becomes a slave to his object: firstly he receives an object of labour, that is he receives labour, and secondly, he receives the means of subsistence. Thus it is his object that permits him to exist first as a worker and secondly as a physical subject. The climax of this slavery is that only as a worker can he maintain himself as a physical subject and it is only as a physical subject that he is a worker.

(According to the laws of political economy the alienation of the worker in his object is expressed as follows: the more the worker produces the less he has to consume, the more values he creates the more valueless and worthless he becomes, the more formed the product the more deformed the worker, the more civilized the product, the more barbaric the worker, the more powerful the work the more powerless becomes the worker, the more cultured the work the more philistine the worker becomes and more of a slave to nature.)

Political economy hides the alienation in the essence of labour by not considering the immediate relationship between the worker (labour) and production. Labour produces works of wonder for the rich, but nakedness for the worker. It produces palaces, but only hovels for the worker; it produces beauty, but cripples the worker; it replaces labour by machines but throws a part of the workers back to a barbaric labour and turns the other part into machines. It produces culture, but also imbecility and cretinism for the worker.

The immediate relationship of labour to its products is the relationship of the worker to the objects of his production. The relationship of the man of means to the objects of production and to production itself is only a consequence of this first relationship. And it confirms it. We shall examine this other aspect later.

So when we ask the question: what relationship is essential to labour, we are asking about the relationship of the worker to production.

Up to now we have considered only one aspect of the alienation or externalization of the worker, his relationship to the products of his labour. But alienation shows itself not only in the result, but also in the act of production, inside productive activity itself. How would the worker be able to affront the product of his work as an alien being if he did not alienate himself in the act of production itself? For the product is merely the summary of the activity of production. So if the product of labour is externalization, production itself must be active externalization, the externalization of activity, the activity of externalization. The alienation of the object of labour is only the résumé of the alienation, the externalization in the activity of labour itself.

What does the externalization of labour consist of then?

Firstly, that labour is exterior to the worker, that is, it does not belong to his essence. Therefore he does not confirm himself in his work, he denies himself, feels miserable instead of happy, deploys no free physical and intellectual energy, but mortifies his body and ruins his mind. Thus the worker only feels a stranger. He is at home when he is not working and when he works he is not at home. His labour is therefore not voluntary but compulsory, forced labour. It is therefore not the satisfaction of a need but only a means to satisfy needs outside itself. How alien it really is is very evident from the fact that when there is no physical or other compulsion, labour is avoided like the plague. External labour, labour in which man externalizes himself, is a labour of self-sacrifice and mortification. Finally, the external character of labour for the worker shows itself in the fact that it is not his own but someone else's, that it does not belong to him, that he does not belong to himself in his labour but to someone else. As in religion the human imagination's own activity, the activity of man's head and his heart, reacts independently on the individual as an alien activity of gods or devils, so the activity of the worker is not his own spontaneous activity. It belongs to another and is the loss of himself.

The result we arrive at then is that man (the worker) only feels himself freely active in his animal functions of eating, drinking, and procreating, at most also in his dwelling and dress, and feels himself an animal in his human functions.

Eating, drinking, procreating, etc. are indeed truly human functions. But in the abstraction that separates them from the other round of human activity and makes them into final and exclusive ends they become animal.

We have treated the act of alienation of practical human activity, labour, from two aspects. 1. The relationship of the worker to the product of his labour as an alien object that has power over him. This relationship is at the same time the relationship to the sensuous exterior world and to natural objects as to an alien and hostile world opposed to him. 2. The relationship of labour to the act of production inside labour. This relationship is the relationship of the worker to his own activity as something that is alien and does not belong to him; it is activity that is passivity, power that is weakness, procreation that is castration, the worker's own physical and intellectual energy, his personal life (for what is life except activity?) as an activity directed against himself, independent of him and not belonging to him. It is self-alienation, as above it was the alienation of the object.

We now have to draw a third characteristic of alienated labour from the two previous ones.

Man is a species-being not only in that practically and theoretically he makes both his own and other species into his objects, but also, and this is only another way of putting the same thing, he relates to himself as to the present, living species, in that he relates to himself as to a universal and therefore free being.

Both with man and with animals the species-life consists physically in the fact that man (like animals) lives from inorganic nature, and the more universal man is than animals the more universal is the area of inorganic nature from which he lives. From the theoretical point of view, plants, animals, stones, air, light, etc. form part of human consciousness, partly as objects of natural science, partly as objects of art; they are his intellectual inorganic nature, his intellectual means of subsistence, which he must first prepare before he can enjoy and assimilate them. From the practical point of view, too, they form a part of human life and activity. Physically man lives solely from these products of nature, whether they appear as food, heating, clothing, habitation, etc. The universality of man appears in practice precisely in the universality that makes the whole of nature into his inorganic body in that it is both (i) his immediate means of subsistence and also (ii) the material object and tool of his vital activity. Nature is the inorganic body of a man, that is, in so far as it is not itself a human body. That man lives from nature means that nature is his body with which he must maintain a constant interchange so as not to die. That man's physical and intellectual life depends on nature merely means that nature depends on itself, for man is a part of nature.

While alienated labour alienates (1) nature from man, and (2) man from himself, his own active function, his vital activity, it also alienates the species from man; it turns his species-life into a means towards his individual life. Firstly it alienates species-life and individual life, and secondly in its abstraction it makes the latter into the aim of the former which is also conceived of in its abstract and alien form. For firstly, work, vital activity, and productive life itself appear to man only as a means to the satisfaction of a need, the need to preserve his physical existence. But productive life is species-life. It is life producing life. The whole character of a species, its generic character, is contained in its manner of vital activity, and free conscious activity is the species-characteristic of man. Life itself appears merely as a means to life.

The animal is immediately one with its vital activity. It is not distinct from it. They are identical. Man makes his vital activity itself into an object of his will and consciousness. He has a conscious vital activity. He is not immediately identical to any of his characterizations. Conscious vital activity differentiates man immediately from animal vital activity. It is this and this alone that makes man a species-being. He is only a conscious being, that is, his own life is an object to him, precisely because he is a species-being. This is the only reason for his activity being free activity. Alienated labour reverses the relationship so that, just because he is a conscious being, man makes his vital activity and essence a mere means to his existence.

The practical creation of an objective world, the working-over of inorganic nature, is the confirmation of man as a conscious species-being, that is, as a being that relates to the species as to himself and to himself as to the species. It is true that the animal, too, produces. It builds itself a nest, a dwelling, like the bee, the beaver, the ant, etc. But it only produces what it needs immediately for itself or its offspring; it produces one-sidedly whereas man produces universally; it produces only under the pressure of immediate physical need, whereas man produces freely from physical need and only truly produces when he is thus free; it produces only itself whereas man reproduces the whole of nature. Its product belongs immediately to its physical body whereas man can freely separate himself from his product. The animal only fashions things according to the standards and needs of the species it belongs to, whereas man knows how to produce according to the measure of every species and knows everywhere how to apply its inherent standard to the object; thus man also fashions things according to the laws of beauty.

Thus it is in the working over of the objective world that man first really affirms himself as a species-being. This production is his active species-life. Through it nature appears as his work and his reality. The object of work is therefore the objectification of the species-life of man; for he duplicates himself not only intellectually, in his mind, but also actively in reality and thus can look at his image in a world he has created. Therefore when alienated labour tears from man the object of his production, it also tears from him his species-life, the real objectivity of his species and turns the advantage he has over animals into a disadvantage in that his inorganic body, nature, is torn from him.

Similarly, in that alienated labour degrades man's own free activity to a means, it turns the species-life of man into a means for his physical existence.

Thus consciousness, which man derives from his species, changes itself through alienation so that species-life becomes a means for him.

Therefore alienated labour:

3. makes the species-being of man, both nature and the intellectual faculties of his species, into a being that is alien to him, into a means for his individual existence. It alienates from man his own body, nature exterior to him, and his intellectual being, his human essence.

4. An immediate consequence of man's alienation from the product of his work, his vital activity and his species-being, is the alienation of man from man. When man is opposed to himself, it is another man that is opposed to him. What is valid for the relationship of a man to his work, of the product of his work and himself, is also valid for the relationship of man to other men and of their labour and the objects of their labour.

In general, the statement that man is alienated from his species-being, means that one man is alienated from another as each of them is alienated from the human essence.

The alienation of man and in general of every relationship in which man stands to himself is first realized and expressed in the relationship with which man stands to other men.

Thus in the situation of alienated labour each man measures his relationship to other men by the relationship in which he finds himself placed as a worker.

We began with a fact of political economy, the alienation of the worker and his production. We have expressed this fact in conceptual terms: alienated, externalized labour. We have analysed this concept and thus analysed a purely economic fact.

Let us now see further how the concept of alienated, externalized labour must express and represent itself in reality.

If the product of work is alien to me, opposes me as an alien power, whom does it belong to then?

If my own activity does not belong to me and is an alien, forced activity to whom does it belong then?

To another being than myself.

Who is this being?

The gods? Of course in the beginning of history the chief production, as for example, the building of temples etc. in Egypt, India, and Mexico was both in the service of the gods and also belonged to them. But the gods alone were never the masters of the work. And nature just as little. And what a paradox it would be if, the more man mastered nature through his work and the more the miracles of the gods were rendered superfluous by the miracles of industry, the more man had to give up his pleasure in producing and the enjoyment in his product for the sake of these powers.

The alien being to whom the labour and the product of the labour belongs, whom the labour serves and who enjoys its product, can only be man himself. If the product of labour does not belong to the worker but stands over against him as an alien power, this is only possible in that it belongs to another man apart from the worker.

If his activity torments him it must be a joy and a pleasure to someone else. This alien power above man can be neither the gods nor nature, only man himself.

Consider further the above sentence that the relationship of man to himself first becomes objective and real to him through his relationship to other men. So if he relates to the product of his labour, his objectified labour, as to an object that is alien, hostile, powerful, and independent of him, this relationship implies that another man is the alien, hostile, powerful, and independent master of this object. If he relates to his own activity as to something unfree, it is a relationship to an activity that is under the domination, oppression, and yoke of another man.

Every self-alienation of man from himself and nature appears in the relationship in which he places himself and nature to other men distinct from himself. Therefore religious self-alienation necessarily appears in the relationship of layman to priest, or, because here we are dealing with a spiritual world, to a mediator, etc. In the practical, real world, the self-alienation can only appear through the practical, real relationship to other men. The means through which alienation makes progress are themselves practical. Through alienated labour, then, man creates not only his relationship to the object and act of production, as to alien and hostile men; he creates too the relationship in which other men stand to his production and his product and the relationship in which he stands to these other men. Just as he turns his production into his own loss of reality and punishment and his own product into a loss, a product that does not belong to him, so he creates the domination of the man who does not produce over the production and the product. As he alienates his activity from himself, so he hands over to an alien person an activity that does not belong to him.

Up till now we have considered the relationship only from the side of the worker and we will later consider it from the side of the non-worker.

Thus through alienated, externalized labour the worker creates the relationship to this labour of a man who is alien to it and remains exterior to it. The relationship of the worker to his labour creates the relationship to it of the capitalist, or whatever else one wishes to call the master of the labour. Private property is thus the product, result, and necessary consequence of externalized labour, of the exterior relationship of the worker to nature and to himself.

Thus private property is the result of the analysis of the concept of externalized labour, i.e. externalized man, alienated work, alienated life, alienated man.

We have, of course, obtained the concept of externalized labour (externalized life) from political economy as the result of the movement of private property. But it is evident from the analysis of this concept that, although private property appears to be the ground and reason for externalized labour, it is rather a consequence of it, just as the gods are originally not the cause but the effect of the aberration of the human mind, although later this relationship reverses itself.

It is only in the final culmination of the development of private property that these hidden characteristics come once more to the fore, in that firstly it is the product of externalized labour and secondly it is the means through which labour externalizes itself, the realization of this externalization.

This development sheds light at the same time on several previously unresolved contradictions.

1. Political economy starts from labour as the veritable soul of production, and yet it attributes nothing to labour and everything to private property. Proudhon has drawn a conclusion from this contradiction that is favourable to labour and against private property. But we can see that this apparent contradiction is the contradiction of alienated labour with itself and that political economy has only expressed the laws of alienated labour.

We can therefore also see that wages and private property are identical: for wages, in which the product, the object of the labour, remunerates the labour itself, are just a necessary consequence of the alienation of labour. In the wage system the labour does not appear as the final aim but only as the servant of the wages. We will develop this later and for the moment only draw a few consequences.

An enforced raising of wages (quite apart from other difficulties, apart from the fact that, being an anomaly, it could only be maintained by force) would only mean a better payment of slaves and would not give this human meaning and worth either to the worker or to his labour.

Indeed, even the equality of wages that Proudhon demands only changes the relationship of the contemporary worker to his labour into that of all men to labour. Society is then conceived of as an abstract capitalist.

Wages are an immediate consequence of alienated labour and alienated labour is the immediate cause of private property. Thus the disappearance of one entails also the disappearance of the other.

2. It is a further consequence of the relationship of alienated labour to private property that the emancipation of society from private property, etc., from slavery, is expressed in its political form by the emancipation of the workers. This is not because only their emancipation is at stake but because general human emancipation is contained in their emancipation. It is contained within it because the whole of human slavery is involved in the relationship of the worker to his product and all slave relationships are only modifications and consequences of this relationship.

Just as we have discovered the concept of private property through an analysis of the concept of alienated, externalized labour, so all categories of political economy can be deduced with the help of these two factors. We shall recognize in each category of market, competition, capital, money, only a particular and developed expression of these first two fundamental elements.

1.2 THE THESES ON FEUERBACH

These eleven points were jotted down by Marx sometime in 1845 and set out the differences between his materialism and that of Ludwig Feuerbach (1804–72) whose book *The Essence of Christianity* (1841) caused great controversy at the time. In that book Feuerbach outlined a materialist understanding of religion claiming that people project their humanness into a God, their own creation, which subsequently confronts them as something alien and detached and not as the product of their own collective thought. This notion, that the products of human minds and hands stand in relation to them as something detached and unconnected, recalls the previous discussion of alienation and foreshadows Marx's later discussion of the 'fetishism of commodities'. The first thesis clearly demonstrates Marx's dissatisfaction with materialism up to that point, with its fixed and mechanical portrayal of human activity. The last, most famous, 'thesis' has been something of a 'call-to-arms' for Marxists ever since it was written.

From: D. McLellan, *Karl Marx: Selected Writings* (Oxford University Press, 1977 pp.156–8).

I

The chief defect of all hitherto existing materialism (that of Feuerbach included) is that the thing, reality, sensuousness, is conceived only in the form of the object or of contemplation, but not as sensuous human activity, practice, not subjectively. Hence, in contradistinction to materialism, the active side was developed abstractly by idealism – which, of course, does not know real, sensuous activity as such. Feuerbach wants sensuous objects, really distinct from the thought objects, but he does not conceive human activity itself as objective activity. Hence, in *Das Wesen des Christentums*, he regards the theoretical attitude as the only genuinely human attitude, while practice is conceived and fixed only in its dirty-judaical manifestation. Hence he does not grasp the significance of 'revolutionary', of 'practical-critical', activity.

II

The question whether objective truth can be attributed to human thinking is not a question of theory but is a practical question. Man must prove the truth, i.e. the reality and power, the this-sidedness of his thinking in practice. The dispute over the reality or non-reality of thinking that is isolated from practice is a purely scholastic question.

III

The materialist doctrine concerning the changing of circumstances and up-bringing forgets that circumstances are changed by men and that it is essential to educate the educator himself. This doctrine must, therefore, divide society into two parts, one of which is superior to society.

The coincidence of the changing of circumstances and of human activity or self-changing can be conceived and rationally understood only as revolutionary practice.

IV

Feuerbach starts out from the fact of religious self-alienation, of the duplication of the world into a religious world and a secular one. His work consists in resolving the religious world into its secular basis. But that the secular basis detaches itself from itself and establishes itself as an independent realm in the clouds can only be explained by the cleavages and self-contradictions within this secular basis. The latter must, therefore, in itself be both under stood in its contradiction and revolutionized in practice. Thus, for instance, after the earthly family is discovered to be the secret of the holy family, the former must then itself be destroyed in theory and in practice.

V

Feuerbach, not satisfied with abstract thinking, wants contemplation; but he does not conceive sensuousness as practical, human-sensuous activity.

VI

Feuerbach resolves the religious essence into the human essence. But the human essence is no abstraction inherent in each single individual. In its reality it is the ensemble of the social relations.

Feuerbach, who does not enter upon a criticism of this real essence, is consequently compelled:

1. To abstract from the historical process and to fix the religious sentiment as something by itself and to presuppose an abstract – isolated human individual.
2. Essence, therefore, can be comprehended only as 'genus', as an internal dumb generality which naturally unites the many individuals.

VII

Feuerbach, consequently, does not see that the 'religious sentiment' is itself a social product, and that the abstract individual whom he analyses belongs to a particular form of society.

VIII

All social life is essentially practical. All mysteries which lead theory to mysticism find their rational solution in human practice and in the comprehension of this practice.

IX

The highest point reached by contemplative materialism, that is, materialism which does not comprehend sensuousness as practical activity, is the contemplation of single individuals and of civil society.

X

The standpoint of the old materialism is civil society; the standpoint of the new is human society, or social humanity.

XI

The philosophers have only interpreted the world, in various ways; the point is to change it.

1.3 *THE GERMAN IDEOLOGY* AND HISTORICAL MATERIALISM

The German Ideology was written by Marx (mostly) and Engels in 1846 in an attempt to 'settle accounts' with German philosophical positions. The massive manuscript runs to over 600 pages but is generally best known for containing the first, and one of the clearest, accounts of their 'materialist conception of history' – 'historical materialism' (Marx himself never actually used this phrase). In this passage we get a hint of the power and force of Marx's (and Engels') historical vision and method. The discussion of the growth of the 'division of labour', the development of private property, the separation of town and country, the growth of manufacturing and the subordination of (wage) labour is done with a masterful sense of the dynamics of history and a keen eye for historical detail. At the end of the extract we find Marx sketching out the tension between the newly emerging forces of production and the existing relations of production and the role of the working class as an agent of revolutionary change.

From: C. J. Arthur, *Marx: The German Ideology: Students Edition* (Lawrence and Wishart: London, 1970 pp.42–8, 72–9, 91–5.

First Premises of Materialist Method

The premises from which we begin are not arbitrary ones, not dogmas, but real premises from which abstraction can only be made in the imagination. They are the real individuals, their activity and the material conditions under which they live, both those which they find already existing and those produced by their activity. These premises can thus be verified in a purely empirical way.

The first premise of all human history is, of course, the existence of living human individuals. Thus the first fact to be established is the physical organisation of these individuals and their consequent relation to the rest of nature. Of course, we cannot here go either into the actual physical nature of man, or into the natural conditions in which man finds himself – geological, orohydrographical, climatic and so on. The writing of history must always set out from these natural bases and their modification in the course of history through the action of men.

Men can be distinguished from animals by consciousness, by religion or anything else you like. They themselves begin to distinguish themselves from animals as soon as they begin to *produce* their means of subsistence, a step which is conditioned by their physical organisation. By producing their means of subsistence men are indirectly producing their actual material life.

The way in which men produce their means of subsistence depends first of all on the nature of the actual means of subsistence they find in existence and have to reproduce. This mode of production must not be considered simply as being the production of the physical existence of the individuals. Rather it is a definite form of activity of these individuals, a definite form of expressing their life, a definite *mode of life* on their part. As individuals express their life, so they are. What they are, therefore, coincides with their production, both with *what* they produce and with *how* they produce.

The nature of individuals thus depends on the material conditions determining their production.

This production only makes its appearance with the *increase of population.* In its turn this presupposes the *intercourse* of individuals with one another. The form of this intercourse is again determined by production.

The relations of different nations among themselves depend upon the extent to which each has developed its productive forces, the division of labour and internal intercourse. This statement is generally recognised. But not only the relation of one nation to others, but also the whole internal structure of the nation itself depends on the stage of development reached by its production and its internal and external intercourse. How far the productive forces of a nation are developed is shown most manifestly by the degree to which the division of labour has been carried. Each new productive force, insofar as it is not merely a quantitative extension of productive forces already known (for instance the bringing into cultivation of fresh land), causes a further development of the division of labour.

The division of labour inside a nation leads at first to the separation of industrial and commercial from agricultural labour, and hence to the separation of *town* and *country* and to the conflict of their interests. Its further development leads to the separation of commercial from industrial labour. At the same time through the division of labour inside these various branches there develop various divisions among the individuals co-operating in definite kinds of labour. The relative position of these individual groups is determined by the methods employed in agriculture, industry and commerce (patriarchalism, slavery, estates, classes). These same conditions are to be seen (given a more developed intercourse) in the relations of different nations to one another.

The various stages of development in the division of labour are just so many different forms of ownership, i.e. the existing stage in the division of labour determines also the relations of individuals to one another with reference to the material, instrument, and product of labour.

The first form of ownership is tribal ownership. It corresponds to the undeveloped stage of production, at which a people lives by hunting and fishing, by the rearing of beasts or, in the highest stage, agriculture. In the latter case it presupposes a great mass of uncultivated stretches of land. The division of labour is at this stage still very elementary and is confined to a further extension of the natural division of labour existing in the family. The social structure is, therefore, limited to an extension of the family; patriarchal family chieftains, below them the members of the tribe, finally slaves. The slavery latent in the family only develops gradually with the increase of population, the growth of wants, and with the extension of external relations, both of war and of barter.

The second form is the ancient communal and State ownership which proceeds especially from the union of several tribes into a *city* by agreement or by conquest, and which is still accompanied by slavery. Beside communal ownership we already find movable, and later also immovable, private property developing, but as an abnormal form subordinate to communal ownership. The citizens hold power over their labouring slaves only in their community, and on this account alone, therefore, they are bound to the form of communal ownership. It is the communal private property which compels the active citizens to remain in this spontaneously derived form of association over against their slaves. For this reason the whole structure of society based on this communal ownership, and with it the power of the people, decays in the same measure as, in particular, immovable private property evolves. The division of labour is already more developed. We already find the antagonism of town and country; later the antagonism between those states which represent town interests and those which represent country interests, and inside the towns themselves the antagonism between industry and maritime commerce. The class relation between citizens and slaves is now completely developed.

With the development of private property, we find here for the first time the same conditions which we shall find again, only on a more extensive scale, with modern private property. On the one hand, the concentration of private property, which began very early in Rome and proceeded very rapidly from the time of the civil wars and especially under the Emperors; on the other hand, coupled with this, the transformation of the plebeian small peasantry into a proletariat, which, however, owing to its intermediate position between propertied citizens and slaves, never achieved an independent development.

The third form of ownership is feudal or estate property. If antiquity started out from the *town* and its little territory, the Middle Ages started out from the *country*. This different starting-point was determined by the sparseness of the population at that time, which was scattered over a large area and which received no large increase from the conquerors. In contrast to Greece and Rome, feudal development at the outset, therefore, extends over a much wider territory, prepared by the Roman conquests and the spread of agriculture at first associated with it. The last centuries of the declining Roman Empire and its conquest by the barbarians destroyed a number of productive forces; agriculture had declined, industry had decayed for want of a market, trade had died out or been violently suspended, the rural and urban population had decreased. From these conditions and the mode of organisation of the conquest determined by them, feudal property developed under the influence of the Germanic military constitution. Like tribal and communal ownership, it is based again on a community; but the directly producing class standing over against it is not, as in the case of the ancient community, the slaves, but the enserfed small peasantry. As soon as feudalism is fully developed, there also arises antagonism to the towns. The hierarchical structure of landownership, and the armed bodies of retainers associated with it, gave the nobility power over the serfs. This feudal organisation was, just as much as the ancient communal ownership, an association against a subjected producing class; but the form of association and the relation to the direct producers were different because of the different conditions of production.

This feudal system of landownership had its counterpart in the *towns* in the shape of corporative property, the feudal organisation of trades. Here property consisted chiefly in the labour of each individual person. The necessity for association against the organised robber-nobility, the need for communal covered markets in an age when the industrialist was at the same time a merchant, the growing competition of the escaped serfs swarming into the rising towns, the feudal structure of the whole country: these combined to bring about the *guilds*. The gradually accumulated small capital of individual craftsmen and their stable numbers, as against the growing population, evolved the relation of journeyman and apprentice, which brought into being in the towns a hierarchy similar to that in the country.

Thus the chief form of property during the feudal epoch consisted on the one hand of landed property with serf labour chained to it, and on the other of the labour of the individual with small capital commanding the labour of journeymen. The organisation of both was determined by the restricted conditions of production – the small-scale and primitive cultivation of the land, and the craft type of industry. There was little division of labour in the heyday of feudalism. Each country bore in itself the antithesis of town and country; the division into estates was certainly strongly marked; but apart from the differentiation of princes, nobility, clergy and peasants in the country, and masters, journeymen, apprentices and soon also the rabble of casual labourers in the towns, no division of importance took place. In agriculture it was rendered difficult by the strip-system, beside which the cottage industry of the peasants themselves emerged. In industry there was no division of labour at all in the individual trades themselves, and very little between them. The separation of industry and commerce was found already in existence in older towns; in the newer it only developed later, when the towns entered into mutual relations.

The grouping of larger territories into feudal kingdoms was a necessity for the landed nobility as for the towns. The organisation of the ruling class, the nobility, had, therefore, everywhere a monarch at its head.

The fact is, therefore, that definite individuals who are productively active in a definite way enter into these definite social and political relations. Empirical observation must in each separate instance bring out empirically, and without any mystification and speculation, the connection of the social and political structure with production. The social structure and the State are continually evolving out of the life-process of definite individuals, but of individuals, not as they may appear in their own or other people's imagination, but as they *really* are; i.e. as they operate, produce materially, and hence as they work under definite material limits, presuppositions and conditions independent of their will.

The production of ideas, of conceptions, of consciousness, is at first directly interwoven with the material activity and the material intercourse of men, the language of real life. Conceiving, thinking, the mental intercourse of men, appear at this stage as the direct efflux of their material behaviour. The same applies to mental production as expressed in the language of politics, laws, morality, religion, metaphysics, etc. of a people. Men are the producers of their conceptions, ideas, etc. – real, active men, as they are conditioned by a definite development of their productive forces and of the intercourse corresponding to these, up to its furthest forms. Consciousness can never be anything else than conscious existence, and the existence of men is their actual life-process. If in all ideology men and their circumstances appear upside-down as in a *camera obscura*, this phenomenon arises just as much from their historical life-process as the inversion of objects on the retina does from their physical life-process.

In direct contrast to German philosophy which descends from heaven to earth, here we ascend from earth to heaven. That is to say, we do not set out from what men say, imagine, conceive, nor from men as narrated, thought of, imagined, conceived, in order to arrive at men in the flesh. We set out from real, active men, and on the basis of their real life-process we demonstrate the development of the ideological reflexes and echoes of this life-process. The phantoms formed in the human brain are also, necessarily, sublimates of their material life-process, which is empirically verifiable and bound to material premises. Morality, religion, metaphysics, all the rest of ideology and their corresponding forms of consciousness, thus no longer retain the semblance of independence. They have no history, no development; but men, developing their material production and their material intercourse, alter, along with this their real existence, their thinking and the products of their thinking. Life is not determined by consciousness, but consciousness by life. In the first method of approach the starting-point is consciousness taken as the living individual; in the second method, which conforms to real life, it is the real living individuals themselves, and consciousness is considered solely as *their* consciousness.

This method of approach is not devoid of premises. It starts out from the real premises and does not abandon them for a moment. Its premises are men, not in any fantastic isolation and rigidity, but in their actual, empirically perceptible process of development under definite conditions. As soon as this active life-process is described, history ceases to be a collection of dead facts as it is with the empiricists (themselves still abstract), or an imagined activity of imagined subjects, as with the idealists.

Where speculation ends – in real life – there real, positive science begins: the representation of the practical activity, of the practical process of development of men. Empty talk about consciousness ceases, and real knowledge has to take its place. When reality is depicted, philosophy as an independent branch of knowledge loses its medium of existence. At the best its place can only be taken by a summing-up of the most general results, abstractions which arise from the observation of the historical development of men. Viewed apart from real history, these abstractions have in themselves no value whatsoever. They can only serve to facilitate the arrangement of historical material, to indicate the sequence of its separate strata. But they by no means afford a recipe or schema, as does philosophy, for neatly trimming the epochs of history. On the contrary, our difficulties begin only when we set about the observation and the arrangement – the real depiction – of our historical material, whether of a past epoch or of the present. The removal of these difficulties is governed by premises which it is quite impossible to state here, but which only the study of the actual life-process and the activity of the individuals of each epoch will make evident. [. . .]

The Rise of Manufacturing

The immediate consequence of the division of labour between the various towns was the rise of manufactures, branches of production which had outgrown the guild-system. Manufactures first flourished in Italy and later in Flanders, under the historical premise of commerce with foreign nations. In other countries, England and France for example, manufactures were at first confined to the home market. Besides the premises already mentioned manufactures depend on an already advanced concentration of population, particularly in the countryside, and of capital, which began to accumulate in the hands of individuals, partly in the guilds in spite of the guild regulations, partly among the merchants.

That labour which from the first presupposed a machine, even of the crudest sort, soon showed itself the most capable of development. Weaving, earlier carried on in the country by the peasants as a secondary occupation to procure their clothing, was the first labour to receive an impetus and a further development through the extension of commerce. Weaving was the first and remained the principal manufacture. The rising demand for clothing materials, consequent on the growth of population, the growing accumulation and mobilisation of natural capital through accelerated circulation, the demand for luxuries called forth by the latter and favoured generally by the gradual extension of commerce, gave weaving a quantitative and qualitative stimulus, which wrenched it out of the form of production hitherto existing. Alongside the peasants weaving for their own use, who continued, and still continue, with this sort of work, there emerged a new class of weavers in the towns, whose fabrics were destined for the whole home market and usually for foreign markets too.

Weaving, an occupation demanding in most cases little skill and soon splitting up into countless branches, by its whole nature resisted the trammels of the guild. Weaving was, therefore, carried on mostly in villages and market-centres without guild organisation, which gradually became towns, and indeed the most flourishing towns in each land.

With guild-free manufacture, property relations also quickly changed. The first advance beyond naturally derived estate capital was provided by the rise of merchants whose capital was from the beginning movable, capital in the modern sense as far as one can speak of it, given the circumstances of those times. The second advance came with manufacture, which again made mobile a mass of natural capital, and altogether increased the mass of movable capital as against that of natural capital.

At the same time, manufacture became a refuge of the peasants from the guilds which excluded them or paid them badly, just as earlier the guild-towns had [served] as a refuge for the peasants from [the oppressive landed nobility].

Simultaneously with the beginning of manufactures there was a period of vagabondage caused by the abolition of the feudal bodies of retainers, the disbanding of the swollen armies which had flocked to serve the kings against their vassals, the improvement of agriculture, and the transformation of great strips of tillage into pasture land. From this alone it is clear how this vagabondage is strictly connected with the disintegration of the feudal system. As early as the thirteenth century we find isolated epochs of this kind, but only at the end of the fifteenth and beginning of the sixteenth does this vagabondage make a general and permanent appearance. These vagabonds, who were so numerous that, for instance, Henry VIII of England had 72,000 of them hanged, were only prevailed upon to work with the greatest difficulty and through the most extreme necessity, and then only after long resistance. The rapid rise of manufactures, particularly in England, absorbed them gradually.

With the advent of manufactures, the various nations entered into a competitive relationship, the struggle for trade, which was fought out in wars, protective duties and prohibitions, whereas earlier the nations, insofar as they were connected at all, had carried on an inoffensive exchange with each other. Trade had from now on a political significance.

With the advent of manufacture the relationship between worker and employer changed. In the guilds the patriarchal relationship between journeyman and master continued to exist; in manufacture its place was taken by the monetary relation between worker and capitalist – a relationship which in the countryside and in small towns retained a patriarchal tinge, but in the larger, the real manufacturing towns, quite early lost almost all patriarchal complexion.

Manufacture and the movement of production in general received an enormous impetus through the extension of commerce which came with the discovery of America and the sea-route to the East Indies. The new products imported thence, particularly the masses of gold and silver which came into circulation and totally changed the position of the classes towards one another, dealing a hard blow to feudal landed property and to the workers; the expeditions of adventurers, colonisation; and above all the extension of markets into a world market, which had now become possible and was daily becoming more and more a fact, called forth a new phase of historical development, into which in general we cannot here enter further. Through the colonisation of the newly discovered countries the commercial struggle of the nations amongst one another was given new fuel and accordingly greater extension and animosity.

The expansion of trade and manufacture accelerated the accumulation of movable capital, while in the guilds, which were not stimulated to extend their production, natural capital remained stationary or even declined. Trade and manufacture created the big bourgeoisie; in the guilds was concentrated the petty bourgeoisie, which no longer was dominant in the towns as formerly, but had to bow to the might of the great merchants and manufacturers. Hence the decline of the guilds, as soon as they came into contact with manufacture.

The intercourse of nations took on, in the epoch of which we have been speaking, two different forms. At first the small quantity of gold and silver in circulation involved the ban on the export of these metals; and industry, for the most part imported from abroad and made necessary by the need for employing the growing urban population, could not do without those privileges which could be granted not only, of course, against home competition, but chiefly against foreign. The local guild privilege was in these original prohibitions extended over the whole nation. Customs duties originated from the tributes which the feudal lords exacted as protective levies against robbery from merchants passing through their territories, tributes later imposed likewise by the towns, and which, with the rise of the modern states, were the Treasury's most obvious means of raising money.

The appearance of American gold and silver on the European markets, the gradual development of industry, the rapid expansion of trade and the consequent rise of the non-guild bourgeoisie and of money, gave these measures another significance. The State, which was daily less and less able to do without money, now retained the ban on the export of gold and silver out of fiscal considerations; the bourgeois, for whom these masses of money which were hurled onto the market became the chief object of speculative buying, were thoroughly content with this; privileges established earlier became a source of income for the government and were sold for money; in the customs legislation there appeared the export duty, which, since it only [placed] a hindrance in the way of industry, had a purely fiscal aim.

The second period began in the middle of the seventeenth century and lasted almost to the end of the eighteenth. Commerce and navigation had expanded more rapidly than manufacture, which played a secondary role; the colonies were becoming considerable consumers; and after long struggles the separate nations shared out the opening world market among themselves. This period begins with the Navigation Laws and colonial monopolies. The competition of the nations among themselves was excluded as far as possible by tariffs, prohibitions and treaties; and in the last resort the competitive struggle was carried on and decided by wars (especially naval wars). The mightiest maritime nation, the English, retained preponderance in trade and manufacture. Here, already, we find concentration in one country.

Manufacture was all the time sheltered by protective duties in the home market, by monopolies in the colonial market, and abroad as much as possible by differential duties. The working-up of home-produced material was encouraged (wool and linen in England, silk in France), the export of home-produced raw material forbidden (wool in England), and the [working-up] of imported material neglected or suppressed (cotton in England). The nation dominant in sea trade and colonial power naturally secured for itself also the greatest quantitative and qualitative expansion of manufacture. Manufacture could not be carried on without protection, since, if the slightest change takes place in other countries, it can lose its market and be ruined; under reasonably favourable conditions it may easily be introduced into a country, but for this very reason can easily be destroyed. At the same time through the mode in which it is carried on, particularly in the eighteenth century, in the countryside, it is to such an extent interwoven with the vital relationships of a great mass of individuals, that no country dare jeopardise its existence by permitting free competition. Insofar as it manages to export, it therefore depends entirely on the extension or restriction of commerce, and exercises a relatively very small reaction [on the latter]. Hence its secondary [importance] and the influence of [the merchants] in the eighteenth century. It was the merchants and especially the shippers who more than anybody else pressed for State protection and monopolies; the manufacturers also demanded and indeed received protection, but all the time were inferior in political importance to the merchants. The commercial towns, particularly the maritime towns, became to some extent civilised and acquired the outlook of the big bourgeoisie, but in the factory towns an extreme petty-bourgeois outlook persisted. The eighteenth century was the century of trade.

This period is also characterised by the cessation of the bans on the export of gold and silver and the beginning of the trade in money; by banks, national debts, paper money; by speculation in stocks and shares and stockjobbing in all articles; by the development of finance in general. Again capital lost a great part of the natural character which had still clung to it.

The concentration of trade and manufacture in one country, England, developing irresistibly in the seventeenth century, gradually created for this country a relative world market, and thus a demand for the manufactured products of this country, which could no longer be met by the industrial productive forces hitherto existing. This demand, outgrowing the productive forces, was the motive power which, by producing big industry – the application of elemental forces to industrial ends, machinery and the most complex division of labour – called into existence the third period of private ownership since the Middle Ages. There already existed in England the other pre-conditions of this new phase: freedom of competition inside the nation, the development of theoretical mechanics, etc. (Indeed, the science of mechanics perfected by Newton was altogether the most popular science in France and England in the eighteenth century.) (Free competition inside the nation itself had everywhere to be conquered by a revolution – 1640 and 1688 in England, 1789 in France.) Competition soon compelled every country that wished to retain its historical role to protect its manufactures by renewed customs regulations (the old duties were no longer any good against big industry) and soon after to introduce big industry under protective duties. Big industry universalised competition in spite of these protective measures (it is practical free trade; the protective duty is only a palliative, a measure of defence *within* free trade), established means of communication and the modern world market, subordinated trade to itself, transformed all capital into industrial capital, and thus produced the rapid circulation (development of the financial system) and the centralisation of capital. By universal competition it forced all individuals to strain their energy to the utmost. It destroyed as far as possible ideology, religion, morality, etc. and where it could not do this, made them into a palpable lie. It produced world history for the first time, insofar as it made all civilised nations and every individual member of them dependent for the satisfaction of their wants on the whole world, thus destroying the former natural exclusiveness of separate nations. It made natural science subservient to capital and took from the division of labour the last semblance of its natural character. It destroyed natural growth in general, as far as this is possible while labour exists, and resolved all natural relationships into money relationships. In the place of naturally grown towns it created the modern, large industrial cities which have sprung up overnight. Wherever it penetrated, it destroyed the crafts and all earlier stages of industry. It completed the victory of the commercial town over the countryside. [Its first premise] was the automatic system. [Its development] produced a mass of productive forces, for which private [property] became just as much a fetter as the guild had been for manufacture and the small, rural workshop for the developing craft. These productive forces received under the system of private property a one-sided development only, and became for the majority destructive forces; moreover, a great multitude of such forces could find no application at all within this system. Generally speaking, big industry created everywhere the same relations between the classes of society, and thus destroyed the peculiar individuality of the various nationalities. And finally, while the bourgeoisie of each nation still retained separate national interests, big industry created a class, which in all nations has the same interest and with which nationality is already dead; a class which is really rid of all the old world and at the same time stands pitted against it. Big industry makes for the worker not only the relation to the capitalist, but labour itself, unbearable.

It is evident that big industry does not reach the same level of development in all districts of a country. This does not, however, retard the class movement of the proletariat, because the proletarians created by big industry assume leadership of this movement and carry the whole mass along with them, and because the workers excluded from big industry are placed by it in a still worse situation than the workers in big industry itself. The countries in which big industry is developed act in a similar manner upon the more or less non-industrial countries, insofar as the latter are swept by universal commerce into the universal competitive struggle.

These different forms are just so many forms of the organisation of labour, and hence of property. In each period a unification of the existing productive forces takes place, insofar as this has been rendered necessary by needs. [. . .]

Contradictions of Big Industry: Revolution

Our investigation hitherto started from the instruments of production, and it has already shown that private property was a necessity for certain industrial stages. In *industrie extractive* private property still coincides with labour; in small industry and all agriculture up till now property is the necessary consequence of the existing instruments of production; in big industry the contradiction between the instrument of production and private property appears from the first time and is the product of big industry; moreover, big industry must be highly developed to produce this contradiction. And thus only with big industry does the abolition of private property become possible.

In big industry and competition the whole mass of conditions of existence, limitations, biases of individuals, are fused together into the two simplest forms: private property and labour. With money every form of intercourse, and intercourse itself, is considered fortuitous for the individuals. Thus money implies that all previous intercourse was only intercourse of individuals under particular conditions, not of individuals as individuals. These conditions are reduced to two: accumulated labour or private property, and acrual labour. If both or one of these ceases, then intercourse comes to a standstill. The modern economists themselves, e.g. Sismondi, Cherbuliez, etc., oppose association of individuals to association of capital. On the other hand, the individuals themselves are entirely subordinated to the division of labour and hence are brought into the most complete dependence on one another. Private property, insofar as within labour itself it is opposed to labour, evolves out of the necessity of accumulation, and has still, to begin with, rather the form of the communality; but in its further development it approaches more and more the modern form of private property. The division of labour implies from the outset the division of the *conditions* of labour, of tools and materials, and thus the splitting-up of accumulated capital among different owners, and thus, also, the division between capital and labour, and the different forms of property itself. The more the division of labour develops and accumulation grows, the sharper are the forms that this process of differentiation assumes. Labour itself can only exist on the premise of this fragmentation.

Thus two facts are here revealed. First the productive forces appear as a world for themselves, quite independent of and divorced from the individuals, alongside the individuals: the reason for this is that the individuals, whose forces they are, exist split up and in opposition to one another, whilst, on the other hand, these forces are only real forces in the intercourse and association of these individuals. Thus, on the one hand, we have a totality of productive forces, which have, as it were, taken on a material form and are for the individuals no longer the forces of the individuals but of private property, and hence of the individuals only insofar as they are owners of private property themselves. Never, in any earlier period, have the productive forces taken on a form so indifferent to the intercourse of individuals *as* individuals, because their intercourse itself was formerly a restricted one. On the other hand, standing over against these productive forces, we have the majority of the individuals from whom these forces have been wrested away, and who, robbed thus of all real life-content, have become abstract individuals, but who are, however, only by this fact put into a position to enter into relation with one another *as individuals.*

The only connection which still links them with the productive forces and with their own existence – labour – has lost all semblance of self-activity and only sustains their life by stunting it. While in the earlier periods self-activity and the production of material life were separated, in that they devolved on different persons, and while, on account of the narrowness of the individuals themselves, the production of material life was considered as a subordinate mode of self-activity, they now diverge to such an extent that altogether material life appears as the end, and what produces this material life, labour (which is now the only possible but, as we see, negative form of self-activity), as the means.

Thus things have now come to such a pass that the individuals must appropriate the existing totality of productive forces, not only to achieve self-activity, but, also, merely to safeguard their very existence. This appropriation is first determined by the object to be appropriated, the productive forces, which have been developed to a totality and which only exist within a universal intercourse. From this aspect alone, therefore, this appropriation must have a universal character corresponding to the productive forces and the intercourse.

The appropriation of these forces is itself nothing more than the development of the individual capacities corresponding to the material instruments of production. The appropriation of a totality of instruments of production is, for this very reason, the development of a totality of capacities in the individuals themselves.

This appropriation is further determined by the persons appropriating. Only the proletarians of the present day, who are completely shut off from all self-activity, are in a position to achieve a complete and no longer restricted self-activity, which consists in the appropriation of a totality of productive forces and in the thus postulated development of a totality of capacities. All earlier revolutionary appropriations were restricted; individuals, whose self-activity was restricted by a crude instrument of production and a limited intercourse, appropriated this crude instrument of production, and hence merely achieved a new state of limitation. Their instrument of production became their property, but they themselves remained subordinate to the division of labour and their own instrument of production. In all expropriations up to now, a mass of individuals remained subservient to a single instrument of production; in the appropriation by the proletarians, a mass of instruments of production must be made subject to each individual, and property to all. Modern universal intercourse can be controlled by individuals, therefore, only when controlled by all.

This appropriation is further determined by the manner in which it must be effected. It can only be effected through a union, which by the character of the proletariat itself can again only be a universal one, and through a revolution, in which, on the one hand, the power of the earlier mode of production and intercourse and social organisation is overthrown, and, on the other hand, there develops the universal character and the energy of the proletariat, without which the revolution cannot be accomplished; and in which, further, the proletariat rids itself of everything that still clings to it from its previous position in society.

Only at this stage does self-activity coincide with material life, which corresponds to the development of individuals into complete individuals and the casting-off of all natural limitations. The transformation of labour into self-activity corresponds to the transformation of the earlier limited intercourse into the intercourse of individuals as such. With the appropriation of the total productive forces through united individuals, private property comes to an end. Whilst previously in history a particular condition always appeared as accidental, now the isolation of individuals and the particular private gain of each man have themselves become accidental.

The individuals, who are no longer subject to the division of labour, have been conceived by the philosophers as an ideal, under the name 'Man'. They have conceived the whole process which we have outlined as the evolutionary process of 'Man', so that at every historical stage 'Man' was substituted for the individuals and shown as the motive force of history. The whole process was thus conceived as a process of the self-estrangement of 'Man', and this was essentially due to the fact that the average individual of the later stage was always foisted on to the earlier stage, and the consciousness of a later age on to the individuals of an earlier. Through this inversion, which from the first is an abstract image of the actual conditions, it was possible to transform the whole of history into an evolutionary process of consciousness.

Finally, from the conception of history we have sketched we obtain these further conclusions:

1. In the development of productive forces there comes a stage when productive forces and means of intercourse are brought into being, which, under the existing relationships, only cause mischief, and are no longer productive but destructive forces (machinery and money); and connected with this a class is called forth, which has to bear all the burdens of society without enjoying its advantages, which, ousted

from society, is forced into the most decided antagonism to all other classes; a class which forms the majority of all members of society, and from which emanates the consciousness of the necessity of a fundamental revolution, the communist consciousness, which may, of course, arise among the other classes too through the contemplation of the situation of this class.

2. The conditions under which definite productive forces can be applied are the conditions of the rule of a definite class of society, whose social power, deriving from its property, has its *practical*-idealistic expression in each case in the form of the State; and, therefore, every revolutionary struggle is directed against a class, which till then has been in power.
3. In all revolutions up till now the mode of activity always remained unscathed and it was only a question of a different distribution of this activity, a new distribution of labour to other persons, whilst the communist revolution is directed against the preceding *mode* of activity, does away with *labour*, and abolishes the rule of all classes with the classes themselves, because it is carried through by the class which no longer counts as a class in society, is not recognised as a class, and is in itself the expression of the dissolution of all classes, nationalities, etc. within present society; and
4. Both for the production on a mass scale of this communist consciousness, and for the success of the cause itself, the alteration of men on a mass scale is necessary, an alteration which can only take place in a practical movement, a *revolution*; this revolution is necessary, therefore, not only because the *ruling* class cannot be overthrown in any other way, but also because the class *overthrowing* it can only in a revolution succeed in ridding itself of all the muck of ages and become fitted to found society anew.

1.4 *The Communist Manifesto*

The Communist League was established, largely due to the efforts of Marx and Engels, in 1847 and the duo were given the task of outlining the League's position and vision in a manifesto. The *Communist Manifesto* (essentially the work of Marx alone) was the result, and although it made little impact at the time it went on to become one of the most famous and influential books ever written. The text is comprised of four sections, however it is the first part that is the best known and is reproduced here. This piece contains some of the most stirring and searing passages ever committed to paper – as well as being one of the most quoted! Although the *Manifesto* contains nothing of real originality it still stands as a brilliantly written and compelling summation of historical materialism. It is to be borne in mind that this was the manifesto of a political organisation and it is in that light that we should understand some of the claims made within its pages: e.g. that the dividing-up of society into two great classes (the 'polarisation thesis') and the overthrow of capitalism are inevitable processes.

From: D. McLellan, *Karl Marx: Selected Writings* (Oxford University Press, 1977) pp. 222–31.

Bourgeois and Proletarians

The history of all hitherto existing society is the history of class struggles.

Freeman and slave, patrician and plebeian, lord and serf, guild-master and journeyman – in a word, oppressor and oppressed, stood in constant opposition to one another, carried on an uninterrupted, now hidden, now open fight, a fight that each time ended either in a revolutionary re-constitution of society at large or in the common ruin of the contending classes.

In the earlier epochs of history, we find almost everywhere a complicated arrangement of society into various orders, a manifold gradation of social rank. In ancient Rome we have patricians, knights, plebeians, slaves; in the Middle Ages, feudal lords, vassals, guild-masters, journeymen, apprentices, serfs; in almost all of these classes, again, subordinate gradations.

The modern bourgeois society that has sprouted from the ruins of feudal society has not done away with class antagonisms. It has but established new classes, new conditions of oppression, new forms of struggle in place of the old ones.

Our epoch, the epoch of the bourgeoisie, possesses, however, this distinctive feature: it has simplified the class antagonisms. Society as a whole is more and more splitting up into two great hostile camps, into two great classes directly facing each other: Bourgeoisie and Proletariat.

From the serfs of the Middle Ages sprang the chartered burghers of the earliest towns. From these burgesses the first elements of the bourgeoisie were developed.

The discovery of America, the rounding of the Cape, opened up fresh ground for the rising bourgeoisie. The East Indian and Chinese markets, the colonization of America, trade with the colonies, the increase in the means of exchange and in commodities generally, gave to commerce, to navigation, to industry, an impulse never before known, and thereby, to the revolutionary element in the tottering feudal society, a rapid development.

The feudal system of industry, under which industrial production was monopolized by closed guilds, now no longer sufficed for the growing wants of the new markets. The manufacturing system took its place. The guild-masters were pushed on one side by the manufacturing middle class; division of labour between the different corporate guilds vanished in the face of division of labour in each single workshop.

Meantime the markets kept ever growing, the demand ever rising. Even manufacture no longer sufficed. Thereupon, steam and machinery revolutionized industrial production. The place of manufacture was taken by the giant, Modern Industry, the place of the industrial middle class, by industrial millionaires, the leaders of whole industrial armies, the modern bourgeois.

Modern industry has established the world-market, for which the discovery of America paved the way. This market has given an immense development to commerce, to navigation, to communication by land. This development has, in its turn, reacted on the extension of industry; and in proportion as industry, commerce, navigation, railways extended, in the same proportion the bourgeoisie developed, increased its capital, and pushed into the background every class handed down from the Middle Ages.

We see, therefore, how the modern bourgeoisie is itself the product of a long course of development, of a series of revolutions in the modes of production and of exchange.

Each step in the development of the bourgeoisie was accompanied by a corresponding political advance of that class. An oppressed class under the sway of the feudal nobility, an armed and self-governing association in the medieval commune; here independent urban republic (as in Italy and Germany), there taxable 'third estate' of the monarchy (as in France), afterwards, in the period of manufacture proper, serving either the semi-feudal or the absolute monarchy as a counterpoise against the nobility, and, in fact, corner-stone of the great monarchies in general, the bourgeoisie has at last, since the establishment of Modern Industry and of the world-market, conquered for itself, in the modern representative State, exclusive political sway. The executive of the modern State is but a committee for managing the common affairs of the whole bourgeoisie.

The bourgeoisie, historically, has played a most revolutionary part.

The bourgeoisie, wherever it has got the upper hand, has put an end to all feudal, patriarchal, idyllic relations. It has pitilessly torn asunder the motley feudal ties that bound man to his 'natural superiors', and has left remaining no other nexus between man and man than naked self-interest, than callous 'cash payment'. It has drowned the most heavenly ecstasies of religious fervour, of chivalrous enthusiasm, of philistine sentimentalism, in the icy water of egotistical calculation. It has resolved personal worth into exchange value, and in place of the numberless indefeasible chartered freedoms, has set up that single, unconscionable freedom – Free Trade. In one word, for exploitation, veiled by religious and political illusions, it has substituted naked, shameless, direct, brutal exploitation.

The bourgeoisie has stripped of its halo every occupation hitherto honoured and looked up to with reverent awe. It has converted the physician, the lawyer, the priest, the poet, the man of science into its paid wage-labourers.

The bourgeoisie has torn away from the family its sentimental veil, and has reduced the family relation to a mere money relation.

The bourgeoisie has disclosed how it came to pass that the brutal display of vigour in the Middle Ages, which Reactionists so much admire, found its fitting complement in the most slothful indolence. It has been the first to show what man's activity can bring about. It has accomplished wonders far surpassing Egyptian pyramids, Roman aqueducts, and Gothic cathedrals; it has conducted expeditions that put in the shade all former Exoduses of nations and crusades.

The bourgeoisie cannot exist without constantly revolutionizing the instruments of production, and thereby the relations of production, and with them the whole relations of society. Conservation of the old modes of production in unaltered form, was, on the contrary, the first condition of existence for all earlier industrial classes. Constant revolutionizing of production, uninterrupted disturbance of all social conditions, everlasting uncertainty and agitation distinguish the bourgeois epoch from all earlier ones. All fixed, fast-frozen relations, with their train of ancient and venerable prejudices and opinions, are swept away, all new-formed ones become antiquated before they can ossify. All that is solid melts into air, all that is holy is profaned, and man is at last compelled to face with sober senses, his real conditions of life, and his relations with his kind.

The need of a constantly expanding market for its products chases the bourgeoisie over the whole surface of the globe. It must nestle everywhere, settle everywhere, establish connections everywhere.

The bourgeoisie has through its exploitation of the world-market given a cosmopolitan character to production and consumption in every country. To the great chagrin of Reactionists, it has drawn from under the feet of industry the national ground on which it stood. All old-established national industries have been destroyed or are daily being destroyed. They are dislodged by new industries, whose introduction becomes a life-and-death question for all civilized nations, by industries that no longer work up indigenous raw material, but raw material drawn from the remotest zones; industries whose products are consumed, not only at home, but in every quarter of the globe. In place of the old wants, satisfied by the productions of the country, we find new wants, requiring for their satisfaction the products of distant lands and climes. In place of the old local and national seclusion and self-sufficiency, we have intercourse in every direction, universal interdependence of nations. And as in material, so also in intellectual production. The intellectual creations of individual nations become common property. National one-sidedness and narrow-mindedness become more and more impossible, and from the numerous national and local literatures, there arises a world literature.

The bourgeoisie, by the rapid improvement of all instruments of production, by the immensely facilitated means of communication, draws all, even the most barbarian, nations into civilization. The cheap prices of its commodities are the heavy artillery with which it batters down all Chinese walls, with which it forces the barbarians' intensely obstinate hatred of foreigners to capitulate. It compels all nations, on pain of extinction, to adopt the bourgeois mode of production; it compels them to introduce what it calls civilization into their midst, i.e., to become bourgeois themselves. In one word, it creates a world after its own image.

The bourgeoisie has subjected the country to the rule of the towns. It has created enormous cities, has greatly increased the urban population as compared with the rural, and has thus rescued a considerable part of the population from the idiocy of rural life. Just as it has made the country dependent on the towns, so it has made barbarian and semi-barbarian countries dependent on the civilized ones, nations of peasants on nations of bourgeois, the East on the West.

The bourgeoisie keeps more and more doing away with the scattered state of the population, of the means of production, and of property. It has agglomerated population, centralized means of production, and has concentrated property in a few hands. The necessary consequence of this was political centralization. Independent or but loosely connected provinces, with separate interests, laws, governments, and systems of taxation, became lumped together into one nation, with one government, one code of laws, one national class-interest, one frontier, and one customs-tariff.

The bourgeoisie, during its rule of scarcely one hundred years, has created more massive and more colossal productive forces than have all preceding generations together. Subjection of Nature's forces to man, machinery, application of chemistry to industry and agriculture, steam-navigation, railways, electric telegraphs, clearing of whole continents for cultivation, canalization of rivers, whole populations conjured out of the ground – what earlier century had even a presentiment that such productive forces slumbered in the lap of social labour?

We see then that the means of production and of exchange, on whose foundation the bourgeoisie built itself up, were generated in feudal society. At a certain stage in the development of these means of production and of exchange, the conditions under which feudal society produced and exchanged, the feudal organization of agriculture and manufacturing industry, in one word, the feudal relations of property become no longer compatible with the already developed productive forces; they became so many fetters. They had to be burst asunder; they were burst asunder.

Into their place stepped free competition, accompanied by a social and political constitution adapted to it, and by the economical and political sway of the bourgeois class.

A similar movement is going on before our own eyes. Modern bourgeois society with its relations of production, of exchange and of property, a society that has conjured up such gigantic means of production and of exchange, is like the sorcerer, who is no longer able to control the powers of the nether world which he has called up by his spells. The history of industry and commerce for many a decade past is but the history of the revolt of modern productive forces against modern conditions of production, against the property relations that are the conditions for the existence of the bourgeoisie and of its rule. It is enough to mention the commercial crises that by their periodical return put on trial, each time more threateningly, the existence of the entire bourgeois society. In these crises a great part not only of the existing products, but also of the previously created productive forces, are periodically destroyed. In these crises there breaks out an epidemic that, in all earlier epochs, would have seemed an absurdity – the epidemic of over-production. Society suddenly finds itself put back into a state of momentary barbarism; it appears as if a famine, a universal war of devastation, has cut off the supply of every means of subsistence; industry and commerce seem to be destroyed; and why? Because there is too much civilization, too much means of subsistence, too much industry, too much commerce. The productive forces at the disposal of society no longer tend to further the development of the conditions of bourgeois property; on the contrary, they have become too powerful for these conditions, by which they are fettered, and so soon as they overcome these fetters, they bring disorder into the whole of bourgeois society, endanger the existence of bourgeois property. The conditions of bourgeois society are too narrow to comprise the wealth created by them. And how does the bourgeoisie get over these crises? On the one hand by enforced destruction of a mass of productive forces; on the other, by the conquest of new markets, and by the more thorough exploitation of the old ones. That is to say, by paving the way for more extensive and more destructive crises, and by diminishing the means whereby crises are prevented.

The weapons with which the bourgeoisie felled feudalism to the ground are now turned against the bourgeoisie itself.

But not only has the bourgeoisie forged the weapons that bring death to itself; it has also called into existence the men who are to wield those weapons – the modern working class – the proletarians.

In proportion as the bourgeoisie, i.e., capital, is developed, in the same proportion is the proletariat, the modern working class, developed – a class of labourers, who live only so long as they find work, and who find work only so long as their labour increases capital. These labourers, who must sell themselves piecemeal, are a commodity, like every other article of commerce, and are consequently exposed to all the vicissitudes of competition, to all the fluctuations of the market.

Owing to the extensive use of machinery and to division of labour, the work of the proletarians has lost all individual character, and, consequently, all charm for the workman. He becomes an appendage of the machine, and it is only the most simple, most monotonous, and most easily acquired knack, that is required of him. Hence, the cost of production of a workman is restricted, almost entirely, to the means of subsistence that he requires for his maintenance, and for the propagation of his race. But the price of a commodity, and therefore also of labour, is equal to its cost of production. In proportion, therefore, as the repulsiveness of the work increases, the wage decreases. Nay more, in proportion as the use of machinery and division of labour increases, in the same proportion the burden of toil also increases, whether by prolongation of the working hours, by increase of the work exacted in a given time or by increased speed of the machinery, etc.

Modern industry has converted the little workshop of the patriarchal master into the great factory of the industrial capitalist. Masses of labourers, crowded into the factory, are organized like soldiers. As privates of the industrial army they are placed under the command of a perfect hierarchy of officers and sergeants. Not only are they slaves of the bourgeois class, and of the bourgeois State; they are daily and hourly enslaved by the machine, by the overlooker, and, above all, by the individual bourgeois manufacturer himself. The more openly this despotism proclaims gain to be its end and aim, the more petty, the more hateful, and the more embittering it is.

The less the skill and exertion of strength implied in manual labour, in other words, the more modern industry becomes developed, the more is the labour of men superseded by that of women. Differences of age and sex have no longer any distinctive social validity for the working class. All are instruments of labour, more or less expensive to use, according to their age and sex.

No sooner is the exploitation of the labourer by the manufacturer, so far, at an end, and he receives his wages in cash, than he is set upon by the other portions of the bourgeoisie, the landlord, the shopkeeper, the pawnbroker, etc.

The lower strata of the middle class – the small tradespeople, shopkeepers, and retired tradesmen generally, the handicraftsmen and peasants – all these sink gradually into the proletariat, partly because their diminutive capital does not suffice for the scale on which Modern Industry is carried on, and is swamped in the competition with the large capitalists, partly because their specialized skill is rendered worthless by new methods of production. Thus the proletariat is recruited from all classes of the population.

The proletariat goes through various stages of development. With its birth begins its struggle with the bourgeoisie. At first the contest is carried on by individual labourers, then by the workpeople of a factory, then by the operatives of one trade, in one locality, against the individual bourgeois who directly exploits them. They direct their attacks not against the bourgeois conditions of production, but against the instruments of production themselves; they destroy imported wares that compete with their labour, they smash to pieces machinery, they set factories ablaze, they seek to restore by force the vanished status of the workman of the Middle Ages.

At this stage the labourers still form an incoherent mass scattered over the whole country, and broken up by their mutual competition. If anywhere they unite to form more compact bodies, this is not yet the consequence of their own active union, but of the union of the bourgeoisie, which class, in order to attain its own political ends, is compelled to set the whole proletariat in motion, and is moreover yet, for a time, able to do so. At this stage, therefore, the proletarians do not fight their enemies, but the enemies of their enemies, the remnants of absolute monarchy, the landowners, the non-industrial bourgeois, the petty bourgeoisie. Thus the whole historical movement is concentrated in the hands of the bourgeoisie; every victory so obtained is a victory for the bourgeoisie.

But with the development of industry the proletariat not only increases in number; it becomes concentrated in greater masses, its strength grows, and it feels that strength more. The various interests and conditions of life within the ranks of the proletariat are more and more equalized, in proportion as machinery obliterates all distinctions of labour, and nearly everywhere reduces wages to the same low level. The growing competition among the bourgeois, and the resulting commercial crises, make the wages of the workers ever more fluctuating. The unceasing improvement of machinery, ever more rapidly developing, makes their livelihood more and more precarious; the collisions between individual workmen and individual bourgeois take more and more the character of collisions between two classes. Thereupon the workers begin to form combinations (Trades' Unions) against the bourgeois; they club together in order to keep up the rate of wages; they found permanent associations in order to make provision beforehand for these occasional revolts. Here and there the contest breaks out into riots.

Now and then the workers are victorious, but only for a time. The real fruit of their battles lies, not in the immediate result, but in the ever-expanding union of the workers. This union is helped on by the improved means of communication that are created by modern industry and that place the workers of different localities in contact with one another. It was just this contact that was needed to centralize the numerous local struggles, all of the same character, into one national struggle between classes. But every class struggle is a political struggle. And that union, to attain which the burghers of the Middle Ages, with their miserable highways, required centuries, the modern proletarians, thanks to railways, achieve in a few years.

This organization of the proletarians into a class, and consequently into a political party, is continually being upset again by the competition between the workers themselves. But it ever rises up again, stronger, firmer, mightier. It compels legislative recognition of particular interests of the workers, by taking advantage of the divisions among the bourgeoisie itself. Thus the ten-hours' bill in England was carried.

Altogether, collisions between the classes of the old society further in many ways the course of development of the proletariat. The bourgeoisie finds itself involved in a constant battle. At first with the aristocracy; later on, with those portions of the bourgeoisie itself whose interests have become antagonistic to the progress of industry; at all times, with the bourgeoisie of foreign countries. In all these battles it sees itself compelled to appeal to the proletariat, to ask for its help, and thus to drag it into the political arena. The bourgeoisie itself, therefore, supplies the proletariat with its own elements of political and general education, in other words, it furnishes the proletariat with weapons for fighting the bourgeoisie.

Further, as we have already seen, entire sections of the ruling classes are, by the advance of industry, precipitated into the proletariat, or are at least threatened in their conditions of existence. These also supply the proletariat with fresh elements of enlightenment and progress.

Finally, in times when the class struggle nears the decisive hour, the process of dissolution going on within the ruling class, in fact within the whole range of old society, assumes such a violent, glaring character, that a small section of the ruling class cuts itself adrift, and joins the revolutionary class, the class that holds the future in its hands. Just as, therefore, at an earlier period, a section of the nobility went over to the bourgeoisie, so now a portion of the bourgeoisie goes over to the proletariat, and in particular, a portion of the bourgeois ideologists, who have raised themselves to the level of comprehending theoretically the historical movement as a whole.

Of all the classes that stand face to face with the bourgeoisie today, the proletariat alone is a really revolutionary class. The other classes decay and finally disappear in the face of Modern Industry; the proletariat is its special and essential product.

The lower middle class, the small manufacturer, the shopkeeper, the artisan, the peasant, all these fight against the bourgeoisie, to save from extinction their existence as fractions of the middle class. They are therefore not revolutionary, but conservative. Nay more, they are reactionary, for they try to roll back the wheel of history. If by chance they are revolutionary, they are so only in view of their impending transfer into the proletariat; they thus defend not their present, but their future interests, they desert their own standpoint to place themselves at that of the proletariat.

The 'dangerous class', the social scum, that passively rotting mass thrown off by the lowest layers of old society, may, here and there, be swept into the movement by a proletarian revolution; its conditions of life, however, prepare it far more for the part of a bribed tool of reactionary intrigue.

In the conditions of the proletariat, those of old society at large are already virtually swamped. The proletarian is without property; his relation to his wife and children has no longer anything in common with the bourgeois family relations; modern industrial labour, modern subjection to capital, the same in England as in France, in America as in Germany, has stripped him of every trace of national character. Law, morality, religion are to him so many bourgeois prejudices, behind which lurk in ambush just as many bourgeois interests.

All the preceding classes that got the upper hand, sought to fortify their already acquired status by subjecting society at large to their conditions of appropriation. The proletarians cannot become masters of the productive forces of society, except by abolishing their own previous mode of appropriation, and thereby also every other previous mode of appropriation. They have nothing of their own to secure and to fortify; their mission is to destroy all previous securities for, and insurances of, individual property.

All previous historical movements were movements of minorities, or in the interests of minorities. The proletarian movement is the self-conscious, independent movement of the immense majority, in the interests of the immense majority. The proletariat, the lowest stratum of our present society, cannot stir, cannot raise itself up, without the whole superincumbent strata of official society being sprung into the air.

Though not in substance, yet in form, the struggle of the proletariat with the bourgeoisie is at first a national struggle. The proletariat of each country must, of course, first of all settle matters with its own bourgeoisie.

In depicting the most general phases of the development of the proletariat, we traced the more or less veiled civil war, raging within existing society, up to the point where that war breaks out into open revolution, and where the violent overthrow of the bourgeoisie lays the foundation for the sway of the proletariat.

Hitherto, every form of society has been based, as we have already seen, on the antagonism of oppressing and oppressed classes. But in order to oppress a class, certain conditions must be assured to it under which it can, at least, continue its slavish existence. The serf, in the period of serfdom, raised himself to membership in the commune, just as the petty bourgeois, under the yoke of feudal absolutism, managed to develop into a bourgeois. The modern labourer, on the contrary, instead of rising with the progress of industry, sinks deeper and deeper below the conditions of existence of his own class. He becomes a pauper, and pauperism develops more rapidly than population and wealth. And here it becomes evident, that the bourgeoisie is unfit any longer to be the ruling class in society, and to impose its conditions of existence upon society as an overriding law. It is unfit to rule because it is incompetent to assure an existence to its slave within his slavery, because it cannot help letting him sink into such a state, that it has to feed him, instead of being fed by him. Society can no longer live under this bourgeoisie, in other words, its existence is no longer compatible with society.

The essential condition for the existence, and for the sway of the bourgeois class, is the formation and augmentation of capital; the condition for capital is wage-labour. Wage-labour rests exclusively on competition between the labourers. The advance of industry, whose involuntary promoter is the bourgeoisie, replaces the isolation of the labourers, due to competition, by their revolutionary combination, due to association. The development of Modern Industry, therefore, cuts from under its feet the very foundation on which the bourgeoisie produces and appropriates products. What the bourgeoisie, therefore, produces, above all, is its own grave-diggers. Its fall and the victory of the proletariat are equally inevitable.

1.5 WAGE LABOUR AND CAPITAL

The following selection originally appeared in 1849 as a series of articles in the Cologne-based paper the *Neue Rheinische Zeitung*, of which Marx was the editor. The articles were in turn based on a series of lectures that Marx gave at the German Workers' Society (founded by Marx and Engels in 1847) in Brussels. Given that they were aimed at non-specialists the lectures that make up *Wage Labour and Capital* stand as a clear and systematic account of Marxist economic theory.

From: K. Marx and F. Engels, *Selected Works* (Lawrence and Wishart: London, 1968) pp.71–93.

Now, after our readers have seen the class struggle develop in colossal political forms in 1848, the time has come to deal more closely with the economic relations themselves on which the existence of the bourgeoisie and its class rule, as well as the slavery of the workers, are founded.

We shall present in three large sections:

1. the relation of *wage labour to capital*, the slavery of the worker, the domination of the capitalist;
2. *the inevitable destruction of the middle bourgeois classes and of the so-called peasant estate under the present system*;
3. *the commercial subjugation and exploitation of the bourgeois classes of the various European nations* by the despot of the world market – England.

We shall try to make our presentation as simple and popular as possible and shall not presuppose even the most elementary notions of political economy. We wish to be understood by the workers. Moreover, the most remarkable ignorance and confusion of ideas prevails in Germany in regard to the simplest economic relations, from the accredited defenders of the existing state of things down to the *socialist miracle workers* and the *unrecognised political geniuses* in which fragmented Germany is even richer than in sovereign princes.

Now, therefore, for the first question:

What are Wages? How are they Determined?

If workers were asked: 'How much are your wages?' one would reply: 'I get a mark a day from my employer'; another, 'I get two marks,' and so on. According to the different trades to which they belong, they would mention different sums of money which they receive from their respective employers for the performance of a particular piece of work, for example, weaving a yard of linen or type-setting a printed sheet. In spite of the variety of their statements, they would all agree on one point: wages are the sum of money paid by the capitalist for a particular labour time or for a particular output of labour.

The capitalist, it seems, therefore, *buys* their labour with money. They *sell* him their labour for money. But this is merely the appearance. In reality what they sell to the capitalist for money is their labour *power.* The capitalist buys this labour power for a day, a week, a month, etc. And after he has bought it, he uses it by having the workers work for the stipulated time. For the same sum with which the capitalist has bought their labour power, for example, two marks, he could have bought two pounds of sugar or a definite amount of any other commodity. The two marks, with which he bought two pounds of sugar, are the *price* of the two pounds of sugar. The two marks, with which he bought twelve hours' use of labour power, are the price of twelve hours' labour. Labour power, therefore, is a commodity, neither more nor less than sugar. The former is measured by the clock, the latter by the scales.

The workers exchange their commodity, labour power, for the commodity of the capitalist, for money, and this exchange takes place in a definite ratio. So much money for so long a use of labour power. For twelve hours' weaving, two marks. And do not the two marks represent all the other commodities which I can buy for two marks? In fact, therefore, the worker has exchanged his commodity, labour power, for other commodities of all kinds and that in a definite ratio. By giving him two marks, the capitalist has given him so much meat, so much clothing, so much fuel, light, etc., in exchange for his day's labour. Accordingly, the two marks express the ratio in which labour power is exchanged for other commodities, the *exchange value* of his labour power. The exchange value of a commodity, reckoned in *money*, is what is called its *price. Wages* are only a special name for the price of labour power, commonly called the *price of labour*, for the price of this peculiar commodity which has no other repository than human flesh and blood.

Let us take any worker, say, a weaver. The capitalist supplies him with the loom and yarn. The weaver sets to work and the yarn is converted into linen. The capitalist takes possession of the linen and sells it, say, for twenty marks. Now are the wages of the weaver a *share* in the linen, in the twenty marks, in the product of his labour? By no means. Long before the linen is sold, perhaps long before its weaving is finished, the weaver has received his wages. The capitalist, therefore, does not pay these wages with the money which he will obtain from the linen, but with money already in reserve. Just as the loom and the yarn are not the product of the weaver to whom they are supplied by his employer, so likewise with the commodities which the weaver receives in exchange for his commodity, labour power. It was possible that his employer found no purchaser at all for his linen. It was possible that he did not get even the amount of the wages by its sale. It is possible that he sells it very profitably in comparison with the weaver's wages. All that has nothing to do with the weaver. The capitalist buys the labour power of the weaver with a part of his available wealth, of his capital, just as he has bought the raw material – the yarn – and the instrument of labour – the loom – with another part of his wealth. After he has made these purchases, and these purchases include the labour power necessary for the production of linen, he produces only with the *raw materials and instruments of labour belonging to him.* For the latter include now, true enough, our good weaver as well, who has as little share in the product or the price of the product as the loom has.

Wages are, therefore, not the worker's share in the commodity produced by him. Wages are the part of already existing commodities with which the capitalist buys for himself a definite amount of productive labour power.

Labour power is, therefore, a commodity which its possessor, the wage-worker, sells to capital. Why does he sell it? In order to live.

But the exercise of labour power, labour, is the worker's own life-activity, the manifestation of his own life. And this *life-activity* he sells to another person in order to secure the necessary *means of subsistence.* Thus his life-activity is for him only a means to enable him to exist. He works in order to live. He does not even reckon labour as part of his life, it is rather a sacrifice of his life. It is a commodity which he has made over to another. Hence, also, the product of his activity is not the object of his activity. What he produces for himself is not the silk that he weaves, not the gold that he draws from the mine, not the palace that he builds. What he produces for himself is *wages*, and silk, gold, palace resolve themselves for him into a definite quantity of the means of subsistence, perhaps into a cotton jacket, some copper coins and a lodging in a cellar. And the worker, who for twelve hours weaves, spins, drills, turns, builds, shovels, breaks stones, carries loads, etc. – does he consider this twelve hours' weaving, spinning, drilling, turning, building, shovelling, stone breaking as a manifestation of his life, as life? On the contrary, life begins for him where this activity ceases, at table, in the public house, in bed. The twelve hours' labour, on the other hand, has no meaning for him as weaving, spinning, drilling, etc., but as *earnings*, which bring him to the table, to the public house, into bed. If the silk worm were to spin in order to continue its existence as a caterpillar, it would be a complete wage-worker. Labour power was not always a *commodity*. Labour was not always wage labour, that is, *free labour.* The *slave* did not sell his labour power to the slave owner, any more than the ox sells its services to the peasant. The slave, together with his labour power, is sold once and for all to his owner. He is a commodity which can pass from the hand of one owner to that of another. He is *himself* a commodity, but the labour power is not *his* commodity. The *serf* sells only a part of his labour power. He does not receive a wage from the owner of the land; rather the owner of the land receives a tribute from him.

The serf belongs to the land and turns over to the owner of the land the fruits thereof. The *free labourer*, on the other hand, sells himself and, indeed, sells himself piecemeal. He sells at auction eight, ten, twelve, fifteen hours of his life, day after day, to the highest bidder, to the owner of the raw materials, instruments of labour and means of subsistence, that is, to the capitalist. The worker belongs neither to an owner nor to the land, but eight, ten, twelve, fifteen hours of his daily life belong to him who buys them. The worker leaves the capitalist to whom he hires himself whenever he likes, and the capitalist discharges him whenever he thinks fit, as soon as he no longer gets any profit out of him, or not the anticipated profit. But the worker, whose sole source of livelihood is the sale of his labour power, cannot leave the *whole class of purchasers, that is, the capitalist class*, without renouncing his existence. He belongs not to this or that capitalist but to the *capitalist class*, and, moreover, it is his business to dispose of himself, that is, to find a purchaser within this capitalist class.

Now, before going more closely into the relation between capital and wage labour, we shall present briefly the most general relations which come into consideration in the determination of wages.

Wages, as we have seen, are the *price* of a definite commodity, of labour power. Wages are, therefore, determined by the same laws that determine the price of every other commodity. The question, therefore, is *how is the price of a commodity determined?*

By What is the Price of a Commodity Determined?

By competition between buyers and sellers, by the relation of inquiry to delivery, of demand to supply. Competition, by which the price of a commodity is determined, is *three-sided.*

The same commodity is offered by various sellers. With goods of the same quality, the one who sells most cheaply is certain of driving the others out of the field and securing the greatest sale for himself. Thus, the sellers mutually contend among themselves for sales, for the market. Each of them desires to sell, to sell as much as possible and, if possible, to sell alone, to the exclusion of the other sellers. Hence, one sells cheaper than another. Consequently, *competition* takes place *among the sellers*, which *depresses* the price of the *commodities* offered by them.

But *competition* also takes place *among the buyers*, which in its turn *causes* the commodities offered to *rise* in price.

Finally *competition* occurs *between buyers and sellers*: the former desire to buy as cheaply as possible, the latter to sell as dearly as possible. The result of this competition between buyers and sellers will depend upon how the two above-mentioned sides of the competition are related, that is, whether the competition is stronger in the army of buyers or in the army of sellers. Industry leads two armies into the field against each other, each of which again carries on a battle within its own ranks, among its own troops. The army whose troops beat each other up the least gains the victory over the opposing hots.

Let us suppose there are 100 bales of cotton on the market and at the same time buyers for 1,000 bales of cotton. In this case, therefore, the demand is ten times as great as the supply. Competition will be very strong among the buyers, each of whom desires to get one, and if possible all, of the hundred bales for himself. This example is no arbitrary assumption. We have experienced periods of cotton crop failure in the history of the trade when a few capitalists in alliance have tried to buy, not one hundred bales, but all the cotton stocks of the world. Hence, in the example mentioned, one buyer will seek to drive the other from the field by offering a relatively higher price per bale of cotton. The cotton sellers, who see that the troops of the enemy army are engaged in the most violent struggle among themselves and that the sale of all their hundred bales is absolutely certain, will take good care not to fall out among themselves and depress the price of cotton at the moment when their adversaries are competing with one another to force it up. Thus, peace suddenly descends on the army of the sellers. They stand facing the buyers as one man, fold their arms philosophically, and there would be no bounds to their demands were it not that the offers of even the most persistent and eager buyers have very definite limits.

If, therefore, the supply of a commodity is lower than the demand for it, then only slight competition, or none at all, takes place among the sellers. In the same proportion as this competition decreases, competition increases among the buyers. The result is a more or less considerable rise in commodity prices.

It is well known that the reverse case with a reverse result occurs more frequently. Considerable surplus of supply over demand; desperate competition among the sellers; lack of buyers; disposal of goods at ridiculously low prices.

But what is the meaning of a rise, a fall in prices; what is the meaning of high price, low price? A grain of sand is high when examined through a microscope, and a tower is low when compared with a mountain. And if price is determined by the relation between supply and demand, what determines the relation between supply and demand?

Let us turn to the first bourgeois we meet. He will not reflect for an instant but, like another Alexander the Great, will cut this metaphysical knot with the multiplication table. If the production of the goods which I sell has cost me 100 marks, he will tell us, and if I get 110 marks from the sale of these goods, within the year of course – then that is sound, honest, legitimate profit. But if I get in exchange 120 or 130 marks, that is a high profit; and if I get as much as 200 marks, that would be an extraordinary, an enormous profit. What, therefore, serves the bourgeois as his *measure* of profit? The *cost of production* of his commodity. If he receives in exchange for this commodity an amount of other commodities which it has cost less to produce, he has lost. If he receives in exchange for his commodity an amount of other commodities the production of which has cost more, he has gained. And he calculates the rise or fall of the profit according to the degree in which the exchange value of his commodity stands above or below zero – the *cost of production.*

We have thus seen how the changing relation of supply and demand causes now a rise and now a fall of prices, now high, now low prices. If the price of a commodity rises considerably because of inadequate supply or disproportionate increase of the demand, the price of some other commodity must necessarily have fallen proportionately, for the price of a commodity only expresses in money the ratio in which other commodities are given in exchange for it. If, for example, the price of a yard of silk material rises from five marks to six marks, the price of silver in relation to silk material has fallen and likewise the prices of all other commodities that have remained at their old prices have fallen in relation to the silk. One has to give a larger amount of them in exchange to get the same amount of silks. What will be the consequence of the rising price of a commodity? A mass of capital will be thrown into that flourishing branch of industry and this influx of capital into the domain of the favoured industry will continue until it yields the ordinary profits or, rather, until the price of its products, through overproduction, sinks below the cost of production.

Conversely, if the price of a commodity falls below its cost of production, capital will be withdrawn from the production of this commodity. Except in the case of a branch of industry which has become obsolete and must, therefore, perish, the production of such a commodity, that is, its supply, will go on decreasing owing to this flight of capital until it corresponds to the demand, and consequently its price is again on a level with its cost of production or, rather, until the supply has sunk below the demand, that is, until its price rises again above its cost of production, *for the current price of a commodity is always either above or below its cost of production.*

We see how capital continually migrates in and out, out of the domain of one industry into that of another. High prices bring too great an immigration and low prices too great an emigration.

We could show from another point of view how not only supply but also demand is determined by the cost of production. But this would take us too far away from our subject.

We have just seen how the fluctuations of supply and demand continually bring the price of a commodity back to the cost of production. *The real price of a commodity, it is true, is always above or below its cost of production; but rise and fall reciprocally balance each other*, so that within a certain period of time, taking the ebb and flow of the industry together, commodities are exchanged for one another in accordance with their cost of production, their price, therefore, being determined by their cost of production.

This determination of price by cost of production is not to be understood in the sense of the economists. The economists say that the *average price* of commodities is equal to the cost of production; that this is a *law*. The anarchical movement, in which rise is compensated by fall and fall by rise, is regarded by them as chance. With just as much right one could regard the fluctuations as the law and the determination by the cost of production as chance, as has actually been done by other economists. But it is solely these fluctuations, which, looked at more closely, bring with them the most fearful devastations and, like earthquakes, cause bourgeois society to tremble to its foundations – it is solely in the course of these fluctuations that prices are determined by the cost of production. The total movement of this disorder is its order. In the course of this industrial anarchy, in this movement in a circle, competition compensates, so to speak, for one excess by means of another.

We see, therefore, that the price of a commodity is determined by its cost of production in such manner that the periods in which the price of this commodity rises above its cost of production are compensated by the periods in which it sinks below the cost of production, and vice versa. This does not hold good, of course, for separate, particular industrial products but only for the whole branch of industry. Consequently, it also does not hold good for the individual industrialist but only for the whole class of industrialists.

The determination of price by the cost of production is equivalent to the determination of price by the labour time necessary for the manufacture of a commodity, for the cost of production consists of 1. raw materials and depreciation of instruments, that is, of industrial products the production of which has cost a certain amount of labour days and which, therefore, represent a certain amount of labour time, and 2. of direct labour, the measure of which is, precisely, time.

Now, the same general laws that regulate the price of commodities in general of course also regulate *wages*, the *price of labour.*

Wages will rise and fall according to the relation of supply and demand, according to the turn taken by the competition between the buyers of labour power, the capitalists, and the sellers of labour power, the workers. The fluctuations in wages correspond in general to the fluctuations in prices of commodities. *Within these fluctuations, however, the price of labour will be determined by the cost of production, by the labour time necessary to produce this commodity – labour power.*

What, then, is the cost of production of labour power?

It is the cost required for maintaining the worker as a worker and of developing him into a worker.

The less the period of training, therefore, that any work requires the smaller is the cost of production of the worker and the lower is the price of his labour, his wages. In those branches of industry in which hardly any period of apprenticeship is required and where the mere bodily existence of the worker suffices, the cost necessary for his production is almost confined to the commodities necessary for keeping him alive and capable of working. The *price of his labour* will, therefore, be determined by the *price of the necessary means of subsistence.*

Another consideration, however, also comes in. The manufacturer in calculating his cost of production and, accordingly, the price of the products takes into account the wear and tear of the instruments of labour. If, for example, a machine costs him 1,000 marks and wears out in ten years, he adds 100 marks annually to the price of the commodities so as to be able to replace the wornout machine by a new one at the end of ten years. In the same way, in calculating the cost of production of simple labour power, there must be included the cost of reproduction, whereby the race of workers is enabled to multiply and to replace worn-out workers by new ones. Thus the depreciation of the worker is taken into account in the same way as the depreciation of the machine.

The cost of production of simple labour power, therefore, amounts to the *cost of existence and reproduction of the worker.* The price of this cost of existence and reproduction constitutes wages. Wages so determined are called the *wage minimum.* This wage minimum, like the determination of the price of commodities by the cost of production in general, does not hold good for the *single individual* but for the *species.* Individual workers, millions of workers, do not get enough to be able to exist and reproduce themselves; *but the wages of the whole working class* level down, within their fluctuations, to this minimum.

Now that we have arrived at an understanding of the most general laws which regulate wages like the price of any other commodity, we can go into our subject more specifically.

Capital consists of raw materials, instruments of labour and means of subsistence of all kinds, which are utilised in order to produce new raw materials, new instruments of labour and new means of subsistence. All these component parts of capital are creations of labour, products of labour, *accumulated labour.* Accumulated labour which serves as a means of new production is capital.

So say the economists.

What is a Negro slave? A man of the black race. The one explanation is as good as the other.

A Negro is a Negro. He only becomes a slave in a certain relations. A cotton-spinning jenny is a machine for spinning cotton. It becomes *capital* only in certain relations. Torn from these relationships it is no more capital than gold in itself is *money* or sugar the price of sugar.

In production, men not only act on nature but also on one another. They produce only by co-operating in a certain way and mutually exchanging their activities. In order to produce, they enter into definite connections and relations with one another and only within these social connections and relations does their action on nature, does production, take place.

These social relations into which the producers enter with one another, the conditions under which they exchange their activities and participate in the whole act of production, will naturally vary according to the character of the means of production. With the invention of a new instrument of warfare, firearms, the whole internal organisation of the army necessarily changed; the relationships within which individuals can constitute an army and act as an army were transformed and the relations of different armies to one another also changed.

Thus the social relations within which individuals produce, *the social relations of production, change, are transformed, with the change and development of the material means of production, the productive forces. The relations of production in their totality constitute what are called the social relations, society, and, specifically, a society at a definite stage of historical development,* a society with a peculiar, distinctive character. *Ancient* society, *feudal* society, *bourgeois* society are such totalities of production relations, each of which at the same time denotes a special stage of development in the history of mankind.

Capital, also, is a social relation of production. *It is a bourgeois production relation,* a production relation of bourgeois society. Are not the means of subsistence, the instruments of labour, the raw materials of which capital consists, produced and accumulated under given social conditions, in definite social relations? Are they not utilised for new production under given social conditions, in definite social relations? And is it not just this definite social character which turns the products serving for new production into *capital*?

Capital consists not only of means of subsistence, instruments of labour and raw materials, not only of material products; it consists just as much of *exchange values.* All the products of which it consists are *commodities.* Capital is, therefore, not only a sum of material products; it is a sum of commodities, of exchange values, *of social magnitudes.*

Capital remains the same, whether we put cotton in place of wool, rice in place of wheat or steamships in place of railways, provided only that the cotton, the rice, the steamships – the body of capital – have the same exchange value, the same price as the wool, the wheat, the railways in which it was previously incorporated. The body of capital can change continually without the capital suffering the slightest alteration.

But while all capital is a sum of commodities, that is, of exchange values, not every sum of commodities, of exchange values, is capital.

Every sum of exchange values is an exchange value. Every separate exchange value is a sum of exchange values. For instance, a house that is worth 1,000 marks is an exchange value of 1,000 marks. A piece of paper worth a pfennig is a sum of exchange values of one-hundred hundredths of a pfennig. Products which are exchangeable for others are *commodities*. The particular ratio in which they are exchangeable constitutes their *exchange value* or, expressed in money, their *price*. The quantity of these products can change nothing in their quality of being *commodities* or representing an *exchange value* or having a definite price. Whether a tree is large or small it is a tree. Whether we exchange iron for other products in ounces or in hundred-weights, does this make any difference in its character as commodity, as exchange value? It is a commodity of greater or lesser value, of higher or lower price, depending upon the quantity.

How, then, does any amount of commodities, of exchange values, become capital?

By maintaining and multiplying itself as an independent social *power*, that is, as the power *of a portion of society*, by means of its *exchange for direct, living, labour power*. The existence of a class which possesses nothing but its capacity to labour is a necessary prerequisite of capital.

It is only the domination of accumulated, past, materialised labour over direct, living labour that turns accumulated labour into capital.

Capital does not consist in accumulated labour serving living labour as a means for new production. It consists in living labour serving accumulated labour as a means for maintaining and multiplying the exchange value of the latter.

What takes place in the exchange between capitalist and wage-worker?

The worker receives means of subsistence in exchange for his labour power, but the capitalist receives in exchange for his means of subsistence labour, the productive activity of the worker, the creative power whereby the worker not only replaces what he consumes but *gives to the accumulated labour a greater value than it previously possessed*. The worker receives a part of the available means of subsistence from the capitalist. For what purpose do these means of subsistence serve him? For immediate consumption. As soon, however, as I consume the means of subsistence, they are irretrievably lost to me unless I use the time during which I am kept alive by them in order to produce new means of subsistence, in order during consumption to create by my labour new values in place of the values which perish in being consumed. But it is just this noble reproductive power that the worker surrenders to the capitalist in exchange for means of subsistence received. He has, therefore, lost it for himself.

Let us take an example: a tenant farmer gives his day labourer five silver groschen a day. For these five silver groschen the labourer works all day on the farmer's field and thus secures him a return of ten silver groschen. The farmer not only gets the value replaced that he has to give the day labourer; he doubles it. He has therefore employed, consumed, the five silver groschen that he gave to the labourer in a fruitful, productive manner. He has bought with the five silver groschen just that labour and power of the labourer which produces agricultural products of double value and makes ten silver groschen out of five. The day labourer, on the other hand, receives in place of his productive power, the effect of which he has bargained away to the farmer, five silver groschen, which he exchanges for means of subsistence, and these he consumes with greater or less rapidity. The five silver groschen have, therefore, been consumed in a double way *reproductively* for capital, for they have been exchanged for labour power which produced ten silver groschen, *unproductively* for the worker, for they have been exchanged for means of subsistence which have disappeared forever and the value of which he can only recover by repeating the same exchange with the farmer. *Thus capital presupposes wage labour; wage labour presupposes capital. They reciprocally condition the existence of each other; they reciprocally bring forth each other.*

Does a worker in a cotton factory produce merely cotton textiles? No, he produces capital. He produces values which serve afresh to command his labour and by means of it to create new values.

Capital can only increase by exchanging itself for labour power, by calling wage labour to life. The labour power of the wage-worker can only be exchanged for capital by increasing capital, by strengthening the power whose slave it is. *Hence, increase of capital is increase of the proletariat, that is, of the working class.*

The interests of the capitalist and those of the worker are, therefore, *one and the same*, assert the bourgeois and their economists. Indeed! The worker perishes if capital does not employ him. Capital perishes if it does not exploit labour power, and in order to exploit it, it must buy it. The faster capital intended for production, productive capital, increases, the more, therefore, industry prospers, the more the bourgeoisie enriches itself and the better business is, the more workers does the capitalist need, the more dearly does the worker sell himself.

The indispensable condition for a tolerable situation of the worker *is, therefore, the fastest possible growth of productive capital.*

But what is the growth of productive capital? Growth of the power of accumulated labour over living labour. Growth of the domination of the bourgeoisie over the working class. If wage labour produces the wealth of others that rules over it, the power that is hostile to it, capital, then the means of employment, that is, the means of subsistence, flow back to it from this hostile power, on condition that it makes itself afresh into a part of capital, into the lever which hurls capital anew into an accelerated movement of growth.

To say that the interests of capital and those of the workers are one and the same is only to say that capital and wage labour are two sides of one and the same relation. The one conditions the other, just as usurer and squanderer condition each other.

As long as the wage-worker is a wage-worker his lot depends upon capital. That is the much-vaunted community of interests between worker and capitalist.

If capital grows, the mass of wage labour grows, the number of wage-workers grows; in a word, the domination of capital extends over a greater number of individuals. Let us assume the most favourable case: when productive capital grows, the demand for labour grows; consequently, the price of labour, wages, goes up.

A house may be large or small; as long as the surrounding houses are equally small it satisfies all social demands for a dwelling. But let a palace arise beside the little house, and it shrinks from a little house to a hut. The little house shows now that its owner has only very slight or no demands to make; and however high it may shoot up in the course of civilisation, if the neighbouring palace grows to an equal or even greater extent, the occupant of the relatively small house will feel more and more uncomfortable, dissatisfied and cramped within its four walls.

A noticeable increase in wages presupposes a rapid growth of productive capital. The rapid growth of productive capital brings about an equally rapid growth of wealth, luxury, social wants, social enjoyments. Thus, although the enjoyments of the worker have risen, the social satisfaction that they give has fallen in comparison with the increased enjoyments of the capitalist, which are inaccessible to the worker, in comparison with the state of development of society in general. Our desires and pleasures spring from society; we measure them, therefore, by society and not by the objects which serve for their satisfaction. Because they are of a social nature, they are of a relative nature.

In general, wages are determined not only by the amount of commodities for which I can exchange them. They embody various relations.

What the workers receive for their labour power is, in the first place, a definite sum of money. Are wages determined only by this money price?

In the sixteenth century, the gold and silver circulating in Europe increased as a result of the discovery of richer and more easily worked mines in America. Hence, the value of gold and silver fell in relation to other commodities. The workers received the same amount of coined silver for their labour power as before. The money price of their labour remained the same, and yet their wages had fallen, for in exchange for the same quantity of silver they received a smaller amount of other commodities. This was one of the circumstances which furthered the growth of capital and the rise of the bourgeoisie in the sixteenth century.

Let us take another case. In the winter of 1847, as a result of a crop failure, the most indispensable means of subsistence, cereals, meat, butter, cheese, etc., rose considerably in price. Assume that the workers received the same sum of money for their labour power as before. Had not their wages fallen? Of course. For the same money they received less bread, meat, etc., in exchange. Their wages had fallen, not because the value of silver had diminished, but because the value of the means of subsistence had increased.

Assume, finally, that the money price of labour remains the same while all agricultural and manufactured goods have fallen in price owing to the employment of new machinery, a favourable season, etc. For the same money the workers can now buy more commodities of all kinds. Their wages, therefore, have risen, just because the money value of their wages has not changed.

Thus, the money price of labour, nominal wages, do not coincide with real wages, that is, with the sum of commodities which is actually given in exchange for the wages. If, therefore, we speak of a rise or fall of wages, we must keep in mind not only the money price of labour, the nominal wages.

But neither nominal wages, that is, the sum of money for which the worker sells himself to the capitalist, nor real wages, that is, the sum of commodities which he can buy for this money, exhaust the relations contained in wages.

Wages are, above all, also determined by their relation to the gain, to the profit of the capitalist – comparative, relative wages.

Real wages express the price of labour in relation to the price of other commodities; relative wages, on the other hand, express the share of direct labour in the new value it has created in relation to the share which falls to accumulated labour, to capital.

We said above: 'Wages are not the worker's share in the commodity produced by him. Wages are the part of already existing commodities with which the capitalist buys for himself a definite amount of productive labour power.' But the capitalist must replace these wages out of the price at which he sells the product produced by the worker; he must replace it in such a way that there remains to him, as a rule, a surplus over the cost of production expended by him, a profit. For the capitalist, the selling price of the commodities produced by the worker is divided into three parts: *first*, the replacement of the price of the raw materials advanced by him together with replacement of the depreciation of the tools, machinery and other means of labour also advanced by him; *secondly*, the replacement of the wages advanced by him, and *thirdly*, the surplus left over, the capitalist's profit. While the first part only replaces *previously existing values*, it is clear that both the replacement of the wages and also the surplus profit of the capitalist are, on the whole, taken from the *new value created by the worker's labour* and added to the raw materials. And *in this sense*, in order to compare them with one another, we can regard both wages and profit as shares in the product of the worker.

Real wages may remain the same, they may even rise, and yet relative wages may fall. Let us suppose, for example, that all means of subsistence have gone down in price by two-thirds while wages per day have only fallen by one-third, that is to say, for example, from three marks to two marks. Although the worker can command a greater amount of commodities with these two marks than he previously could with three marks, yet his wages have gone down in relation to the profit of the capitalist. The profit of the capitalist (for example, the manufacturer) has increased by one mark; that is, for a smaller sum of exchange values which he pays to the worker, the latter must produce a greater amount of exchange values than before. The share of capital relative to the share of labour has risen. The division of social wealth between capital and labour has become still more unequal. With the same capital, the capitalist commands a greater quantity of labour. The power of the capitalist class over the working class has grown, the social position of the worker has deteriorated, has been depressed one step further below that of the capitalist.

What, then, is the general law which determines the rise and fall of wages and profit in their reciprocal relation?

They stand in inverse ratio to each other. Capital's share, profit, rises in the same proportion as labour's share, wages, falls, and vice versa. Profit rises to the extent that wages fall; it falls to the extent that wages rise.

The objection will, perhaps, be made that the capitalist can profit by a favourable exchange of his products with other capitalists, by increase of the demand for his commodities, whether as a result of the opening of new markets, or as a result of a momentarily increased demand in the old markets, etc.; that the capitalist's profit can, therefore, increase by overreaching other capitalists, independently of the rise and fall of wages, of the exchange value of labour power; or that the capitalist's profit may also rise owing to the improvement of the instruments of labour, a new application of natural forces, etc.

First of all, it will have to be admitted that the result remains the same, although it is brought about in reverse fashion. True, the profit has not risen because wages have fallen, but wages have fallen because the profit has risen. With the same amount of other people's labour, the capitalist has acquired a greater amount of exchange values, without having paid more for the labour on that account; that is, therefore, labour is paid less in proportion to the net profit which it yields the capitalist.

In addition, we recall that, in spite of the fluctuations in prices of commodities, the average price of every commodity, the ratio in which it is exchanged for other commodities, is determined by its *cost of production.* Hence the overreachings within the capitalist class necessarily balance one another. The improvement of machinery, new application of natural forces in the service of production, enable a larger amount of products to be created in a given period of time with the same amount of labour and capital, but not by any means a larger amount of exchange values. If, by the use of the spinning jenny, I can turn out twice as much yarn in an hour as before its invention, say, one hundred pounds instead of fifty, then in the long run I will receive for these hundred pounds no more commodities in exchange than formerly for the fifty pounds, because the cost of production has fallen by one-half, or because I can deliver double the product at the same cost.

Finally, in whatever proportion the capitalist class, the bourgeoisie, whether of one country or of the whole world market, shares the net profit of production within itself, the total amount of this net profit always consists only of the amount by which, on the whole, accumulated labour has been increased by direct labour. This total amount grows, therefore, in the proportion in which labour augments capital, that is, in the proportion in which profit rises in comparison with wages.

We see, therefore, that even if we remain *within the relation of capital and wage labour, the interests of capital and the interests of wage labour are diametrically opposed.*

A rapid increase of capital is equivalent to a rapid increase of profit. Profit can only increase rapidly if the price of labour, if relative wages, decrease just as rapidly. Relative wages can fall although real wages rise simultaneously with nominal wages, with the money value of labour, if they do not rise, however, in the same proportion as profit. If, for instance, in times when business is good, wages rise by five per cent, profit on the other hand by thirty per cent, then the comparative, the relative wages, have not *increased* but *decreased.*

Thus if the income of the worker increases with the rapid growth of capital, the social gulf that separates the worker from the capitalist increases at the same time, and the power of capital over labour, the dependence of labour on capital, likewise increases at the same time.

To say that the worker has an interest in the rapid growth of capital is only to say that the more rapidly the worker increases the wealth of others, the richer will be the crumbs that fall to him, the greater is the number of workers that can be employed and called into existence, the more can the mass of slaves dependent on capital be increased.

We have thus seen that:

Even the *most favourable situation* for the working class, the *most rapid possible growth of capital*, however much it may improve the material existence of the worker, does not remove the antagonism between his interests and the interests of the bourgeoisie, the interests of the capitalists. *Profit and wages* remain as before in *inverse proportion.*

If capital is growing rapidly, wages may rise; the profit of capital rises incomparably more rapidly. The material position of the worker has improved, but at the cost of his social position. The social gulf that divides him from the capitalist has widened.

Finally:

To say that the most favourable condition for wage labour is the most rapid possible growth of productive capital is only to say that the more rapidly the working class increases and enlarges the power that is hostile to it, the wealth that does not belong to it and that rules over it, the more favourable will be the conditions under which it is allowed to labour anew at increasing bourgeois wealth, at enlarging the power of capital, content with forging for itself the golden chains by which the bourgeoisie drags it in its train.

Are *growth of productive capital and rise of wages* really so inseparably connected as the bourgeois economists maintain? We must not take their word for it. We must not even believe them when they say that the fatter capital is, the better will its slave be fed. The bourgeoisie is too enlightened, it calculates too well, to share the prejudices of the feudal lord who makes a display by geoisie compel it to calculate.

We must, therefore, examine more closely:

How does the growth of productive capital affect wages?

If, on the whole, the productive capital of bourgeois society grows, a *more manifold* accumulation of labour takes place. The capitals increase in number and extent. The *numerical increase* of the capitals increases the *competition between the capitalists.* The *increasing extent* of the capitals provides the means for *bringing more powerful labour armies with more gigantic instruments of war into the industrial battlefield.*

One capitalist can drive another from the field and capture his capital only by selling more cheaply. In order to be able to sell more cheaply without ruining himself, he must produce more cheaply, that is, raise the productive power of labour as much as possible. But the productive power of labour is raised, above all, by *a greater division of labour*, by a more universal introduction and continual improvement of *machinery*. The greater the labour army among whom labour is divided, the more gigantic the scale on which machinery is introduced, the more does the cost of production proportionately decrease, the more fruitful is labour. Hence, a general rivalry arises among the capitalists to increase the division of labour and machinery and to exploit them on the greatest possible scale.

If, now, by a greater division of labour, by the utilisation of new machines and their improvement, by more profitable and extensive exploitation of natural forces, one capitalist has found the means of producing with the same amount of labour or of accumulated labour a greater amount of products, of commodities, than his competitors, if he can, for example, produce a whole yard of linen in the same labour time in which his competitors weave half a yard, how will this capitalist operate?

He could continue to sell half a yard of linen at the old market price; this would, however, be no means of driving his opponents from the field and of enlarging his own sales. But in the same measure in which his production has expanded, his need to sell has also increased. The more powerful and costly means of production that he has called into life *enable* him, indeed, to sell his commodities more cheaply, they *compel* him, however, at the same time *to sell more commodities*, to conquer a much *larger* market for his commodities; consequently, our capitalist will sell his half yard of linen more cheaply than his competitors.

The capitalist will not, however, sell a whole yard as cheaply as his competitors sell half a yard, although the production of the whole yard does not cost him more than the half yard costs the others. Otherwise he would not gain anything extra but only get back the cost of production by the exchange. His possibly greater income would be derived from the fact of having set a larger capital into motion, but not from having made more of his capital than the others. Moreover, he attains the object he wishes to attain, if he puts the price of his goods only a small percentage lower than that of his competitors. He drives them from the field, he wrests from them at least a part of their sales, by *underselling* them. And, finally, it will be remembered that the current price always stands *above or below the cost of production*, according to whether the sale of the commodity occurs in a favourable or unfavourable industrial season. The percentage at which the capitalist who has employed new and more fruitful means of production sells above his real cost of production will vary, depending upon whether the market price of a yard of linen stands below or above its hitherto customary cost of production.

However, the *privileged position* of our capitalist is not of long duration; other competing capitalists introduce the same machines, the same division of labour, introduce them on the same or on a larger scale, and this introduction will become so general that the price of linen *is reduced* not only *below its old*, but *below its new cost of production.*

The capitalists find themselves, therefore, in the same position relative to one another as *before* the introduction of the new means of production, and if they are able to supply by these means double the production at the same price, they are *now* forced to supply the double product *below* the old price. On the basis of this new cost of production, the same game begins again. More division of labour, more machinery, enlarged scale of exploitation of machinery and division of labour. And again competition brings the same counteraction against this result.

We see how in this way the mode of production and the means of production are continually transformed, revolutionised, *how the division of labour is necessarily followed by greater division of labour, the application of machinery by still greater application of machinery, work on a large scale by work on a still larger scale.*

That is the law which again and again throws bourgeois production out of its old course and which compels capital to intensify the productive forces of labour, *because* it has intensified them, it, the law which gives capital no rest and continually whispers in its ear: 'Go on! Go on!'

This law is none other than that which, within the fluctuations of trade periods, necessarily *levels out* the price of a commodity to its *cost of production.*

However powerful the means of production which a capitalist brings into the field, competition will make these means of production universal and from the moment when it has made them universal, the only result of the greater fruitfulness of his capital is that he must now supply *for the same price* ten, twenty, a hundred times as much as before. But, as he must sell perhaps a thousand times as much as before in order to outweigh the lower selling price by the greater amount of the product sold, because a more extensive sale is now necessary, not only in order to make more profit but in order to replace the cost of production – the instrument of production itself, as we have seen, becomes more and more expensive – and because this mass sale becomes a question of life and death not only for him but also for his rivals, the old struggle begins again *all the more violently the more fruitful the already discovered means of production are. The division of labour and the application of machinery, therefore, will go on anew on an incomparably greater scale.*

Whatever the power of the means of production employed may be, competition seeks to rob capital of the golden fruits of this power by bringing the price of the commodities back to the cost of production, by thus making cheaper production – the supply of ever greater amounts of products for the same total price – an imperative law to the same extent as production can be cheapened, that is, as more can be produced with the same amount of labour. Thus the capitalist would have won nothing by his own exertions but the obligation to supply more in the same labour time, in a word, *more difficult conditions for augmentation of the value of his capital.* While, therefore, competition continually pursues him with its law of the cost of production and every weapon that he forges against his rivals recoils against himself, the capitalist continually tries to get the better of competition by incessantly introducing new machines, more expensive, it is true, but producing more cheaply, and new division of labour in place of the old, and by not waiting until competition has rendered the new ones obsolete.

If now we picture to ourselves this feverish simultaneous agitation on the *whole world market*, it will be comprehensible how the growth, accumulation and concentration of capital results in an uninterrupted division of labour, and in the application of new and the perfecting of old machinery precipitately and on an ever more gigantic scale.

But how do these circumstances, which are inseparable from the growth of productive capital, affect the determination of wages?

The greater *division of labour* enables *one* worker to do the work of five, ten or twenty; it therefore multiplies, competition among the workers fivefold, tenfold and twentyfold. The workers do not only compete by one selling himself cheaper than another; they compete by *one* doing the work of five, ten, twenty; and the *division of labour*, introduced by capital and continually increased, compels the workers to compete among themselves in this way.

Further, as the *division of labour* increases, labour *is simplified.* The special skill of the worker becomes worthless. He becomes transformed into a simple, monotonous productive force that does not have to use intense bodily or intellectual faculties. His labour becomes a labour that anyone can perform. Hence, competitors crowd upon him on all sides, and besides we remind the reader that the more simple and easily learned the labour is, the lower the cost of production needed to master it, the lower do wages sink, for, like the price of every other commodity, they are determined by the cost of production.

Therefore, as labour becomes more unsatisfying, more repulsive, competition increases and wages decrease. The worker tries to keep up the amount of his wages by working more, whether by working longer hours or by producing more in one hour. Driven by want, therefore, he still further increases the evil effects of the division of labour. The result is that *the more he works the less wages he receives*, and for the simple reason that he competes to that extent with his fellow workers, hence makes them into so many competitors who offer themselves on just the same bad terms as he does himself, and that, therefore, in the last resort he *competes with himself, with himself as a member of the working class.*

Machinery brings about the same results on a much greater scale, by replacing skilled workers by unskilled, men by women, adults by children. It brings about the same results, where it is newly introduced, by throwing the hand workers on to the streets in masses, and, where it is developed, improved and replaced by more productive machinery, by discharging workers in smaller batches. We have portrayed above, in a hasty sketch, the industrial war of the capitalists among themselves; *this war has the peculiarity that its battles are won less by recruiting than by discharging the army of labour. The generals, the capitalists, compete with one another as to who can discharge most soldiers of industry.*

The economists tell us, it is true, that the workers rendered superfluous by machinery find *new* branches of employment.

They dare not assert directly that the same workers who are discharged find places in the new branches of labour. The facts cry out too loudly against this lie. They really only assert that new means of employment will open up for *other component sections of the working class*, for instance, for the portion of the young generation of workers that was ready to enter the branch of industry which has gone under. That is, of course, a great consolation for the disinherited workers. The worshipful capitalists will never want for fresh exploitable flesh and blood, and will let the dead bury their dead. This is a consolation which the bourgeois give themselves rather than one which they give the workers. If the whole class of wage-workers were to be abolished owing to machinery, how dreadful that would be for capital which, without wage labour, ceases to be capital!

Let us suppose, however, that those directly driven out of their jobs by machinery, and the entire section of the new generation that was already on the watch for this employment, *find a new occupation.* Does any one imagine that it will be as highly paid as that which has been lost? *That would contradict all the laws of economics.* We have seen how modern industry always brings with it the substitution of a more simple, subordinate occupation for the more complex and higher one.

How, then, could a mass of workers who have been thrown out of one branch of industry owing to machinery find refuge in another, unless the latter *is lower, worse paid?*

The workers who work in the manufacture of machinery itself have been cited as an exception. As soon as more machinery is demanded and used in industry, it is said, there must necessarily be an increase of machines, consequently of the manufacture of machines, and consequently of the employment of workers in the manufacture of machines; and the workers engaged in this branch of industry are claimed to be skilled, even educated workers.

Since the year 1840 this assertion, which even before was only half true, has lost all semblance of truth because ever more versatile machines have been employed in the manufacture of machinery, no more and no less than in the manufacture of cotton yarn, and the workers employed in the machine factories, confronted by highly elaborate machines, can only play the part of highly unelaborate machines.

But in place of the man who has been discharged owing to the machine, the factory employs maybe *three* children and *one* woman. And did not the man's wages have to suffice for the three children and a woman? Did not the minimum of wages have to suffice to maintain and to propagate the race? What, then, does this favourite bourgeois phrase prove? Nothing more than that now four times as many workers' lives are used up in order to gain a livelihood for one worker's family.

Let us sum up: *The more productive capital grows, the more the division of labour and the application of machinery expands. The more the division of labour and the application of machinery expands, the more competition among the workers expands and the more their wages contract.*

In addition, the working class gains recruits from the *higher strata of society* also; a mass of petty industrialists and small rentiers are hurled down into its ranks and have nothing better to do than urgently stretch out their arms alongside those of the workers. Thus the forest of uplifted arms demanding work becomes ever thicker, while the arms themselves become ever thinner.

That the small industrialist cannot survive in a contest one of the first conditions of which is to produce on an ever greater scale, that is, precisely to be a large and not a small industrialist, is self-evident.

That the interest on capital decreases in the same measure as the mass and number of capitals increase, as capital grows; that, therefore, the small rentier can no longer live on his interest but must throw himself into industry, and, consequently, help to swell the ranks of the small industrialists and thereby of candidates for the proletariat – all this surely requires no further explanation.

Finally, as the capitalists are compelled, by the movement described above, to exploit the already existing gigantic means of production on a larger scale and to set in motion all the mainsprings of credit to this end, there is a corresponding increase in industrial earthquakes, in which the trading world can only maintain itself by sacrificing a part of wealth, of products and even of productive forces to the gods of the nether world – in a word, *crises* increase. They become more frequent and more violent, if only because, as the mass of production, and consequently the need for extended markets, grows, the world market becomes more and more contracted, fewer and fewer new markets remain available for exploitation, since every preceding crisis has subjected to world trade a market hitherto unconquered or only superficially exploited. But capital does not *live* only on labour. A lord, at once aristocratic and barbarous, it drags with it into the grave the corpses of its slaves, whole hecatombs of workers who perish in the crises. Thus we see: *if capital grows rapidly, competition among the workers grows incomparably more rapidly, that is, the means of employment, the means of subsistence, of the working class decrease proportionately so much the more, and, nevertheless, the rapid growth of capital is the most favourable condition for wage labour.*

1.6 The Preface to *A Critique of Political Economy*

The '1859 Preface' is one of the most famous, oft quoted and controversial pieces of Marx's writing. The preface contains a superbly written and succinct précis of historical materialism and the connection between production relations and social life. Often this passage is used to confirm the 'base-superstructure' metaphor as being a valid one for understanding Marx's method. However this is suggestive of a rather mechanical and simplistic conception of society which is rarely employed in Marx's detailed historical writing – we should recall the 'living human individuals' Marx discusses in *The German Ideology*. The '1859 Preface' is best seen as a useful summary but not the classic statement of his position.

From: D. McLellan, *Karl Marx: Selected Writings* (Oxford University Press, 1977) pp. 389–90.

In the social production of life, men enter into definite relations that are indispensable and independent of their will, relations of production which correspond to a definite stage of development of their material productive forces. The sum total of these relations of production constitutes the economic structure of society, the real foundation, on which rises a legal and political superstructure and to which correspond definite forms of social consciousness. The mode of production of material life conditions the social, political, and intellectual life process in general. It is not the consciousness of men that determines their being, but, on the contrary, their social being that determines their consciousness. At a certain stage of their development, the material productive forces of society come in conflict with the existing relations of production, or – what is but a legal expression for the same thing – with the property relations within which they have been at work hitherto. From forms of development of the productive forces these relations turn into their letters. Then begins an epoch of social revolution. With the change of the economic foundations the entire immense superstructure is more or less rapidly transformed. In considering such transformations a distinction should always be made between the material transformation of the economic conditions of production, which can be determined with the precision of natural science, and the legal, political, religious, aesthetic, or philosophic – in short, ideological forms in which men become conscious of this conflict and fight it out. Just as our opinion of an individual is not based on what he thinks of himself, so can we not judge of such a period of transformation by its own consciousness; on the contrary, this consciousness must be explained rather from the contradictions of material life, from the existing conflict between the social productive forces and the relations of production. No social order ever perishes before all the productive forces for which there is room in it have developed; and new, higher relations of production never appear before the material conditions of their existence have matured in the womb of the old society itself. Therefore mankind always sets itself only such tasks as it can solve; since, looking at the matter more closely, it will always be found that the task itself arises only when the material conditions for its solution already exist or are at least in the process of formation. In broad outlines Asiatic, ancient, feudal, and modern bourgeois modes of production can be designated as progressive epochs in the economic formation of society. The bourgeois relations of production are the last antagonistic form of the social process of production – antagonistic not in the sense of individual antagonism, but of one arising from the social conditions of life of the individuals; at the same time the productive forces developing in the womb of bourgeois society create the material conditions for the solution of that antagonism. This social formation brings, therefore, the prehistory of human society to a close.

1.7 The Fetishism of Commodities

This extract is taken from *Capital, Volume 1* (1867) and is concerned with the 'mystical character of commodities'. The circulation of commodities within capitalism has the effect of masking the social relations of production within which they are initially produced. So the capitalist market appears to us as a world of prices, profits, cash transactions and the flitting of figures on stock market computer screens, and relations between people are lost and assume the 'fantastic form' of relations between 'things'. There are clearly parallels and lines of continuity between the discussion of 'fetishism' and Marx's earlier concerns with 'alienation'.

From: D. McLellan, *Karl Marx: Selected Writings* (Oxford University Press, 1977) pp. 435–9.

A commodity appears, at first sight, a very trivial thing, and easily understood. Its analysis shows that it is, in reality, a very queer thing, abounding in metaphysical subtleties and theological niceties. So far as it is a value in use, there is nothing mysterious about it, whether we consider it from the point of view that by its properties it is capable of satisfying human wants, or from the point that those properties are the product of human labour. It is as clear as noonday, that man, by his industry, changes the forms of the materials furnished by Nature, in such a way as to make them useful to him. The form of wood, for instance, is altered, by making a table out of it. Yet, for all that, the table continues to be that common, everyday thing, wood. But, so soon as it steps forth as a commodity, it is changed into something transcendent. It not only stands with its feet on the ground, but, in relation to all other commodities, it stands on its head, and evolves out of its wooden brain grotesque ideas, far more wonderful than 'table-turning' ever was.

The mystical character of commodities does not originate, therefore, in their use-value. Just as little does it proceed from the nature of the determining factors of value. For, in the first place, however varied the useful kinds of labour, or productive activities, may be, it is a physiological fact, that they are functions of the human organism, and that each such function, whatever may be its nature or form, is essentially the expenditure of human brain, nerves, muscles, etc. Secondly, with regard to that which forms the groundwork for the quantitative determination of value, namely, the duration of that expenditure, or the quantity of labour, it is quite clear that there is a palpable difference between its quantity and the quality. In all states of society, the labour time that it costs to produce the means of subsistence must necessarily be an object of interest to mankind, though not of equal interest in different stages of development. And lastly, from the moment that men in any way work for one another, their labour assumes a social form.

Whence, then, arises the enigmatical character of the product of labour, so soon as it assumes the form of commodities? Clearly from this form itself. The equality of all sorts of human labour is expressed objectively by their products all being equally values; the measure of the expenditure of labour power by the duration of that expenditure takes the form of the quantity of value of the products of labour; and finally, the mutual relations of the producers, within which the social character of their labour affirms itself, take the form of a social relation between the products.

A commodity is therefore a mysterious thing, simply because in it the social character of men's labour appears to them as an objective character stamped upon the product of that labour; because the relation of the producers to the sum total of their own labour is presented to them as a social relation, existing not between themselves, but between the products of their labour. This is the reason why the products of labour become commodities, social things whose qualities are at the same time perceptible and imperceptible by the senses. In the same way the light from an object is perceived by us not as the subjective excitation of our optic nerve, but as the objective form of something outside the eye itself. But, in the act of seeing, there is at all events, an actual passage of light from one thing to another, from the external object to the eye. There is a physical relation between physical things. But it is different with commodities. There, the existence of the things *qua* commodities, and the value relation between the products of labour which stamps them as commodities, have absolutely no connection with their physical properties and with the material relations arising therefrom. There it is a definite social relation between men, that assumes, in their eyes, the fantastic form of a relation between things. In order, therefore, to find an analogy, we must have recourse to the mist-enveloped regions of the religious world. In that world the productions of the human brain appear as independent beings endowed with life, and entering into relation both with one another and the human race. So it is in the world of commodities with the products of men's hands. This I call the Fetishism which attaches itself to the products of labour, so soon as they are produced as commodities, and which is therefore inseparable from the production of commodities.

This Fetishism of commodities has its origin in the peculiar social character of the labour that produces them.

As a general rule, articles of utility become commodities, only because they are products of the labour of private individuals or groups of individuals who carry on their work independently of each other. The sum total of the labour of all these private individuals forms the aggregate labour of society. Since the producers do not come into social contact with each other until they exchange their products, the specific social character of each producer's labour does not show itself except in the act of exchange. In other words, the labour of the individual asserts itself as a part of the labour of society only by means of the relations which the act of exchange establishes directly between the products, and indirectly, through them, between the producers. To the latter, therefore, the relations connecting the labour of one individual with that of the rest appear, not as direct social relations between individuals at work, but as what they really are, material relations between persons and social relations between things. It is only by being exchanged that the products of labour acquire, as values, one uniform social status, distinct from their varied forms of existence as objects of utility. This division of a product into a useful thing and a value becomes practically important, only when exchange has acquired such an extension that useful articles are produced for the purpose of being exchanged, and their character as values has therefore to be taken into account, beforehand, during production. From this moment the labour of the individual producer acquires socially a twofold character. On the one hand, it must, as a definite useful kind of labour, satisfy a definite social want, and thus hold its place as part and parcel of the collective labour of all, as a branch of a social division of labour that has sprung up spontaneously. On the other hand, it can satisfy the manifold wants of the individual producer himself, only in so far as the mutual exchangeability of all kinds of useful private labour is an established social fact, and therefore the private useful labour of each producer ranks on an equality with that of all others. The equalization of the most different kinds of labour can be the result only of an abstraction from their inequalities, or of reducing them to their common denominator, viz., expenditure of human labour power or human labour in the abstract. The twofold social character of the labour of the individual appears to him, when reflected in his brain, only under those forms which are impressed upon that labour in everyday practice by the exchange of products. In this way, the character that his own labour possesses of being socially useful takes the form of the condition that the product must be not only useful, but useful for others, and the social character that his particular labour has of being the equal of all other particular kinds of labour, takes the form that all the physically different articles that are the products of labour have one common quality, viz., that of having value.

Hence, when we bring the products of our labour into relation with each other as values, it is not because we see in these articles the material receptacles of homogeneous human labour. Quite the contrary: whenever, by an exchange, we equate as values our different products, by that very act, we also equate, as human labour, the different kinds of labour expended upon them. We are not aware of this, nevertheless we do it. Value, therefore, does not stalk about with a label describing what it is. It is value, rather, that converts every product into a social hieroglyphic. Later on, we try to decipher the hieroglyphic, to get behind the secret of our own social products; for to stamp an object of utility as a value, is just as much a social product as language. The recent scientific discovery that the products of labour, so far as they are values, are but material expressions of the human labour spent in their production marks, indeed, an epoch in the history of the development of the human race, but by no means dissipates the mist through which the social character of labour appears to us to be an objective character of the products themselves. The fact that in the particular form of production with which we are dealing, viz., the production of commodities, the specific social character of private labour carried on independently, consists in the equality of every kind of that labour, by virtue of its being human labour, which character, therefore, assumes in the product the form of value – this fact appears to the producers, notwithstanding the discovery above referred to, to be just as real and final, as the fact that, after the discovery by science of the component gases of air, the atmosphere itself remained unaltered.

What, first of all, practically concerns producers when they make an exchange, is the question, how much of some other product they get for their own? in what proportions are the products exchangeable? When these proportions have, by custom, attained a certain stability, they appear to result from the nature of the products, so that, for instance, one ton of iron and two ounces of gold appear as naturally to be of equal value as a pound of gold and a pound of iron, in spite of their different physical and chemical qualities, appear to be of equal weight. The character of having value, when once impressed upon products, obtains fixity only by reason of their acting and reacting upon each other as quantities of value. These quantities vary continually, independently of the will, foresight, and action of the producers. To them, their own social action takes the form of the action of objects, which rule the producers instead of being ruled by them. It requires a fully developed production of commodities before, from accumulated experience alone, the scientific conviction springs up that all the different kinds of private labour, which are carried on independently of each other, and yet as spontaneously developed branches of the social division of labour, are continually being reduced to the quantitative proportions in which society requires them. And why? Because, in the midst of all the accidental and ever fluctuating exchange-relations between the products, the labour time socially necessary for their production forcibly asserts itself like an overriding law of Nature. The law of gravity thus asserts itself when a house falls about our ears. The determination of the magnitude of value by labour time is therefore a secret, hidden under the apparent fluctuations in the relative values of commodities. Its discovery, while removing all appearance of mere accidentality from the determination of the magnitude of the values of products, yet in no way alters the mode in which that determination takes place.

Man's reflections on the forms of social life, and consequently, also, his scientific analysis of those forms, take a course directly opposite to that of their actual historical development. He begins, *post festum* [sic: after the event], with the results of the process of development ready to hand before him. The characters that stamp products as commodities, and whose establishment is a necessary preliminary to the circulation of commodities, have already acquired the stability of natural, self-understood forms of social life, before man seeks to decipher, not their historical character, for in his eyes they are immutable, but their meaning. Consequently it was the analysis of the prices of commodities that alone led to the determination of the magnitude of value, and it was the common expression of all commodities in money that alone led to the establishment of their characters as values. It is, however, just this ultimate money-form of the world of commodities that actually conceals, instead of disclosing, the social character of private labour, and the social relations between the individual producers. When I state that coats or boots stand in a relation to linen, because it is the universal incarnation of abstract human labour, the absurdity of the statement is self-evident. Nevertheless, when the producers of coats and boots compare those articles with linen, or, what is the same thing, with gold or silver, as the universal equivalent, they express the relation between their own private labour and the collective labour of society in the same absurd form.

The categories of bourgeois economy consist of such like forms. They are forms of thought expressing with social validity the conditions and relations of a definite, historically determined mode of production, viz., the production of commodities. The whole mystery of commodities, all the magic and necromancy that surrounds the products of labour as long as they take the form of commodities, vanishes therefore, as soon as we come to other forms of production.

1.8 THE SO-CALLED PRIMITIVE ACCUMULATION

This section forms 'Part VIII' of *Capital Volume 1* and is a brilliant and stirring account of the development of the capitalist mode of production. Rich in historical detail and displaying a virtuoso use of statistical evidence, this section is also one of Marx's best examples of 'historical materialism' put into practice.

From: K. Marx, *Capital Volume 1* (Lawrence and Wishart: London, 1954) pp. 667–712.

The Secret of Primitive Accumulation

We have seen how money is changed into capital; how through capital surplus-value is made, and from surplus-value more capital. But the accumulation of capital pre-supposes surplus-value; surplus-value pre-supposes capitalistic production; capitalistic production pre-supposes the pre-existence of considerable masses of capital and of labour-power in the hands of producers of commodities. The whole movement, therefore, seems to turn in a vicious circle, out of which we can only get by supposing a primitive accumulation (previous accumulation of Adam Smith) preceding capitalistic accumulation; an accumulation not the result of the capitalist mode of production, but its starting point.

This primitive accumulation plays in Political Economy about the same part as original sin in theology. Adam bit the apple, and thereupon sin fell on the human race. Its origin is supposed to be explained when it is told as an anecdote of the past. In times long gone by there were two sorts of people; one, the diligent, intelligent, and, above all, frugal élite; the other, lazy rascals, spending their substance, and more, in riotous living. The legend of theological original sin tells us certainly how man came to be condemned to eat his bread in the sweat of his brow; but the history of economic original sin reveals to us that there are people to whom this is by no means essential. Never mind! Thus it came to pass that the former sort accumulated wealth, and the latter sort had at last nothing to sell except their own skins. And from this original sin dates the poverty of the great majority that, despite all labour, has up to now nothing to sell but itself, and the wealth of the few that increases constantly although they have long ceased to work. Such insipid childishness is every day preached to us in the defence of property. M. Thiers, e.g., had the assurance to repeat it with all the solemnity of a stateman, to the French people, once so *spirituel*. But as soon as the question of property crops up, it becomes a sacred duty to proclaim the intellectual food of the infant as the one thing fit for all ages and for all stages of development. In actual history it is notorious that conquest, enslavement, robbery, murder, briefly force, play the great part. In the tender annals of Political Economy, the idyllic reigns from time immemorial. Right and 'labour' were from all time the sole means of enrichment, the present year of course always excepted. As a matter of fact, the methods of primitive accumulation are anything but idyllic.

In themselves money and commodities are no more capital than are the means of production and of subsistence. They want transforming into capital. But this transformation itself can only take place under certain circumstances that centre in this, viz., that two very different kinds of commodity-possessors must come face to face and into contact; on the one hand, the owners of money, means of production, means of subsistence, who are eager to increase the sum of values they possess, by buying other people's labour-power; on the other hand, free labourers, the sellers of their own labour-power, and therefore the sellers of labour. Free labourers, in the double sense that neither they themselves form part and parcel of the means of production, as in the case of slaves, bondsmen, etc., nor do the means of production belong to them, as in the case of peasant-proprietors; they are, therefore, free from, unencumbered by, any means of production of their own. With this polarisation of the market for commodities, the fundamental conditions of capitalist production are given. The capitalist system pre-supposes the complete separation of the labourers from all property in the means by which they can realise their labour. As soon as capitalist production is once on its own legs, it not only maintains this separation, but reproduces it on a continually extending scale. The process, therefore, that clears the way for the capitalist system, can be none other than the process which takes away from the labourer the possession of his means of production; a process that transforms, on the one hand, the social means of subsistence and of production into capital, on the other, the immediate producers into wage-labourers. The so-called primitive accumulation, therefore, is nothing else than the historical process of divorcing the producer from the means of production. It appears as primitive, because it forms the pre-historic stage of capital and of the mode of production corresponding with it.

The economic structure of capitalistic society has grown out of the economic structure of feudal society. The dissolution of the latter set free the elements of the former.

The immediate producer, the labourer, could only dispose of his own person after he had ceased to be attached to the soil and ceased to be the slave, serf, or bondman of another. To become a free seller of labour-power, who carries his commodity wherever he finds a market, he must further have escaped from the regime of the guilds, their rules for apprentices and journeymen, and the impediments of their labour regulations. Hence, the historical movement which changes the producers into wage-workers, appears, on the one hand, as their emancipation from serfdom and from the fetters of the guilds, and this side alone exists for our bourgeois historians. But, on the other hand, these new freedmen became sellers of themselves only after they had been robbed of all their own means of production, and of all the guarantees of existence afforded by the old feudal arrangements. And the history of this, their expropriation, is written in the annals of mankind in letters of blood and fire.

The industrial capitalists, these new potentates, had on their part not only to displace the guild masters of handicrafts, but also the feudal lords, the possessors of the sources of wealth. In this respect their conquest of social power appears as the fruit of a victorious struggle both against feudal lordship and its revolting prerogatives, and against the guilds and the fetters they laid on the free development of production and the free exploitation of man by man. The chevaliers d'industrie, however, only succeeded in supplanting the chevaliers of the sword by making use of events of which they themselves were wholly innocent. They have risen by means as vile as those by which the Roman freedman once on a time made himself the master of his *patronus.*

The starting-point of the development that gave rise to the wage-labourer as well as to the capitalist, was the servitude of the labourer. The advance consisted in a change of form of this servitude, in the transformation of feudal exploitation into capitalist exploitation. To understand its march, we need not go back very far. Although we come across the first beginnings of capitalist production as early as the fourteenth or fifteenth century, sporadically, in certain towns of the Mediterranean, the capitalistic era dates from the sixteenth century. Wherever it appears, the abolition of serfdom has been long effected, and the highest development of the middle ages, the existence of sovereign towns, has been long on the wane.

In the history of primitive accumulation, all revolutions are epoch-making that act as levers for the capitalist class in course of formation; but, above all, those moments when great masses of men are suddenly and forcibly torn from their means of subsistence, and hurled as free and 'unattached' proletarians on the labour-market. The expropriation of the agricultural producer, of the peasant, from the soil, is the basis of the whole process. The history of this expropriation, in different countries, assumes different aspects, and runs through its various phases in different orders of succession, and at different periods. In England alone, which we take as our example, has it the classic form.[1]

Expropriation of the Agricultural Population from the Land

In England, serfdom had practically disappeared in the last part of the fourteenth century. The immense majority of the population[2] consisted then, and to a still larger extent, in the fifteenth century, of free peasant proprietors, whatever was the feudal title under which their right of property was hidden. In the larger seignorial domains, the old bailiff, himself a serf, was displaced by the free farmer. The wage-labourers of agriculture consisted partly of peasants, who utilised their leisure time by working on the large estates, partly of an independent special class of wage-labourers, relatively and absolutely few in numbers. The latter also were practically at the same time peasant farmers, since, besides their wages, they had allotted to them arable land to the extent of four or more acres, together with their cottages. Besides they, with the rest of the peasants, enjoyed the usufruct of the common land, which gave pasture to their cattle, furnished them with timber, fire-wood, turf, etc.[3] In all countries of Europe, feudal production is characterised by division of the soil amongst the greatest possible number of sub-feudatories. The might of the feudal lord, like that of the sovereign, depended not on the length of his rent-roll, but on the number of his subjects, and the latter depended on the number of peasant proprietors.[4] Although, therefore, the English land, after the Norman conquest, was distributed in gigantic baronies, one of which often included some 900 of the old Anglo-Saxon lordships, it was bestrewn with small peasant properties, only here and there interspersed with great seignorial domains. Such conditions, together with the prosperity of the towns so characteristic of the fifteenth century, allowed of that wealth of the people which

Chancellor Fortescue so eloquently paints in his 'Laudes legum Angliæ; but it excluded the possibility of capitalistic wealth.

The prelude of the revolution that laid the foundation of the capitalist ist mode of production, was played in the last third of the fifteenth, and the first decade of the sixteenth century. A mass of free proletarians was hurled on the labour-market by the breaking-up of the bands of feudal retainers, who, as Sir James Steuart well says, 'everywhere uselessly filled house and castle.' Although the royal power, itself a product of bourgeois development, in its strife after absolute sovereignty forcibly hastened on the dissolution of these bands of retainers, it was by no means the sole cause of it. In insolent conflict with king and parliament, the great feudal lords created an incomparably larger proletariat by the forcible driving of the peasantry from the land, to which the latter had the same feudal right as the lord himself, and by the usurpation of the common lands. The rapid rise of the Flemish wool manufactures, and the corresponding rise in the price of wool in England, gave the direct impulse to these evictions. The old nobility had been devoured by the great feudal wars. The new nobility was the child of its time, for which money was the power of all powers. Transformation of arable land into sheepwalks was, therefore, its cry. Harrison, in his 'Description of England, prefixed to Holinshed's Chronicles,' describes how the expropriation of small peasants is ruining the country. 'What care our great encroachers?' The dwellings of the peasants and the cottages of the labourers were razed to the ground or doomed to decay. 'If,' says Harrison, 'the old records of euerie manour be sought . . . it will soon appear that in some manour seventeene, eighteene, or twentie houses are shrunk . . . that England was neuer less furnished with people then at the present . . . Of cities and townes either utterly decaied or more than a quarter or half diminished, though some one be a little increased here or there; of townes pulled downe for sheepe-walks, and no more but the lordships now standing in them . . . I could saie somewhat. The complaints of these old chroniclers are always exaggerated, but they reflect faithfully the impression made on contemporaries by the revolution in the conditions of production. A comparison of the writings of Chancellor Fortescue and Thomas More reveals the gulf between the fifteenth and sixteenth century. As Thornton rightly has it, the English working-class was precipitated without any transition from its golden into its iron age.

Legislation was terrified at this revolution. It did not yet stand on that height of civilisation where the 'wealth of the nation' (i.e., the formation of capital, and the reckless exploitation and impoverishing of the mass of the people figure as the *ultima Thule* of all state-craft. In his history of Henry VIII, Bacon says: 'Inclosures at that time (1489) began to be more frequent, whereby arable land (which could not be manured without people and families) was turned into pasture, which was easily rid by a few herdsmen; and tenancies for years, lives, and at will (whereupon much of the yeomanry lived) were turned into demesnes. This bred a decay of people, and (by consequence) a decay of towns, churches, tithes and the like . . . In remedying of this inconvenience the king's wisdom was admirable, and the parliament's at that time . . . they took a course to take away depopulating inclosures, and depopulating pasturage.' An Act of Henry VII., 1489, cap. 19, forbad the destruction of all 'houses of husbandry' to which at least 20 acres of land belonged. By an Act, 25 Henry VIII., the same law was renewed. It recites, among other things, that many farms and large flocks of cattle, especially of sheep, are concentrated in the hands of a few men, whereby the rent of land has much risen and tillage has fallen off, churches and houses have been pulled down, and marvellous numbers of people have been deprived of the means wherewith to maintain themselves and their families. The Act, therefore, ordains the rebuilding of the decayed farm-steads, and fixes a proportion between corn land and pasture land, etc. An Act of 1533 recites that some owners possess 24,000 sheep, and limits the number to be owned to 2,000.[5] The cry of the people and the legislation directed, for 150 years after Henry VII., against the expropriation of the small farmers and peasants, were alike fruitless. The secret of their inefficiency Bacon, without knowing it, reveals to us. The device of King Henry VII,' says Bacon, in his Essays, Civil and Moral, Essay 29, was profound and admirable, in making farms and houses of husbandry of a standard; that is, maintained with such a proportion of land unto them as may breed a subject to live in convenient plenty, and no servile condition, and to keep the plough in the hands of the owners and not mere hirelings.'[6] What the capitalist system demanded was, on the other hand, a degraded and almost servile condition of the mass of the people, the transformation of them into mercenaries and of their means of labour into capital. During this transformation period, legislation also strove to retain the 4 acres of land by the cottage of the agricultural wage-labourer, and forbad him to take lodgers into his cottage. In the reign of James I, 1627, Roger Crocker of Front Mill, was condemned for having built a cottage on the manor of Front Mill without 4 acres of land attached to the same in perpetuity. As late as Charles I's reign, 1633, a royal commission was appointed to enforce the carrying out of the old laws, especially that referring to the 4 acres of land. Even in Cromwell's time, the building of a house within 4 miles of London was forbidden unless it was endowed with 4 acres of land. As late as the first half of the eighteenth century complaint is made if the cottage of the agricultural labourer has not an adjunct of one or two acres of land. Nowadays he is lucky if it is furnished with a little garden, or if he may rent, far away from his cottage, a few roods. Landlords and farmers, says Dr Hunter, work here hand in hand. A few acres to the cottage would make the labourers too independent.[7]

The process of forcible expropriation of the people received in the sixteenth century a new and frightful impulse from the Reformation, and from the consequent colossal spoliation of the church property. The Catholic church was, at the time of the Reformation, feudal proprietor of a great part of the English land. The suppression of the monasteries etc., hurled their inmates into the proletariat. The estates of the church were to a large extent given away to rapacious royal favourites, or sold at a nominal price to speculating farmers and citizens, who drove out, *en mass*, the hereditary sub-tenants and threw their holdings into one. The legally guaranteed property of the poorer folk in a part of the church's tithes was tacitly confiscated.[8] 'Pauper ubique jacet,' cried Queen Elizabeth, after a journey through England. In the 43rd year of her reign the nation was obliged to recognise pauperism officially by the introduction of a poor-rate. 'The authors of this law seem to have been ashamed to state the grounds of it, for [contrary to traditional usage] it has no preamble whatever.[9] By the 16th of

Charles I, ch. 4, it was declared perpetual, and in fact only in 1834 did it take a new and harsher form.[10] These immediate results of the Reformation were not its most lasting ones. The property of the church formed the religious bulwark of the traditional conditions of landed property. With its fall these were no longer tenable.[11]

Even in the last decade of the seventeenth century, the yeomanry, the class of independent peasants, were more numerous than the class of farmers. They had formed the backbone of Cromwell's strength, and, even according to the confession of Macaulay, stood in favourable contrast to the drunken squires and to their servants, the country clergy, who had to marry their masters' cast-off mistresses. About 1750, the yeomanry had disappeared,[12] and so had, in the last decade of the eighteenth century, the last trace of the common land of the agricultural labourer. We leave on one side here the purely economic causes of the agricultural revolution. We deal only with the forcible means employed.

After the restoration of the Stuarts, the landed proprietors carried, by legal means, an act of usurpation, effected everywhere on the Continent without any legal formality. They abolished the feudal tenure of land, i.e. they got rid of all its obligations to the State, 'indemnified' the State by taxes on the peasantry and the rest of the mass of the people, vindicated for themselves the rights of modern private property in estates to which they had only a feudal title, and, finally, passed those laws of settlement, which, *mutatis mutandis*, had the same effect on the English agricultural labourer, as the edict of the Tartar Boris Godunof on the Russian peasantry.

The 'glorious Revolution' brought into power, along with William of Orange, the landlord and capitalist appropriators of surplus-value.[13] They inaugurated the new era by practising on a colossal scale thefts of state lands, thefts that had been hitherto managed more modestly. These estates were given away, sold at a ridiculous figure, or even annexed to private estates by direct seizure.[14] All this happened without the slightest observation of legal etiquette. The Crown lands thus fraudulently appropriated, together with the robbery of the Church estates, as far as these had not been lost again during the republican revolution, form the basis of the to-day princely domains of the English oligarchy.[15] The bourgeois capitalists favoured the operation with the view, among others, to promoting free trade in land, to extending the domain of modern agriculture on the large farm-system, and to increasing their supply of the free agricultural proletarians ready to hand. Besides, the new landed aristocracy was the natural ally of the new bankocracy, of the newly-hatched *haute finance*, and of the large manufacturers, then depending on protective duties. The English bourgeoisie acted for its own interest quite as wisely as did the Swedish bourgeoisie who, reversing the process, hand in hand with their economic allies, the peasantry, helped the kings in the forcible resumption of the Crown lands from the oligarchy. This happened since 1604 under Charles X and Charles XI.

Communal property – always distinct from the State property just dealt with – was an old Teutonic institution which lived on under cover of feudalism. We have seen how the forcible usurpation of this, generally accompanied by the turning of arable into pasture land, begins at the end of the fifteenth and extends into the sixteenth century. But, at that time, the process was carried on by means of individual acts of violence against which legislation, for a hundred and fifty years, fought in vain. The advance made by the eighteenth century shows itself in this, that the law itself becomes now the instrument of the theft of the people's land, although the large farmers make use of their little independent methods as well.[16] The parliamentary form of the robbery is that of Acts for enclosures of Commons, in other words, decrees by which the landlords grant themselves the people's land as private property, decrees of expropriation of the people. Sir F. M. Eden refutes his own crafty special pleading, in which he tries to represent communal property as the private property of the great landlords who have taken the place of the feudal lords, when he, himself, demands a 'general Act of Parliament for the enclosure of Commons' (admitting thereby that a parliamentary *coup d'état* is necessary for its transformation into private property), and moreover calls on the legislature for the indemnification for the expropriated poor.[17]

Whilst the place of the independent yeoman was taken by tenants at will, small farmers on yearly leases, a servile rabble dependent on the pleasure of the landlords, the systematic robbery of the Communal lands helped especially, next to the theft of the State domains, to swell those large farms, that were called in the eighteenth century capital farms[18] or merchant farms,[19] and to 'set free' the agricultural population as proletarians for manufacturing industry.

The eighteenth century, however, did not yet recognise as fully as the nineteenth, the identity between national wealth and the poverty of the people. Hence the most vigorous polemic, in the economic literature of that time, on the 'enclosure of commons.' From the mass of materials that lie before me, I give a few extracts that will throw a strong light on the circumstances of the time. 'In several parishes of Hertfordshire,' writes one indignant person, '24 farms, numbering on the average 50–150 acres, have been melted up into three farms.'[20] 'In Northamptonshire and Leicestershire the enclosure of common lands has taken place on a very large scale, and most of the new lordships, resulting from the enclosure, have been turned into pasturage, in consequence of which many lordships have not now 50 acres ploughed yearly, in which 1,500 were ploughed formerly. The ruins of former dwelling-houses, barns, stables, etc.,' are the sole traces of the former inhabitants. 'An hundred houses and families have in some open-field villages . . . dwindled to eight or ten. . . . The landholders in most parishes that have been enclosed only 15 or 20 years, are very few in comparison of the numbers who occupied them in their open-field state. It is no uncommon thing for 4 or 5 wealthy graziers to engross a large enclosed lordship which was before in the hands of 20 or 30 farmers, and as many smaller tenants and proprietors. All these are hereby thrown out of their livings with their families and many other families who were chiefly employed and supported by them.'[21] It was not only the land that lay waste, but often land cultivated either in common or held under a definite rent paid to the community, that was annexed by the neighbouring landlords under pretext of enclosure. 'I have here in view enclosures of open fields and lands already improved. It is acknowledged by even the writers in defence of enclosures that these diminished villages increase the monopolies of farms, raise the prices of provisions, and produce depopulation . . . and even the enclosure of waste lands (as now carried on) bears hard on the poor, by depriving them of a part of their subsistence, and only goes towards increasing farms already too large.'[22] 'When,' says Dr Price, 'this land gets into the hands of a few great farmers, the consequence must be that the little farmers' (earlier designated by him 'a multitude of little proprietors and tenants, who maintain themselves and families by the produce of the ground they occupy by sheep kept on a common, by poultry, hogs, etc., and who therefore have little occasion to purchase any of the means of subsistence') 'will be converted into a body of men who earn their subsistence by working for others, and who will be under a necessity of going to market for all they want . . . There will, perhaps, be more labour, because there will be more compulsion to it . . . Towns and manufactures will increase, because more will be driven to them in quest of places and employment. This is the way in which the engrossing of farms naturally operates. And this is the way in which, for many years, it has been actually operating in this kingdom.'[23] He sums up the effect of the enclosures thus: 'Upon the whole, the circumstances of the lower ranks of men are altered in almost every respect for the worse. From little occupiers of land, they are reduced to the state of day-labourers and hirelings; and, at the same time, their subsistence in that state has become more difficult.'[24] In fact, usurpation of the common lands and the revolution in agriculture accompanying this, told so acutely on the agricultural labourers that, even according to Eden, between 1765 and 1780, their wages began to fall below the minimum, and to be supplemented by official poor-law relief. Their wages, he says, 'were not more than enough for the absolute necessaries of life.'

Let us hear for a moment a defender of enclosures and an opponent of Dr Price. 'Not is it a consequence that there must be depopulation, because men are not seen wasting their labour in the open field. . . . If, by converting the little farmers into a body of men who must work for others, more labour is produced, it is an advantage which the nation' (to which, of course, the 'converted' ones do not belong) 'should wish for . . . the produce being greater when their joint labours are employed on one farm, there will be a surplus for manufactures, and by this means manufactures, one of the mines of the nation, will increase, in proportion to the quantity of corn produced.'[25]

The stoical peace of mind with which the political economist regards the most shameless violation of the 'sacred rights of property' and the grossest acts of violence to persons, as soon as they are necessary to lay the foundations of the capitalistic mode of production, is shown by Sir F. M. Eden, philanthropist and tory to boot. The whole series of thefts, outrages, and popular misery, that accompanied the forcible expropriation of the people, from the last third of the fifteenth to the end the eighteenth century, lead him merely to the comfortable conclusion: 'The due proportion between arable land and pasture had to be established. During the whole of the fourteenth and the greater part of the fifteenth century, there was one acre of pasture to 2, 3, and even 4 of arable land. About the middle of the sixteenth century the proportion was changed of 2 acres of pasture to 2, later on, of 2 acres of pasture to one of arable, until at last the just proportion of 3 acres of pasture to one of arable land was attained.'

In the nineteenth century, the very memory of the connexion between the agricultural labourer and the communal property had, of course, vanished. To say nothing of more recent times, have the agricultural population received a farthing of compensation for the 3,511,770 acres of common land which between 1801 and 1831 were stolen from them and by parliamentary devices presented to the landlords by the landlords?

The last process of wholesale expropriation of the agricultural population from the soil is, finally, the so-called clearing of estates, i.e., sweeping men off them. All the English methods hitherto considered culminated in 'clearing.' As we saw in the picture of modern conditions given in a former chapter, where there are no more independent peasants to get rid of, the 'cleaning' of cottages begins; so that the agricultural labourers do not find on the soil cultivated by them even the spot necessary for their own housing. But what 'clearing of estates' really and properly signifies, we learn only in the promised land of modern romance, the Highlands of Scotland. There the process is distinguished by its systematic character, by the magnitude of the scale on which it is carried out at one blow (in Ireland landlords have gone to the length of sweeping away several villages at once; in Scotland areas as large as German principalities are dealt with), finally by the peculiar form of property, under which the embezzled lands were held.

The Highland Celts were organised in clans, each of which was the owner of the land on which it was settled. The representative of the clan, its chief or 'great man,' was only the titular owner of this property, just as the Queen of England is the titular owner of all the national soil. When the English government succeeded in suppressing the intestine wars of these 'great men,' and their constant incursions into the Lowland plains, the chiefs of the clans by no means gave up their time-honoured trade as robbers; they only changed its form. On their own authority they transformed their nominal right into a right of private property, and as this brought them into collision with their clansmen, resolved to drive them out by open force. 'A king of England might as well claim to drive his subjects into the sea,' says Professor Newman.[26] This revolution, which began in Scotland after the last rising of the followers of the Pretender, can be followed through its first phases in the writings of Sir James Steuart[27] and James Anderson[28] In the eighteenth century the hunted-out Gaels were forbidden to emigrate from the country, with a view to driving them by force to Glasgow and other manufacturing towns.[29] As an example of the method[30] obtaining in the nineteenth century, the 'clearing' made by the Duchess of Sutherland will suffice here. This person, well instructed in economy, resolved, on entering upon her government, to effect a radical cure, and to turn the whole country, whose population had already been, by earlier processes of the like kind, reduced to 15,000, into a sheep-walk. From 1814 to 1820 these 15,000 inhabitants, about 3,000 families, were systematically hunted and rooted out. All their villages were destroyed and burnt, all their fields turned into pasturage. British soldiers enforced this eviction, and came to blows with the inhabitants. One old woman was burnt to death in the flames of the hut, which she refused to leave. Thus this fine lady appropriated 794,000 acres of land that had from time immemorial belonged to the clan. She assigned to the expelled inhabitants about 6,000 acres on the sea-shore – 2 acres per family. The 6,000 acres had until this time lain waste, and brought in no income to their owners. The Duchess, in the nobility of her heart, actually went so far as to let these at an average rent of 2s. 6d. per acre to the clansmen, who for centuries had shed their blood for her family. The whole of the stolen clanland she divided into 29 great sheep farms, each inhabited by a single family, for the most part imported English farm-servants. In the year 1835 the 15,000 Gaels were already replaced by 131,000 sheep. The remnant of the aborigines flung on the sea-shore, tried to live by catching fish. They became amphibious and lived, as an English author says, half on land and half on water, and withal only half on both.[31]

But the brave Gaels must expiate yet more bitterly their idolatry, romantic and of the mountains, for the 'great men' of the clan. The smell of their fish rose to the noses of the great men. They scented some profit in it, and let the sea-shore to the great fishmongers of London. For the second time the Gaels were hunted out.[32]

But, finally, part of the sheep-walks are turned into deer preserves. Every one knows that there are no real forests in England. The deer in the parks of the great are demurely domestic cattle, fat as London aldermen. Scotland is therefore the last refuge of the 'noble passion.' 'In the Highlands,' says Somers in 1848, 'new forests are springing up like mushrooms. Here, on one side of Gaick, you have the new forest of Glenfeshie; and there on the other you have the new forest of Ardverikie. In the same line you have the Black plount, an immense waste also recently, erected. From east to west – from the neighbourhood of Aberdeen to the crags of Oban – you have now a continuous line of forests; while in other parts of the Highlands there are the new forests of Loch Archaig, Glengarry, Glenmoriston, etc. Sheep were introduced into glens which had been the seats of communities of small farmers; and the latter were driven to seek subsistence on coarser and more sterile tracs of soil. Now deer are supplanting sheep; and these are once more dispossessing the small tenants, who will necessarily be driven down upon still coarser land and to more grinding penury. Deer-forests[33] and the people cannot co-exist. One or other of the two must yield. Let the forests be increased in number and extent during the next quarter of a century, as they have been in the last, and the Gaels will perish from their native soil . . . This movement among the Highland proprietors is with some a matter of ambition . . . with some love of sport . . . while others, of a more practical cast, follow the trade in deer with an eye solely to profit. For it is a fact, that a mountain range laid out in forest is, in many cases, more profitable to the proprietor than when let as a sheep-walk . . . The huntsman who wants a deer-forest limits his offers by no other calculation than the extent of his purse . . . Sufferings have been inflicted in the Highlands scarcely less severe than those occasioned by the policy of the Norman kings. Deer have received extended ranges, while men have been hunted within a narrower and still narrower circle . . . One after one the liberties of the people have been cloven down . . . And the oppressions are daily on the increase . . . The clearance and dispersion of the people is pursued by the proprietors as a settled principle, as an agricultural necessity, just as trees and brushwood are cleared from the wastes of America or Australia; and the operation goes on in a quiet, business like way, etc.'[34]

The spoliation of the church's property, the fraudulent alienation of the State domains, the robbery of the common lands, the usurpation of feudal and clan property, and its transformation into modern private property under circumstances of reckless terrorism, were just so many idyllic methods of primitive accumulation. They conquered the field for capitalistic agriculture, made the soil part and parcel of capital, and created for the town industries the necessary supply of a 'free' and outlawed proletariat.

Bloody Legislation Against The Expropriated, from the end of the 15th Century. Forcing Down of Wages by Acts Of Parliament

The proletariat created by the breaking up of the bands of feudal retainers and by the forcible expropriation of the people from the soil, this 'free' proletariat could not possibly be absorbed by the nascent manufactures as fast as it was thrown upon the world. On the other hand, these men, suddenly dragged from their wonted mode of life, could not as suddenly adapt themselves to the discipline of their new condition. They were turned *en masse* into beggars, robbers, vagabonds, partly from inclination, in most cases from stress of circumstances. Hence at the end of the fifteenth and during the whole of the sixteenth century, throughout Western Europe a bloody legislation against vagabondage. The fathers of the present working-class were chastised for their enforced transformation into vagabonds and paupers. Legislation treated them as 'voluntary' criminals, and assumed that it depended on their own good will to go on working under the old conditions that no longer existed.

In England this legislation began under Henry VII.

Henry VIII 1530: Beggars old and unable to work receive a beggar's licence. On the other hand, whipping and imprisonment for sturdy vagabonds. They are to be tied to the cart-tail and whipped until the blood streams from their bodies, then to swear an oath to go back to their birthplace or to where they have lived the last three years and to 'put themselves to labour.' What grim irony! In 27 Henry VIII the former statute is repeated, but strengthened with new clauses. For the second arrest for vagabondage the whipping is to be repeated and half the ear sliced off; but for the third relapse the offender is to be executed as a hardened criminal and enemy of the common weal.

Edward VI: A statute of the first year of his reign, 1547, ordains that if anyone refuses to work, he shall be condemned as a slave to the person who has denounced him as an idler. The master shall feed his slave on bread and water, weak broth and such refuse meat as he thinks fit. He has the right to force him to do any work, no matter how disgusting, with whip and chains. If the slave is absent a fortnight, he is condemned to slavery for life and is to be branded on forehead or back with the letter S; if he runs away thrice, he is to be executed as a felon. The master can sell him, bequeath him, let him out on hire as a slave, just as any other personal chattel or cattle. If the slaves attempt anything against the masters, they are also to be executed. Justices of the peace, on information, are to hunt the rascals down. If it happens that a vagabond has been idling about for three days, he is to be taken to his birthplace, branded with a redhot iron with the letter V on the breast and be set to work, in chains, in the streets or at some other labour. If the vagabond gives a false birthplace, he is then to become the slave for life of this place, of its inhabitants, or its corporation, and to be branded with an S. All persons have the right to take away the children of the vagabonds and to keep them as apprentices, the young men until the twenty-fourth year, the girls until the twentieth. If they run away, they are to become up to this age the slaves of their masters, who can put them in irons, whip them, etc., if they like. Every master may put an iron ring round the neck, arms or legs of his slave, by which to know him more easily and to be more certain of him.[35] The last part of this statute provides, that certain poor people may be employed by a place or by persons, who are willing to give them food and drink and to find them work. This kind of parish-slaves was kept up in England until far into the nineteenth century under the name of 'roundsmen.'

Elizabeth, 1572: Unlicensed beggars above 14 years of age are to be severely flogged and branded on the left ear unless some one will take them into service for two years; in case of a repetition of the offence, if they are over 18, they are to be executed, unless some one will take them into service for two years; but for the third offence they are to be executed without mercy as felons. Similar statutes: 18 Elizabeth, c. 13, and another of 1597.[36]

James I: Any one wandering about and begging is declared a rogue and a vagabond. Justices of the peace in petty sessions are authorised to have them publicly whipped and for the first offence to imprison them for 6 months, for the second for 2 years. Whilst in prison they are to be whipped as much and as often as the justices of the peace think fit . . . Incorrigible and dangerous rogues are to be branded with an R on the left shoulder and set to hard labour, and if they are caught begging again, to be executed without mercy. These statutes, legally binding until the beginning of the eighteenth century, were only repealed by 12 Anne, C. 23.

Similar laws in France, where by the middle of the seventeenth century a kingdom of vagabonds (truands) was established in Paris. Even at the beginning of Louis XVI's reign (Ordinance of July 13th, 1777) every man in good health from 16 to 60 years of age, if without means of subsistence and not practising a trade, is to be sent to the galleys. Of the same nature are the statute of Charles V, for the Netherlands (October, 1537), the first edict of the States and Towns of Holland (March 10, 1614), the 'Plakaat' of the United Provinces (June 26, 1649), etc.

Thus were the agricultural people, first forcibly expropriated from the soil, driven from their homes, turned into vagabonds, and then whipped, branded, tortured by laws grotesquely terrible, into the discipline necessary for the wage system.

It is not enough that the conditions of labour are concentrated in a mass, in the shape of capital, at the one pole of society, while at the other are grouped masses of men, who have nothing to sell but their labour-power. Neither is it enough that they are compelled to sell it voluntarily. The advance of capitalist production develops a working-class, which by education, tradition, habit, looks upon the conditions of that mode of production as self-evident laws of Nature. The organisation of the capitalist process of production, once fully developed, breaks down all resistance. The constant generation of a relative surplus-population keeps the law of supply and demand of labour, and therefore keeps wages, in a rut that corresponds with the wants of capital. The dull compulsion of economic relations completes the subjection of the labourer to the capitalist. Direct force, outside economic conditions, is of course still used, but only exceptionally. In the ordinary run of things, the labourer can be left to the 'natural laws of production,' i.e., to his dependence on capital, a dependence springing from, and guaranteed in perpetuity by, the conditions of production themselves. It is otherwise during the historic genesis of capitalist production. The bourgeoisie, at its rise, wants and uses the power of the state to 'regulate' wages, i.e., to force them within the limits suitable for surplus-value making, to lengthen the working-day and to keep the labourer himself in the normal degree of dependence. This is an essential element of the so-called primitive accumulation.

The class of wage-labourers, which arose in the latter half of the 14th century, formed then and in the following century only a very small part of the population, well protected in its position by the independent peasant proprietary in the country and the guild-organisation in the town. In country and town master and workmen stood close together socially. The subordination of labour to capital was only formal – i.e., the mode of production itself had as yet no specific capitalistic character. Variable capital preponderated greatly over constant. The demand for wage-labour grew, therefore, rapidly with every accumulation of capital, whilst the supply of wage-labour followed but slowly. A large part of the national product, changed later into a fund of capitalist accumulation, then still entered into the consumption-fund of the labourer.

Legislation on wage-labour (from the first, aimed at the exploitation of the labourer and, as it advanced, always equally hostile to him),[37] is started in England by the Statute of Labourers, of Edward III, 1349. The ordinance of 1350 in France, issued in the name of King John, corresponds with it. English and French legislation run parallel and are identical in purport. So far as the labour-statutes aim at compulsory extension of the working-day, I do not return to them, as this point was treated earlier (Chap. X, Section 5).

The Statute of Labourers was passed at the urgent instance of the House of Commons. A Tory says naïvely: 'Formerly the poor demanded such *high* wages as to threaten industry and wealth. Next, their wages are so *low* as to threaten industry and wealth equally and perhaps more, but in another way.'[38] A tariff of wages was fixed by law for town and country, for piece-work and day-work. The agricultural labourers were to hire themselves out by the year, the town ones 'in open market.' It was forbidden, under pain of imprisonment, to pay higher wages than those fixed by the statute, but the taking of higher wages was more severely punished than the giving them. [So also in Sections 18 and 19 of the Statute of Apprentices of Elizabeth, ten days' imprisonment is decreed for him that pays the higher wages, but twenty-one days for him that receives them.] A statute of 1360 increased the penalties and authorised the masters to extort labour at the legal rate of wages by corporal punishment. All combinations, contracts, oaths, etc., by which masons and carpenters reciprocally bound themselves, were declared null and void. Coalition of the labourers is treated as a heinous crime from the fourteenth century to 1825, the year of the repeal of the laws against Trades' Unions. The spirit of the Statute of Labourers of 1349 and of its offshoots, comes out clearly in the fact, that indeed a maximum of wages is dictated by the State, but on no account a minimum.

In the sixteenth century, the condition of the labourers had, as we know, become much worse. The money wage rose, but not in proportion to the depreciation of money and the corresponding rise in the prices of commodities. Wages, therefore, in reality fell. Nevertheless, the laws for keeping them down remained in force, together with the ear-clipping and branding of those 'whom no one was willing to take into service.' By the Statute of Apprentices 5 Elizabeth, c. 3, the justices of the peace were empowered to fix certain wages and to modify them according to the time of the year and the price of commodities. James I extended these regulations of labour also to weavers, spinners, and all possible categories of workers.[39] George II extended the laws against coalitions of labourers to manufacturers. In the manufacturing period *per excellence*, the capitalist mode of production had become sufficiently strong to render legal regulation of wages as impracticable as it was unnecessary; but the ruling classes were unwilling in case of necessity to be without the weapons of the old arsenal. Still, 8 George II forbade a higher day's wage than 2s. 7½d. for journeymen tailors in and around London, except in cases of general mourning; still, 13 George III., c. 68, gave the regulation of the wages of silk-weavers to the justices of the peace; still, in 1706, it required two judgments of the higher courts to decide, whether the mandates of justices of the peace as to wages held good also for non-agricultural labourers; still, in 1799, an act of Parliament ordered that the wages of the Scotch miners should continue to be regulated by a statute of Elizabeth and two Scotch acts of 1661 and 1671. How completely in the meantime circumstances had changed, is proved by an occurrence unheard-of before in the English Lower House. In that place, where for more than 400 years laws had been made for the maximum, beyond which wages absolutely must not rise, Whitbread in 1796 proposed a legal minimum wage for agricultural labourers. Pitt opposed this, but confessed that the 'condition of the poor was cruel.' Finally, in 1813, the laws for the regulation of wages were repealed. They were an absurd anomaly, since the capitalist regulated his factory by his private legislation, and could by the poor-rates make up the wage of the agricultural labourer to the indispensable minimum. The provisions of the labour statutes as to contracts between master and workman, as to giving notice and the like, which only allow of a civil action against the contract-breaking master, but on the contrary permit a criminal action against the contract-breaking workman, are to this hour (1873) in full force. The barbarous laws against Trades' Unions fell in 1825 before the threatening bearing of the proletariat. Despite this, they fell only in part. Certain beautiful fragments of the old statute vanished only in 1859. Finally, the act of Parliament of June 29, 1871, made a pretence of removing the last traces of this class of legislation by legal recognition of Trades' Unions. But an act of Parliament of the same date (an act to amend the criminal law relating to violence, threats, and molestation), re-established, in point of fact, the former state of things in a new shape. By this Parliamentary escamotage the means which the labourers could use in a strike or lock-out were withdrawn from the laws common to all citizens, and placed under exceptional penal legislation, the interpretation of which fell to the masters themselves in their capacity as justices of the peace. Two years earlier, the same House of Commons and the same Mr Gladstone in the well-known straightforward fashion brought in a bill for the abolition of all exceptional penal legislation against the working-class. But this was never allowed to go beyond the second reading, and the matter was thus protracted until at last the 'great Liberal party,' by an alliance with the Tories, found courage to turn against the very proletariat that had carried it into power. Not content with this treachery, the 'great Liberal party' allowed the English judges, ever complaisant in the service of the ruling classes, to dig up again the earlier laws against 'conspiracy,' and to apply them to coalitions of labourers. We see that only against its will and under the pressure of the masses did the English Parliament give up the laws against Strikes and Trades' Unions, after it had itself, for 500 years, held, with shameless egoism, the position of a permanent Trades' Union of the capitalists against the labourers.

During the very first storms of the revolution, the French bourgeoisie dared to take away from the workers the right of association but just acquired. By a decree of June 14, 1791, they declared all coalition of the workers as 'an attempt against liberty and the declaration of the rights of man,' punishable by a fine of 500 livres, together with deprivation of the rights of an active citizen for one year.[40] This law which, by means of State compulsion, confined the struggle between capital and labour within limits comfortable for capital, has outlived revolutions and changes of dynasties. Even the Reign of Terror left it untouched. It was but quite recently struck out of the Penal Code. Nothing is more characteristic than the pretext for this bourgeois *coup d'état.* 'Granting,' says Chapelier, the reporter of the Select Committee on this law, 'that wages ought to be a little higher than they are, . . . that they ought to be high enough for him that receives them, to be free from that state of absolute dependence due to the want of the necessaries of life, and which is almost that of slavery,' yet the workers must not be allowed to come to any understanding about their own interests, nor to act in common and thereby lessen their 'absolute dependence, which is almost that of slavery;' because, forsooth, in doing this they injure 'the freedom of their cidevant masters, the present entrepreneurs,' and because a coalition against the despotium of the quondam masters of the corporations is – guess what! – is a restoration of the corporations abolished by the French constitution.

Genesis of The Capitalist Farmer

Now that we have considered the forcible creation of a class of outlawed proletarians, the bloody discipline that turned them into wage-labourers, the disgraceful action of the State which employed the police to accelerate the accumulation of capital by increasing the degree of exploitation of labour, the question remains: whence came the capitalists originally? For the expropriation of the agricultural population creates, directly, none but great landed proprietors. As far, however, as concerns the genesis of the farmer, we can, so to say, put our hand on it, because it is a slow process evolving through many centuries. The serfs, as well as the free small proprietors, held land under very different tenures, and were therefore emancipated under very different economic conditions. In England the first form of the farmer is the bailiff, himself a serf. His position is similar to that of the old Roman *villicus*, only in a more limited sphere of action. During the second half of the fourteenth century he is replaced by a farmer, whom the landlord provides with seed, cattle and implements. His condition is not very different from that of the peasant. Only he exploits more wage-labour. Soon he becomes a métayer, a half-farmer. He advances one part of the agricultural stock, the landlord the other. The two divide the total product in proportions determined by contract. This form quickly disappears in England, to give place to the farmer proper, who makes his own capital breed by employing wage-labourers, and pays a part of the surplus-product, in money or in kind, to the landlord as rent. So long, during the fifteenth century, as the independent peasant and the farm-labourer working for himself as well as for wages, enriched themselves by their own labour, the circumstances of the farmer, and his field of production, were equally mediocre. The agricultural revolution which commenced in the last third of the fifteenth century, and continued during almost the whole of the sixteenth (excepting, however, its last decade), enriched him just as speedily as it impoverished the mass of the agricultural people.[41]

The usurpation of the common lands allowed him to augment greatly his stock of cattle, almost without cost, whilst they yielded him a richer supply of manure for the tillage of the soil. To this, was added in the sixteenth century, a very important element. At that time the contracts for farms ran for a long time, often for 99 years. The progressive fall in the value of the precious metals, and therefore of money, brought the farmers golden fruit. Apart from all the other circumstances discussed above, it lowered wages. A portion of the latter was now added to the profits of the farm. The continuous rise in the price of corn, wool, meat, in a word of all agricultural produce, swelled the money capital of the farmer without any action on his part, whilst the rent he paid (being calculated on the old value of money) diminished in reality.[42] Thus they grew rich at the expense both of their labourers and their landlords. No wonder therefore, that England, at the end of the sixteenth century, had a class of capitalist farmers, rich, considering the circumstances of the time.[43]

Reaction of the Agricultural Revolution on Industry. Creation of the Home-Market for Industrial Capital

The expropriation and expulsion of the agricultural population, intermittent but renewed again and again, supplied, as we saw, the town industries with a mass of proletarians entirely unconnected with the corporate guilds and unfettered by them; a fortunate circumstance that makes old A. Anderson (not to be confounded with James Anderson) in his 'History of Commerce,' believe in the direct intervention of Providence. We must still pause a moment on this element of primitive accumulation. The thinning-out of the independent, self-supporting peasants not only brought about the crowding together of the industrial proletariat, in the way that Geoffroy Saint Hilaire explained the condensation of cosmical matter at one place, by its rarefaction at another.[44] In spite of the smaller number of its cultivators, the soil brought forth as much or more produce, after as before, because the revolution in the conditions of landed property was accompanied by improved methods of culture, greater co-operation, concentration of the means of production, etc., and because not only were the agricultural wage-labourers put on the strain more intensely,[45] but the field of production on which they worked for themselves, became more and more contracted. With the setting free of a part of the agricultural population, therefore, their former means of nourishment were also set free. They were now transformed into material elements of variable capital. The peasant, expropriated and cast adrift, must buy their value in the form of wages, from his new master, the industrial capitalist. That which holds good of the means of subsistence holds with the raw materials of industry dependent upon home agriculture. They were transformed into an element of constant capital. Suppose, e.g., a part of the Westphalian peasants, who, at the time of Frederick II, all span flax, forcibly expropriated and hunted from the soil; and the other part that remained, turned into day-labourers of large farmers. At the same time arise large establishments for flax-spinning and weaving, in which the men 'set free' now work for wages. The flax looks exactly as before. Not a fibre of it is changed, but a new social soul has popped into its body. It forms now a part of the constant capital of the master manufacturer. Formerly divided among a number of small producers, who cultivated it themselves and with their families spun it in retail fashion, it is now concentrated in the hand of one capitalist, who sets others to spin and weave it for him. The extra labour expended in flax-spinning realised itself formerly in extra income to numerous peasant families, or maybe, in Frederick IIs time, in taxes *pour le roi de Prusse*. It realises itself now in profit for a few capitalists. The spindles and looms, formerly scattered over the face of the country, are now crowded together in a few great labour-barracks, together with the labourers and the raw material. And spindles, looms, raw material, are now transformed, from means of independent existence for the spinners and weavers, into means for commanding them and sucking out of them unpaid labour[46] One does not perceive, when looking at the large manufactories and the large farms, that they have originated from the throwing into one of many small centres of production, and have been built up by the expropriation of many small independent producers. Nevertheless, the popular intuition was not at fault. In the time of Mirabeau, the lion of the Revolution, the great manufactories were still called manufactures réunies, workshops thrown into one, as we speak of fields thrown into one. Says Mirabeau: 'We are only paying attention to the grand manufactories, in which hundreds of men work under a director and which are commonly called *manufactures réunies*. Those where a very large number of labourers work, each separately and on his own account, are hardly considered; they are placed at an infinite distance from the others. This is a great error, as the latter alone make a really important object of national prosperity . . . The large workshop (*manufacture réunie*) will enrich prodigiously one or two entrepreneurs, but the labourers will only be journeymen, paid more or less, and will not have any share in the success of the undertaking. In the discrete workshop (*manufacture* séparée), on the contrary, no one will become rich, but many labourers will be comfortable; the saving and the industrious will be able to amass a little capital, to put by a little for a birth of a child, for an illness, for themselves or their belongings. The number of saving and industrious labourers will increase, because they will see in good conduct, in activity, a means of essentially bettering their condition, and not of obtaining a small rise of wages that can never be of any importance of the future, and whose sole result is to place men in the position to live a little better, but only from day to day. . . . The large workshops, undertakings of certain private persons who pay labourers from day to day to work for their gain, may be able to put these private individuals at their ease, but they will never be an object worth the attention of governments. Discrete workshops, for the most part combined with cultivation of small holdings, are the only free ones.'[47] (The expropriation and eviction of a part of the agricultural population not only set free for industrial capital, the labourers, their means of subsistence, and material for labour; it also created the home-market.)

In fact, the events that transformed the small peasants into wagelabourers, and their means of subsistence and of labour into material elements of capital, created, at the same time, a home-market for the latter. Formerly, the peasant family produced the means of subsistence and the raw materials, which they themselves, for the most part, consumed. These raw materials and means of subsistence have now become commodities; the large farmer sells them, he finds his market in manufactures. Yarn, linen, coarse woollen stuffs – things whose raw materials had been within the reach of every peasant family, had been spun and woven by it for its own use – were now transformed into articles of manufacture, to which the country districts at once served for markets. The many scattered customers, whom stray artisans until now had found in the numerous small producers working on their own account, concentrate themselves now into one great market provided for by industrial *capital*.[48] Thus, hand in hand with the expropriation of the self-supporting peasants, with their separation from their means of production, goes the destruction of rural domestic industry, the process of separation between manufacture and agriculture. And only the destruction of rural domestic industry can give the internal market of a country that extension and consistence which the capitalist mode of production requires. Still the manufacturing period, properly so called, does not succeed in carrying out this transformation radically and completely. It will be remembered that manufacture, properly so called, conquers but partially the domain of national production, and always rests on the handicrafts of the town and the domestic industry of the rural districts as its ultimate basis. If it destroys these in one form, in particular branches, at certain points, it calls them up again elsewhere, because it needs them for the preparation of raw material up to a certain point. It produces, therefore, a new class of small villagers who, while following the cultivation of the soil as an accessary calling, find their chief occupation in industrial labour, the products of which they sell to the manufacturers directly, or through the medium of merchants. This is one, though not the chief, cause of a phenomenon which, at first, puzzles the student of English history. From the last third of the fifteenth century he finds continually complaints, only interrupted at certain intervals, about the encroachment of capitalist farming in the country districts, and the progressive destruction of the peasantry. On the other hand, he always finds this peasantry turning up again, although in diminished number, and always under worse conditions.[49] The chief reason is: England is at one time chiefly a cultivator of corn, at another chiefly a breeder of cattle, in alternate periods, and with these the extent of peasant cultivation fluctuates. Modern Industry alone, and finally, supplies, in machinery, the lasting basis of capitalistic agriculture, expropriates radically the enormous majority of the agricultural population, and completes the separation between agriculture and rural domestic industry, whose roots – spinning and weaving – it tears up.[50] It therefore also, for the first time, conquers for industrial capital the entire homemarket.[51]

Genesis of The Industrial Capitalist

The genesis of the industrial[52] capitalist did not proceed in such a gradual way as that of the farmer. Doubtless many small guild-masters, and yet more independent small artisans, or even wage-labourers, transformed themselves into small capitalists, and (by gradually extending exploitation of wage-labour and corresponding accumulation) into full-blown capitalists. In the infancy of capitalist production, things often happened as in the infancy of mediaeval towns, where the question, which of the escaped serfs should be master and which servant, was in great part decided by the earlier or later date of their flight. The snail's pace of this method corresponded in no wise with the commercial requirements of the new world-market that the great discoveries of the end of the fifteenth century created. But the middle ages had handed down two distinct forms of capital, which mature in the most different economic social formations, and which, before the era of the capitalist mode of production, are considered as capital *quand même* – usurer's capital and merchant's capital.

'At present, all the wealth of society goes first into the possession of the capitalist . . . he pays the landowner his rent, the labourer his wages, the tax and tithe gatherer their claims, and keeps a large, indeed the largest, and a continually augmenting share, of the annual produce of labour for himself. The capitalist may now be said to be the first owner of all the wealth of the community, though no law has conferred on him the right to this property . . . this change has been effected by the taking of interest on capital . . . and it is not a little curious that all the law-givers of Europe endeavoured to prevent this by statutes, viz., statutes against usury. . . . The power of the capitalist over all the wealth of the country is a complete change in the right of property, and by what law, or series of laws, was it effected?'[53] The author should have remembered that revolutions are not made by laws.

The money capital formed by means of usury and commerce was prevented from turning into industrial capital, in the country by the feudal constitution, in the towns by the guild organisation.[54] These fetters vanished with the dissolution of feudal society, with the expropriation and partial eviction of the country population. The new manufactures were established at sea-ports, or at inland points beyond the control of the old municipalities and their guilds. Hence in England an embittered struggle of the corporate towns against these new industrial nurseries.

The discovery of gold and silver in America, the extirpation, enslavement and entombment in mines of the aboriginal population, the beginning of the conquest and looting of the East Indies, the turning of Africa into a warren for the commercial hunting of black-skins, signalised the rosy dawn of the era of capitalist production. These idyllic proceedings are the chief momenta of primitive accumulation. On their heels treads the commercial war of the European nations, with the globe for a theatre. It begins with the revolt of the Netherlands from Spain, assumes giant dimensions in England's Anti-Jacobin War, and is still going on in the opium wars against China, etc.

The different momenta of primitive accumulation distribute themselves now, more or less in chronological order, particularly over Spain, Portugal, Holland, France, and

England. In England at the end of the seventeenth century, they arrive at a systematical combination, embracing the colonies, the national debt, the modern mode of taxation, and the protectionist system. These methods depend in part on brute force, e.g., the colonial system. But they all employ the power of the State, the concentrated and organised force of society, to hasten, hot-house fashion, the process of transformation of the feudal mode of production into the capitalist mode, and to shorten the transition. Force is the midwife of every old society pregnant with a new one. It is itself an economic power.

Of the Christian colonial system, W. Howitt, a man who makes a speciality of Christianity, says: 'The barbarities and desperate outrages of the so-called Christian race, throughout every region of the world, and upon every people they have been able to subdue, are not to be paralleled by those of any other race, however fierce, however untaught, and however reckless of mercy and of shame, in any age of the earth.'[55] The history of the colonial administration of Holland – and Holland was the head capitalistic nation of the seventeenth century – 'is one of the most extraordinary relations of treachery, bribery, massacre, and meanness.'[56] Nothing is more characteristic than their system of stealing men, to get slaves for Java. The men stealers were trained for this purpose. The thief, the interpreter, and the seller, were the chief agents in this trade, native princes the chief sellers. The young people stolen, were thrown into the secret dungeons of Celebes, until they were ready for sending to the slave-ships. An official report says: 'This one town of Macassar, e.g., is full of secret prisons, one more horrible than the other, crammed with unfortunates, victims of greed and tyranny fettered in chains, forcibly torn from their families.' To secure Malacca, the Dutch corrupted the Portuguese governor. He let them into the town in 1641. They hurried at once to his house and assassinated him, to 'abstain' from the payment of £21,875, the price of his treason. Wherever they set foot, devastation and depopulation followed. Banjuwangi, a province of Java, in 1750 numbered over 80,000 inhabitants, in 1811 only 18,000. Sweet commerce!

The English East India Company, as is well known, obtained, besides the political rule in India, the exclusive monopoly of the tea-trade, as well as of the Chinese trade in general, and of the transport of goods to and from Europe. But the coasting trade of India and between the islands, as well as the internal trade of India, were the monopoly of the higher employés of the company. The monopolies of salt, opium, betel and other commodities, were inexhaustible mines of wealth. The employés themselves fixed the price and plundered at will the unhappy Hindus. The Governor-General took part in this private traffic. His favourites received contracts under conditions whereby they, cleverer than the alchemists, made gold out of nothing. Great fortunes sprang up like mushrooms in a day; primitive accumulation went on without the advance of a shilling. The trial of Warren Hastings swarms with such cases. Here is an instance. A contract for opium was given to a certain Sullivan at the moment of his departure on an official mission to a part of India far removed from the opium district. Sullivan sold his contract to one Binn for £40,000; Binn sold it the same day for £60,000, and the ultimate purchaser who carried out the contract declared that after all he realised an enormous gain. According to one of the lists laid before Parliament, the Company and its employés from 1757–66 got £6,000,000 from the Indians as gifts. Between 1769 and 1770, the English manufactured a famine by buying up all the rice and refusing to sell it again, except at fabulous prices.[57]

The treatment of the aborigines was, naturally, most frightful in plantation-colonies destined for export trade only, such as the West Indies, and in rich and well-populated countries, such as Mexico and India, that were given over to plunder. But even in the colonies properly so called, the Christian character of primitive accumulation did not belie itself. Those sober virtuosi of Protestantism, the Puritans of New England, in 1703, by decrees of their assembly set a premium of £40 on every Indian scalp and every captured red-skin: in 1720 a premium of £100 on every scalp; in 1744, after Massachusetts-Bay had proclaimed a certain tribe as rebels, the following prices: for a male scalp of 12 years and upwards £100 (new currency), for a male prisoner £105, for women and children prisoners £50, for scalps of women and children £50. Some decades later, the colonial system took its revenge on the descendants of the pious pilgrim fathers, who had grown seditious in the meantime. At English instigation and for English pay they were tomahawked by red-skins. The British Parliament proclaimed blood-hounds and scalping as 'means that God and Nature had given into its hand.'

The colonial system ripened, like a hot-house, trade and navigation. The 'societies Monopolia' of Luther were powerful levers for concentration of capital. The colonies secured a market for the budding manufactures, and, through the monopoly of the market, an increased accumulation. The treasures captured outside Europe by undisguised looting, enslavement, and murder, floated back to the mother-country and were there turned into capital. Holland, which first fully developed the colonial system, in 1648 stood already in the acme of its commercial greatness. It was 'in almost exclusive possession of the East Indian trade and the commerce between the south-east and north-west of Europe. Its fisheries, marine, manufactures, surpassed those of any other country. The total capital of the Republic was probably more important than that of all the rest of Europe put together.' Gülich forgets to add that by 1648, the people of Holland were more over-worked, poorer and more brutally oppressed than those of all the rest of Europe put together.

To-day industrial supremacy implies commercial supremacy. In the period of manufacture properly so called, it is, on the other hand, the commercial supremacy that gives industrial predominance. Hence the preponderant rôle that the colonial system plays at that time. It was 'the strange God' who perched himself on the altar cheek by jowl with the old Gods of Europe, and one fine day with a shove and a kick chucked them all of a heap. It proclaimed surplus-value making as the sole end and aim of humanity.

The system of public credit, i.e., of national debts, whose origin we discover in Genoa and Venice as early as the middle ages, took possession of Europe generally during the manufacturing period. The colonial system with its maritime trade and commercial wars served as a forcing-house for it. Thus it first took root in Holland. National debts, i.e., the alienation of the state – whether despotic, constitutional or republican – marked with its stamp the capitalistic era. The only part of the so-called national wealth that actually enters into the collective possessions of modern peoples is – their national debt.[58] Hence, as a necessary consequence, the modern doctrine that a nation becomes the richer the more deeply it is in debt. Public credit becomes the *credo* of capital. And with the rise of national debt-making, want of faith in the national debt takes the place of the blasphemy against the Holy Ghost, which may not be forgiven.

The public debt becomes one of the most powerful levers of primitive accumulation. As with the stroke of an enchanter's wand, it endows barren money with the power of breeding and thus turns it into capital, without the necessity of its exposing itself to the troubles and risks inseparable from its employment in industry or even in usury. The state-creditors actually give nothing away, for the sum lent is transformed into public bonds, easily negotiable, which go on functioning in their hands just as so much hard cash would. But further, apart from the class of lazy annuitants thus created, and from the improvised wealth of the financiers, middlemen between the government and the nation – as also apart from the tax-farmers, merchants, private manufacturers, to whom a good part of every national loan renders the service of a capital fallen from heaven – the national debt has given rise to joint-stock companies, to dealings in negotiable effects of all kinds, and to agiotage, in a word to stock-exchange gambling and the modern bankocracy.

At their birth the great banks, decorated with national titles, were only associations of private speculators, who placed themselves by the side of governments, and, thanks to the privileges they received, were in a position to advance money to the State. Hence the accumulation of the national debt has no more infallible measure than the successive rise in the stock of these banks, whose full development dates from the founding of the Bank of England in 1694. The Bank of England began with lending its money to the Government at 8 per cent; at the same time it was empowered by Parliament to coin money out of the same capital, by lending it again to the public in the form of banknotes. It was allowed to use these notes for discounting bills, making advances on commodities, and for buying the precious metals. It was not long ere this credit-money, made by the bank itself, became the coin in which the Bank of England made its loans to the State, and paid, on account of the State, the interest on the public debt. It was not enough that the bank gave with one hand and took back more with the other; it remained, even whilst receiving, the eternal creditor of the nation down to the last shilling advanced. Gradually it became inevitably the receptacle of the metallic hoard of the country, and the centre of gravity of all commercial credit. What effect was produced on their contemporaries by the sudden uprising of this brood of bankocrats, financiers, rentiers, brokers, stock-jobbers, etc., is proved by the writings of that time, e.g., by Bolingbroke's.[59]

With the national debt arose an international credit system, which often conceals one of the sources of primitive accumulation in this or that people. Thus the villainies of the Venetian thieving system formed one of the secret bases of the capital-wealth of Holland to whom Venice in her decadence lent large sums of money. So also was it with Holland and England. By the beginning of the eighteenth century the Dutch manufactures were far outstripped. Holland had ceased to be the nation preponderant in commerce and industry. One of its main lines of business, therefore, from 1701–76, is the lending out of enormous amounts of capital, especially to its great rival England. The same thing is going on to-day between England and the United States. A great deal of capital, which appears to-day in the United States without any certificate of birth, was yesterday, in England, the capitalised blood of children.

As the national debt finds its support in the public revenue, which must cover the yearly payments for interest, etc., the modern system of taxation was the necessary complement of the system of national loans. The loans enable the government to meet extraordinary expenses, without the tax-payers feeling it immediately, but they necessitate, as a consequence, increased taxes. On the other hand, the raising of taxation caused by the accumulation of debts contracted one after another, compels the government always to have recourse to new loans for new extraordinary expenses. Modern fiscality, whose pivot is formed by taxes on the most necessary means of subsistence (thereby increasing their price), thus contains within itself the germ of automatic progression. Over-taxation is not an incident, but rather a principle. In Holland, therefore, where this system was first inaugurated, the great patriot, DeWitt, has in his 'Maxims' extolled it as the best system for making the wage-labourer submissive, frugal, industrious, and overburdened with labour. The destructive influence that it exercises on the condition of the wage-labourer concerns us less however, here, than the forcible expropriation, resulting from it, of peasants, artisans, and in a word, all elements of the lower middle-class. On this there are not two opinions, even among the bourgeois economists. Its expropriating efficacy is still further heightened by the system of protection, which forms one of its integral parts.

The great part that the public debt, and the fiscal system corresponding with it, has played in the capitalisation of wealth and the expropriation of the masses, has led many writers, like Cobbett, Doubleday and others, to seek in this, incorrectly, the fundamental cause of the misery of the modern peoples.

The system of protection was an artificial means of manufacturing manufacturers, of expropriating independent labourers, of capitalising the national means of production and subsistence, of forcibly abbreviating the transition from the mediæval to the modern mode of production. The European states tore one another to pieces about the patent of this invention, and, once entered into the service of the surplus-value makers, did not merely lay under contribution in the pursuit of this purpose their own people, indirectly through protective duties, directly through export premiums. They also forcibly rooted out, in their dependent countries, all industry, as, e.g., England did with the Irish woollen manufacture. On the continent of Europe, after Colbert's example, the process was much simplified. The primitive industrial capital, here, came in part directly out of the state treasury. 'Why,' cries Mirabeau, 'why go so far to seek the cause of the manufacturing glory of Saxony before the war? 180,000,000 of debts contracted by the sovereigns!'[60]

Colonial system, public debts, heavy taxes, protection, commercial wars, etc., these children of the true manufacturing period, increase gigantically during the infancy of Modern Industry. The birth of the latter is heralded by a great slaughter of the innocents. Like the royal navy, the factories were recruited by means of the press-gang.

Blasé as Sir F. M. Eden is as to the horrors of the expropriation of the agricultural population from the soil, from the last third of the fifteenth century to his own time; with all the self-satisfaction with which he rejoices in this process, 'essential' for establishing capitalistic agriculture and 'the due proportion between arable and pasture land' – he does not show, however, the same economic insight in respect to the necessity of child-stealing and child-slavery for the transformation of manufacturing exploitation into factory exploitation, and the establishment of the 'true relation' between capital and labour-power. He says: 'It may, perhaps, be worthy the attention of the public to consider, whether any manufacture, which, in order to be carried on successfully, requires that cottages and workhouses should be ransacked for poor children; that they should be employed by turns during the greater part of the night and robbed of that rest which, though indispensable to all, is most required by the young; and that numbers of both sexes, of different ages and dispositions, should be collected together in such a manner that the contagion of example cannot but lead to profligacy and debauchery; will add to the sum of individual or national felicity?'[61]

'In the counties of Derbyshire, Nottinghamshire, and more particularly in Lancashire,' says Fielden, 'the newly-invented machinery was used in large factories built on the sides of streams capable of turning the water-wheel. Thousands of hands were suddenly required in these places, remote from towns; and Lancashire, in particular, being, till then, comparatively thinly populated and barren, a population was all that she now wanted. The small and nimble fingers of little children being be very far the most in request, the custom instantly sprang up of procuring *apprentices* from the different parish workhouses of London, Birmingham, and elsewhere. Many, many thousands of these little, hapless creatures were sent down into the north, being from the age of 7 to the age of 13 or 14 years old. The custom was for the master to clothe his apprentices and to feed and lodge them in an 'apprentice house' near the factory; overseers were appointed to see to the works, whose interest it was to work the children to the utmost, because their pay was in proportion to the quantity of work that they could exact. Cruelty was, of course, the consequence . . . In many of the manufacturing districts, but particularly, I am afraid, in the guilty county to which I belong [Lancashire], cruelties the most heart-rending were practised upon the unoffending and friendless creatures who were thus consigned to the charge of master-manufacturers; they were harassed to the brink of death by excess of labour . . . were flogged, fettered and tortured in the most exquisite refinement of cruelty; . . . they were in many cases starved to the bone while flogged to their work and . . . even in some instances . . . were driven to commit suicide . . . The beautiful and romantic valleys of Derbyshire, Nottinghamshire and Lancashire, secluded from the public eye, became the dismal solitudes of torture, and of many a murder. The profits of manufacturers were enormous; but this only whetted the appetite that it should have satisfied, and therefore the manufacturers had recourse to an expedient that seemed to secure to them those profits without any possibility of limit; they began the practice of what is termed 'night-working,' that is having tired one set of hands, by working them throughout the day, they had another set ready to go on working throughout the night; the day-set getting into the beds that the night-set had just quitted, and in their turn again, the night-set getting into the beds that the day-set quitted in the morning. It is a common tradition in Lancashire, that the beds *never get cold*'[62]

With the development of capitalist production during the manufacturing period, the public opinion of Europe had lost the last remnant of shame and conscience. The nations bragged cynically of every infamy that served them as a means to capitalistic accumulation. Read, e.g., the naïve Annals of Commerce of the worthy A. Anderson. Here it is trumpeted forth as a triumph of English statecraft that at the Peace of Utrecht, England extorted from the Spaniards by the Asiento Treaty the privilege of being allowed to ply the negro-trade, until then only carried on between Africa and the English West Indies, between Africa and Spanish America as well. England thereby acquired the right of supplying Spanish America until 1743 with 4,800 negroes yearly. This threw, at the same time, an official cloak over British smuggling Liverpool waxed fat on the slave-trade. This was its method of primitive accumulation. And, even to the present day, Liverpool 'respectability' is the Pindar of the slave-trade which – compare the work of Aikin [1795] already quoted – 'has coincided with that spirit of bold adventure which has characterised the trade of Liverpool and rapidly carried it to its present state of prosperity; has occasioned vast employment for shipping and sailors, and greatly augmented the demand for the manufactures of the country' (p. 339). Liverpool employed in the slave-trade, in 1730, 15 ships; in 1751, 53; in 1760, 74; in 1770, 96; and in 1792, 132.

Whilst the cotton industry introduced child-slavery in England, it gave in the United States a stimulus to the transformation of the earlier, more or less patriarchal slavery, into a system of commercial exploitation. In fact, the veiled slavery of the wage-workers in Europe needed, for its pedestal, slavery pure and simple in the new world.[63]

Tantæ molis erat, to establish the 'eternal laws of Nature' of the capitalist mode of production, to complete the process of separation between labourers and conditions of labour, to transform, at one pole, the social means of production and subsistence into capital, at the opposite pole, the mass of the population into wage-labourers, into 'free labouring poor,' that artificial product of modern society.[64] *If money, according to Augier*,[65] 'comes into the world with a congenital blood-stain on one cheek,' capital comes dripping from head to foot, from every pore, with blood and dirt.[66]

Notes

1. In Italy, where capitalistic production developed earliest, the dissolution of serfdom also took place earlier than elsewhere. The serf was emancipated in that country before he had acquired any prescriptive right to the soil. His emancipation at once transformed him into a free proletarian, who, moreover, found his master ready waiting for him in the towns, for the most part handed down as legacies from the Roman time. When the revolution of the world-market, about the end of the 15th century, annihilated Northern Italy's commercial supremacy, a movement in the reverse direction set in. The labourers of the towns were driven *en masse* into the country, and gave an impulse, never before seen, to the *petite culture*, carried on in the form of gardening.
2. 'The pretty proprietors who cultivated their own fields with their own hands, and enjoyed a modest competence . . . then formed a much more important part of the nation than

at present. If we may trust the best statistical writers of that age, not less than 160,000 proprietors who, with their families, must have made up more than a seventh of the whole population, derived their subsistence from little freehold estates. The average income of these small landlords ... was estimated at between £60 and £70 a year. It was computed that the number of persons who tilled their own land was greater than the number of those who farmed the land of others.' Macaulay: *History of England*, 10th ed., 1854, I. pp.333, 334. Even in the last third of the 17th century, 4/5 of the English people were agricultural. (l. c., p. 413.) I quote Macaulay, because as systematic falsifier of history he minimises as much as possible facts of this kind.

3. We must never forget that even the serf was not only the owner, if but a tribute-paying owner, of the piece of land attached to his house, but also a co-possessor of the common land. 'Le paysan (in Silesia, under Frederick II) est serf.' Nevertheless, these serfs possess common lands. 'On n'a pas pu encore engager les Silésiens au partage des communes, tandis que dans la Nouvelle Marche, il n'y a guère de village où ce partage ne soit exécuté avec le plus grand succès.' (Mirabeau: *De la Monarchie Prussienne.* Londres, 1788, t. ii, pp. 125, 126.)
4. Japan, with its purely feudal organisation of landed property and its developed *petite culture*, gives a much truer picture of the European middle ages than all our history books, dictated as these are, for the most part, by bourgeois prejudices. It is very convenient to be 'liberal' at the expense of the middle ages.
5. In his 'Utopia', Thomas More says, that in England 'your shepe that were wont to be so meke and tame, and so smal eaters, now, as I heare saye, become so great devourers and so wylde that they eate up, and swallow downe', the very men themselfes.' 'Utopia' transl. by Robinson, ed., Arber, Lond., 1869, p. 41.
6. Bacon shows the connexion between a free, well-to-do peasantry and good infantry. 'This did wonderfully concern the might and mannerhood of the kingdom to have farms as it were of a standard sufficient to maintain an able body out of penury, and did in effect amortise a grat part of the lands of the kingdom unto the hold and occupation of the yeomanry or middle people, of a condition between gentlemen, and cottagers and peasants ... For it hath been held by the general opinion of men of best judgment in the wars ... that the principal strength of an army consisteth in the infantry or foot. And to make good infantry it requireth men bred, not in a servile or indigent fashion, but in some free and plentiful manner. Therefore, if a state run most to noblemen and gentlemen, and that the husbandmen and ploughmen be but as their workfolk and labourers, or else mere cottagers (which are but hous'd beggars), you may have a good cavalry, but never good stable bands of foot ... And this is to be seen in France, and Italy, and some other parts abroad, where in effect all is noblesse or peasantry ... insomuch that they are inforced to employ mercenary bands of Switzers and the like, for their battalions of foot; whereby also it comes to pass that those nations have much people and few soldiers.' ('The Reign of Hentry VII.' Verbatim reprint from Kennet's England. Ed. 1719. Lond., 1870, p. 308.)
7. Dr Hunter, 1. c., p. 134. 'The quantity of land assigned (in the old laws) would now be judged too great for labourers, and rather as likely to convert them into small farmers.' (George Roberts: 'The Social History of the People of the Southern Counties of England in Past Centuries.' Lond., 1856, pp. 184–5.)
8. 'The right of the poor to share in the tithe, is established by the tenour of ancient statutes.' (Tuckett, 1. c., Vol. II, pp. 804–5.)
9. William Cobbett: 'A History of the Protestant Reformation,' ‡ 471.
10. The 'spirit' of Protestantism may be seen from the following, among other things. In the south of England certain landed proprietors and well-to-do farmers put their heads together and propounded ten questions as to the right interpretation of the poor-law of Elizabeth. These they laid before a celebrated jurist of that time, Sergeant Snigge (later a judge under James I) for his opinion. 'Question 9 – some of the more wealthy farmers in the parish have devised a skilful mode by which all the trouble of executing this Act (the 43rd of Elizabeth) might be avoided. They have proposed that we shall erect a prison in the parish, and then give notice to the neighbourhood, that if any persons are disposed to farm the poor of this parish, they do give in sealed proposals, on a certain day, of the lowest price at which they will take them off our hands; and that they will be authorised to refuse to any one unless he be shut up in the aforesaid prison. The proposers of this plan conceive that there will be

found in the adjoining counties, persons, who, being unwilling to labour and not possessing substance or credit to take a farm or ship, so as to live without labour, may be induced to make a very advantageous offer to the parish. If any of the poor perish under the contractor's care, the sin will lie at his door, as the parish will have done its duty by them. We are, however, apprehensive that the present Act (43rd of Elizabeth) will not warrant a prudential measure of this kind; but you are to learn that the rest of the freeholders of the county, and of the adjoining county of B, will very readily join in instructing their members to propose an Act to enable the parish to contract with a person to lock up and work the poor; and to declare that if any person shall refuse to be so locked up and worked, he shall be entitled to no relief. This, it is hoped, will prevent persons in distress from wanting relief, and be the means of keeping down parishes.' (R. Blakey: 'The History of Political Literature from the Earliest Times.' Lond., 1855, Vol. II, pp. 84–5.) In Scotland, the abolition of serfdom took place some centuries later than in England. Even in 1698, Fletcher of Saltoun, declared in the Scotch parliament, 'The number of beggars in Scotland is reckoned at not less than 200,000. The only remedy that I, a republican on principle, can suggest, is to restore the old state of serfdom, to make slaves of all those who are unable to provide for their own subsistence.' Eden, 1. c., Book 1., ch. 1, pp. 60–61, says, 'The decrease of villenage seems necessarily to have been the era of the origin of the poor. Manufactures and commerce are the two parents of our national poor.' Eden, like our Scotch republican on principle, errs only in this: not the abolition of villenage, but the abolition of the property of the agricultural labourer in the soil made him a proletarian, and eventually a pauper. In France, where the expropriation was effected in another way, the ordonnance of Moulins, 1566, and the Edict of 1656, correspond to the English poor-laws.

11. Professor Rogers, although formerly Professor of Political Economy in the University of Oxford, the hotbed of Protestant orthodoxy, in his preface to the 'History of Agriculture' lays stress on the fact of the pauperisation of the mass of the people by the Reformation.
12. 'A Letter to Sir. F. C. Bunbury, Bart., on the High Price of Provisions. By a Suffolk Gentleman.' Ipswich, 1795, p. 4. Even the fanatical advocate of the system of l arge farms, the author of the 'Inquiry into the Connexion between the Present Price of Provisions,' London, 1773, p. 139, says: 'I most lament the loss of our yeomanry, that set of men who really kept up the independence of this nation; and sorry I am to see their lands now in the hands of monopolising lords, tenanted out to small farmers, who hold their leases on such conditions as to be little better than vassals ready to attend a summons on every mischievous occasion.'
13. On the private moral character of this bourgeois hero, among other things: 'The large grant of lands in Ireland to Lady Orkney, in 1695, is a public instance of the king's affection, and the lady's influence . . . Lady Orkney's endearing offices are supposed to have been – foeda laborium ministeria.' (In the Sloane Manuscript Collection, at the British Museum, No.4224. The Manuscript is entitled: 'The character and behaviour of King William, Sunderland, etc., as represented in Original Letters to the Duke of Shrewsbury from Somers, Halifax, Oxford, Secretary Vernon, etc.' It is full of curiosa.)
14. 'The illegal alienation of the Crown Estates, partly by sale and partly by gift, is a scandalous chapter in English history . . . a gigantic fraud on the nation.' (F. W. Newman, 'Lectures on Political Economy.' London, 1851, pp. 129, 130.) [For details as to how the present large landed proprietors of England came into their possessions see 'Our Old Nobility. By Noblesse Oblige.' London, 1879. – *F.E.*]
15. Read, e.g., E. Burke's Pamphlet on the ducal house of Bedford, whose offshoot was Lord John Russell, the 'tomtit of Liberalism.'
16. 'The farmers forbid cottagers to keep any living creatures besides themselves and children, under the pretence that if they keep any beasts or poultry, they will steal from the farmers' barns for their support; they also say, keep the cottagers poor and you will keep them industrious, etc., but the real fact I believe, is that the farmers may have the whole right of common to themselves.' ('A Political Inquiry into the Consequences of Enclosing Waste Lands.' London, 1785, p. 75.)
17. Eden, 1. c., preface.
18. 'Capital Farms.' Two letters on the Flour Trade and the Dearness of Corn. By a person in business. London, 1767, pp. 19, 20.

19. 'Merchant Farms.' 'An Enquiry into the Causes of the Present High Price of Provisions.' London, 1767, p. 11. Note. – This excellent work, that was published anonymously, is by the Rev. Nathaniel Forster.
20. Thomas Wright: 'A Short Address to the Public on the Monopoly of Large Farms,' 1779, pp. 2, 3.
21. Rev Addington: 'Inquiry into the Reasons for or against Enclosing Open Fields,' London, 1772, pp. 37, 43 passim.
22. Dr. R. Price, 1 c., v. ii., p. 155, Forster Addington, Kent, Price, and James Anderson, should be read and compared with the miserable prattle of Sycophant MacCulloch in his catalogue: 'The Literature of Political Economy,' London, 1845.
23. Price, 1. c., p. 147.
24. Price, 1. c., p. 159. We are reminded of ancient Rome. 'The rich had got possession of the greater part of the undivided land. They trusted in the conditions of the time, that these possessions would not be again taken from them, and bought, therefore, some of the pieces of land lying near theirs, and belonging to the poor, with the acquiescence of their owners, and took some by force, so that they now were cultivating widely extended domains, instead of isolated fields. Then they employed slaves in agriculture and cattle-breeding, because freemen would have been taken from labour for military service. The possession of slaves brought them great gain, inasmuch as these, on account of their immunity from military service, could freely multiply and have a multitude of children. Thus the powerful men drew all wealth to themselves, and all the land swarmed with slaves. The Italians, on the other hand, were always decreasing in number, destroyed as they were by poverty, taxes, and military service. Even when times of peace came, they were doomed to complete inactivity, because the rich were in possession of the soil, and used slaves instead of freemen in the tilling of it.' (Appian: 'Civil Wars,' I 7.) This passage refers to the time before the Licinian rogations. Military service, which hastened to so great an extent the ruin of the Roman plebeians, was also the chief means by which, as in a forcing-house, Charlemagne brought about the transformation of free German peasants into serfs and bondsmen.
25. 'An Inquiry into the Connexion between the Present Price of Provisions, etc.,' pp. 124, 129. To the like effect, but with an opposite tendency: 'Working-men are driven from their cottages and forced into the towns to seek for employment; but then a larger surplus is obtained, and thus capital is augmented.' ('The Perils of the Nation,' 2nd ed. London, 1843, p. 14.)
26. l. c., p. 132.
27. Steuart says: 'If you compare the rent of these lands' (he erroneously includes in this economic category the tribute of the taskmen to the clanchief) 'with the extent, it appears very small. If you compare it with the numbers fed upon the farm, you will find that an estate in the Highlands maintains, perhaps, ten times as many people as another of the same value in good and fertile province.' (l. c., vol.i, ch.xvi., p. 104.)
28. James Anderson: 'Observations on the Means of Exciting a Spirit of National Industry, etc.,' Edinburgh, 1777.
29. In 1860 the people expropriated by force were exported to Canada under false pretences. Some fled to the mountains and neighbouring islands. They were followed by the police, came to blows with them and escaped.
30. 'In the Highlands of Scotland,' says Buchanan, the commentator on Adam Smith, 1814, 'the ancient state of property is daily subverted. . . . The landlord, without regard to the hereditary tenant (a category used in error here), now often his land to the highest bidder, who, if he is an improver, instantly adopts a new system of cultivation. The land, formerly overspread with small tenants or labourers, was peopled in proportion to its produce, but under the new system of improved cultivation and increased rents, the largest possible produce is obtained at the least possible expense: and the useless hands being, with this view, removed, the population is reduced, not to what the land will maintain, but to what it will employ. The dispossessed tenants either seek a subsistence in the neighbouring towns,' etc. (David Buchanan: 'Observations on, etc., A Smith's Wealth of Nations.' Edinburgh, 1814, vol.iv, p. 144.) 'The Scotch grandees dispossessed families as they would grub up coppice-wood, and they treated villages and their people as Indians harassed with wild beasts do, in their vengeance, a jungle with tigers . . . Man is bartered for a fleece or a carcase of mutton, nay,

held cheaper . . . Why, how much worse is it than the intention of the Moguls, who, when they had broken into the northern provinces of China, proposed in council to exterminate the inhabitants, and convert the land into pasture. This proposal many Highland proprietors have effected in their own country against their own countrymen' (George Ensor: 'An Inquiry Concerning the Population of Nations.' Lond, 1818, pp. 215, 216.)

31. When the present Duchess of Sutherland entertained Mrs Beecher Stowe, authoress of 'Uncle Tom's Cabin,' with great magnificence in London to show her sympathy for the negro slaves of the American republic – a sympathy that she prudently forgot, with her fellow-aristocrats, during the civil war, in which every 'noble' English heart beat for the slave-owner – I gave in the *New York Tribune* the facts about the Sutherland slaves. (Epitomised in part by Carey in 'The Slave Trade.' Philadelphia, 1853, pp. 203, 204.) My article was reprinted in a Scotch newspaper, and led to a pretty polemic between the latter and the sycophants of the Sutherlands.
32. Interesting details on this fish trade will be found in Mr David Urquhart's Portfolio, new series. – Nassau W. Senior, in his posthumous work, already quoted, terms 'the proceedings in Sutherlandshire one of the most beneficent clearings since the memory of man.' (l. c.)
33. The deer-forests of Scotland contain not a single tree. The sheep are driven from, and then the deer driven to, the naked hills, and then it is called a deer-forest. Not even timber-planting and real forest culture.
34. Robert Somers: 'Letters from the Highlands: or the Famine of 1847.' London, 1848, pp. 12–28 passim. These letters originally appeared in *The Times*. The English economists of course explained the famine of the Gaels in 1847, by their over-population. At all events, they 'were pressing on their food-supply.' The 'clearing of estates,' or as it is called in Germany, 'Bauernlegen,' occurred in Germany especially after the 30 years' war, and led to peasant-revolts as late as 1790 in Kursachsen. It obtained especially in East Germany. In most of the Prussian provinces, Frederick II for the first time secured right of property for the peasants. After the conquest of Silesia he forced the landlords to rebuild the huts, barns, etc., and to provide the peasants with cattle and implements. He wanted soldiers for his army and tax-payers for his treasury. For the rest, the pleasant life that the peasant led under Frederick's system of finance and hodge-podge rule of despotism, bureaucracy and feudalism, may be seen from the following quotation from his admirer, Mirabeau: 'Le lin fait donc une des grandes richesses du cultivateur dans le Nord de l'Allemagne. Malheureusement pour l'espèce humanine, ce n'est qu'une ressource contre la misère et non un moyen de bien-être. Les impôts directs, les corvées, les servitudes de tout genre, écrasent le cultivateur allemand, qui paie encore des impôts indirects dans tout ce qu'il achète . . . et pour comble de ruine, il n'ose pas vendre ses productions où et comme il le veut; il n'ose pas acheter ce dont il a besoin aux marchands qui pourraient le lui livrer au meilleur prix. Toutes ces causes le ruinent insensiblement, et il se trouverait hors d'état de payer les impôts directs à l'échéance sans la filerie; elle lui offre une ressource, en occupant utilement sa femme, ses enfants, ses servants, ses valets, et lui-même; mais quelle pénible vie, même aidée de ce secours. En été, il travaille comme un forcat au labourage et à la récolte; il se couche à 9 heures et se lève à deux, pour suffire aux travaux; en hiver il devrait réparer ses forces par un plus grand repos; mais il manquera de grains pour le pain et les semailles, s'il se défait des denrées qu'il faudrait vendre pour payer les impôts. Il faut donc filer pour suppléer à ce vide . . . il faut y apporter la plus grande assiduité. Aussi le paysan se couche-t-il en hiver à minuit, une heure, et se lève à cinq ou six; ou bien il se couche à neuf, et se lève à deux, et cela tous les jours de la vie si ce n'est le dimanche. Ces excès de veille et de travail usent la nature humaine, et de là vien qu'hommes et femmes vieillissent beaucoup plutôt dans les campagnes que dans les villes.' (Mirabeau, l. c., t. III. pp. 212 sqq.)

Note to the second edition. In April 1866, 18 years after the publication of the work of robert Somers quoted above, Professor Leone Levi gave a lecture before the Society of Arts on the transformation of sheep-walks into deer-forest, in which he depicts the advance in the devastation of the Scottish Highlands. He says, with other things: 'Depopulation and transformation into sheep-walks were the most convenient means for getting an income without expenditure . . . A deer-forest in place of a sheep-walk was a common change in the Highlands. The landowners turned out the sheep as they once turned out the men from their estates, and welcomed the new tenants – the wild beasts and the feathered birds . . . One can walk from the Earl of Dalhousie's estates in Forfarshire to John o'Groats, without ever leaving forest land . . . In many of these woods the fox, the wild cat, the marten, the polecat, the weasel and the Apline hare are common; whilst the rabbit, the squirrel and the rat have lately made their way into the country. Immense tracts of land, much of which is described in the statistical account of Scotland as having a pasturage in richness and extent of very superior description, are thus shut out from all cultivation and improvement, and are solely devoted to the sport of a few persons for a very brief period of the year.' The London *Economist* of June 2, 1866, says, 'Amongst the items of news in a Scotch paper of last week, we read . . . "One of the finest sheep farms in Sutherlandshire, for which a rent of £1,200 a year was recently offered, on the expiry of the existing lease this year, is to be converted into a deer-forest," Here we see the modern instincts of feudalism . . . operating pretty much as they did when the Norman Conqueror . . . destroyed 36 villages to create the New Forest . . . Two millions of acres . . . totally laid waste, embracing within their area some of the most fertile lands of Scotland. The natural grass of Glen Tilt was among the most nutritive in the country of Perth. The deer-forest of Ben Aulder was by far the best grazing ground in the wide district of Badenoch; a part of the Black Mount forest was the best pasture for black-faced sheep in Scotland. Some idea of the ground laid waste for purely sporting purposes in Scotland may be formed from the fact that it embraced an area larger than the whole country of Perth. The resources of the forest of Ben Aulder might give some idea of the loss sustained from the forced desolations. The ground would pasture 15,000 sheep, and as it was not more than one-thirtieth part of the old forest ground in Scotland . . . it might, etc. . . . All that forest land is as totally unproductive . . . It might thus as well have been submerged under the waters of the German Ocean . . . Such extemporised wildernesses or deserts ought to be put down by the decided interference of the Legislature.

35. The author of the 'Essay on Trade, etc.,' 1770, says, 'In the reign of Edward VI indeed the English seem to have set, in good earnest, about encouraging manufactures and employing the poor. This we learn from a remarkable statute which runs thus: "That all vagrants shall be branded, etc.,"' l. c., p. 5.

36. Thomas More says in his 'Utopia': 'Therefore that on covetous and unsatiable cormaraunte and very plage of his native contrey maye compasse aboute and inclose many thousand akers of grounde together within one pale or hedge, the husbandmen be thrust owte of their owne, or els either by coneyne and fraude, or by violent oppression they be put besydes it, or by wrongs and iniuries thei be so weried that they be compelled to sell all: by one meanes, therfore, or by other, either by hooke or crooke they muste needes departe awaye, poore, selye, wretched soules, men, women, husbands, wiues, fatherlesse children, widowes, wofull mothers with their youge babes, and their whole householde smal in substance, and muche in numbre, as husbandrye requireth many handes. Awaye thei trudge, I say, owte of their knowen accustomed houses, fyndynge no place to reste in. All their housholde stuffe, which is very little woorthe, thoughe it might well abide the sale: yet beeynge sodainely thruste owte, they be constrayned to sell it for a thing of nought. And when they haue wandered abrode tyll that be spent, what cant they then els doe but steale, and then iustly pardy be hanged, or els go about beggyng. And yet then also they be caste in prison as vagaboundes, because they go aboute and worke not: whom no man wyl set a worke though thei neuer so willyngly profre themselues therto.' Of these poor fugitives of whom Thomas More says that they were forced to thieve, '7, 200 great and petty thieves were put to death,' in the reign of Henry VIII. (Holinshed, 'Description of England,' Vol.1, p. 186.) In Elizabeth's time, 'rogues were trussed up apace, and that there was not one year commonly wherein three or four hundred were not devoured and eaten up by the gallowes.' (Strype's 'Annals of the Reformation and Establishment of Religion and other Various Occurrences in the Church of England during Queen Elizabeth's Happy Reign.' Second ed., 1725, Vol. 2.) According to this same Strype, in Somersetshire, in one year, 40 persons were executed, 35 robbers burnt in the hand, 37 whipped, and 183 discharged as 'incorrigible vagabonds.' Nevertheless, he is of opinion that this large number of prisoners does not comprise even a fifth of the actual criminals, thanks to the negligence of the justices and the foolish compassion of the people; and the other counties of England were not better off in this respect than Somersetshire, while some were even worse.

37. Whenever the legislature attempts to regulate the differences between masters and their workmen, its counsellors are always the masters,' says A. Smith. 'L'esprit des lois, c'est la propriété,' says Linguet.
38. 'Sophisms of Free Trade.' By a Barrister. Lond., 1850, p. 206. He adds maliciously: 'We were ready enough to interfere for the employer, can nothing now be done for the employed?'
39. From a clause of Statute 2 James I, c. 6, we see that certain clothmakers took upon themselves to dictate, in their capacity of justices of the peace, the official tariff of wages in their own shops. In Germany, especially after the Thirty Years' War, statutes for keeping down wages were general. 'The want of servants and labourers was very troublesome to the landed proprietors in the depopulated districts. All villagers were forbidden to let rooms to single men and women; all the latter were to be reported to the authorities and cast into prison if they were unwilling to become servants, even if they were employed at any other work, such as sowing seeds for the peasants at a daily wage, or even buying and selling corn. (Imperial privileges and sanctions for Silesia, I., 25.) For a whole century in the decrees of the small German potentates a bitter cry goes up again and again about the wicked and impertinent rabble that will not reconcile itself to its hard lot, will not be content with the legal wage; the individual landed proprietors are forbidden to pay more than the State had fixed by a tariff. And yet the conditions of service were at times better after the war than 100 years later; the farm servants of Silesia had, in 1652, meat twice a week, whilst even in our century, districts are known where they have it only three times a year. Further, wages after the war were higher than in the following century.' (G. Freytag.)
40. Article I. of this law runs: 'L'anéantissement de toute espèce de corporations du même état et profession étant l'une des bases fondamentales de la constitution française, il est défendu de les rétablir de fait sous quelque prétexte et sous quelque forme que ce soit.' Article IV. declares, that if 'des citoyens attachés aux mêmes professions, arts et métiers prenaient des délibérations, faisaient entre eux des conventions tendantes à refuser de concert ou à n'accorder qu'à un prix déterminé le secours de leur industrie ou de leurs travaux, les dites délibérations et conventions . . . seront déclarées inconstitutionnelles, attentatoires à la liberté et à la declaration des droits de l'homme, &c.' felony, therefore, as in the old labour-statutes. ('Révolutions des Paris,' Paris, 1791, t.III, p. 523.)
41. Harrison in his 'Description of England,' says 'although peradventure foure pounds of old rent be improved to fortie, toward the end of his term, if he have not six or seven yeares rent lieng by him, fiftie or a hundred pounds, yet will the farmer thinke his gaines verie small.'
42. On the influence of the depreciation of money in the 16th century, on the different classes of society, see 'A Compendious or Briefe Examination of Certayne Ordinary Complaints of Divers of our Countrymen in these our Days.' By W. S., Gentleman. (London 1581.) The dialogue form of this work led people for a long time to ascribe it to Shakespeare, and even in 1751, it was published under his name. Its author is William Stafford. In one place the knight reasons as follows:

['Knight:] You, my neighbour, the husbandman, you Maister Mercer, and you Goodman Cooper, with other artificers, may save yourselves metely well. For as much as all things are dearer than they were, so much do you arise in the pryce of your wares and occupations that ye sell agayne. But we have nothing to sell whereby we might advance ye price there of, to countervaile those things that we must buy agayne.' In another place the knight asks the doctor: 'I pray you, what be those sorts that ye meane. And first, of those that ye thinke should have no losse thereby? – Doctor: I mean all those that live by buying and selling, for as they buy deare, they sell thereafter. Knight: What is the next sort that ye say would win by it? Doctor: Marry, all such as have takings of fearmes in their owne manurance [cultivation] at the old rent, for where they pay after the olde rate they sell after the newe – that is, they paye for theire lande good cheape, and sell all things growing thereof deare. Knight: What sorte is that which, ye sayde should have greater losse hereby, than these men had profit? Doctor: It is all noblemen, gentlemen, and all other that live either by a stinted rent or stypend, or do not manure [cultivation] the ground, or doe occupy no buying and selling.'

43. In France, the régisseur, steward, collector of dues for the feudal lords during the earlier part of the middle ages, soon became an homme d'affaires, who by extortion, cheating, etc., swindled himself into a capitalist. These régisseurs themselves were sometimes noblemen. E.g., 'C'est li compte que messire Jacques de Thoraine, chevalier chastelain sor Besancon rent

ès-seigneur tenant les comptes à Dijon pour monseigneur le duc et comte de Bourgoigne, des rentes appartenant à la dite chastellenie, depuis xxve jour de décembre MCCCLIX jusqu'au xxviiie jour de décembre MCCCLX.' (Alexis Monteil: 'Traité de Matériaux Manuscrits etc.,' pp. 234, 235.) Already it is evident here how in all spheres of social life the lion's share falls to the middleman. In the economic domain, *e.g.*, financiers, stock-exchange speculators, merchants, shoopkeepers skim the cream; in civil matters, the lawyer fleeces his clients; in politics the representative is of more importance than the voters, the minister than the sovereign; in religion God is pushed into the background by the 'Mediator,' and the latter again is shoved back by the priests, the inevitable middlemen between the good shepherd and his sheep. In France, as in England, the great feudal territories were divided into innumerable small homesteads, but under conditions incomparably more unfavourable for the people. During the 14th century arose the farms or *terriers*. Their number grew constantly, far beyond 100,000. They paid rents varying from one-twelfth to one-fifth of the product in money or in kind. These farms were fiefs, sub-fiefs, etc., according the value and extent of the domains, many of them only containing a few acres. But these farmers had rights of jurisdiction in some degree over the dwellers on the soil; there were four grades. The oppression of the agricultural population under all these petty tyrants will be understood. Monteil says that there were once in France 160,000 judges, where to-day, 4,000 tribunals, including justices of the peace, suffice.

44. In his 'Notions de Philosophie Naturelle.' Paris, 1838.
45. A point that Sir James Steuart emphasises.
46. 'Je permettrai,' says the capitalist, 'que vous ayez l'honneur de me servir, à condition que vous me donnez le peu qui vous reste pour la peine que je prends de vous commander.' (J. J. Rousseau: 'Discours sur l'Economie Politique.')
47. Mirabeau, l. c., t.iii., pp. 20–109 passim. That Mirabeau considers the separate workshops more economical and productive than the 'combined,' and sees in the latter merely artificial exotics under government cultivation, is explained by the position at that time of a great part of the continental manufactures.
48. 'Twenty pounds of wool converted unobtrusively into the yearly clothing of a labourer's family by its own industry in the intervals of other work – this makes no show; but bring it to market, send it to the factory, thence to the broker, thence to the dealer, and you will have great commercial operations, and nominal capital engaged to the amount or twenty times its value . . . The working-class is thus emersed to support a wretched factory population, a parasitical shop-keeping class, and a fictitious commercial, monetary, and financial system. (David Urquhart, 1. c., p. 120.)
49. Cromwell's time forms an exception. So long as the Republic lasted, the mass of the English people of all grades rose from the degradation into which they had sunk under the Tudors.
50. Tuckett is aware that the modern woollen industry has sprung, with the introduction of machinery, from manufacture proper and from the destruction of rural and domestic industries. 'The plough, the yoke, were "the invention of gods, and the occupation of heroes;" are the loom, the spindle, the distaff, of less noble parentage. You sever the distaff and the plough, the spindle and the yoke, and you get factories and poor-houses, credit and panics, two hostile nations, agricultural and commercial.' (David Urquhart, l. c., p. 122). But now comes Carey, and cries out upon England, surely not with unreason, that it is trying to turn every other country into a mere agricultural nation, whose manufacturer is to be England. He pretends that in this way Turkey has been ruined, because 'the owners and occupants of land have never been permitted by England to strengthen themselves by the formation of that natural alliance between the plough and the loom, the hammer and the harrow.' ('The Slave Trade,' p. 125.) According to him, Urquhart himself is one of the chief agents in the ruin of Turkey, where he had made Free-trade propaganda in the English interest. The best of it is that Carey, a great Russophile by the way, wants to prevent the process of separation by that very system of protection which accelerates it.
51. Philanthropic English economists, like Mill, Rogers, Goldwin Smith, Fawcett, etc., and liberal manufacturers like John Bright, and Co., ask the English landed proprietors, as God asked Cain after Abel, Where are our thousands of freeholders gone? But where do *you* come from, then? From the destruction of those freeholders. Why don't you ask further, where are the independent weavers, spinners, and artisans gone?

52. Industrial here in contradistinction to agricultural. In the 'categoric' sense the farmer is an industrial capitalist as much as the manufacturer.
53. 'The Natural and Artificial Rights of Property Contrasted.' Lond:, 1832, pp. 98–9. Author of the anonymous work: 'Th. Hodgskin.'
54. [Even] as late as 1794, the small cloth-makers of Leeds sent a deputation to Parliament, with a petition for a law to forbid any merchant from becoming a manufacturer. (Dr Aikin, l. c.)
55. William Howitt: 'Colonisation and Christianity: A Popular History of the Treatment of the Natives by the Europeans in all their Colonies.' London, 1838, p. 9. On the treatment of the slaves there is a good compilation in Charles Comte, 'Traité de la Législation.' 3me éd. Bruxelles, 1837. This subject one must study in detail, to see what the bourgeoisie makes of itself and of the labourer, wherever it can, without restraint, model the world after its own image.
56. Thomas Stamford Raffles, late Lieut-Gov. of that island: 'The History of Java,' Lond., 1817.
57. In the year 1866 more than a million Hindus died of hunger in the province of Orissa alone. Nevertheless, the attempt was made to enrich the Indian treasury by the price at which the necessaries of life were sold to the starving people.
58. William Cobbett remarks that in England all public institutions are designated 'royal'; as compensation for this, however, there is the 'national' debt.
59. 'Si les Tartares inondaient l'Europe aujourd'hui, il faudrait bien des affaires pour leur faire entendre ce que c'est qu'un financier parmi nous.' Montesquieu, 'Esprit des lois,' t.iv., p. 33, ed. Londres, 1769.
60. Mirabeau. l. c., t.vi., p. 101.
61. Eden, l. c., Vol. i., Book ii., Ch. i., p. 421.
62. John Fielden, l. c., pp. 5, 6. On the earlier infamies of the factory system, cf. Dr Aikin (1795), l. c.,p. 219 and Gisborne: 'Enquiry into the Duties of Men,' 1795, Vol. ii. When the steam-engine transplanted the factories from the country waterfalls to the middle of towns, the 'abstemious' surplus-value maker found the child-material ready to his hand, without being forced to seek slaves from the workhouses. When Sir R. Peel (father of the 'minister of plausibility'), brought in his bill for the protection of children, in 1815, Francis Horner, lumen of the Billion Committee and intimate friend of Ricardo, said in the House of Commons: 'It is notorious, that with a bankrupt's effects, a gang, if he might use the word, of these children had been put up to sale, and were advertised publicly as part of the property. A most atrocious instance had been brought before the Court of King's Bench two years before, in which a number of these boys, apprenticed by a parish in London to one manufacturer, had been transferred to another, and had been found by some benevolent persons in a state of absolute famine. Another case more horrible had come to his knowledge while on a [Parliamentary] Committee . . . that not many years ago, an agreement had been made between a London parish and a Lancashire manufacturer, by which it was stipulated, that with every 20 sound children one idiot should be taken.'
63. In 1790, there were in the English West Indies ten slaves for one free man, in the French fourteen for one, in the Dutch twenty-three for one. (Henry Brougham: 'An Inquiry into the Colonial Policy of the European Powers.' Edin. 1803, vol. ii, p. 74.)
64. The phrase, 'labouring poor,' is found in English legislation from the moment when the class of wage-labourers becomes noticeable. This term is used in opposition, on the one hand, to the 'idle poor,' beggars, etc., on the other to those labourers, who, pigeons not yet plucked, are still possessors of their own means of labour. From the Statute Book it passed into Political Economy, and was handed down by Culpeper, J. Child, etc., to Adam Smith and Eden. After this, one can judge of the good faith of the 'execrable political cant-monger,' Edmund Burke, when he called the expression, 'labouring poor,' – 'execrable political cant.' This sycophant who, in the pay of the English oligarchy, played the romantic laudator temporis acti against the French Revolution, just as, in the pay of the North American Colonies, at the beginning of the American troubles, he had played the Liberal against the English oligarchy, was an out and out vulgar bourgeois. 'The laws of commerce are the laws of Nature, and therefore the laws of God.' (E. Burke, l. c., pp 31, 32.) No wonder that, true to the laws of God and of Nature, he always sold himself in the best market. A very good portrait of this Edmund Burke, during his liberal time, is to be found in the writings of the Rev. Mr Tucker. Tucker was a parson and a Tory, but, for the rest, an honourable man and a competent political

economist. In face of the infamous cowardice of character that reigns to-day, and believes most devoutly in 'the laws of commerce,' it is our bounden duty again and again to brand the Burkes, who only differ from their successors in one thing – talent.

65. Marie Augier: 'Du Crédit Public.' Paris, 1842.
66. 'Capital is said by a Quarterly Reviewer to fly turbulence and strife, and to be timid, which is very true; but this is very incompletely stating the question. Capital eschews no profit, or very small profit, just as Nature was formerly said to abhor a vacuum. With adequate profit, capital is very bold. A certain 10 per cent. will ensure its employment anywhere; 20 per cent. certain will produce eagerness; 50 per cent., positive audacity; 100 per cent. will make it ready to trample on all human laws; 300 per cent., and there is not a crime at which it will scruple, nor a risk it will not run, even to the chance of its owner being hanged. If turbulence and strife will bring a profit, it will freely encourage both. Smuggling and the slave-trade have amply proved all that is here stated.' (T. J. Dunning, l. c., pp. 35, 36.)

1.9 Selected Correspondence

In between his political activities and his research and writing, Marx somehow found time to produce an enormous amount of correspondence. Three of his letters are printed here.

Letter to Annenkov: Paul Vasilyevich Annenkov (1812–87) was a liberal Russian landowner and a friend of Marx. This letter was sent in 1846 and is of interest for Marx's answer to his own question: 'what is society'? (NB: Pierre-Joseph Proudhon, 1809–65, was a French economist and one of the founders of the anarchist movement.)

From: K. Marx and F. Engels *Selected Works* (Lawrence and Wishart: London, 1968) pp. 660–1.

Letter to Weydemyer: Joseph Weydemyer (1818–66) was a prominent figure in the American and German working-class movement. In this famous letter of 1852 Marx dismisses any notion that he 'discovered' the existence of classes within society.

From: K. Marx and F. Engels *Selected Works* (Lawrence and Wishart: London, 1968) p. 669.

Letter to Mikhailovski: Nikolai Mikhailovski (1842–1904), a writer, sociologist and journalist within the Russian Populist movement was critical of Marx's arguments in *Capital Volume 1* as he thought that they denied the possibility of Russia developing without first going through a capitalist phase. Marx's reply (in 1877) emphasises the historically specific nature of his theories and their application to developments in Western Europe and argues that they cannot be seen as a source of prediction or a historical 'master key' for unlocking the secrets of all social development from different historical epochs.

From: D. McLellan, *Karl Marx: Selected Writings* (Oxford University Press, 1977): pp. 571–2.

Letter to Annenkov

What is society, whatever its form may be? The product of men's reciprocal action. Are men free to choose this or that form of society? By no means. Assume a particular state of development in the productive faculties of man and you will get a particular form of commerce and consumption. Assume particular stages of development in production, commerce and consumption and you will have a corresponding social constitution, a corresponding organisation of the family, of orders or of classes, in a word, a corresponding civil society. Assume a particular civil society and you will get particular political conditions which are only the official expression of civil society. M. Proudhon will never understand this because he thinks he is doing something great by appealing from the state to civil society – that is to say, from the official résumé of society to official society.

It is superfluous to add that men are not free to choose *their productive forces* – which are the basis of all their history – for every productive force is an acquired force, the product of former activity. The productive forces are therefore the result of practical human energy; but this energy is itself conditioned by the circumstances in which men find themselves, by the productive forces already acquired, by the social form which exists before they do, which they do not create, which is the product of the preceding generation. Because of this simple fact that every succeeding generation finds itself in possession of the productive forces acquired by the previous generation, which serve it as the raw material for new production, a coherence arises in human history, a history of humanity takes shape which is all the more a history of humanity as the productive forces of man and therefore his social relations have been more developed. Hence it necessarily follows that the social history of men is never anything but the history of their individual development, whether they are conscious of it or not. Their material relations are the basis of all their relations. These material relations are only the necessary forms in which their material and individual activity is realised.

M. Proudhon mixes up ideas and things. Men never relinquish what they have won, but this does not mean that they never relinquish the social form in which they have acquired certain productive forces. On the contrary, in order that they may not be deprived of the result attained and forfeit the fruits of civilisation, they are obliged, from the moment when their mode of carrying on commerce no longer corresponds to the productive forces acquired, to change all their traditional social forms.

Letter to Weydemyer

> And now as to myself, no credit is due to me for discovering the existence of classes in modern society or the struggle between them. Long before me bourgeois historians had described the historical development of this class struggle and bourgeois economists the economic anatomy of the classes. What I did that was new was to prove: 1. that the *existence of classes* is only bound up with *particular historical phases in the development of production*, 2. that the class struggle necessarily leads to *the dictatorship of the proletariat*, 3. that this dictatorship itself only constitutes the transition to the *abolition of all classes and to a classless society* . . .

Letter to Mikhailovski

The chapter on primitive accumulation does not pretend to do more than trace the path by which, in Western Europe, the capitalist order of economy emerged from the womb of the feudal order of economy. It therefore describes the historical movement which by divorcing the producers from their means of production converts them into wage workers (proletarians in the modern sense of the word) while it converts those who possess the means of production into capitalists. In that history 'all revolutions are epoch-making that act as levers for the advancement of the capitalist class in course of formation; above all, those which, by stripping great masses of men of their traditional means of production and subsistence, suddenly hurl them on the labour market. But the basis of this whole development is the expropriation of the agricultural producer. This has been accomplished in radical fashion only in England . . . but all the countries of Western Europe are going through the same movement', etc. (*Capital*, French edition, pp. 315.) At the end of the chapter the historical tendency of production is summed up thus: That it 'itself begets its own negation with the inexorability which governs the metamorphoses of nature'; that it has itself created the elements of a new economic order, by giving the greatest impulse at once to the productive forces of social labour and to the integral development of every individual producer; that capitalist property, resting already, as it actually does, on a collective mode of production, cannot but transform itself into social property. At this point I have not furnished any proof, for the good reason that this statement is itself nothing else but a general summary of long expositions previously given in the chapters on capitalist production.

Now what application to Russia could my critic make of this historical sketch? Only this: If Russia is tending to become a capitalist nation after the example of the West European countries – and during the last few years she has been taking a lot of trouble in this direction – she will not succeed without having first transformed a good part of her peasants into proletarians; and after that, once taken to the bosom of the capitalist regime, she will experience its pitiless laws like other profane peoples. That is all. But that is too little for my critic. He feels he absolutely must metamorphose my historical sketch of the genesis of capitalism in Western Europe into a historico-philosophic theory of the general path every people is fated to tread, whatever the historical circumstances in which it finds itself, in order that it may ultimately arrive at the form of economy which ensures, together with the greatest expansion of the productive powers of social labour, the most complete development of man. But I beg his pardon. (He is both honouring and shaming me too much.) Let us take an example.

In several parts of *Capital* I allude to the fate which overtook the plebeians of ancient Rome. They were originally free peasants, each cultivating his own piece of land on his own account. In the course of Roman history they were expropriated. The same movement which divorced them from their means of production and subsistence involved the formation not only of big landed property but also of big money capital. And so one fine morning there were to be found on the one hand free men, stripped of everything except their labour power, and on the other, in order to exploit this labour, those who held all the acquired wealth in their possession. What happened? The Roman proletarians became not wage-labourers but a mob of do-nothings more abject than the former 'poor whites' in the South of the United States, and alongside of them there developed a mode of production which was not capitalist but based on slavery. Thus events strikingly analogous but taking place in different historical surroundings led to totally different results. By studying each of these forms of evolution separately and then comparing them one can easily find the clue to this phenomenon, but one will never arrive there by using as one's master key a general historico-philosophical theory, the supreme virtue of which consists in being super-historical . . .

Guide To Further Reading

[The original date of publication is given in brackets where appropriate]

Early Writings (Penguin: Harmondsworth, 1975)

(with Engels) *The German Ideology: Student's Edition* (ed C. J. Arthur). Lawrence and Wishart: London, 1977) [originally written 1846–7]

The Poverty of Philosophy (International Publishers: New York, 1982) [1847]

Grundrisse: Foundations of the Critique of Political Economy (Penguin: Harmondsworth, 1973) [originally written 1857–8]

Pre-Capitalist Economic Formations (Lawrence and Wishart: London, 1964) A Contribution to the Critique of Political Economy (Progress Publishers: Moscow, 1977) [1859]

Capital: A Critique of Political Economy Volume 1 (Lawrence and Wishart: London, 1954) [1867]

Capital: A Critique of Political Economy Volume 2 (Foreign Languages Publications: Moscow, 1957) [1885]

Capital: A Critique of Political Economy Volume 3 (Penguin: Harmondsworth, 1981) [1894]

Marx and Engels: Selected Works (Lawrence and Wishart: London, 1968; includes, amongst others, *The Communist Manifesto* [1848], *The 18th Brumaire of Louis Bonaparte* [1852], *The Civil War in France* [1871])

The literature on Marx is vast. Here I can only suggest reading for those relatively new to his work and I will refrain from compiling a dishearteningly long list.

After reading this book (!) it would be worthwhile dipping further into *Capital, Volume* 1, much of which is more accessible than is often imagined – particularly the chapters on the 'Working Day' and 'Machinery and Modern Industry'. A useful collection of Marx' and Engels' writings is contained in *Selected Works* (Lawrence and Wishart: London, 1968) which includes, amongst other things, *The Communist Manifesto, The Civil War in France, The 18th Brumaire of Louis Bonaparte, Wages, Price Profit* and a selection from Marx and Engels, vast amount of correspondence. David McLellan's *Karl Marx: Selected Writings* (Oxford University Press, 1977) is also an excellent source. T. B. Bottomore and M. Rubel's *Selected Writings in Sociology and Social Philosophy* (Watts: London, 1956) contains two interesting introductory essays and an edited collection of Marx's more 'sociological' writings. Derek Sayer's *Readings From Karl Marx* (Routledge: London, 1989) is an interesting collection of Marx's writings. There are hundreds, at least, of commentaries about Marx. The new edition of Alex Callinicos' *The Revolutionary Ideas of Karl Marx* (Bookmarks: London, 1995) is an excellent introduction to Marx's life and work and emphasises the fact that first and foremost Marx was a revolutionary. David McLellan's *The Thought of Karl Marx*, (Macmillan: London, second edition, 1980) is a superbly organised and invaluable account of the development and context of Marx's thought and contains a mixture of biography, commentary and selected readings. Peter Worsley's *Marx and Marxism* (Tavistock: London, 1982) has the virtue of being a useful introduction that barely gets over 100 pages. *Karl Marx: Man and Fighter* (Penguin: Harmondsworth, 1973) by Boris Nicolaievsky and Otto Maenchen-Helfen is a detailed and readable single volume biography of Marx, as is Isaiah Berlin's *Karl Marx: His Life and Environment* (Oxford University Press: Oxford, 1963).

Marxism and Philosophy (Oxford University Press: Oxford, 1983) by Alex Callinicos investigates Marx's (and Marxism's), at times strained, relationship to philosophy. Ralph Milliband's *Marxism and Politics* (Oxford University Press, 1977) investigates the 'politics of Marxism' and a recent book by Jules Townsend, *The Politics of Marxism* (Leicester University Press, 1996), surveys Marxist debates through the twentieth century.

SECTION TWO
MAX WEBER

MAX WEBER: A BRIEF BIOGRAPHY

Weber was born in 1864 in Erfurt, Germany. His father, a lawyer and a prominent politician, came from a family of prosperous textile manufacturers. His mother was a deeply religious woman and was involved in a range of humanitarian activities. In 1868 the Weber family moved to Berlin, where his father became a National Liberal member of the German Reichstag, and the Weber household became something of a centre for debate and socialising for the Berlin intelligentsia.

At seventeen Weber went to Heidelberg University to study law and also took a range of other subjects including history, economics, theology and philosophy. We get a fascinating glimpse of Weber's student days from one of his letters:

> The logic course at seven in the morning forces me to rise early. Then I rush around the fencing hall for an hour each morning and [then] conscientiously sit through my lectures. At half past twelve I eat next door for one mark, sometimes drinking a quarter litre of wine or beer with my lunch. Then I often play a solid game of skat [a card game] with Otto and Herr Ickrath, the innkeeper . . . I look through my notes and read Straus' *Der alte und der neue Glaube.* In the afternoon we sometimes go hiking in the mountains. In the evening we are together again at Ickrath's, where we get a pretty good supper for eight pfennigs, and afterward we regularly read Lotze's *Mikrokosmos*, about which we have the most heated arguments. (M. Weber *Max Weber: A Biography*, Wiley Interscience: New York, 1957 p. 68)

It was during this time that Weber received the 'obligatory' duelling scar on his face as well as a reputation for being able to drink vast amounts of alcohol.

At nineteen Weber moved to Strasbourg to serve his year in the army. He returned to his studies in Berlin and Göttingen and in 1884 he qualified as a junior barrister. Five years later he completed his PhD. thesis on *The History of Trading Companies in the Middle Ages* – for the research of which he taught himself Italian and Spanish. Weber took up a lecturing post in Berlin and in 1892 completed his first 'sociological' work on the *Situation of Farm Workers in Germany East of the River Elbe.* A year later he married Marianne Schnitger, who went on to write his definitive biography. At the age of thirty, and by now an academic of formidable reputation, Weber accepted a Chair in Economics at Freiburg and two years later he became Professor at Heidelberg. It was at this time, soon after the death of his father, that Weber suffered a series of debilitating attacks of anxiety, sleeplessness and exhaustion which culminated in a complete nervous breakdown. It was several years before he was able to resume his academic work; even then this was often interrupted by relapses, fatigue and even temporary paralysis. From around 1903, despite his illness, Weber went into a new phase of activity and output from which most of his 'sociological' writings emerged, such as his work on *The Protestant Ethic and the Spirit of Capitalism* and, published shortly after his death, the three volume *Sociology of Religion* and the two volume *Economy and Society*. He also edited the important and influential journal *The Archive for Social Science and Social Policy* and helped found the *German Sociological Society* in 1910. He even managed to teach himself Russian in order to observe and write about the 1905 Russian revolution. In 1919 Weber took a Chair at Munich (he never held a post as a 'sociologist') and lectured to packed theatres on an astonishing range of subjects. The *General Economic History*, mainly based on students lecture notes, gives an indication of Weber's almost unimaginable, when viewed from the compartmentalised and specialised world of academia today, intellectual versatility and virtuosity.

Weber was also a well known public figure and was involved in a range of political activities, most notably as a member of the German peace delegation at Versailles at the end of the First World War – a war which he, as a staunch nationalist, supported. In 1920, at the age of fifty-six, Weber died of pneumonia.

2.1 *The Protestant Ethic and the Spirit of Capitalism*

The Protestant Ethic and the Spirit of Capitalism comprises two essays published in 1904–5 and is probably Weber's most famous piece of work. It certainly contains some of his most vivid and accessible writing.

Weber thought that it was pointless to search for underlying laws of historical development as the unfolding of history is as much about chance and contingency as about certainty and predictability. The economic determinism he thought characterised Marxism was the best example of this one-sided or mono-causal form of historical explanation. In *The Protestant Ethic* he sought to illustrate the power of ideas as a catalyst for historical and social change and to give the realm of ideas some autonomy from the economic or material world. Weber wanted to explain why modern capitalism emerged first in the West–particularly England. For modern rational capitalism in the West to develop there had to be not only the correct 'external' conditions – e.g. wage-labour, markets, etc. – but also the creation of the correct mental attitude and personality. For Weber the widespread influence of Protestantism after the Reformation helped explain why full blown rational capitalism developed where and when it did. Protestantism, in its various guises, overcame internal psychological obstacles – such as the mysticism, ceremony and magic central to some religions like Catholicism – and helped foster an approach to life very useful for the development and expansion of capitalism, although Weber did not believe that Protestantism and the Reformation 'caused' capitalism. As the religious input dwindled we are left with a pure 'spirit of capitalism', encapsulated in a phrase coined by the American politician and scientist Benjamin Franklin (1706–90) 'time is money' and our secularised modern world becomes an 'iron cage' of rationality.

Although Weber's 'Protestant ethic thesis' has generated much controversy and debate it still stands as a compelling and brilliantly insightful argument and a good example of Weber's 'sociology'.

From: M. Weber, *The Protestant Ethic and the Spirit of Capitalism* (Allen and Unwin: London, 1978) pp. 17–22, 144–51, 155–83.

And the same is true of the most fateful force in our modern life, capitalism. The impulse to acquisition, pursuit of gain, of money, of the greatest possible amount of money, has in itself nothing to do with capitalism. This impulse exists and has existed among waiters, physicians, coachmen, artists, prostitutes, dishonest officials, soldiers, nobles, crusaders, gamblers, and beggars. One may say that it has been common to all sorts and conditions of men at all times and in all countries of the earth, wherever the objective possibility of it is or has been given. It should be taught in the kindergarten of cultural history that this naïve idea of capitalism must be given up once and for all. Unlimited greed for gain is not in the least identical with capitalism, and is still less its spirit. Capitalism *may* even be identical with the restraint, or at least a rational tempering, of this irrational impulse. But capitalism is identical with the pursuit of profit, and forever *renewed* profit, by means of continuous, rational, capitalistic enterprise. For it must be so: in a wholly capitalistic order of society, an individual capitalistic enterprise which did not take advantage of its opportunities for profit-making would be doomed to extinction.

Let us now define our terms somewhat more carefully than is generally done. We will define a capitalistic economic action as one which rests on the expectation of profit by the utilization of opportunities for exchange, that is on (formally) peaceful chances of profit. Acquisition by force (formally and actually) follows its own particular laws, and it is not expedient, however little one can forbid this, to place it in the same category with action which is, in the last analysis, oriented to profits from exchange. Where capitalistic acquisition is rationally pursued, the corresponding action is adjusted to calculations in terms of capital. This means that the action is adapted to a systematic utilization of goods or personal services as means of acquisition in such a way that, at the close of a business period, the balance of the enterprise in money assets (or, in the case of a continuous enterprise, the periodically estimated money value of assets) exceeds the capital, i.e. the estimated value of the material means of production used for acquisition in exchange. It makes no difference whether it involves a quantity of goods entrusted *in natura* to a travelling merchant, the proceeds of which may consist in other goods *in natura* acquired by trade, or whether it involves a manufacturing enterprise, the assets of which consist of buildings, machinery, cash, raw materials, partly and wholly manufactured goods, which are balanced against liabilities. The important fact is always that a calculation of capital in terms of money is made, whether by modern book-keeping methods or in any other way, however primitive and crude. Everything is done in terms of balances: at the beginning of the enterprise an initial balance, before every individual decision a calculation to ascertain its probable profitableness, and at the end a final balance to ascertain how much profit has been made. For instance, the initial balance of a *commenda* transaction would determine an agreed money value of the assets put into it (so far as they were not in money form already), and a final balance would form the estimate on which to base the distribution of profit and loss at the end. So far as the transactions are rational, calculation underlies every single action of the partners. That a really accurate calculation or estimate may not exist, that the procedure is pure guess-work, or simply traditional and conventional, happens even to-day in every form of capitalistic enterprise where the circumstances do not demand strict accuracy. But these are points affecting only the *degree* of rationality of capitalistic acquisition.

For the purpose of this conception all that matters is that an actual adaptation of economic action to a comparison of money income with money expenses takes place, no matter how primitive the form. Now in this sense capitalism and capitalistic enterprises, even with a considerable rationalization of capitalistic calculation, have existed in all civilized countries of the earth, so far as economic documents permit us to judge. In China, India, Babylon, Egypt, Mediterranean antiquity, and the Middle Ages, as well as in modern times. These were not merely isolated ventures, but economic enterprises which were entirely dependent on the continual renewal of capitalistic undertakings, and even continuous operations. However, trade especially was for a long time not continuous like our own, but consisted essentially in a series of individual undertakings. Only gradually did the activities of even the large merchants acquire an inner cohesion (with branch organizations, etc.). In any case, the capitalistic enterprise and the capitalistic entrepreneur, not only as occasional but as regular entrepreneurs, are very old and were very widespread.

Now, however, the Occident has developed capitalism both to a quantitative extent, and (carrying this quantitative development) in types, forms, and directions which have never existed elsewhere. All over the world there have been merchants, wholesale and retail, local and engaged in foreign trade. Loans of all kinds have been made, and there have been banks with the most various functions, at least comparable to ours of, say, the sixteenth century. Sea loans, *commenda*, and transactions and associations similar to the *Kommanditgesellschaft*, have all been widespread, even as continuous businesses. Whenever money finances of public bodies have existed, money-lenders have appeared, as in Babylon, Hellas, India, China, Rome. They have financed wars and piracy, contracts and building operations of all sorts. In overseas policy they have functioned as colonial entrepreneurs, as planters with slaves, or directly or indirectly forced labour, and have farmed domains, offices, and, above all, taxes. They have financed party leaders in elections and *condottieri* in civil wars. And, finally, they have been speculators in chances for pecuniary gain of all kinds. This kind of entrepreneur, the capitalistic adventurer, has existed everywhere. With the exception of trade and credit and banking transactions, their activities were predominantly of an irrational and speculative character, or directed to acquisition by force, above all the acquisition of booty, whether directly in war or in the form of continuous fiscal booty by exploitation of subjects.

The capitalism of promoters, large-scale speculators, concession hunters, and much modern financial capitalism even in peace time, but, above all, the capitalism especially concerned with exploiting wars, bears this stamp even in modern Western countries, and some, but only some, parts of large-scale international trade are closely related to it, to-day as always.

But in modern times the Occident has developed, in addition to this, a very different form of capitalism which has appeared nowhere else: the rational capitalistic organization of (formally) free labour. Only suggestions of it are found elsewhere. Even the organization of unfree labour reached a considerable degree of rationality only on plantations and to a very limited extent in the *Ergasteria* of antiquity. In the manors, manorial workshops, and domestic industries on estates with serf labour it was probably somewhat less developed. Even real domestic industries with free labour have definitely been proved to have existed in only a few isolated cases outside the Occident. The frequent use of day labourers led in a very few cases – especially State monopolies, which are, however, very different from modern industrial organization – to manufacturing organizations, but never to a rational organization of apprenticeship in the handicrafts like that of our Middle Ages.

Rational industrial organization, attuned to a regular market, and neither to political nor irrationally speculative opportunities for profit, is not, however, the only peculiarity of Western capitalism. The modern rational organization of the capitalistic enterprise would not have been possible without two other important factors in its development: the separation of business from the household, which completely dominates modern economic life, and closely connected with it, rational book-keeping. A spatial separation of places of work from those of residence exists elsewhere, as in the Oriental bazaar and in the *ergasteria* of other cultures. The development of capitalistic associations with their own accounts is also found in the Far East, the Near East, and in antiquity. But compared to the modern independence of business enterprises, those are only small beginnings. The reason for this was particularly that the indispensable requisites for this independence, our rational business book-keeping and our legal separation of corporate from personal property, were entirely lacking, or had only begun to develop. The tendency everywhere else was for acquisitive enterprises to arise as parts of a royal or manorial *household* (of the *oikos*), which is, as Rodbertus has perceived, with all its superficial similarity, a fundamentally different, even opposite, development.

However, all these peculiarities of Western capitalism have derived their significance in the last analysis only from their association with the capitalistic organization of labour. Even what is generally called commercialization, the development of negotiable securities and the rationalization of speculation, the exchanges, etc., is connected with it. For without the rational capitalistic organization of labour, all this, so far as it was possible at all, would have nothing like the same significance, above all for the social structure and all the specific problems of the modern Occident connected with it. Exact calculation – the basis of everything else – is only possible on a basis of free labour.

The Baptist Sects

The Pietism of the Continent of Europe and the Methodism of the Anglo-Saxon peoples are, considered both in their content of ideas and their historical significance, secondary movements. On the other hand, we find a second independent source of Protestant asceticism besides Calvinism in the Baptist movement and the sects which, in the course of the sixteenth and seventeenth centuries, came directly from it or adopted its forms of religious thought, the Baptists, Mennonites, and, above all, the Quakers. With them we approach religious groups whose ethics rest upon a basis differing in principle from the Calvinistic doctrine. The following sketch, which only emphasizes what is important for us, can give no true impression of the diversity of this movement. Again we lay the principal emphasis on the development in the older capitalistic countries.

The feature of all these communities, which is both historically and in principle most important, but whose influence on the development of culture can only be made quite clear in a somewhat different connection, is something with which we are already familiar, the believer's Church. This means that the religious community, the visible Church in the language of the Reformation Churches, was no longer looked upon as a sort of trust foundation for supernatural ends, an institution, necessarily including both the just and the unjust, whether for increasing the glory of God (Calvinistic) or as a medium for bringing the means of salvation to men (Catholic and Lutheran), but solely as a community of personal believers of the reborn, and only these. In other words, not as a Church but as a sect. This is all that the principle, in itself purely external, that only adults who have personally gained their own faith should be baptized, is meant to symbolize. The justification through this faith was for the Baptists, as they have insistently repeated in all religious discussions, radically different from the idea of work in the world in the service of Christ, such as dominated the orthodox dogma of the older Protestantism. It consisted rather in taking spiritual possession of His gift of salvation. But this occurred through individual revelation, by the working of the Divine Spirit in the individual, and only in that way. It was offered to everyone, and it sufficed to wait for the Spirit, and not to resist its coming by a sinful attachment to the world. The significance of faith in the sense of knowledge of the doctrines of the Church, but also in that of a repentant search for divine grace, was consequently quite minimized, and there took place, naturally with great modifications, a renaissance of Early Christian pneumatic doctrines. For instance, the sect to which Menno Simons in his *Fondamentboek* (1539) gave the first reasonably consistent doctrine, wished, like the other Baptist sects, to be the true blameless Church of Christ; like the apostolic community, consisting entirely of those personally awakened and called by God. Those who have been born again, and they alone, are brethren of Christ, because they, like Him, have been created in spirit directly by God. A strict avoidance of the world, in the sense of all not strictly necessary intercourse with worldly people, together with the strictest bibliocracy in the sense of taking the life of the first generations of Christians as a model, were the results for the first Baptist communities, and this principle of avoidance of the world never quite disappeared so long as the old spirit remained alive.

As a permanent possession, the Baptist sects retained from these dominating motives of their early period a principle with which, on a somewhat different foundation, we have already become acquainted in Calvinism, and the fundamental importance of which will again and again come out. They absolutely repudiated all idolatry of the flesh, as a detraction from the reverence due to God alone. The Biblical way of life was conceived by the first Swiss and South German Baptists with a radicalism similar to that of the young St Francis, as a sharp break with all the enjoyment of life, a life modelled directly on that of the Apostles. And, in truth, the life of many of the earlier Baptists is reminiscent of that of St Giles. But this strict observation of Biblical precepts was not on very secure foundations in its connection with the pneumatic character of the faith. What God had revealed to the prophets and apostles was not all that He could and would reveal. On the contrary, the continued life of the Word, not as a written document, but as the force of the Holy Spirit working in daily life, which speaks directly to any individual who is willing to hear, was the sole characteristic of the true Church. That, as Schwenkfeld taught as against Luther and later Fox against the Presbyterians, was the testimony of the early Christian communities. From this idea of the continuance of revelation developed the well-known doctrine, later consistently worked out by the Quakers, of the (in the last analysis decisive) significance of the inner testimony of the Spirit in reason and conscience. This did away, not with the authority, but with the sole authority, of the Bible, and started a development which in the end radically eliminated all that remained of the doctrine of salvation through the Church; for the Quakers even with Baptism and the Communion.

The Baptist denominations along with the predestinationists, especially the strict Calvinists, carried out the most radical devaluation of all sacraments as means to salvation, and thus accomplished the religious rationalization of the world in its most extreme form. Only the inner light of continual revelation could enable one truly to understand even the Biblical revelations of God. On the other hand, at least according to the Quaker doctrine which here drew the logical conclusion, its effects could be extended to people who had never known revelation in its Biblical form. The proposition *extra ecclesiam nulla salus* held only for this *in*visible Church of those illuminated by the Spirit. Without the inner light, the natural man, even the man guided by natural reason, remained purely a creature of the flesh, whose godlessness was condemned by the Baptists, including the Quakers, almost even more harshly than by the Calvinists. On the other hand, the new birth caused by the Spirit, if we wait for it and open our hearts to it, may, since it is divinely caused, lead to a state of such complete conquest of the power of sin, that relapses, to say nothing of the loss of the state of grace, become practically impossible. However, as in Methodism at a later time, the attainment of that state was not thought of as the rule, but rather the degree of perfection of the individual was subject to development.

But all Baptist communities desired to be pure Churches in the sense of the blameless conduct of their members. A sincere repudiation of the world and its interests, and unconditional submission to God as speaking through the conscience, were the only unchallengeable signs of true rebirth, and a corresponding type of conduct was thus indispensable to salvation. And hence the gift of God's grace could not be earned, but only one who followed the dictates of his conscience could be justified in considering himself reborn. Good works in this sense were a *causa sine qua non.* As we see, this last reasoning of Barclay, to whose exposition we have adhered, was again the equivalent in practice of the Calvinistic doctrine, and was certainly developed under the influence of the Calvinistic asceticism, which surrounded the Baptist sects in England and the Netherlands. George Fox devoted the whole of his early missionary activity to the preaching of its earnest and sincere adoption.

But, since predestination was rejected, the peculiarly rational character of Baptist morality rested psychologically above all on the idea of expectant waiting for the Spirit to descend, which even to-day is characteristic of the Quaker meeting, and is well analysed by Barclay. The purpose of this silent waiting is to overcome everything impulsive and irrational, the passions and subjective interests of the natural man. He must be stilled in order to create that deep repose of the soul in which alone the word of God can be heard. Of course, this waiting might result in hysterical conditions, prophecy, and, as long as eschatological hopes survived, under certain circumstances even in an outbreak of chiliastic enthusiasm, as is possible in all similar types of religion. That actually happened in the movement which went to pieces in Münster.

But in so far as Baptism affected the normal workaday world, the idea that God only speaks when the flesh is silent evidently meant an incentive to the deliberate weighing of courses of action and their careful justification in terms of the individual conscience. The later Baptist communities, most particularly the Quakers, adopted this quiet, moderate, eminently conscientious character of conduct. The radical elimination of magic from the world allowed no other psychological course than the practice of worldly asceticism. Since these communities would have nothing to do with the political powers and their doings, the external result also was the penetration of life in the calling with these ascetic virtues. The leaders of the earliest Baptist movement were ruthlessly radical in their rejection of worldliness. But naturally, even in the first generation, the strictly apostolic way of life was not maintained as absolutely essential to the proof of rebirth for everyone. Well-to-do bourgeois there were, even in this generation and even before Menno, who definitely defended the practical worldly virtues and the system of private property; the strict morality of the Baptists had turned in practice into the path prepared by the Calvinistic ethic. This was simply because the road to the otherworldly monastic form of asceticism had been closed as unbiblical and savouring of salvation by works since Luther, whom the Baptists also followed in this respect.

Nevertheless, apart from the half-communistic communities of the early period, one Baptist sect, the socalled Dunckards (*Tunker, dompelaers*), has to this day maintained its condemnation of education and of every form of possession beyond that indispensable to life. And even Barclay looks upon the obligation to one's calling not in Calvinistic or even Lutheran terms, but rather Thomistically, as *naturali ratione*, the necessary consequence of the believers having to live in the world.

This attitude meant a weakening of the Calvinistic conception of the calling similar to those of Spener and the German Pietists. But, on the other hand, the intensity of interest in economic occupations was considerably increased by various factors at work in the Baptist sects. In the first place, by the refusal to accept office in the service of the State, which originated as a religious duty following from the repudiation of everything worldly. After its abandonment in principle it still remained, at least for the Mennonites and Quakers, effective in practice, because the strict refusal to bear arms or to take oaths formed a sufficient disqualification for office. Hand in hand with it in all Baptists' denominations went an invincible antagonism to any sort of aristocratic way of life. Partly, as with the Calvinists, it was a consequence of the prohibition of all idolatry of the flesh, partly a result of the aforementioned unpolitical or even anti-political principles. The whole shrewd and conscientious rationality of Baptist conduct was thus forced into non-political callings.

At the same time, the immense importance which was attributed by the Baptist doctrine of salvation to the rôle of the conscience as the revelation of God to the individual gave their conduct in worldly callings a character which was of the greatest significance for the development of the spirit of capitalism. We shall have to postpone its consideration until later, and it can then be studied only in so far as this is possible without entering into the whole political and social ethics of Protestant asceticism. But, to anticipate this much, we have already called attention to that most important principle of the capitalistic ethic which is generally formulated 'honesty is the best policy'. Its classical document is the tract of Franklin quoted above. And even in the judgment of the seventeenth century the specific form of the worldly asceticism of the Baptists, especially the Quakers, lay in the practical adoption of this maxim. On the other hand, we shall expect to find that the influence of Calvinism was exerted more in the direction of the liberation of energy for private acquisition. For in spite of all the formal legalism of the elect, Goethe's remark in fact applied often enough to the Calvinist: 'The man of action is always ruthless; no one has a conscience but an observer.' [. . .]

Asceticism and the Spirit of Capitalism

In order to understand the connection between the fundamental religious ideas of ascetic Protestantism and its maxims for everyday economic conduct, it is necessary to examine with especial care such writings as have evidently been derived from ministerial practice. For in a time in which the beyond meant everything, when the social position of the Christian depended upon his admission to the communion, the clergyman, through his ministry, Church discipline, and preaching, exercised an influence (as a glance at collections of *consilia, casus conscientiæ*, etc., shows) which we modern men are entirely unable to picture. In such a time the religious forces which express themselves through such channels are the decisive influences in the formation of national character.

For the purposes of this chapter, though by no means for all purposes, we can treat ascetic Protestantism as a single whole. But since that side of English Puritanism which was derived from Calvinism gives the most consistent religious basis for the idea of the calling, we shall, following our previous method, place one of its representatives at the centre of the discussion. Richard Baxter stands out above many other writers on Puritan ethics, both because of his eminently practical and realistic attitude, and, at the same time, because of the universal recognition accorded to his works, which have gone through many new editions and translations. He was a Presbyterian and an apologist of the Westminster Synod, but at the same time, like so many of the best spirits of his time, gradually grew away from the dogmas of pure Calvinism. At heart he opposed Cromwell's usurpation as he would any revolution. He was unfavourable to the sects and the fanatical enthusiasm of the saints, but was very broad-minded about external peculiarities and objective towards his opponents. He sought his field of labour most especially in the practical promotion of the moral life through the Church. In the pursuit of this end, as one of the most successful ministers known to history, he placed his services at the disposal of the Parliamentary Government, of Cromwell, and of the Restoration, until he retired from office under the last, before St Bartholomew's day. His *Christian Directory* is the most complete compendium of Puritan ethics, and is continually adjusted to the practical experiences of his own ministerial activity. In comparison we shall make use of Spener's *Theologische Bedenken*, as representative of German Pietism, Barclay's *Apology* for the Quakers, and some other representatives of ascetic ethics, which, however, in the interest of space, will be limited as far as possible.

Now, in glancing at Baxter's *Saints' Everlasting Rest*, or his *Christian Directory*, or similar works of others, one is struck at first glance by the emphasis placed, in the discussion of wealth and its acquisition, on the ebionitic elements of the New Testament. Wealth as such is a great danger; its temptations never end, and its pursuit is not only senseless as compared with the dominating importance of the Kingdom of God, but it is morally suspect. Here asceticism seems to have turned much more sharply against the acquisition of earthly goods than it did in Calvin, who saw no hindrance to the effectiveness of the clergy in their wealth, but rather a thoroughly desirable enhancement of their prestige. Hence he permitted them to employ their means profitably. Examples of the condemnation of the pursuit of money and goods may be gathered without end from Puritan writings, and may be contrasted with the late mediæval ethical literature, which was much more open-minded on this point.

Moreover, these doubts were meant with perfect seriousness; only it is necessary to examine them somewhat more closely in order to understand their true ethical significance and implications. The real moral objection is to relaxation in the security of possession, the enjoyment of wealth with the consequence of idleness and the temptations of the flesh, above all of distraction from the pursuit of a righteous life. In fact, it is only because possession involves this danger of relaxation that it is objectionable at all. For the saints' everlasting rest is in the next world; on earth man must, to be certain of his state of grace, 'do the works of him who sent him, as long as it is yet day'. Not leisure and enjoyment, but only activity serves to increase the glory of God, according to the definite manifestations of His will.

Waste of time is thus the first and in principle the deadliest of sins. The span of human life is infinitely short and precious to make sure of one's own election Loss of time through sociability, idle talk, luxury, even more sleep than is necessary for health, six to at most eight hours, is worthy of absolute moral condemnation. It does not yet hold, with Franklin, that time is money, but the proposition is true in a certain spiritual sense. It is infinitely valuable because every hour lost is lost to labour for the glory of God. Thus inactive contemplation is also valueless, or even directly reprehensible if it is at the expense of one's daily work. For it is less pleasing to God than the active performance of His will in a calling. Besides, Sunday is provided for that, and, according to Baxter, it is always those who are not diligent in their callings who have no time for God when the occasion demands it.

Accordingly, Baxter's principal work is dominated by the continually repeated, often almost passionate preaching of hard, continuous bodily or mental labour. It is due to a combination of two different motives. Labour is, on the one hand, an approved ascetic technique, as it always has been in the Western Church, in sharp contrast not only to the Orient but to almost all monastic rules the world over. It is in particular the specific defence against all those temptations which Puritanism united under the name of the unclean life, whose rôle for it was by no means small. The sexual asceticism of Puritanism differs only in degree, not in fundamental principle, from that of monasticism; and on account of the Puritan conception of marriage, its practical influence is more far-reaching than that of the latter. For sexual intercourse is permitted, even within marriage, only as the means willed by God for the increase of His glory according to the commandment, 'Be fruitful and multiply.' Along with a moderate vegetable diet and cold baths, the same prescription is given for all sexual temptations as is used against religious doubts and a sense of moral unworthiness: 'Work hard in your calling.' But the most important thing was that even beyond that labour came to be considered in itself the end of life, ordained as such by God. St Paul's 'He who will not work shall not eat' holds unconditionally for everyone. Unwillingness to work is symptomatic of the lack of grace.

Here the difference from the mediæval view-point becomes quite evident. Thomas Aquinas also gave an interpretation of that statement of St Paul. But for him labour is only necessary *naturali ratione* for the maintenance of individual and community. Where this end is achieved, the precept ceases to have any meaning. Moreover, it holds only for the race, not for every individual. It does not apply to anyone who can live without labour on his possessions, and of course contemplation, as a spiritual form of action in the Kingdom of God, takes precedence over the commandment in its literal sense. Moreover, for the popular theology of the time, the highest form of monastic productivity lay in the increase of the *Thesaurus ecclesiæ* through prayer and chant.

Now only do these exceptions to the duty to labour naturally no longer hold for Baxter, but he holds most emphatically that wealth does not exempt anyone from the unconditional command. Even the wealthy shall not eat without working, for even though they do not need to labour to support their own needs, there is God's commandment which they, like the poor, must obey. For everyone without exception God's Providence has prepared a calling, which he should profess and in which he should labour. And this calling is not, as it was for the Lutheran, a fate to which he must submit and which he must make the best of, but God's commandment to the individual to work for the divine glory. This seemingly subtle difference had far-reaching psychological consequences, and became connected with a further development of the providential interpretation of the economic order which had begun in scholasticism.

The phenomenon of the division of labour and occupations in society had, among others, been interpreted by Thomas Aquinas, to whom we may most conveniently refer, as a direct consequence of the divine scheme of things. But the places assigned to each man in this cosmos follow *ex causis naturalibus* and are fortuitous (contingent in the Scholastic terminology). The differentiation of men into the classes and occupations established through historical development became for Luther, as we have seen, a direct result of the divine will. The perseverance of the individual in the place and within the limits which God had assigned to him was a religious duty. This was the more certainly the consequence since the relations of Lutheranism to the world were in general uncertain from the beginning and remained so. Ethical principles for the reform of the world could not be found in Luther's realm of ideas; in fact it never quite freed itself from Pauline indifference. Hence the world had to be accepted as it was, and this alone could be made a religious duty.

But in the Puritan view, the providential character of the play of private economic interests takes on a somewhat different emphasis. True to the Puritan tendency to pragmatic interpretations, the providential purpose of the division of labour is to be known by its fruits. On this point Baxter expresses himself in terms which more than once directly recall Adam Smith's well-known apotheosis of the division of labour. The specialization of occupations leads, since it makes the development of skill possible, to a quantitative and qualitative improvement in production, and thus serves the common good, which is identical with the good of the greatest possible number. So far, the motivation is purely utilitarian, and is closely related to the customary view-point of much of the secular literature of the time.

But the characteristic Puritan element appears when Baxter sets at the head of his discussion the statement that 'outside of a well-marked calling the accomplishments of a man are only casual and irregular, and he spends more time in idleness than at work', and when he concludes it as follows: 'and he [the specialized worker] will carry out his work in order while another remains in constant confusion, and his business knows neither time nor place . . . therefore is a certain calling the best for everyone'. Irregular work, which the ordinary labourer is often forced to accept, is often unavoidable, but always an unwelcome state of transition. A man without a calling thus lacks the systematic, methodical character which is, as we have seen, demanded by worldly asceticism.

The Quaker ethic also holds that a man's life in his calling is an exercise in ascetic virtue, a proof of his state of grace through his conscientiousness, which is expressed in the care and method with which he pursues his calling. What God demands is not labour in itself, but rational labour in a calling. In the Puritan concept of the calling the emphasis is always placed on this methodical character of worldly asceticism, not, as with Luther, on the acceptance of the lot which God has irretrievably assigned to man.

Hence the question whether anyone may combine several callings is answered in the affirmative, if it is useful for the common good or one's own, and not injurious to anyone, and if it does not lead to unfaithfulness in one of the callings. Even a change of calling is by no means regarded as objectionable, if it is not thoughtless and is made for the purpose of pursuing a calling more pleasing to God, which means, on general principles, one more useful.

It is true that the usefulness of a calling, and thus its favour in the sight of God, is measured primarily in moral terms, and thus in terms of the importance of the goods produced in it for the community. But a further, and, above all, in practice the most important, criterion is found in private profitableness. For if that God, whose hand the Puritan sees in all the occurrences of life, shows one of His elect a chance of profit, he must do it with a purpose. Hence the faithful Christian must follow the call by taking advantage of the opportunity. 'If God show you a way in which you may lawfully get more than in another way (without wrong to your soul or to any other), if you refuse this, and choose the less gainful way, you cross one of the ends of your calling, and you refuse to be God's steward, and to accept His gifts and use them for Him when He requireth it: you may labour to be rich for God, though not for the flesh and sin.'

Wealth is thus bad ethically only in so far as it is a temptation to idleness and sinful enjoyment of life, and its acquisition is bad only when it is with the purpose of later living merrily and without care. But as a performance of duty in a calling it is not only morally permissible, but actually enjoined. The parable of the servant who was rejected because he did not increase the talent which was entrusted to him seemed to say so directly. To wish to be poor was, it was often argued, the same as wishing to be unhealthy; it is objectionable as a glorification of works and derogatory to the glory of God. Especially begging, on the part of one able to work, is not only the sin of slothfulness, but a violation of the duty of brotherly love according to the Apostle's own word.

The emphasis on the ascetic importance of a fixed calling provided an ethical justification of the modern specialized division of labour. In a similar way the providential interpretation of profit-making justified the activities of the business man. The superior indulgence of the *seigneur* and the parvenu ostentation of the *nouveau riche* are equally detestable to asceticism. But, on the other hand, it has the highest ethical appreciation of the sober, middle-class, self-made man. 'God blesseth His trade' is a stock remark about those good men who had successfully followed the divine hints. The whole power of the God of the Old Testament, who rewards His people for their obedience in this life, necessarily exercised a similar influence on the Puritan who, following Baxter's advice, compared his own state of grace with that of the heroes of the Bible, and in the process interpreted the statements of the Scriptures as the articles of a book of statutes. [. . .]

As far as the influence of the Puritan outlook extended, under all circumstances – and this is, of course, much more important than the mere encouragement of capital accumulation – it favoured the development of a rational bourgeois economic life; it was the most important, and above all the only consistent influence in the development of that life. It stood at the cradle of the modern economic man.

To be sure, these Puritanical ideals tended to give way under excessive pressure from the temptations of wealth, as the Puritans themselves knew very well. With great regularity we find the most genuine adherents of Puritanism among the classes which were rising from a lowly status, the small bourgeois and farmers, while the *beati possidentes*, even among Quakers, are often found tending to repudiate the old ideals. It was the same fate which again and again befell the predecessor of this worldly asceticism, the monastic asceticism of the Middle Ages. In the latter case, when rational economic activity had worked out its full effects by strict regulation of conduct and limitation of consumption, the wealth accumulated either succumbed directly to the nobility, as in the time before the Reformation, or monastic discipline threatened to break down, and one of the numerous reformations became necessary.

In fact the whole history of monasticism is in a certain sense the history of a continual struggle with the problem of the secularizing influence of wealth. The same is true on a grand scale of the worldly asceticism of Puritanism. The great revival of Methodism, which preceded the expansion of English industry toward the end of the eighteenth century, may well be compared with such a monastic reform. We may hence quote here a passage from John Wesley himself which might well serve as a motto for everything which has been said above. For it shows that the leaders of these ascetic movements understood the seemingly paradoxical relationships which we have here analysed perfectly well, and in the same sense that we have given them. He wrote:

> I fear, wherever riches have increased, the essence of religion has decreased in the same proportion. Therefore I do not see how it is possible, in the nature of things, for any revival of true religion to continue long. For religion must necessarily produce both industry and frugality, and these cannot but produce riches. But as riches increase, so will pride, anger, and love of the world in all its branches. How then is it possible that Methodism, that is, a religion of the heart, though it flourishes now as a green bay tree, should continue in this state? For the Methodists in every place grow diligent and frugal; consequently they increase in goods. Hence they proportionately increase in pride, in anger, in the desire of the flesh, the desire of the eyes, and the pride of life. So, although the form of religion remains, the spirit is swiftly vanishing away. Is there no way to prevent this – this continual decay of pure religion? We ought not to prevent people from being diligent frugal; *we must exhort all Christians to gain all they can, and to save all they can; that is, in effect, to grow rich.*

There follows the advice that those who gain all they can and save all they can should also give all they can, so that they will grow in grace and lay up a treasure in heaven. It is clear that Wesley here expresses, even in detail, just what we have been trying to point out.

As Wesley here says, the full economic effect of those great religious movements, whose significance for economic development lay above all in their ascetic educative influence, generally came only after the peak of the purely religious enthusiasm was past. Then the intensity of the search for the Kingdom of God commenced gradually to pass over into sober economic virtue; the religious roots died out slowly, giving way to utilitarian worldliness. Then, as Dowden puts it, as in *Robinson Crusoe*, the isolated economic man who carries on missionary activities on the side takes the place of the lonely spiritual search for the Kingdom of Heaven of Bunyan's pilgrim, hurrying through the market-place of Vanity.

When later the principle 'to make the most of both worlds' became dominant in the end, as Dowden has remarked, a good conscience simply became one of the means of enjoying a comfortable bourgeois life, as is well expressed in the German proverb about the soft pillow. What the great religious epoch of the seventeenth century bequeathed to its utilitarian successor was, however, above all an amazingly good, we may even say a pharisaically good, conscience in the acquisition of money, so long as it took place legally. Every trace of the *deplacere vix potest* has disappeared.

A specifically bourgeois economic ethic had grown up. With the consciousness of standing in the fullness of God's grace and being visibly blessed by Him, the bourgeois business man, as long as he remained within the bounds of formal correctness, as long as his moral conduct was spotless and the use to which he put his wealth was not objectionable, could follow his pecuniary interests as he would and feel that he was fulfilling a duty in doing so. The power of religious asceticism provided him in addition with sober, conscientious, and unusually industrious workmen, who clung to their work as to a life purpose willed by God.

Finally, it gave him the comforting assurance that the unequal distribution of the goods of this world was a special dispensation of Divine Providence, which in these differences, as in particular grace, pursued secret ends unknown to men. Calvin himself had made the much-quoted statement that only when the people, i.e. the mass of labourers and craftsmen, were poor did they remain obedient to God. In the Netherlands (Pieter de la Court and others), that had been secularized to the effect that the mass of men only labour when necessity forces them to do so. This formulation of a leading idea of capitalistic economy later entered into the current theories of the productivity of low wages. Here also, with the dying out of the religious root, the utilitarian interpretation crept in unnoticed, in the line of development which we have again and again observed.

Mediæval ethics not only tolerated begging but actually glorified it in the mendicant orders. Even secular beggars, since they gave the person of means opportunity for good works through giving alms, were sometimes considered an estate and treated as such. Even the Anglican social ethic of the Stuarts was very close to this attitude. It remained for Puritan Asceticism to take part in the severe English Poor Relief Legislation which fundamentally changed the situation. And it could do that, because the Protestant sects and the strict Puritan communities actually did not know any begging in their own midst.

On the other hand, seen from the side of the workers, the Zinzendorf branch of Pietism, for instance, glorified the loyal worker who did not seek acquisition, but lived according to the apostolic model, and was thus endowed with the *charisma* of the disciples. Similar ideas had originally been prevalent among the Baptists in an even more radical form.

Now naturally the whole ascetic literature of almost all denominations is saturated with the idea that faithful labour, even at low wages, on the part of those whom life offers no other opportunities, is highly pleasing to God. In this respect Protestant Asceticism added in itself nothing new. But it not only deepened this idea most powerfully, it also created the force which was alone decisive for its effectiveness: the psychological sanction of it through the conception of this labour as a calling, as the best, often in the last analysis the only means of attaining certainty of grace. And on the other hand it legalized the exploitation of this specific willingness to work, in that it also interpreted the employer's business activity as a calling. It is obvious how powerfully the exclusive search for the Kingdom of God only through the fulfilment of duty in the calling, and the strict asceticism which Church discipline naturally imposed, especially on the propertyless classes, was bound to affect the productivity of labour in the capitalistic sense of the word. The treatment of labour as a calling became as characteristic of the modern worker as the corresponding attitude toward acquisition of the business man. It was a perception of this situation, new at his time, which caused so able an observer as Sir William Petty to attribute the economic power of Holland in the seventeenth century to the fact that the very numerous dissenters in that country (Calvinists and Baptists) 'are for the most part thinking, sober men, and such as believe that Labour and Industry is their duty towards God'.

Calvinism opposed organic social organization in the fiscal-monopolistic form which it assumed in Anglicanism under the Stuarts, especially in the conceptions of Laud, this alliance of Church and State with the monopolists on the basis of a Christian-social ethical foundation. Its leaders were universally among the most passionate opponents of this type of politically privileged commercial, putting-out, and colonial capitalism. Over against it they placed the individualistic motives of rational legal acquisition by virtue of one's own ability and initiative. And, while the politically privileged monopoly industries in England all disappeared in short order, this attitude played a large and decisive part in the development of the industries which grew up in spite of and against the authority of the State. The Puritans (Prynne, Parker) repudiated all connection with the large-scale capitalistic courtiers and projectors as an ethically suspicious class. On the other hand, they took pride in their own superior middle-class business morality, which formed the true reason for the persecutions to which they were subjected on the part of those circles. Defoe proposed to win the battle against dissent by boycotting bank credit and withdrawing deposits. The difference of the two types of capitalistic attitude went to a very large extent hand in hand with religious differences. The opponents of the Nonconformists, even in the eighteenth century, again and again ridiculed them for personifying the spirit of shopkeepers, and for having ruined the ideals of old England. Here also lay the difference of the Puritan economic ethic from the Jewish; and contemporaries (Prynne) knew well that the former and not the latter was the bourgeois capitalistic ethic.

One of the fundamental elements of the spirit of modern capitalism, and not only of that but of all modern culture: rational conduct on the basis of the idea of the calling, was born – that is what this discussion has sought to demonstrate – from the spirit of Christian asceticism. One has only to re-read the passage from Franklin, quoted at the beginning of this essay, in order to see that the essential elements of the attitude which was there called the spirit of capitalism are the same as what we have just shown to be the content of the Puritan worldly asceticism, only without the religious basis, which by Franklin's time had died away. The idea that modern labour has an ascetic character is of course not new. Limitation to specialized work, with a renunciation of the Faustian universality of man which it involves, is a condition of any valuable work in the modern world; hence deeds and renunciation inevitably condition each other today. This fundamentally ascetic trait of middle-class life, if it attempts to be a way of life at all, and not simply the absence of any, was what Goethe wanted to teach, at the height of his wisdom, in the *Wanderjahren*, and in the end which he gave to the life of his *Faust*. For him the realization meant a renunciation, a departure from an age of full and beautiful humanity, which can no more be repeated in the course of our cultural development than can the flower of the Athenian culture of antiquity.

The Puritan wanted to work in a calling; we are forced to do so. For when asceticism was carried out of monastic cells into everyday life, and began to dominate worldly morality, it did its part in building the tremendous cosmos of the modern economic order. This order is now bound to the technical and economic conditions of machine production which to-day determine the lives of all the individuals who are born into this mechanism, not only those directly concerned with economic acquisition, with irresistible force. Perhaps it will so determine them until the last ton of fossilized coal is burnt. In Baxter's view the care for external goods should only lie on the shoulders of the 'saint like a light cloak, which can be thrown aside at any moment'. But fate decreed that the cloak should become an iron cage.

Since asceticism undertook to remodel the world and to work out its ideals in the world, material goods have gained an increasing and finally an inexorable power over the lives of men as at no previous period in history. To-day the spirit of religious asceticism – whether finally, who knows? – has escaped from the cage. But victorious capitalism, since it rests on mechanical foundations, needs its support no longer. The rosy blush of its laughing heir, the Enlightenment, seems also to be irretrievably fading, and the idea of duty in one's calling prowls about in our lives like the ghost of dead religious beliefs. Where the fulfilment of the calling cannot directly be related to the highest spiritual and cultural values, or when, on the other hand, it need not be felt simply as economic compulsion, the individual generally abandons the attempt to justify it at all. In the field of its highest development, in the United States, the pursuit of wealth, stripped of its religious and ethical meaning, tends to become associated with purely mundane passions, which often actually give it the character of sport.

No one knows who will live in this cage in the future, or whether at the end of this tremendous development entirely new prophets will arise, or there will be a great rebirth of old ideas and ideals, or, if neither, mechanized petrification, embellished with a sort of convulsive self-importance. For of the last stage of this cultural development, it might well be truly said: 'Specialists without spirit, sensualists without heart; this nullity imagines that it has attained a level of civilization never before achieved.'

But this brings us to the world of judgments of value and of faith, with which this purely historical discussion need not be burdened. The next task would be rather to show the significance of ascetic rationalism, which has only been touched in the foregoing sketch, for the content of practical social ethics, thus for the types of organization and the functions of social groups from the conventicle to the State. Then its relations to humanistic rationalism, its ideals of life and cultural influence; further to the development of philosophical and scientific empiricism, to technical development and to spiritual ideals would have to be analysed. Then its historical development from the mediæval beginnings of worldly asceticism to its dissolution into pure utilitarianism would have to be traced out through all the areas of ascetic religion. Only then could the quantitative cultural significance of ascetic Protestantism in its relation to the other plastic elements of modern culture be estimated.

Here we have only attempted to trace the fact and the direction of its influence to their motives in one, though a very important point. But it would also further be necessary to investigate how Protestant Asceticism was in turn influenced in its development and its character by the totality of social conditions, especially economic. The modern man is in general, even with the best will, unable to give religious ideas a significance for culture and national character which they deserve. But it is, of course, not my aim to substitute for a one-sided materialistic an equally one-sided spiritualistic causal interpretation of culture and of history. Each is equally possible, but each, if it does not serve as the preparation, but as the conclusion of an investigation, accomplishes equally little in the interest of historical truth.

2.2 CLASS, STATUS AND PARTY

This famous segment of the massive *Economy and Society* (2 volumes), published after Weber's death, deals with 'the distribution of power within a community'. In it Weber argues that 'status', which is not reducible to economic factors, can be a more important source of individual and collective action and power than 'class'. Indeed 'status groupings', according to this view, can cut across class-based organisations and provide formidable obstacles for the realisation of effective 'class struggle' and 'class consciousness'. Weber's discussion of 'class', 'status' and 'parties' continues to exert a major influence on theoretical debate about, and empirical investigation of, 'social stratification' within modern societies and is often seen to be an essential corrective to Marxist accounts of stratification and class mobilisation.

From: H. H. Gerth and C. Wright Mills, *From Max Weber: Essays in Sociology* (Routledge: London, 1991) pp. 180–90, 194–5.

Economically Determined Power and the Social Order

Law exists when there is a probability that an order will be upheld by a specific staff of men who will use physical or psychical compulsion with the intention of obtaining conformity with the order, or of inflicting sanctions for infringement of it. The structure of every legal order directly influences the distribution of power, economic or otherwise, within its respective community. This is true of all legal orders and not only that of the state. In general, we understand by 'power' the chance of a man or of a number of men to realize their own will in a communal action even against the resistance of others who are participating in the action.

'Economically conditioned' power is not, of course, identical with 'power' as such. On the contrary, the emergence of economic power may be the consequence of power existing on other grounds. Man does not strive for power only in order to enrich himself economically. Power, including economic power, may be valued 'for its own sake.' Very frequently the striving for power is also conditioned by the social 'honor' it entails. Not all power, however, entails social honor: The typical American Boss, as well as the typical big speculator, deliberately relinquishes social honor. Quite generally, 'mere economic' power, and especially 'naked' money power, is by no means a recognized basis of social honor. Nor is power the only basis of social honor. Indeed, social honor, or prestige, may even be the basis of political or economic power, and very frequently has been. Power, as well as honor, may be guaranteed by the legal order, but, at least normally, it is not their primary source. The legal order is rather an additional factor that enhances the chance to hold power or honor; but it cannot always secure them.

The way in which social honor is distributed in a community between typical groups participating in this distribution we may call the 'social order.' The social order and the economic order are, of course, similarly related to the 'legal order.' However, the social and the economic order are not identical. The economic order is for us merely the way in which economic goods and services are distributed and used. The social order is of course conditioned by the economic order to a high degree, and in its turn reacts upon it.

Now: 'classes,' 'status groups,' and 'parties' are phenomena of the distribution of power within a community.

Determination of Class-Situation by Market-Situation

In our terminology, 'classes' are not communities; they merely represent possible, and frequent, bases for communal action. We may speak of a 'class' when 1. a number of people have in common a specific causal component of their life chances, in so far as 2. this component is represented exclusively by economic interests in the possession of goods and opportunities for income, and 3. is represented under the conditions of the commodity or labor markets. [These points refer to 'class situation,' which we may express more briefly as the typical chance for a supply of goods, external living conditions, and personal life experiences, in so far as this chance is determined by the amount and kind of power, or lack of such, to dispose of goods or skills for the sake of income in a given economic order. The term 'class' refers to any group of people that is found in the same class situation.]

It is the most elemental economic fact that the way in which the disposition over material property is distributed among a plurality of people, meeting competitively in the market for the purpose of exchange, in itself creates specific life chances. According to the law of marginal utility this mode of distribution excludes the non-owners from competing for highly valued goods; it favors the owners and, in fact, gives to them a monopoly to acquire such goods. Other things being equal, this mode of distribution monopolizes the opportunities for profitable deals for all those who, provided with goods, do not necessarily have to exchange them. It increases, at least generally, their power in price wars with those who, being propertyless, have nothing to offer but their services in native form or goods in a form constituted through their own labor, and who above all are compelled to get rid of these products in order barely to subsist. This mode of distribution gives to the propertied a monopoly on the possibility of transferring property from the sphere of use as a 'fortune,' to the sphere of 'capital goods'; that is, it gives them the entrepreneurial function and all chances to share directly or indirectly in returns on capital. All this holds true within the area in which pure market conditions prevail. 'Property' and 'lack of property' are, therefore, the basic categories of all class situations. It does not matter whether these two categories become effective in price wars or in competitive struggles.

Within these categories, however, class situations are further differentiated: on the one hand, according to the kind of property that is usable for returns; and, on the other hand, according to the kind of services that can be offered in the market. Ownership of domestic buildings; productive establishments; warehouses; stores; agriculturally usable land, large and small holdings – quantitative differences with possibly qualitative consequences – ; ownership of mines; cattle; men (slaves); disposition over mobile instruments of production, or capital goods of all sorts, especially money or objects that can be exchanged for money easily and at any time; disposition over products of one's own labor or of others' labor differing according to their various distances from consumability; disposition over transferable monopolies of any kind – all these distinctions differentiate the class situations of the propertied just as does the 'meaning' which they can and do give to the utilization of property, especially to property which has money equivalence. Accordingly, the propertied, for instance, may belong to the class of rentiers or to the class of entrepreneurs.

Those who have no property but who offer services are differentiated just as much according to their kinds of services as according to the way in which they make use of these services, in a continuous or discontinuous relation to a recipient. But always this is the generic connotation of the concept of class: that the kind of chance in the *market* is the decisive moment which presents a common condition for the individual's fate. 'Class situation' is, in this sense, ultimately 'market situation.' The effect of naked possession *per se*, which among cattle breeders gives the non-owning slave or serf into the power of the cattle owner, is only a fore-runner of real 'class' formation. However, in the cattle loan and in the naked severity of the law of debts in such communities, for the first time mere 'possession' as such emerges as decisive for the fate of the individual. This is very much in contrast to the agricultural communities based on labor. The creditor-debtor relation becomes the basis of 'class situations' only in those cities where a 'credit market,' however primitive, with rates of interest increasing according to the extent of dearth and a factual monopolization of credits, is developed by a plutocracy. Therewith 'class struggles' begin.

Those men whose fate is not determined by the chance of using goods or services for themselves on the market, e.g. slaves, are not, however, a 'class' in the technical sense of the term. They are, rather, a 'status group.'

Communal Action Flowing from Class Interest

According to our terminology, the factor that creates 'class' is unambiguously economic interest, and indeed, only those interests involved in the existence of the 'market.' Nevertheless, the concept of 'class-interest' is an ambiguous one: even as an empirical concept it is ambiguous as soon as one understands by it something other than the factual direction of interests following with a certain probability from the class situation for a certain 'average' of those people subjected to the class situation. The class situation and other circumstances remaining the same, the direction in which the individual worker, for instance, is likely to pursue his interests may vary widely, according to whether he is constitutionally qualified for the task at hand to a high, to an average, or to a low degree. In the same way, the direction of interests may vary according to whether or not a *communal* action of a larger or smaller portion of those commonly affected by the 'class situation,' or even an association among them, e.g. a 'trade union,' has grown out of the class situation from which the individual may or may not expect promising results. [Communal action refers to that action which is oriented to the feeling of the actors that they belong together. Societal action, on the other hand, is oriented to a rationally motivated adjustment of interests.] The rise of societal or even of communal action from a common class situation is by no means a universal phenomenon.

The class situation may be restricted in its effects to the generation of essentially *similar* reactions, that is to say, within our terminology, of 'mass actions.' However, it may not have even this result. Furthermore, often merely an amorphous communal action emerges. For example, the 'murmuring' of the workers known in ancient oriental ethics: the moral disapproval of the work-master's conduct, which in its practical significance was probably equivalent to an increasingly typical phenomenon of precisely the latest industrial development, namely, the 'slow down' (the deliberate limiting of work effort) of laborers by virtue of tacit agreement. The degree in which 'communal action' and possibly 'societal action,' emerges from the 'mass actions' of the members of a class is linked to general cultural conditions, especially to those of an intellectual sort. It is also linked to the extent of the contrasts that have already evolved, and is especially linked to the *transparency* of the connections between the causes and the consequences of the 'class situation.' For however different life chances may be, this fact in itself, according to all experience, by no means gives birth to 'class action' (communal action by the members of a class). The fact of being conditioned and the results of the class situation must be distinctly recognizable. For only then the contrast of life chances can be felt not as an absolutely given fact to be accepted, but as a resultant from either 1. the given distribution of property, or 2. the structure of the concrete economic order. It is only then that people may react against the class structure not only through acts of an intermittent and irrational protest, but in the form of rational association. There have been 'class situations' of the first category (1), of a specifically naked and transparent sort, in the urban centers of Antiquity and during the Middle Ages; especially then, when great fortunes were accumulated by factually monopolized trading in industrial products of these localities or in foodstuffs. Furthermore, under certain circumstances, in the rural economy of the most diverse periods, when agriculture was increasingly exploited in a profit-making manner. The most important historical example of the second category (2) is the class situation of the modern 'proletariat.'

Types of 'Class Struggle'

Thus every class may be the carrier of any one of the possibly in numerable forms of 'class action,' but this is not necessarily so. In any case, a class does not in itself constitute a community. To treat 'class' conceptually as having the same value as 'community' leads to distortion. That men in the same class situation regularly react in mass actions to such tangible situations as economic ones in the direction of those interests that are most adequate to their average number is an important and after all simple fact for the understanding of historical events. Above all, this fact must not lead to that kind of pseudo-scientific operation with the concepts of 'class' and 'class interests' so frequently found these days, and which has found its most classic expression in the statement of a talented author, that the individual may be in error concerning his interests but that the 'class' is 'infallible' about its interests. Yet, if classes as such are not communities, nevertheless class situations emerge only on the basis of communalization. The communal action that brings forth class situations, however, is not basically action between members of the identical class; it is an action between members of different classes. Communal actions that directly determine the class situation of the worker and the entrepreneur are: the labor market, the commodities market, and the capitalistic enterprise. But, in its turn, the existence of a capitalistic enterprise presupposes that a very specific communal action exists and that it is specifically structured to protect the possession of goods *per se*, and especially the power of individuals to dispose, in principle freely, over the means of production. The existence of a capitalistic enterprise is preconditioned by a specific kind of 'legal order.' Each kind of class situation, and above all when it rests upon the power of property *per se*, will become most clearly efficacious when all other determinants of reciprocal relations are, as far as possible, eliminated in their significance. It is in this way that the utilization of the power of property in the market obtains its most sovereign importance.

Now 'status groups' hinder the strict carrying through of the sheer market principle. In the present context they are of interest to us only from this one point of view. Before we briefly consider them, note that not much of a general nature can be said about the more specific kinds of antagonism between 'classes' (in our meaning of the term). The great shift, which has been going on continuously in the past, and up to our times, may be summarized although at the cost of some precision: the struggle in which class situations are effective has progressively shifted from consumption credit toward, first, competitive struggles in the commodity market and, then, toward price wars on the labor market. The 'class struggles' of antiquity – to the extent that they were genuine class struggles and not struggles between status groups – were initially carried on by indebted peasants, and perhaps also by artisans threatened by debt bondage and struggling against urban creditors. For debt bondage is the normal result of the differentiation of wealth in commercial cities, especially in seaport cities. A similar situation has existed among cattle breeders. Debt relationships as such produced class action up to the time of Cataline. Along with this, and with an increase in provision of grain for the city by transporting it from the outside, the struggle over the means of sustenance emerged. It centered in the first place around the provision of bread and the determination of the price of bread. It lasted throughout antiquity and the entire Middle Ages. The propertyless as such flocked together against those who actually and supposedly were interested in the dearth of bread. This fight spread until it involved all those commodities essential to the way of life and to handicraft production. There were only incipient discussions of wage disputes in antiquity and in the Middle Ages. But they have been slowly increasing up into modern times. In the earlier periods they were completely secondary to slave rebellions as well as to fights in the commodity market.

The propertyless of antiquity and of the Middle Ages protested against monopolies, pre-emption, forestalling, and the withholding of goods from the market in order to raise prices. Today the central issue is the determination of the price of labor.

This transition is represented by the fight for access to the market and for the determination of the price of products. Such fights went on between merchants and workers in the putting-out system of domestic handicraft during the transition to modern times. Since it is quite a general phenomenon we must mention here that the class antagonisms that are conditioned through the market situation are usually most bitter between those who actually and directly participate as opponents in price wars. It is not the rentier, the share-holder, and the banker who suffer the ill will of the worker, but almost exclusively the manufacturer and the business executives who are the direct opponents of workers in price wars. This is so in spite of the fact that it is precisely the cash boxes of the rentier, the share-holder, and the banker into which the more or less 'unearned' gains flow, rather than into the pockets of the manufacturers or of the business executives. This simple state of affairs has very frequently been decisive for the role the class situation has played in the formation of political parties. For example, it has made possible the varieties of patriarchal socialism and the frequent attempts – formerly, at least – of threatened status groups to form alliances with the proletariat against the 'bourgeoisie.'

Status Honor

In contrast to classes, *status groups* are normally communities. They are, however, often of an amorphous kind. In contrast to the purely economically determined 'class situation' we wish to designate as 'status situation' every typical component of the life fate of men that is determined by a specific, positive or negative, social estimation of *honor*. This honor may be connected with any quality shared by a plurality, and, of course, it can be knit to a class situation: class distinctions are linked in the most varied ways with status distinctions. Property as such is not always recognized as a status qualification, but in the long run it is, and with extraordinary regularity. In the subsistence economy of the organized neighborhood, very often the richest man is simply the chieftain. However, this often means only an honorific preference. For example, in the so-called pure modern 'democracy,' that is, one devoid of any expressly ordered status privileges for individuals, it may be that only the families coming under approximately the same tax class dance with one another. This example is reported of certain smaller Swiss cities. But status honor need not necessarily be linked with a 'class situation.' On the contrary, it normally stands in sharp opposition to the pretensions of sheer property.

Both propertied and propertyless people can belong to the same status group, and frequently they do with very tangible consequences. This 'equality' of social esteem may, however, in the long run become quite precarious. The 'equality' of status among the American 'gentlemen,' for instance, is expressed by the fact that outside the subordination determined by the different functions of 'business,' it would be considered strictly repugnant – wherever the old tradition still prevails – if even the richest 'chief,' while playing billiards or cards in his club in the evening, would not treat his 'clerk' as in every sense fully his equal in birthright. It would be repugnant if the American 'chief' would bestow upon his 'clerk' the condescending 'benevolence' marking a distinction of 'position,' which the German chief can never dissever from his attitude. This is one of the most important reasons why in America the German 'clubby-ness' has never been able to attain the attraction that the American clubs have.

Guarantees of Status Stratification

In content, status honor is normally expressed by the fact that above all else a specific *style of life* can be expected from all those who wish to belong to the circle. Linked with this expectation are restrictions on 'social' intercourse (that is, intercourse which is not subservient to economic or any other of business's 'functional' purposes). These restrictions may confine normal marriages to within the status circle and may lead to complete endogamous closure. As soon as there is not a mere individual and socially irrelevant imitation of another style of life, but an agreed-upon communal action of this closing character, the 'status' development is under way.

In its characteristic form, stratification by 'status groups' on the basis of conventional styles of life evolves at the present time in the United States out of the traditional democracy. For example, only the resident of a certain street ('the street') is considered as belonging to 'society,' is qualified for social intercourse, and is visited and invited. Above all, this differentiation evolves in such a way as to make for strict submission to the fashion that is dominant at a given time in society. This submission to fashion also exists among men in America to a degree unknown in Germany. Such submission is considered to be an indication of the fact that a given man *pretends* to qualify as a gentleman. This submission decides, at least *prima facie*, that he will be treated as such. And this recognition becomes just as important for his employment chances in 'swank' establishments, and above all, for social intercourse and marriage with 'esteemed' families, as the qualification for dueling among Germans in the Kaiser's day. As for the rest: certain families resident for a long time, and, of course, correspondingly wealthy, e.g. 'F. F. V., i.e. First Families of Virginia,' or the actual or alleged descendants of the 'Indian Princess' Pocahontas, of the Pilgrim fathers, or of the Knicker-bockers, the members of almost inaccessible sects and all sorts of circles setting themselves apart by means of any other characteristics and badges . . . all these elements usurp 'status' honor. The development of status is essentially a question of stratification resting upon usurpation. Such usurpation is the normal origin of almost all status honor. But the road from this purely conventional situation to legal privilege, positive or negative, is easily traveled as soon as a certain stratification of the social order has in fact been 'lived in' and has achieved stability by virtue of a stable distribution of economic power.

'Ethnic' Segregation and 'Caste'

Where the consequences have been realized to their full extent, the status group evolves into a closed 'caste.' Status distinctions are then guaranteed not merely by conventions and laws, but also by *rituals*. This occurs in such a way that every physical contact with a member of any caste that is considered to be 'lower' by the members of a 'higher' caste is considered as making for a ritualistic impurity and to be a stigma which must be expiated by a religious act. Individual castes develop quite distinct cults and gods.

In general, however, the status structure reaches such extreme consequences only where there are underlying differences which are held to be 'ethnic.' The 'caste' is, indeed, the normal form in which ethnic communities usually live side by side in a 'societalized' manner. These ethnic communities believe in blood relationship and exclude exogamous marriage and social intercourse. Such a caste situation is part of the phenomenon of 'pariah' peoples and is found all over the world. These people form communities, acquire specific occupational traditions of handicrafts or of other arts, and cultivate a belief in their ethnic community. They live in a 'diaspora' strictly segregated from all personal intercourse, except that of an unavoidable sort, and their situation is legally precarious. Yet, by virtue of their economic indispensability, they are tolerated, indeed, frequently privileged, and they live in interspersed political communities. The Jews are the most impressive historical example.

A 'status' segregation grown into a 'caste' differs in its structure from a mere 'ethnic' segregation: the caste structure transforms the horizontal and unconnected coexistences of ethnically segregated groups into a vertical social system of super- and subordination. Correctly formulated: a comprehensive societalization integrates the ethnically divided communities into specific political and communal action. In their consequences they differ precisely in this way: ethnic coexistences condition a mutual repulsion and disdain but allow each ethnic community to consider its own honor as the highest one; the caste structure brings about a social subordination and an acknowledgment of 'more honor' in favor of the privileged caste and status groups. This is due to the fact that in the caste structure ethnic distinctions as such have become 'functional' distinctions within the political societalization (warriors, priests, artisans that are politically important for war and for building, and so on). But even pariah people who are most despised are usually apt to continue cultivating in some manner that which is equally peculiar to ethnic and to status communities: the belief in their own specific 'honor.' This is the case with the Jews.

Only with the negatively privileged status groups does the 'sense of dignity' take a specific deviation. A sense of dignity is the precipitation in individuals of social honor and of conventional demands which a positively privileged status group raises for the deportment of its members. The sense of dignity that characterizes positively privileged status groups is naturally related to their 'being' which does not transcend itself, that is, it is to their 'beauty and excellence' (χαλο-χάγαθα). Their kingdom is 'of this world.' They live for the present and by exploiting their great past. The sense of dignity of the negatively privileged strata naturally refers to a future lying beyond the present, whether it is of this life or of another. In other words, it must be nurtured by the belief in a providential 'mission' and by a belief in a specific honor before God. The 'chosen people's' dignity is nurtured by a belief either that in the beyond 'the last will be the first,' or that in this life a Messiah will appear to bring forth into the light of the world which has cast them out the hidden honor of the pariah people. This simple state of affairs, and not the 'resentment' which is so strongly emphasized in Nietzsche's much admired construction in the *Genealogy of Morals*, is the source of the religiosity cultivated by pariah status groups. In passing, we may note that resentment may be accurately applied only to a limited extent; for one of Nietzsche's main examples, Buddhism, it is not at all applicable.

Incidentally, the development of status groups from ethnic segregations is by no means the normal phenomenon. On the contrary, since objective 'racial differences' are by no means basic to every subjective sentiment of an ethnic community, the ultimately racial foundation of status structure is rightly and absolutely a question of the concrete individual case. Very frequently a status group is instrumental in the production of a thoroughbred anthropological type. Certainly a status group is to a high degree effective in producing extreme types, for they select personally qualified individuals (e.g. the Knighthood selects those who are fit for warfare, physically and psychically). But selection is far from being the only, or the predominant, way in which status groups are formed: Political membership or class situation has at all times been at least as frequently decisive. And today the class situation is by far the predominant factor, for of course the possibility of a style of life expected for members of a status group is usually conditioned economically. [. . .]

Parties

Whereas the genuine place of 'classes' is within the economic order, the place of 'status groups' is within the social order, that is, within the sphere of the distribution of 'honor.' From within these spheres, classes and status groups influence one another and they influence the legal order and are in turn influenced by it. But 'parties' live in a house of 'power.'

Their action is oriented toward the acquisition of social 'power,' that is to say, toward influencing a communal action no matter what its content may be. In principle, parties may exist in a social 'club' as well as in a 'state.' As over against the actions of classes and status groups, for which this is not necessarily the case, the communal actions of 'parties' always mean a societalization. For party actions are always directed toward a goal which is striven for in planned manner. This goal may be a 'cause' (the party may aim at realizing a program for ideal or material purposes), or the goal may be 'personal' (sinecures, power, and from these, honor for the leader and the followers of the party). Usually the party action aims at all these simultaneously. Parties are, therefore, only possible within communities that are societalized, that is, which have some rational order and a staff of persons available who are ready to enforce it. For parties aim precisely at influencing this staff, and if possible, to recruit it from party followers.

In any individual case, parties may represent interests determined through 'class situation' or 'status situation,' and they may recruit their following respectively from one or the other. But they need be neither purely 'class' nor purely 'status' parties. In most cases they are partly class parties and partly status parties, but sometimes they are neither. They may represent ephemeral or enduring structures. Their means of attaining power may be quite varied, ranging from naked violence of any sort to canvassing for votes with coarse or subtle means: money, social influence, the force of speech, suggestion, clumsy hoax, and so on to the rougher or more artful tactics of obstruction in parliamentary bodies.

The sociological structure of parties differs in a basic way according to the kind of communal action which they struggle to influence. Parties also differ according to whether or not the community is stratified by status or by classes. Above all else, they vary according to the structure of domination within the community. For their leaders normally deal with the conquest of a community. They are, in the general concept which is maintained here, not only products of specially modern forms of domination. We shall also designate as parties the ancient and medieval 'parties,' despite the fact that their structure differs basically from the structure of modern parties. By virtue of thes structural differences of domination it is impossible to say anything about the structure of parties without discussing the structural forms of social domination *per se*. Parties, which are always structures struggling for domination, are very frequently organized in a very strict 'authoritarian' fashion . . .

Concerning 'classes,' 'status groups,' and 'parties,' it must be said in general that they necessarily presuppose a comprehensive societalization, and especially a political framework of communal action, within which they operate. This does not mean that parties would be confined by the frontiers of any individual political community. On the contrary, at all times it has been the order of the day that the societalization (even when it aims at the use of military force in common) reaches beyond the frontiers of politics. This has been the case in the solidarity of interests among the Oligarchs and among the democrats in Hellas, among the Guelfs and among Ghibellines in the Middle Ages, and within the Calvinist party during the period of religious struggles. It has been the case up to the solidarity of the landlords (international congress of agrarian landlords), and has continued among princes (holy alliance, Karlsbad decrees), socialist workers, conservatives (the longing of Prussian conservatives for Russian intervention in 1850). But their aim is not necessarily the establishment of new international political, i.e. *territorial*, dominion. In the main they aim to influence the existing dominion.

2.3 BUREAUCRACY

For Weber the construction of 'ideal types' is unavoidable if we are to investigate social life. 'Ideal types' are conceptual abstractions that social scientists can use to help explain the complexities of the world around them, even though the 'ideal types' do not actually exist, in 'reality', in their pure form. They are indispensable analytical and investigative tools. One of Weber's most famous 'ideal types' is that of bureaucracy, and in this extract he outlines its central features and the conditions necessary for its development.

The bureaucratic form for Weber was a central feature of, and growing tendency within, modern societies and the most explicit and recognisable aspect of the inexorable development of 'rationality' throughout all of social and economic life. Bureaucracy is the clearest example of Weber's 'iron cage' of rationality and is a social arrangement which becomes extremely difficult both to do without and destroy. This extract also displays Weber's pessimism – he was once described as a 'petrified liberal' – about our fate within modern societies and unlike Marx and, to a lesser extent, Durkheim he offers us 'no way out'. For example, socialist revolution would only lead, for Weber, to more bureaucratic structures evolving and a further suppression of individual freedoms and rights.

Weber's discussion of Bureaucracy has formed the basis for much subsequent study into organisations.

From: H. H. Gerth and C. Wright Mills, *From Max Weber: Essays in Sociology* (Routledge: London, 1991) pp.196–205, 228–35, 244.

Characteristics of Bureaucracy

Modern officialdom functions in the following specific manner:

I. There is the principle of fixed and official jurisdictional areas, which are generally [ordered] by rules, that is, by laws or administrative regulations.

1. The regular activities required for the purposes of the bureaucratically governed structure are distributed in a fixed way as official duties.
2. The authority to give the commands required for the discharge of these duties is distributed in a stable way and is strictly delimited by rules concerning the coercive means, physical, sacerdotal, or otherwise, which may be placed at the disposal of officials.
3. Methodical provision is made for the regular and continuous fulfilment of these duties and for the execution of the corresponding rights; only persons who have the generally regulated qualifications to serve are employed.

In public and lawful government these three elements constitute 'bureaucratic authority.' In private economic domination, they constitute bureaucratic 'management.' Bureaucracy, thus understood, is fully developed in political and ecclesiastical communities only in the modern state, and, in the private economy, only in the most advanced institutions of capitalism. Permanent and public office authority, with fixed jurisdiction, is not the historical rule but rather the exception. This is so even in large political structures such as those of the ancient Orient, the Germanic and Mongolian empires of conquest, or of many feudal structures of state. In all these cases, the ruler executes the most important measures through personal trustees, table-companions, or court-servants. Their commissions and authority are not precisely delimited and are temporarily called into being for each case.

II. The principles of office hierarchy and of levels of graded authority mean a firmly ordered system of super and subordination in which there is a supervision of the lower offices by the higher ones. Such a system offers the governed the possibility of appealing the decision of a lower office to its higher authority, in a definitely regulated manner. With the full development of the bureaucratic type, the office hierarchy is monocratically organized. The principle of hierarchical office authority is found in all bureaucratic structures: in state and ecclesiastical structures as well as in large party organizations and private enterprises. It does not matter for the character of bureaucracy whether its authority is called 'private' or 'public.'

When the principle of jurisdictional 'competency' is fully carried through, hierarchical subordination – at least in public office – does not mean that the 'higher' authority is simply authorized to take over the business of the 'lower.' Indeed, the opposite is the rule. Once established and having fulfilled its task, an office tends to continue in existence and be held by another incumbent.

III. The management of the modern office is based upon written documents ('the files'), which are preserved in their original or draught form. There is, therefore, a staff of subaltern officials and scribes of all sorts. The body of officials actively engaged in a 'public' office, along with the respective apparatus of material implements and the files, make up a 'bureau.' In private enterprise, 'the bureau' is often called 'the office.'

In principle, the modern organization of the civil service separates the bureau from the private domicile of the official, and, in general, bureaucracy segregates official activity as something distinct from the sphere of private life. Public monies and equipment are divorced from the private property of the official. This condition is everywhere the product of a long development. Nowadays, it is found in public as well as in private enterprises; in the latter, the principle extends even to the leading entrepreneur. In principle, the executive office is separated from the household, business from private correspondence, and business assets from private fortunes. The more consistently the modern type of business management has been carried through the more are these separations the case. The beginnings of this process are to be found as early as the Middle Ages.

It is the peculiarity of the modern entrepreneur that he conducts himself as the 'first official' of his enterprise, in the very same way in which the ruler of a specifically modern bureaucratic state spoke of himself as 'the first servant' of the state. The idea that the bureau activities of the state are intrinsically different in character from the management of private economic offices is a continental European notion and, by way of contrast, is totally foreign to the American way.

IV. Office management, at least all specialized office management – and such management is distinctly modern – usually presupposes thorough and expert training.

This increasingly holds for the modern executive and employee of private enterprises, in the same manner as it holds for the state official.

V. When the office is fully developed, official activity demands the full working capacity of the official, irrespective of the fact that his obligatory time in the bureau may be firmly delimited. In the normal case, this is only the product of a long development, in the public as well as in the private office. Formerly, in all cases, the normal state of affairs was reversed: official business was discharged as a secondary activity.

VI. The management of the office follows general rules, which are more or less stable, more or less exhaustive, and which can be learned. Knowledge of these rules represents a special technical learning which the officials possess. It involves jurisprudence, or administrative or business management.

The reduction of modern office management to rules is deeply embedded in its very nature. The theory of modern public administration, for instance, assumes that the authority to order certain matters by decree – which has been legally granted to public authorities – does not entitle the bureau to regulate the matter by commands given for each case, but only to regulate the matter abstractly. This stands in extreme contrast to the regulation of all relationships through individual privileges and bestowals of favor, which is absolutely dominant in patrimonialism, at least in so far as such relationships are not fixed by sacred tradition.

The Position of the Official

All this results in the following for the internal and external position of the official:

I. Office holding is a 'vocation.' This is shown, first, in the requirement of a firmly prescribed course of training, which demands the entire capacity for work for a long period of time, and in the generally prescribed and special examinations which are prerequisites of employment. Furthermore, the position of the official is in the nature of a duty. This determines the internal structure of his relations, in the following manner: Legally and actually, office holding is not considered a source to be exploited for rents or emoluments, as was normally the case during the Middle Ages and frequently up to the threshold of recent times. Nor is office holding considered a usual exchange of services for equivalents, as is the case with free labor contracts. Entrance into an office, including one in the private economy, is considered an acceptance of a specific obligation of faithful management in return for a secure existence. It is decisive for the specific nature of modern loyalty to an office that, in the pure type, it does not establish a relationship to a *person*, like the vassal's or disciple's faith in feudal or in patrimonial relations of authority. Modern loyalty is devoted to impersonal and functional purposes. Behind the functional purposes, of course, 'ideas of culture-values' usually stand. These are *ersatz* for the earthly or supra-mundane personal master: ideas such as 'state,' 'church,' 'community,' 'party,' or 'enterprise' are thought of as being realized in a community; they provide an ideological halo for the master.

The political official – at least in the fully developed modern state – is not considered the personal servant of a ruler. Today, the bishop, the priest, and the preacher are in fact no longer, as in early Christian times, holders of purely personal charisma. The supra-mundane and sacred values which they offer are given to everybody who seems to be worthy of them and who asks for them. In former times, such leaders acted upon the personal command of their master; in principle, they were responsible only to him. Nowadays, in spite of the partial survival of the old theory, such religious leaders are officials in the service of a functional purpose, which in the present-day 'church' has become routinized and, in turn, ideologically hallowed.

II. The personal position of the official is patterned in the following way:

1. Whether he is in a private office or a public bureau, the modern official always strives and usually enjoys a distinct *social esteem* as compared with the governed. His social position is guaranteed by the prescriptive rules of rank order and, for the political official, by special definitions of the criminal code against 'insults of officials' and 'contempt' of state and church authorities.

The actual social position of the official is normally highest where, as in old civilized countries, the following conditions prevail: a strong demand for administration by trained experts; a strong and stable social differentiation, where the official predominantly derives from socially and economically privileged strata because of the social distribution of power; or where the costliness of the required training and status conventions are binding upon him. The possession of educational certificates – to be discussed elsewhere – are usually linked with qualification for office. Naturally, such certificates or patents enhance the 'status element' in the social position of the official. For the rest this status factor in individual cases is explicitly and impassively acknowledged; for example, in the prescription that the acceptance or rejection of an aspirant to an official career depends upon the consent ('election') of the members of the official body. This is the case in the German army with the officer corps. Similar phenomena, which promote this guild-like closure of officialdom, are typically found in patrimonial and, particularly, in prebendal officialdoms of the past. The desire to resurrect such phenomena in changed forms is by no means infrequent among modern bureaucrats. For instance, they have played a role among the demands of the quite proletarian and expert officials (the *tretyj* element) during the Russian revolution.

Usually the social esteem of the officials as such is especially low where the demand for expert administration and the dominance of status conventions are weak. This is especially the case in the United States; it is often the case in new settlements by virtue of their wide fields for profit-making and the great instability of their social stratification.

2. The pure type of bureaucratic official is *appointed* by a superior authority. An official elected by the governed is not a purely bureaucratic figure. Of course, the formal existence of an election does not by itself mean that no appointment hides behind the election – in the state, especially, appointment by party chiefs. Whether or not this is the case does not depend upon legal statutes but upon the way in which the party mechanism functions. Once firmly organized, the parties can turn a formally free election into the mere acclamation of a candidate designated by the party chief. As a rule, however, a formally free election is turned into a fight, conducted according to definite rules, for votes in favor of one of two designated candidates.

In all circumstances, the designation of officials by means of an election among the governed modifies the strictness of hierarchical subordination. In principle, an official who is so elected has an autonomous position opposite the superordinate official. The elected official does not derive his position 'from above' but 'from below,' or at least not from a superior authority of the official hierarchy but from powerful party men ('bosses'), who also determine his further career. The career of the elected official is not, or at least not primarily, dependent upon his chief in the administration. The official who is not elected but appointed by a chief normally functions more exactly, from a technical point of view, because, all other circumstances being equal, it is more likely that purely functional points of consideration and qualities will determine his selection and career. As laymen, the governed can become acquainted with the extent to which a candidate is expertly qualified for office only in terms of experience, and hence only after his service. Moreover, in every sort of selection of officials by election, parties quite naturally give decisive weight not to expert considerations but to the services a follower renders to the party boss. This holds for all kinds of procurement of officials by elections, for the designation of formally free, elected officials by party bosses when they determine the slate of candidates, or the free appointment by a chief who has himself been elected. The contrast, however, is relative: substantially similar conditions hold where legitimate monarchs and their subordinates appoint officials, except that the influence of the followings are then less controllable.

Where the demand for administration by trained experts is considerable, and the party followings have to recognize an intellectually developed, educated, and freely moving 'public opinion,' the use of unqualified officials falls back upon the party in power at the next election. Naturally, this is more likely to happen when the officials are appointed by the chief. The demand for a trained administration now exists in the United States, but in the large cities, where immigrant votes are 'corraled,' there is, of course, no educated public opinion. Therefore, popular elections of the administrative chief and also of his subordinate officials usually endanger the expert qualification of the official as well as the precise functioning of the bureaucratic mechanism. It also weakens the dependence of the officials upon the hierarchy. This holds at least for the large administrative bodies that are difficult to supervise. The superior qualification and integrity of federal judges, appointed by the President, as over against elected judges in the United States is well known, although both types of officials have been selected primarily in terms of party considerations. The great changes in American metropolitan administrations demanded by reformers have proceeded essentially from elected mayors working with an apparatus of officials who were appointed by them. These reforms have thus come about in a 'Caesarist' fashion. Viewed technically, as an organized form of authority, the efficiency of 'Caesarism,' which often grows out of democracy, rests in general upon the position of the 'Caesar' as a free trustee of the masses (of the army or of the citizenry), who is unfettered by tradition. The 'Caesar' is thus the unrestrained master of a body of highly qualified military officers and officials whom he selects freely and personally without regard to tradition or to any other considerations. This 'rule of the personal genius,' however, stands in contradiction to the formally 'democratic' principle of a universally elected officialdom.

3. Normally, the position of the official is held for life, at least in public bureaucracies; and this is increasingly the case for all similar structures. As a factual rule, *tenure for life* is presupposed, even where the giving of notice or periodic reappointment occurs. In contrast to the worker in a private enterprise, the official normally holds tenure. Legal or actual life-tenure, however, is not recognized as the official's right to the possession of office, as was the case with many structures of authority in the past. Where legal guarantees against arbitrary dismissal or transfer are developed, they merely serve to guarantee a strictly objective discharge of specific office duties free from all personal considerations. In Germany, this is the case for all juridical and, increasingly, for all administrative officials.

Within the bureaucracy, therefore, the measure of 'independence,' legally guaranteed by tenure, is not always a source of increased status for the official whose position is thus secured. Indeed, often the reverse holds, especially in old cultures and communities that are highly differentiated. In such communities, the stricter the subordination under the arbitrary rule of the master, the more it guarantees the maintenance of the conventional seigneurial style of living for the official. Because of the very absence of these legal guarantees of tenure, the conventional esteem for the official may rise in the same way as, during the Middle Ages, the esteem of the nobility of office rose at the expense of esteem for the freemen, and as the king's judge surpassed that of the people's judge. In Germany, the military officer or the administrative official can be removed from office at any time, or at least far more readily than the 'independent judge,' who never pays with loss of his office for even the grossest offense against the 'code of honor' or against social conventions of the salon. For this very reason, if other things are equal, in the eyes of the master stratum the judge is considered less qualified for social intercourse than are officers and administrative officials, whose greater dependence on the master is a greater guarantee of their conformity with status conventions. Of course, the average official strives for a civil-service law, which would materially secure his old age and provide increased guarantees against his arbitrary removal from office. This striving, however, has its limits. A very strong development of the 'right to the office' naturally makes it more difficult to staff them with regard to technical efficiency, for such a development decreases the career-opportunities of ambitious candidates for office. This makes for the fact that officials, on the whole, do not feel their dependency upon those at the top. This lack of a feeling of dependency, however, rests primarily upon the inclination to depend upon one's equals rather than upon the socially inferior and governed strata. The present conservative movement among the Badenia clergy, occasioned by the anxiety of a presumably threatening separation of church and state, has been expressly determined by the desire not to be turned 'from a master into a servant of the parish.'

4. The official receives the regular *pecuniary* compensation of a normally fixed *salary* and the old age security provided by a pension. The salary is not measured like a wage in terms of work done, but according to 'status,' that is, according to the kind of function (the 'rank') and, in addition, possibly, according to the length of service. The relatively great security of the official's income, as well as the rewards of social esteem, make the office a sought-after position, especially in countries which no longer provide

opportunities for colonial profits. In such countries, this situation permits relatively low salaries for officials.

5. The official is set for a '*career*' within the hierarchical order of the public service. He moves from the lower, less important, and lower paid to the higher positions. The average official naturally desires a mechanical fixing of the conditions of promotion: if not of the offices, at least of the salary levels. He wants these conditions fixed in terms of 'seniority,' or possibly according to grades achieved in a developed system of expert examinations. Here and there, such examinations actually form a character *indelebilis* of the official and have lifelong effects on his career. To this is joined the desire to qualify the right to office and the increasing tendency toward status group closure and economic security. All of this makes for a tendency to consider the offices as 'prebends' of those who are qualified by educational certificates. The necessity of taking general personal and intellectual qualifications into consideration, irrespective of the often subaltern character of the educational certificate, has led to a condition in which the highest political offices, especially the positions of 'ministers,' are principally filled without reference to such certificates.

The Presuppositions and Causes of Bureaucracy

The social and economic presuppositions of the modern structure of the office are as follows:

The development of the *money economy*, in so far as a pecuniary compensation of the officials is concerned, is a presupposition of bureaucracy. Today it not only prevails but is predominant. This fact is of very great importance for the whole bearing of bureaucracy, yet by itself it is by no means decisive for the existence of bureaucracy.

Historical examples of rather distinctly developed and quantitatively large bureaucracies are:

1. Egypt, during the period of the new Empire which, however, contained strong patrimonial elements;
2. the later Roman Principate, and especially the Diocletian monarchy and the Byzantine polity which developed out of it and yet retained strong feudal and patrimonial elements;
3. the Roman Catholic Church, increasingly so since the end of the thirteenth century;
4. China, from the time of Shi Hwangti until the present, but with strong patrimonial and prebendal elements;
5. in ever purer forms, the modern European states and, increasingly, all public corporations since the time of princely absolutism;
6. the large modern capitalist enterprise, the more so as it becomes greater and more complicated.

To a very great extent, partly even predominantly, cases 1. to 4. have rested upon compensation of the officials in kind. Yet they have displayed many other traits and effects characteristic of bureaucracy. The historical model of all later bureaucracies – the new Empire of Egypt – is at the same time one of the most grandiose examples of an organized subsistence economy. Yet this coincidence of bureaucracy and subsistence economy is understandable in view of the quite unique conditions that existed in Egypt. And the reservations – and they are quite considerable – which one must make in classifying this Egyptian structure as a bureaucracy are conditioned by the subsistence economy. A certain measure of a developed money economy is the normal precondition for the unchanged and continued existence, if not for the establishment, of pure bureaucratic administrations. [. . .]

The Permanent Character of the Bureaucratic Machine

Once it is fully established, bureaucracy is among those social structures which are the hardest to destroy. Bureaucracy is *the* means of carrying 'community action' over into rationally ordered 'societal action.' Therefore, as an instrument for 'societalizing' relations of power, bureaucracy has been and is a power instrument of the first order – for the one who controls the bureaucratic apparatus.

Under otherwise equal conditions, a 'societal action,' which is methodically ordered and led, is superior to every resistance of 'mass' or even of 'communal action.' And where the bureaucratization of administration has been completely carried through, a form of power relation is established that is practically unshatterable.

The individual bureaucrat cannot squirm out of the apparatus in which he is harnessed. In contrast to the honorific or avocational 'notable,' the professional bureaucrat is chained to his activity by his entire material and ideal existence. In the great majority of cases, he is only a single cog in an ever-moving mechanism which prescribes to him an essentially fixed route of march. The official is entrusted with specialized tasks and normally the mechanism cannot be put into motion or arrested by him, but only from the very top. The individual bureaucrat is thus forged to the community of all the functionaries who are integrated into the mechanism. They have a common interest in seeing that the mechanism continues its functions and that the societally exercised authority carries on.

The ruled, for their part, cannot dispense with or replace the bureaucratic apparatus of authority once it exists. For this bureaucracy rests upon expert training, a functional specialization of work, and an attitude set for habitual and virtuoso-like mastery of single yet methodically integrated functions. If the official stops working, or if his work is forcefully interrupted, chaos results, and it is difficult to improvise replacements from among the governed who are fit to master such chaos. This holds for public administration as well as for private economic management. More and more the material fate of the masses depends upon the steady and correct functioning of the increasingly bureaucratic organizations of private capitalism. The idea of eliminating these organizations becomes more and more utopian.

Economic and Social Consequences of Bureaucracy

It is clear that the bureaucratic organization of a social structure, and especially of a political one, can and regularly does have far-reaching economic consequences. But what sort of consequences? Of course in any individual case it depends upon the distribution of economic and social power, and especially upon the sphere that is occupied by the emerging bureaucratic mechanism. The consequences of bureaucracy depend therefore upon the direction which the powers using the apparatus give to it. And very frequently a crypto-plutocratic distribution of power has been the result.

In England, but especially in the United States, party donors regularly stand behind the bureaucratic party organizations. They have financed these parties and have been able to influence them to a large extent. The breweries in England, the so-called 'heavy industry,' and in Germany the Hansa League with their voting funds are well enough known as political donors to parties. In modern times bureaucratization and social leveling within political, and particularly within state organizations in connection with the destruction of feudal and local privileges, have very frequently benefited the interests of capitalism. Often bureaucratization has been carried out in direct alliance with capitalist interests, for example, the great historical alliance of the power of the absolute prince with capitalist interests. In general, a legal leveling and destruction of firmly established local structures ruled by notables has usually made for a wider range of capitalist activity. Yet one may expect as an effect of bureaucratization, a policy that meets the petty bourgeois interest in a secured traditional 'subsistence,' or even a state socialist policy that strangles opportunities for private profit. This has occurred in several cases of historical and far-reaching importance, specifically during antiquity; it is undoubtedly to be expected as a future development. Perhaps it will occur in Germany.

The very different effects of political organizations which were, at least in principle, quite similar – in Egypt under the Pharaohs and in Hellenic and Roman times – show the very different economic significances of bureaucratization which are possible according to the direction of other factors. The mere fact of bureaucratic organization does not unambiguously tell us about the concrete direction of its economic effects, which are always in some manner present. At least it does not tell us as much as can be told about its relatively leveling effect socially. In this respect, one has to remember that bureaucracy as such is a precision instrument which can put itself at the disposal of quite varied – purely political as well as purely economic, or any other sort – of interests in domination. Therefore, the measure of its parallelism with democratization must not be exaggerated, however typical it may be. Under certain conditions, strata of feudal lords have also put bureaucracy into their service. There is also the possibility – and often it has become a fact, for instance, in the Roman principate and in some forms of absolutist state structures – that a bureaucratization of administration is deliberately connected with the formation of *estates*, or is entangled with them by the force of the existing groupings of social power. The express reservation of offices for certain status groups is very frequent, and actual reservations are even more frequent. The democratization of society in its totality, and in the *modern* sense of the term, whether actual or perhaps merely formal, is an especially favorable basis of bureaucratization, but by no means the only possible one. After all, bureaucracy strives merely to level those powers that stand in its way and in those areas that, in the individual case, it seeks to occupy. We must remember this fact – which we have encountered several times and which we shall have to discuss repeatedly: that 'democracy' as such is opposed to the 'rule' of bureaucracy, in spite and perhaps because of its unavoidable yet unintended promotion of bureaucratization. Under certain conditions, democracy creates obvious ruptures and blockages to bureaucratic organization. Hence, in every individual historical case, one must observe in what special direction bureaucratization has developed. [. . .]

Every bureaucracy seeks to increase the superiority of the professionally informed by keeping their knowledge and intentions secret. Bureaucratic administration always tends to be an administration of 'secret sessions': in so far as it can, it hides its knowledge and action from criticism. Prussian church authorities now threaten to use disciplinary measures against pastors who make reprimands or other admonitory measures in any way accessible to third parties. They do this because the pastor, in making such criticism available, is 'guilty' of facilitating a possible criticism of the church authorities. The treasury officials of the Persian shah have made a secret doctrine of their budgetary art and even use secret script. The official statistics of Prussia, in general, make public only what cannot do any harm to the intentions of the power-wielding bureaucracy. The tendency toward secrecy in certain administrative fields follows their material nature: everywhere that the power interests of the domination structure toward *the outside* are at stake, whether it is an economic competitor of a private enterprise, or a foreign, potentially hostile polity, we find secrecy. If it is to be successful, the management of diplomacy can only be publicly controlled to a very limited extent. The military administration must insist on the concealment of its most important measures; with the increasing significance of purely technical aspects, this is all the more the case. Political parties do not proceed differently, in spite of all the ostensible publicity of Catholic congresses and party conventions. With the increasing bureaucratization of party organizations, this secrecy will prevail even more. Commercial policy, in Germany for instance, brings about a concealment of production statistics. Every fighting posture of a social structure toward the outside tends to buttress the position of the group in power.

The pure interest of the bureaucracy in power, however, is efficacious far beyond those areas where purely functional interests make for secrecy. The concept of the 'official secret' is the specific invention of bureaucracy, and nothing is so fanatically defended by the bureaucracy as this attitude, which cannot be substantially justified beyond these specifically qualified areas. In facing a parliament, the bureaucracy, out of a sure power instinct, fights every attempt of the parliament to gain knowledge by means of its own experts or from interest groups. The so-called right of parliamentary investigation is one of the means by which parliament seeks such knowledge. Bureaucracy naturally welcomes a poorly informed and hence a powerless parliament – at least in so far as ignorance somehow agrees with the bureaucracy's interests.

The absolute monarch is powerless opposite the superior knowledge of the bureaucratic expert – in a certain sense more powerless than any other political head. All the scornful decrees of Frederick the Great concerning the 'abolition of serfdom' were derailed, as it were, in the course of their realization because the official mechanism simply ignored them as the occasional ideas of a dilettante. When a constitutional king agrees with a socially important part of the governed, he very frequently exerts a greater influence upon the course of administration than does the absolute monarch. The constitutional king can control these experts better because of what is, at least relatively, the public character of criticism, whereas the absolute monarch is dependent for information solely upon the bureaucracy. The Russian czar of the old regime was seldom able to accomplish permanently anything that displeased his bureaucracy and hurt the power interests of the bureaucrats. His ministerial departments, placed directly under him as the autocrat, represented a conglomerate of satrapies, as was correctly noted by Leroy-Beaulieu. These satrapies constantly fought against one another by all the means of personal intrigue, and, especially, they bombarded one another with voluminous 'memorials,' in the face of which, the monarch, as a dilettante, was helpless.

With the transition to constitutional government, the concentration of the power of the central bureaucracy in one head became unavoidable. Officialdom was placed under a monocratic head, the prime minister, through whose hands everything had to go before it got to the monarch. This put the latter, to a large extent, under the tutelage of the chief of the bureaucracy. Wilhelm II, in his well-known conflict with Bismarck, fought against this principle, but he had to withdraw his attack very soon. Under the rule of expert knowledge, the actual influence of the monarch can attain steadiness only by a continuous communication with the bureaucratic chiefs; this intercourse must be methodically planned and directed by the head of the bureaucracy.

At the same time, constitutionalism binds the bureaucracy and the ruler into a community of interests against the desires of party chiefs for power in the parliamentary bodies. And if he cannot find support in parliament the constitutional monarch is powerless against the bureaucracy. The desertion of the 'Great of the Reich,' the Prussian ministers and top officials of the Reich in November 1918, brought a monarch into approximately the same situation as existed in the feudal state in 1056. However, this is an exception, for, on the whole, the power position of a monarch opposite bureaucratic officials is far stronger than it was in any feudal state or in the 'stereotyped' patrimonial state. This is because of the constant presence of aspirants for promotion, with whom the monarch can easily replace inconvenient and independent officials. Other circumstances being equal, only economically independent officials, that is, officials who belong to the propertied strata, can permit themselves to risk the loss of their offices. Today as always, the recruitment of officials from among propertyless strata increases the power of the rulers. Only officials who belong to a socially influential stratum, whom the monarch believes he must take into account as personal supporters, like the so-called *Kanalrebellen* in Prussia, can permanently and completely paralyse the substance of his will.

Only the expert knowledge of private economic interest groups in the field of 'business' is superior to the expert knowledge of the bureaucracy. This is so because the exact knowledge of facts in their field is vital to the economic existence of businessmen. Errors in official statistics do not have direct economic consequences for the guilty official, but errors in the calculation of a capitalist enterprise are paid for by losses, perhaps by its existence. The 'secret,' as a means of power, is, after all, more safely hidden in the books of an enterpriser than it is in the files of public authorities. For this reason alone authorities are held within narrow barriers when they seek to influence economic life in the capitalist epoch. Very frequently the measures of the state in the field of capitalism take unforeseen and unintended courses, or they are made illusory by the superior expert knowledge of interest groups. [. . .]

The bureaucratic structure is everywhere a late product of development. The further back we trace our steps, the more typical is the absence of bureaucracy and officialdom in the structure of domination. Bureaucracy has a 'rational' character: rules, means, ends, and matter-of-factness dominate its bearing. Everywhere its origin and its diffusion have therefore had 'revolutionary' results, in a special sense, which has still to be discussed. This is the same influence which the advance of *rationalism* in general has had. The march of bureaucracy has destroyed structures of domination which had no rational character, in the special sense of the term. Hence, we may ask: What were these structures?

2.4 SCIENCE AS A VOCATION

This was originally a speech given at the University of Munich in 1919 in which Weber calls for resolute intellectual integrity within the lecture theatre and urges academics not to use the university as a forum for airing political views. In this extract Weber implores us to the face up to 'demands of the day' within an increasingly rationalised and soulless world and one which is characterised by 'disenchantment'. A return into the 'arms of the old churches' is a way out for those not up to this task.

From: H. H. Gerth and C. Wright Mills, *From Max Weber: Essays in Sociology* (Routledge: London, 1991) pp. 152–3, 155–6.

Science today is a 'vocation' organized in special disciplines in the service of self-clarification and knowledge of interrelated facts. It is not the gift of grace of seers and prophets dispensing sacred values and revelations, nor does it partake of the contemplation of sages and philosophers about the meaning of the universe. This, to be sure, is the inescapable condition of our historical situation. We cannot evade it so long as we remain true to ourselves. And if Tolstoi's question recurs to you: as science does not, who is to answer the question: 'What shall we do, and, how shall we arrange our lives?' or, in the words used here tonight: 'Which of the warring gods should we serve? Or should we serve perhaps an entirely different god, and who is he?' then one can say that only a prophet or a savior can give the answers. If there is no such man, or if his message is no longer believed in, then you will certainly not compel him to appear on this earth by having thousands of professors, as privileged hirelings of the state, attempt as petty prophets in their lecture-rooms to take over his role. All they will accomplish is to show that they are unaware of the decisive state of affairs: the prophet for whom so many of our younger generation yearn simply does not exist. But this knowledge in its forceful significance has never become vital for them. The inward interest of a truly religiously 'musical' man can never be served by veiling to him and to others the fundamental fact that he is destined to live in a godless and prophetless time by giving him the *ersatz* of armchair prophecy. The integrity of his religious organ, it seems to me, must rebel against this.

Now you will be inclined to say: Which stand does one take towards the factual existence of 'theology' and its claims to be a 'science'? Let us not flinch and evade the answer. To be sure, 'theology' and 'dogmas' do not exist universally, but neither do they exist for Christianity alone. Rather (going backward in time), they exist in highly developed form also in Islam, in Manicheanism, in Gnosticism, in Orphism, in Parsism, in Buddhism, in the Hindu sects, in Taoism, and in the Upanishads, and, of course, in Judaism. To be sure their systematic development varies greatly. It is no accident that Occidental Christianity – in contrast to the theological possessions of Jewry – has expanded and elaborated theology more systematically, or strives to do so. In the Occident the development of theology has had by far the greatest historical significance. This is the product of the Hellenic spirit, and all theology of the West goes back to it, as (obviously) all theology of the East goes back to Indian thought. All theology represents an intellectual *rationalization* of the possession of sacred values. No science is absolutely free from presuppositions, and no science can prove its fundamental value to the man who rejects these presuppositions. Every theology, however, adds a few specific presuppositions for its work and thus for the justification of its existence. Their meaning and scope vary. Every theology, including for instance Hinduist theology, presupposes that the world must have a *meaning*, and the question is how to interpret this meaning so that it is intellectually conceivable.[. . .]

The fate of our times is characterized by rationalization and intellectualization and, above all, by the 'disenchantment of the world.' Precisely the ultimate and most sublime values have retreated from public life either into the transcendental realm of mystic life or into the brotherliness of direct and personal human relations. It is not accidental that our greatest art is intimate and not monumental, nor is it accidental that today only within the smallest and intimate circles, in personal human situations, in *pianissimo*, that something is pulsating that corresponds to the prophetic *pneuma*, which in former times swept through the great communities like a firebrand, welding them together. If we attempt to force and to 'invent' a monumental style in art, such miserable monstrosities are produced as the many monuments of the last twenty years. If one tries intellectually to construe new religions without a new and genuine prophecy, then, in an inner sense, something similar will result, but with still worse effects. And academic prophecy, finally, will create only fanatical sects but never a genuine community.

To the person who cannot bear the fate of the times like a man, one must say: may he rather return silently, without the usual publicity build-up of renegades, but simply and plainly. The arms of the old churches are opened widely and compassionately for him. After all, they do not make it hard for him. One way or another he has to bring his 'intellectual sacrifice' – that is inevitable. If he can really do it, we shall not rebuke him. For such an intellectual sacrifice in favor of an unconditional religious devotion is ethically quite a different matter than the evasion of the plain duty of intellectual integrity, which sets in if one lacks the courage to clarify one's own ultimate standpoint and rather facilitates this duty by feeble relative judgments. In my eyes, such religious return stands higher than the academic prophecy, which does not clearly realize that in the lecture-rooms of the university no other virtue holds but plain intellectual integrity. Integrity, however, compels us to state that for the many who today tarry for new prophets and saviors, the situation is the same as resounds in the beautiful Edomite watchman's song of the period of exile that has been included among Isaiah's oracles:

> He calleth to me out of Seir, Watchman, what of the night? The watchman said, The morning cometh, and also the night: if ye will enquire, enquire ye: return, come.

The people to whom this was said has enquired and tarried for more than two millennia, and we are shaken when we realize its fate. From this we want to draw the lesson that nothing is gained by yearning and tarrying alone, and we shall act differently. We shall set to work and meet the 'demands of the day,' in human relations as well as in our vocation. This, however, is plain and simple, if each finds and obeys the demon who holds the fibers of his very life.

2.5 Definitions of Sociology and Social Action

Another set of 'ideal types' taken from the pages of *Economy and Society*, this passage includes Weber's famous definition of sociology and his discussion of the role of 'understanding' (*verstehen*) within sociology. This had a crucial influence on what became known as the 'interpretative' tradition within sociology, one which seeks to incorporate within its methodology an understanding of how people 'make sense' of the situations they find themselves in.

This extract also includes Weber's typology of 'social action'. Weber emphasised individual 'social action' as being the starting point for sociology – a perspective often given the label of 'methodological individualism'. This contrasts sharply with Durkheim who thought that large-scale phenomena such as 'society', which exists – sui generis – over and above individuals, were the proper object of study for sociology.

From: T. Parsons (ed.), *Max Weber: The Theory of Social and Economic Organisation* (Free Press: New York, 1968), pp. 88–91, 94–6, 112–18).

Sociology (in the sense in which this highly ambiguous word is used here) is a science which attempts the interpretive understanding of social action in order thereby to arrive at a causal explanation of its course and effects. In 'action' is included all human behaviour when and in so far as the acting individual attaches a subjective meaning to it. Action in this sense may be either overt or purely inward or subjective; it may consist of positive intervention in a situation, or of deliberately refraining from such intervention or passively acquiescing in the situation. Action is social in so far as, by virtue of the subjective meaning attached to it by the acting individual (or individuals), it takes account of the behaviour of others and is thereby oriented in its course.

The Methodological Foundations of Sociology

'Meaning' may be of two kinds. The term may refer first to the actual existing meaning in the given concrete case of a particular actor, or to the average or approximate meaning attributable to a given plurality of actors; or secondly to the theoretically conceived *pure type* of subjective meaning attributed to the hypothetical actor or actors in a given type of action. In no case does it refer to an objectively 'correct' meaning or one which is 'true' in some metaphysical sense. It is this which distinguished the empirical sciences of action, such as sociology and history, from the dogmatic disciplines in that area, such as jurisprudence, logic, ethics, and esthetics, which seek to ascertain the 'true' and 'valid' meanings associated with the objects of their investigation.

The line between meaningful action and merely reactive behaviour to which no subjective meaning is attached, cannot be sharply drawn empirically. A very considerable part of all sociologically relevant behaviour, especially purely traditional behaviour, is marginal between the two. In the case of many psychophysical processes, meaningful, i.e. subjectively understandable, action is not to be found at all; in others it is discernible only by the expert psychologist. Many mystical experiences which cannot be adequately communicated in words are, for a person who is not susceptible to such experiences, not fully understandable. At the same time the ability to imagine one's self performing a similar action is not a necessary prerequisite to understanding; 'one need not have been Caesar in order to understand Caesar.' For the verifiable accuracy of interpretation of the meaning of a phenomenon, it is a great help to be able to put one's self imaginatively in the place of the actor and thus sympathetically to participate in his experiences, but this is not an essential condition of meaningful interpretation. Understandable and non-understandable components of a process are often intermingled and bound up together.

All interpretation of meaning, like all scientific observation, strives for clarity and verifiable accuracy of insight and comprehension (*Evidenz*). The basis for certainty in understanding can be either rational, which can be further subdivided into logical and mathematical, or it can be of an emotionally empathic or artistically appreciative quality. In the sphere of action things are rationally evident chiefly when we attain a completely clear intellectual grasp of the action-elements in their intended context of meaning. Empathic or appreciative accuracy is attained when, through sympathetic participation, we can adequately grasp the emotional context in which the action took place. The highest degree of rational understanding is attained in cases involving the meanings of logically or mathematically related propositions; their meaning may be immediately and unambiguously intelligible. We have a perfectly clear understanding of what it means when somebody employs the proposition $2 \times 2 = 4$ or the Pythagorean theorem in reasoning or argument, or when someone correctly carries out a logical train of reasoning according to our accepted modes of thinking. In the same way we also understand what a person is doing when he tries to achieve certain ends by choosing appropriate means on the basis of the facts of the situation as experience has accustomed us to interpret them. Such an interpretation of this type of rationally purposeful action possesses, for the understanding of the choice of means, the highest degree of verifiable certainty. With a lower degree of certainty, which is, however, adequate for most purposes of explanation, we are able to understand errors, including confusion of problems of the sort that we ourselves are liable to, or the origin of which we can detect by sympathetic self-analysis.

On the other hand, many ultimate ends or values toward which experience shows that human action may be oriented, often cannot be understood completely, though sometimes we are able to grasp them intellectually. The more radically they differ from our own ultimate values, however, the more difficult it is for us to make them understandable by imaginatively participating in them. Depending upon the circumstances of the particular case we must be content either with a purely intellectual understanding of such values or when even that fails, sometimes we must simply accept them as given data. Then we can try to understand the action motivated by them on the basis of whatever opportunities for approximate emotional and intellectual interpretation seem to be available at different points in its course. These difficulties apply, for instance, for people not susceptible to the relevant values, to many unusual acts of religious and charitable zeal; also certain kinds of extreme rationalistic fanaticism of the type involved in some forms of the ideology of the 'rights of man' are in a similar position for people who radically repudiate such points of view. [. . .]

It is altogether possible that future research may be able to discover non-understandable uniformities underlying what has appeared to be specifically meaningful action, though little has been accomplished in this direction thus far. Thus, for example, differences in hereditary biological constitution, as of 'races,' would have to be treated by sociology as given data in the same way as the physiological facts of the need of nutrition or the effect of senescence on action. This would be the case if, and in so far as, we had statistically conclusive proof of their influence on sociologically relevant behaviour. The recognition of the causal significance of such factors would naturally not in the least alter the specific task of sociological analysis or of that of the other sciences of action, which is the interpretation of action in terms of its subjective meaning. The effect would be only to introduce certain non-understandable data of the same order as others which, it has been noted above, are already present, into the complex of subjectively understandable motivation at certain points. Thus it may come to be known that there are typical relations between the frequency of certain types of teleological orientation of action or of the degree of certain kinds of rationality and the cephalic index or skin colour or any other biologically inherited characteristic.

Understanding may be of two kinds: the first is the direct observational understanding of the subjective meaning of a given act as such, including verbal utterances. We thus understand by direct observation, in this sense, the meaning of the proposition $2 \times 2 = 4$ when we hear or read it. This is a case of the direct rational understanding of ideas. We also understand an outbreak of anger as manifested by facial expression, exclamations or irrational movements. This is direct observational understanding of irrational emotional reactions. We can understand in a similar observational way the action of a woodcutter or of somebody who reaches for the knob to shut a door or who aims a gun at an animal. This is rational observational understanding of actions.

Understanding may, however, be of another sort, namely explanatory understanding. Thus we understand in terms of *motive* the meaning an actor attaches to the proposition twice two equals four, when he states it or writes it down, in that we understand what makes him do this at precisely this moment and in these circumstances. Understanding in this sense is attained if we know that he is engaged in balancing a ledger or in making a scientific demonstration, or is engaged in some other task of which this particular act would be an appropriate part. This is rational understanding of motivation, which consists in placing the act in an intelligible and more inclusive context of meaning. Thus we understand the chopping of wood or aiming of a gun in terms of motive in addition to direct observation if we know that the woodchopper is working for a wage or is chopping a supply of firewood for his own use or possibly is doing it for recreation. But he might also be 'working off' a fit of rage, an irrational case. Similarly we understand the motive of a person aiming a gun if we know that he has been commanded to shoot as a member of a firing squad, that he is fighting against an enemy, or that he is doing it for revenge. The last is affectually determined and thus in a certain sense irrational. Finally we have a motivational understanding of the outburst of anger if we know that it has been provoked by jealousy, injured pride, or an insult.

The last examples are all affectually determined and hence derived from irrational motives. In all the above cases the particular act has been placed in an understandable sequence of motivation, the understanding of which can be treated as an explanation of the actual course of behaviour. Thus for a science which is concerned with the subjective meaning of action, explanation requires a grasp of the complex of meaning in which an actual course of understandable action thus interpreted belongs. In all such cases, even where the processes are largely affectual, the subjective meaning of the action, including that also of the relevant meaning complexes, will be called the 'intended' meaning. This involves a departure from ordinary usage, which speaks of intention in this sense only in the case of rationally purposive action.

In all these cases understanding involves the interpretive grasp of the meaning present in one of the following contexts: 1. as in the historical approach, the actually intended meaning for concrete individual action; or 2. as in cases of sociological mass phenomena the average of, or an approximation to, the actually intended meaning; or 3. the meaning appropriate to a scientifically formulated pure type (an ideal type) of a common phenomenon. The concepts and 'laws' of pure economic theory are examples of this kind of ideal type. They state what course a given type of human action would take if it were strictly rational, unaffected by errors or emotional factors and if, furthermore, it were completely and unequivocally directed to a single end, the maximization of economic advantage. In reality, action takes exactly this course only in unusual cases, as sometimes on the stock exchange; and even then there is usually only an approximation to the ideal type. [. . .]

The Concept of Social Action

Social action, which includes both failure to act and passive acquiescence, may be oriented to the past, present, or expected future behaviour of others. Thus it may be motivated by revenge for a past attack, defence against present, or measures of defence against future aggression. The 'others' may be individual persons, and may be known to the actor as such, or may constitute an indefinite plurality and may be entirely unknown as individuals. Thus 'money' is a means of exchange which the actor accepts in payment because he orients his action to the expectation that a large but unknown number of individuals he is personally unacquainted with will be ready to accept it in exchange on some future occasion.

Not every kind of action, even of overt action, is 'social in the sense of the present discussion. Overt action is non-social if it is oriented solely to the behaviour of inanimate objects. Subjective attitudes constitute social action only so far as they are oriented to the behaviour of others. For example, religious behaviour is not social if it is simply a matter of contemplation or of solitary prayer. The economic activity of an individual is only social if, and then only in so far as, it takes account of the behaviour of someone else. Thus very generally in formal terms it becomes social in so far as the actor's actual control over economic goods is respected by others. Concretely it is social, for instance, if in relation to the actor's own consumption the future wants of others are taken into account and this becomes one consideration affecting the actor's own saving. Or, in another connexion, production may be oriented to the future wants of other people.

Not every type of contact of human beings has a social character; this is rather confined to cases where the actor's behaviour is meaningfully oriented to that of others. For example, a mere collision of two cyclists may be compared to a natural event. On the other hand, their attempt to avoid hitting each other, or whatever insults, blows, or friendly discussion might follow the collision, would constitute 'social action.'

Social action is not identical either with the similar actions of many persons or with action influenced by other persons. Thus, if at the beginning of a shower a number of people on the street put up their umbrellas at the same time, this would not ordinarily be a case of action mutually oriented to that of each other, but rather of all reacting in the same way to the like need of protection from the rain. It is well known that the actions of the individual are strongly influenced by the mere fact that he is a member of a crowd confined within a limited space. Thus, the subject matter of studies of 'crowd psychology,' such as those of Le Bon, will be called 'action conditioned by crowds.' It is also possible for large numbers, though dispersed, to be influenced simultaneously or successively by a source of influence operating similarly on all the individuals, as by means of the press. Here also the behaviour of an individual is influenced by his membership in the crowd and by the fact that he is aware of being a member. Some types of reaction are only made possible by the mere fact that the individual acts as part of a crowd. Others become more difficult under these conditions. Hence it is possible that a particular event or mode of human behaviour can give rise to the most diverse kinds of feeling – gaiety, anger, enthusiasm, despair, and passions of all sorts – in a crowd situation which would not occur at all or not nearly so readily if the individual were alone. But for this to happen there need not, at least in many cases, be any meaningful relation between the behaviour of the individual and the fact that he is a member of a crowd. It is not proposed in the present sense to call action 'social' when it is merely a result of the effect on the individual of the existence of a crowd as such and the action is not oriented to that fact on the level of meaning. At the same time the borderline is naturally highly indefinite. In such cases as that of the influence of the demagogue there may be a wide variation in the extent to which his mass clientele is affected by a meaningful reaction to the fact of its large numbers; and whatever this relation may be, it is open to varying interpretations.

But furthermore, mere 'imitation' of the action of others, such as that on which Tarde has rightly laid emphasis, will not be considered a case of specifically social action if it is purely reactive so that there is no meaningful orientation to the actor imitated. The borderline is, however, so indefinite that it is often hardly possible to discriminate. The mere fact that a person is found to employ some apparently useful procedure which he learned from someone else does not, however, constitute, in the present sense, social action. Action such as this is not oriented to the action of the other person, but the actor has, through observing the other, become acquainted with certain objective facts; and it is these to which his action is oriented. His action is then *causally* determined by the action of others, but not meaningfully. On the other hand, if the action of others is imitated because it is 'fashionable' or traditional or exemplary, or lends social distinction, or on similar grounds, it is meaningfully oriented either to the behaviour of the source of imitation or of third persons or of both. There are of course all manner of transitional cases between the two types of imitation. Both the phenomena discussed above, the behaviour of crowds and imitation, stand on the indefinite borderline of social action. The same is true, as will often appear, of traditionalism and charisma. The reason for the indefiniteness of the line in these and other cases lies in the fact that both the orientation to the behaviour of others and the meaning which can be imputed to the actor himself, are by no means always capable of clear determination and are often altogether unconscious and seldom fully self-conscious. Mere 'influence' and meaningful orientation cannot therefore always be clearly differentiated on the empirical level. But conceptually it is essential to distinguish them, even though merely 'reactive' imitation may well have a degree of sociological importance at least equal to that of the type which can be called social action in the strict sense. Sociology, it goes without saying, is by no means confined to the study of 'social action'; this is only, at least for the kind of sociology being developed here, its central subject matter, that which may be said to be decisive for its status as a science. But this does not imply any judgment on the comparative importance of this and other factors.

The Types of Social Action

Social action, like other forms of action, may be classified in the following four types according to its mode of orientation:

1. in terms of rational orientation to a system of discrete individual ends (*zweckrational*), that is, through expectations as to the behaviour of objects in the external situation and of other human individuals, making use of these expectations as 'conditions' or 'means' for the successful attainment of the actor's own rationally chosen ends;
2. in terms of rational orientation to an absolute value (*wertrational*); involving a conscious belief in the absolute value of some ethical, aesthetic, religious, or other form of behaviour, entirely for its own sake and independently of any prospects of external success;
3. in terms of affectual orientation, especially emotional, determined by the specific affects and states of feeling of the actor;
4. traditionally oriented, through the habituation of long practice.

Strictly traditional behaviour, like the reactive type of imitation discussed above, lies very close to the borderline of what can justifiably be called meaningfully oriented action, and indeed often on the other side. For it is very often a matter of almost automatic reaction to habitual stimuli which guide behaviour in a course which has been repeatedly followed. The great bulk of all everyday action to which people have become habitually accustomed approaches this type. Hence, its place in a systematic classification is not merely that of a limiting case because, as will be shown later, attachment to habitual forms can be upheld with varying degrees of self-consciousness and in a variety of senses. In this case the type may shade over into number two (*Wertrationalität*).

Purely affectual behaviour also stands on the borderline of what can be considered 'meaningfully' oriented, and often it, too, goes over the line. It may, for instance, consist in an uncontrolled reaction to some exceptional stimulus. It is a case of sublimation when affectually determined action occurs in the form of conscious release of emotional tension. When this happens it is usually, though not always, well on the road to rationalization in one or the other or both of the above senses.

The orientation of action in terms of absolute value is distinguished from the affectual type by its clearly self-conscious formulation of the ultimate values governing the action and the consistently planned orientation of its detailed course to these values. At the same time the two types have a common element, namely that the meaning of the action does not lie in the achievement of a result ulterior to it, but in carrying out the specific type of action for its own sake. Examples of affectual action are the satisfaction of a direct impulse to revenge, to sensual gratification, to devote oneself to a person or ideal, to contemplative bliss, or, finally, toward the working off of emotional tensions. Such impulses belong in this category regardless of how sordid or sublime they may be.

Examples of pure rational orientation to absolute values would be the action of persons who, regardless of possible cost to themselves, act to put into practice their convictions of what seems to them to be required by duty, honour, the pursuit of beauty, a religious call, personal loyalty, or the importance of some 'cause' no matter in what it consists. For the purposes of this discussion, when action is oriented to absolute values, it always involves 'commands' or 'demands' to the fulfilment of which the actor feels obligated. It is only in cases where human action is motivated by the fulfilment of such unconditional demands that it will be described as oriented to absolute values. This is empirically the case in widely varying degrees, but for the most part only to a relatively slight extent. Nevertheless, it will be shown that the occurrence of this mode of action is important enough to justify its formulation as a distinct type; though it may be remarked that there is no intention here of attempting to formulate in any sense an exhaustive classification of types of action.

Action is rationally oriented to a system of discrete individual ends (*zweckrational*) when the end, the means, and the secondary results are all rationally taken into account and weighed. This involves rational consideration of alternative means to the end, of the relations of the end to other prospective results of employment of any given means, and finally of the relative importance of different possible ends. Determination of action, either in affectual or in traditional terms, is thus incompatible with this type. Choice between alternative and conflicting ends and results may well be determined by considerations of absolute value. In that case, action is rationally oriented to a system of discrete individual ends only in respect to the choice of means. On the other hand, the actor may, instead of deciding between alternative and conflicting ends in terms of a rational orientation to a system of values, simply take them as given subjective wants and arrange them in a scale of consciously assessed relative urgency. He may then orient his action to this scale in such a way that they are satisfied as far as possible in order of urgency, as formulated in the principle of 'marginal utility.' The orientation of action to absolute values may thus have various different modes of relation to the other type of rational action, in terms of a system of discrete individual ends. From the latter point of view, however, absolute values are always irrational. Indeed, the more the value to which action is oriented is elevated to the status of an absolute value, the more 'irrational' in this sense the corresponding action is. For, the more unconditionally the actor devotes himself to this value for its own sake, to pure sentiment or beauty, to absolute goodness or devotion to duty, the less is he influenced by considerations of the consequences of his action. The orientation of action wholly to the rational achievement of ends without relation to fundamental values is, to be sure, essentially only a limiting case.

It would be very unusual to find concrete cases of action, especially of social action, which were oriented *only* in one or another of these ways. Furthermore, this classification of the modes of orientation of action is in no sense meant to exhaust the possibilities of the field, but only to formulate in conceptually pure form certain sociologically important types, to which actual action is more or less closely approximated or, in much the more common case, which constitute the elements combining to make it up. The usefulness of the classification for the purposes of this investigation can only be judged in terms of its results.

2.6 Legitimacy and Authority

For Weber 'power' could be defined quite simply as the ability to get others to do what you want. There are a number of ways in which this might be achieved, none of which need involve force or violence if power is invested in an authority that is seen to be 'legitimate' – a concept which Weber discusses at the beginning of this extract. In a famous and influential typology Weber outlines the three main forms of legitimate authority and domination: legal-rational, traditional and charismatic.

Weber's notion of charisma is particularly interesting. Charismatic authority differs markedly from authority and power based on legal-rational and bureaucratic domination as it is not based on a strict hierarchy, rules or expert knowledge. The 'charismatic individual' can engender awe and a faith in her or his miraculous abilities and can offer a partial way out of the 'iron cage' of rationality and provide temporary relief from the 'disenchantment of the world' (a phrase Weber borrows from the German philosopher Friedrich Schiller).

From: H.H. Gerth and C. Wright Mills, *From Max Weber: Essays in Sociology* (Routledge: London, 1991) pp. 245–8) and T. Parsons (ed.) *Max Weber: The Theory of Social and Economic Organisation* (Free Press: New York, 1968) pp. 130–2, 328–33, 341–3.

The Bases of Legitimacy of an Order

Legitimacy may be ascribed to an order by those acting subject to it in the following ways:–

1. By tradition; a belief in the legitimacy of what has always existed;
2. by virtue of affectual attitudes, especially emotional, legitimizing the validity of what is newly revealed or a model to imitate;
3. by virtue of a rational belief in its absolute value, thus lending it the validity of an absolute and final commitment;
4. because it has been established in a manner which is recognized to be *legal.* This legality may be treated as legitimate in either of two ways: on the one hand, it may derive from a voluntary agreement of the interested parties on the relevant terms. On the other hand, it may be imposed on the basis of what is held to be a legitimate authority over the relevant persons and a corresponding claim to their obedience.

All further details, except for a few other concepts to be defined below, belong in the sociology of law and the sociology of authority. For the present, only a few remarks are necessary.

1. The derivation of the legitimacy of an order from a belief in the sanctity of tradition is the most universal and most primitive case. The fear of magical penalties confirms the general psychological inhibitions against any sort of change in customary modes of action. At the same time the multifarious vested interests which tend to become attached to upholding conformity with an order, once it has become established, have worked in the same direction.

2. Conscious departures from tradition in the establishment of a new order have

originally been due almost entirely to prophetic oracles or at least to pronouncements which have been sanctioned as prophetic. This was true as late as the statutes of the Greek Aisymnetes. Conformity has then depended on belief in the legitimacy of the prophet. In times of strict traditionalism a new order, that is one which was *regarded* as new, could, without being revealed in this way, only become legitimized by the claim that it had actually always been valid though not yet rightly known, or that it had been obscured for a time and was now being restored to its rightful place.

3. The type case of legitimacy by virtue of rational belief in an absolute value is that of 'Natural Law.' However limited its actual effect, as compared with its ideal claims, it cannot be denied that its logically developed reasoning has had an influence on actual action which is far from negligible. This mode of influence should be clearly distinguished from that of a revealed law, of one imposed by authority, or of one which is merely traditional.

4. To-day the most usual basis of legitimacy is the belief in legality, the readiness to conform with rules which are formally correct and have been imposed by accepted procedure. The distinction between an order derived from voluntary agreement and one which has been imposed is only relative. For so far as the agreement underlying the order is not unanimous, as in the past has often been held necessary for complete legitimacy, its functioning within a social group will be dependent on the willingness of individuals with deviant wishes to give way to the majority. This is very frequently the case and actually means that the order is imposed on the minority. At the same time, it is very common for minorities, by force or by the use of more ruthless and far-sighted methods, to impose an order which in the course of time comes to be regarded as legitimate by those who originally resisted it. In so far as the ballot is used as a legal means of altering an order, it is very common for the will of a minority to attain a formal majority and for the majority to submit. In this case majority rule is a mere illusion. The belief in the legality of an order as established by voluntary agreement is relatively ancient and is occasionally found among so-called primitive peoples; but in these cases it is almost always supplemented by the authority of oracles.

5. So far as it is not derived merely from fear or from motives of expediency, a willingness to submit to an order imposed by one man or a small group, always in some sense implies a belief in the legitimate *authority* of the source imposing it.

6. Submission to an order is almost always determined by a variety of motives; by a wide variety of interests and by a mixture of adherence to tradition and belief in legality, unless it is a case of entirely new regulations. In a very large proportion of cases, the actors subject to the order are of course not even aware how far it is a matter of custom, of convention, or of law. In such cases the sociologist must attempt to formulate the typical basis of validity. [. . .]

The Three Pure Types of Legitimate Authority

There are three pure types of legitimate authority. The validity of their claims to legitimacy may be based on:

1. Rational grounds – resting on a belief in the 'legality' of patterns of normative rules and the right of those elevated to authority under such rules to issue commands (legal authority).
2. Traditional grounds – resting on an established belief in the sanctity of immemorial traditions and the legitimacy of the status of those exercising authority under them (traditional authority); or finally,
3. Charismatic grounds – resting on devotion to the specific and exceptional sanctity, heroism or exemplary character of an individual person, and of the normative patterns or order revealed or ordained by him (charismatic authority).

In the case of legal authority, obedience is owed to the legally established impersonal order. It extends to the persons exercising the authority of office under it only by virtue of the formal legality of their commands and only within the scope of authority of the office. In the case of traditional authority, obedience is owed to the *person* of the chief who occupies the traditionally sanctioned position of authority and who is (within its sphere) bound by tradition. But here the obligation of obedience is not based on the impersonal order, but is a matter of personal loyalty within the area of accustomed obligations. In the case of charismatic authority, it is the charismatically qualified leader as such who is obeyed by virtue of personal trust in him and his revelation, his heroism or his exemplary qualities so far as they fall within the scope of the individual's belief in his charisma.

1. The usefulness of the above classification can only be judged by its results in promoting systematic analysis. The concept of 'charisma' ('the gift of grace') is taken from the vocabulary of early Christianity. For the Christian religious organization Rudolf Sohm, in his *Kirchenrecht*, was the first to clarify the substance of the concept, even though he did not use the same terminology. Others (for instance, Hollin, *Enthusiasmus und Bussgewalt*) have clarified certain important consequences of it. It is thus nothing new.

2. The fact that none of these three ideal types, the elucidation of which will occupy the following pages, is usually to be found in historical cases in 'pure' form, is naturally not a valid objection to attempting their conceptual formulation in the sharpest possible form. In this respect the present case is no different from many others. Later on the transformation of pure charisma by the process of routinization will be discussed and thereby the relevance of the concept to the understanding of empirical systems of authority considerably increased. But even so it may be said of every empirically historical phenomenon of authority that it is not likely to be 'as an open book.' Analysis in terms of sociological types has, after all, as compared with purely empirical historical investigation, certain advantages which should not be minimized. That is, it can in the particular case of a concrete form of authority determine what conforms to or approximates such types as 'charisma,' 'hereditary charisma', 'the charisma of office,' 'patriarchy', 'bureaucracy', the authority of status groups, and in doing so it can work with relatively unambiguous concepts. But the idea that the whole of concrete historical reality can be exhausted in the conceptual

scheme about to be developed is as far from the author's thoughts as anything could be.

Legal Authority with a Bureaucratic Administrative Staff

The effectiveness of legal authority rests on the acceptance of the validity of the following mutually inter-dependent ideas.

1. That any given legal norm may be established by agreement or by imposition, on grounds of expediency or rational values or both, with a claim to obedience at least on the part of the members of the corporate group. This is, however, usually extended to include all persons within the sphere of authority or of power in question – which in the case of territorial bodies is the territorial area – who stand in certain social relationships or carry out forms of social action which in the order governing the corporate group have been declared to be relevant.

2. That every body of law consists essentially in a consistent system of abstract rules which have normally been intentionally established. Furthermore, administration of law is held to consist in the application of these rules to particular cases; the administrative process in the rational pursuit of the interests which are specified in the order governing the corporate group within the limits laid down by legal precepts and following principles which are capable of generalized formulation and are approved in the order governing the group, or at least not disapproved in it.

3. That thus the typical person in authority occupies an 'office.' In the action associated with his status, including the commands he issues to others, he is subject to an impersonal order to which his actions are oriented. This is true not only for persons exercising legal authority who are in the usual sense 'officials,' but, for instance, for the elected president of a state.

4. That the person who obeys authority does so, as it is usually stated, only in his capacity as a 'member' of the corporate group and what he obeys is only 'the law.' He may in this connexion be the member of an association, of a territorial commune, of a church, or a citizen of a state.

5. In conformity with point 3, it is held that the members of the corporate group, in so far as they obey a person in authority, do not owe this obedience to him as an individual, but to the impersonal order. Hence, it follows that there is an obligation to obedience only within the sphere of the rationally delimited authority which, in terms of the order, has been conferred upon him.

The following may thus be said to be the fundamental categories of rational legal authority:–

(1) A continuous organization of official functions bound by rules.

(2) A specified sphere of competence. This involves (a) a sphere of obligations to perform functions which has been marked off as part of a systematic division of labour. (b) The provision of the incumbent with the necessary authority to carry out these functions. (c) That the necessary means of compulsion are clearly defined and their use is subject to definite conditions. A unit exercising authority which is organized in this way will be called an 'administrative organ.'

There are administrative organs in this sense in large-scale private organizations, in parties and armies, as well as in the state and the church. An elected president, a cabinet of ministers, or a body of elected representatives also in this sense constitute administrative organs. This is not, however, the place to discuss these concepts. Not every administrative organ is provided with compulsory powers. But this distinction is not important for present purposes.

(3) The organization of offices follows the principle of hierarchy; that is, each lower office is under the control and supervision of a higher one. There is a right of appeal and of statement of grievances from the lower to the higher. Hierarchies differ in respect to whether and in what cases complaints can lead to a ruling from an authority at various points higher in the scale, and as to whether changes are imposed from higher up or the responsibility for such changes is left to the lower office, the conduct of which was the subject of complaint.

(4) The rules which regulate the conduct of an office may be technical rules or norms. In both cases, if their application is to be fully rational, specialized training is necessary. It is thus normally true that only a person who has demonstrated an adequate technical training is qualified to be a member of the administrative staff of such an organized group, and hence only such persons are eligible for appointment to official positions. The administrative staff of a rational corporate group thus typically consists of 'officials,' whether the organization be devoted to political, religious, economic – in particular, capitalistic – or other ends.

(5) In the rational type it is a matter of principle that the members of the administrative staff should be completely separated from ownership of the means of production or administration. Officials, employees, and workers attached to the administrative staff do not themselves own the non-human means of production and administration. These are rather provided for their use in kind or in money, and the official is obligated to render an accounting of their use. There exists, furthermore, in principle complete separation of the property belonging to the organization, which is controlled within the sphere of office, and the personal property of the official, which is available for his own private uses. There is a corresponding separation of the place in which official functions are carried out, the 'office' in the sense of premises, from living quarters.

(6) In the rational type case, there is also a complete absence of appropriation of his official position by the incumbent. Where 'rights' to an office exist, as in the case of judges, and recently of an increasing proportion of officials and even of workers, they do not normally serve the purpose of appropriation by the official, but of securing the purely objective and independent character of the conduct of the office so that it is oriented only to the relevant norms.

(7) Administrative acts, decisions, and rules are formulated and recorded in writing, even in cases where oral discussion is the rule or is even mandatory. This applies at least to preliminary discussions and proposals, to final decisions, and to all sorts of orders and rules. The combination of written documents and a continuous organization of official functions constitutes the 'office' which is the central focus of all types of modern corporate action.

(8) Legal authority can be exercised in a wide variety of different forms which will be distinguished and discussed later. The following analysis will be deliberately confined for the most part to the aspect of imperative co-ordination in the structure of the administrative staff. It will consist in an analysis in terms of ideal types of officialdom or 'bureaucracy.'

In the above outline no mention has been made of the kind of supreme head appropriate to a system of legal authority. This is a consequence of certain considerations which can only be made entirely understandable at a later stage in the analysis. There are very important types of rational imperative co-ordination which, with respect to the ultimate source of authority, belong to other categories. This is true of the hereditary charismatic type, as illustrated by hereditary monarchy and of the pure charismatic type of a president chosen by plebiscite. Other cases involve rational elements at important points, but are made up of a combination of bureaucratic and charismatic components, as is true of the cabinet form of government. Still others are subject to the authority of the chief of other corporate groups, whether their character be charismatic or bureaucratic; thus the formal head of a government department under a parliamentary regime may be a minister who occupies his position because of his authority in a party. The type of rational, legal administrative staff is capable of application in all kinds of situations and contexts. It is the most important mechanism for the administration of everyday profane affairs. For in that sphere, the exercise of authority and, more broadly, imperative co-ordination, consists precisely in administration. [. . .]

Traditional Authority

A system of imperative co-ordination will be called 'traditional' if legitimacy is claimed for it and believed in on the basis of the sanctity of the order and the attendant powers of control as they have been handed down from the past, 'have always existed.' The person or persons exercising authority are designated according to traditionally transmitted rules. The object of obedience is the personal authority of the individual which he enjoys by virtue of his traditional status. The organized group exercising authority is, in the simplest case, primarily based on relations of personal loyalty, cultivated through a common process of education. The person exercising authority is not a 'superior,' but a personal 'chief.'

His administrative staff does not consist primarily of officials, but of personal retainers. Those subject to authority are not 'members' of an association, but are either his traditional 'comrades' or his 'subjects.' What determines the relations of the administrative staff to the chief is not the impersonal obligation of office, but personal loyalty to the chief.

Obedience is not owed to enacted rules, but to the person who occupies a position of authority by tradition or who has been chosen for such a position on a traditional basis. His commands are legitimized in one of two ways: 1. partly in terms of traditions which themselves directly determine the content of the command and the objects and extent of authority. In so far as this is true, to overstep the traditional limitations would endanger his traditional status by undermining acceptance of his legitimacy. 2. In part, it is a matter of the chief's free personal decision, in that tradition leaves a certain sphere open for this. This sphere of traditional prerogative rests primarily on the fact that the obligations of obedience on the basis of personal loyalty are essentially unlimited. There is thus a double sphere: on the one hand, of action which is bound to specific tradition; on the other hand, of that which is free of any specific rules.

In the latter sphere, the chief is free to confer 'grace' on the basis of his personal pleasure or displeasure, his personal likes and dislikes, quite arbitrarily, particularly in return for gifts which often become a source of regular income. So far as his action follows principles at all, these are principles of substantive ethical common sense, of justice, or of utilitatrian expediency. They are not, however, as in the case of legal authority, formal principles. The exercise of authority is normally oriented to the question of what the chief and his administrative staff will normally permit, in view of the traditional obedience of the subjects and what will or will not arouse their resistance. When resistance occurs, it is directed against the person of the chief or of a member of his staff. The accusation is that he has failed to observe the traditional limits of his authority. Opposition is not directed against the system as such.

It is impossible in the pure type of traditional authority for law or administrative rules to be deliberately created by legislation. What is actually new is thus claimed to have always been in force but only recently to have become known through the wisdom of the promulgator. The only documents which can play a part in the orientation of legal administration are the documents of tradition; namely, precedents.

A traditional chief exercises authority with or without an administrative staff. The typical administrative staff is recruited from one or more of the following sources:

(1) From persons who are already related to the chief by traditional ties of personal loyalty. This will be called 'patrimonial' recruitment. Such persons may be kinsmen, slaves, dependents who are officers of the household, clients, coloni, or freedmen.

(2) It may be recruited from other sources on an 'extra-patrimonial' basis. This category includes people in a relation of purely personal loyalty, such as all sorts of 'favourites,' people standing in a relation of fealty to their chief – 'vassals' – and, finally, those who have of their own free will entered into a relation of personal loyalty as officials.

In traditionalistic organizations, it is very common for the most important posts to be filled with members of a ruling family or clan.

In patrimonial administrations, it is common for slaves or freedmen to rise even to the highest positions. It has not been uncommon even for Grand Viziers to have been at one time slaves.

The typical household officials have been the following: the senechal, the marshal (once in charge of horses), the chamberlain, the carver, the steward, who was the head of the service personnel and possibly even of the vassals. These are to be found everywhere in Europe. In the Orient, in addition, the head eunuch, who was in charge of the harem, has been particularly important. In the African kingdoms, the executioner is often included. Universally, the body physician, the astrologer, and various others have been common.

In China and in Egypt, the principal source of recruitment for patrimonial officials lay in the clientele of the king. Armies of coloni have been known throughout the Orient and were typical of the Roman nobility. Even in modern times, in the Mohammedan world, armies of slaves have existed.

The regime of 'favourites' is characteristic of every patrimonial system and has often been the occasion for 'traditionalistic' revolutions.

The status of 'vassal' will be dealt with separately.

Bureaucracy has first developed in patrimonial states with a body of officials recruited from extra-patrimonial sources; but, as will be shown presently, these 'officials' have originally been personal followers of their chief.

In the pure type of traditional authority, the following features of a bureaucratic administrative staff are absent: (a) a clearly defined sphere of competence subject to impersonal rules, (b) a rational ordering of relations of superiority and inferiority, (c) a regular system of appointment and promotion on the basis of free contract, (d) technical training as a regular requirement, (e) fixed salaries, in the type case paid in money. [. . .]

Charismatic Authority

Bureaucratic and patriarchal structures are antagonistic in many ways, yet they have in common a most important peculiarity: permanence. In this respect they are both institutions of daily routine. Patriarchal power especially is rooted in the provisioning of recurrent and normal needs of the workaday life. Patriarchal authority thus has its original locus in the economy, that is, in those branches of the economy that can be satisfied by means of normal routine. The patriarch is the 'natural leader' of the daily routine. And in this respect, the bureaucratic structure is only the counter-image of patriarchalism transposed into rationality. As a permanent structure with a system of rational rules, bureaucracy is fashioned to meet calculable and recurrent needs by means of a normal routine.

The provisioning of all demands that go beyond those of everyday routine has had, in principle, an entirely heterogeneous, namely, a *charismatic*, foundation; the further back we look in history, the more we find this to be the case. This means that the 'natural' leaders – in times of psychic, physical, economic, ethical, religious, political distress – have been neither officeholders nor incumbents of an 'occupation' in the present sense of the word, that is, men who have acquired expert knowledge and who serve for remuneration. The natural leaders in distress have been holders of specific gifts of the body and spirit; and these gifts have been believed to be supernatural, not accessible to everybody. The concept of 'charisma' is here used in a completely 'value-neutral' sense.

The capacity of the Irish culture hero, Cuchulain, or of the Homeric Achilles for heroic frenzy is a manic seizure, just as is that of the Arabian berserk who bites his shield like a mad dog – biting around until he darts off in raving bloodthirstiness. For a long time it has been maintained that the seizure of the berserk is artificially produced through acute poisoning. In Byzantium, a number of 'blond beasts,' disposed to such seizures, were kept about, just as war elephants were formerly kept. Shamanist ecstasy is linked to constitutional epilepsy, the possession and the testing of which represents a charismatic qualification. Hence neither is 'edifying' to our minds. They are just as little edifying to us as is the kind of 'revelation,' for instance, of the Sacred Book of the Mormons, which, at least from an evaluative standpoint, perhaps would have to be called a 'hoax.' But sociology is not concerned with such questions. In the faith of their followers, the chief of the Mormons has proved himself to be charismatically qualified, as have 'heroes' and 'sorcerers.' All of them have practiced their arts and ruled by virtue of this gift (charisma) and, where the idea of God has already been clearly conceived, by virtue of the divine mission lying therein. This holds for doctors and prophets, just as for judges and military leaders, or for leaders of big hunting expeditions.

It is to his credit that Rudolf Sohm brought out the sociological peculiarity of this category of domination-structure for a historically important special case, namely, the historical development of the authority of the early Christian church. Sohm performed this task with logical consistency, and hence, by necessity, he was one-sided from a purely historical point of view. In principle, however, the very same state of affairs recurs universally, although often it is most clearly developed in the field of religion.

In contrast to any kind of bureaucratic organization of offices, the charismatic structure knows nothing of a form or of an ordered procedure of appointment or dismissal. It knows no regulated 'career,' 'advancement,' 'salary,' or regulated and expert training of the holder of charisma or of his aids. It knows no agency of control or appeal, no local bailiwicks or exclusive functional jurisdictions; nor does it embrace permanent institutions like our bureaucratic 'departments,' which are independent of persons and of purely personal charisma.

Charisma knows only inner determination and inner restraint. The holder of charisma seizes the task that is adequate for him and demands obedience and a following by virtue of his mission. His success determines whether he finds them. His charismatic claim breaks down if his mission is not recognized by those to whom he feels he has been sent. If they recognize him, he is their master – so long as he knows how to maintain recognition through 'proving' himself. But he does not derive his 'right' from their will, in the manner of an election. Rather, the reverse holds: it is the *duty* of those to whom he addresses his mission to recognize him as their charismatically qualified leader.

In Chinese theory, the emperor's prerogatives are made dependent upon the recognition of the people. But this does not mean recognition of the sovereignty of the people any more than did the prophet's necessity of getting recognition from the believers in the early Christian community. The Chinese theory, rather, characterizes the charismatic nature of the *monarch's position*, which adheres to his *personal* qualification and to his *proved* worth.

Charisma can be, and of course regularly is, qualitatively particularized. This is an internal rather than an external affair, and results in the qualitative barrier of the charisma holder's mission and power. In meaning and in content the mission may be addressed to a group of men who are delimited locally, ethnically, socially, politically, occupationally, or in some other way. If the mission is thus addressed to a limited group of men, as is the rule, it finds its limits within their circle.

In its economic sub-structure, as in everything else, charismatic domination is the very opposite of bureaucratic domination. If bureaucratic domination depends upon regular income, and hence at least *a potiori* on a money economy and money taxes, charisma lives in, though not off, this world. This has to be properly understood. Frequently charisma quite deliberately shuns the possession of money and of pecuniary income *per se*, as did Saint Francis and many of his like; but this is of course not the rule. Even a pirate genius may exercise a 'charismatic' domination, in the value-neutral sense intended here. Charismatic political heroes seek booty and, above all, gold. But charisma, and this is decisive, always rejects as undignified any pecuniary gain that is methodical and rational. In general, charisma rejects all rational economic conduct.

The sharp contrast between charisma and any 'patriarchal' structure that rests upon the ordered base of the 'household' lies in this rejection of rational economic conduct. In its 'pure' form, charisma is never a source of private gain for its holders in the sense of economic exploitation by the making of a deal. Nor is it a source of income in the form of pecuniary compensation, and just as little does it involve an orderly taxation for the material requirements of its mission. If the mission is one of peace, individual patrons provide the necessary means for charismatic structures; or those to whom the charisma is addressed provide honorific gifts, donations, or other voluntary contributions. In the case of charismatic warrior heroes, booty represents one of the ends as well as the material means of the mission. 'Pure' charisma is contrary to all patriarchal domination (in the sense of the term used here). It is the opposite of all ordered economy. It is the very force that disregards economy. This also holds, indeed precisely, where the charismatic leader is after the acquisition of goods, as is the case with the charismatic warrior hero. Charisma can do this because by its very nature it is not an 'institutional' and permanent structure, but rather, where its 'pure' type is at work, it is the very opposite of the institutionally permanent.

In order to do justice to their mission, the holders of charisma, the master as well as his disciples and followers, must stand outside the ties of this world, outside of routine occupations, as well as outside the routine obligations of family life. The statutes of the Jesuit order preclude the acceptance of church offices; the members of orders are forbidden to own property or, according to the original rule of St Francis, the order as such is forbidden to do so. The priest and the knight of an order have to live in celibacy, and numerous holders of a prophetic or artistic charisma are actually single. All this is indicative of the unavoidable separation from this world of those who partake ('χλῆροξ') of charisma. In these respects, the economic conditions of participation in charisma may have an (apparently) antagonistic appearance, depending upon the type of charisma – artistic or religious, for instance – and the way of life flowing from its meaning. Modern charismatic movements of artistic origin represent 'independents without gainful employment' (in everyday language, rentiers). Normally such persons are the best qualified to follow a charismatic leader. This is just as logically consistent as was the medieval friar's vow of poverty, which demanded the very opposite.

Guide To Further Reading

[The original date of publication is given in brackets where appropriate]

The Protestant Ethic and The Spirit of Capitalism (Allen and Unwin: London, 1978) [1904–5]

The City (ed. D. Martindale and G. Neuwrith, Heinemann: London, 1958) [1921]

Economy and Society Volumes 1 and 2 (G. Roth and C. Wittich eds, University of California Press: Berkeley, 1978)

General Economic History (Allen and Unwin: London, 1923) [1922]

The Sociology of Religion (Beacon Press: Boston, 1964) [1922]

The Methodology of the Social Sciences (ed. E. A. Shils and H. A. Finch, The Free Press: New York, 1949)

The Theory of Social and Economic Organisation (ed. T. Parsons, Free Press: New York, 1968)

From Max Weber: Essays in Sociology (ed. H. H. Gerth and C. Wright Mills, Routledge: London, 1991)

The Protestant Ethic and the Spirit of Capitalism is the best place to begin reading Weber. Tackling the volumes of *Economy and Society* can be a daunting experience and looking at collections of his writing, such as this one of course, would probably be the most sensible course of action. Many of the key parts of *Economy and Society*, and other selections, can be found in *From Max Weber: Essays in Sociology* (Routledge: London, 1991) edited by H. H. Gerth and C. Wright Mills, who also provide excellent biographical and introductory essays. W. G. Runciman's *Max Weber: Selections in Transition* (Cambridge University Press: Cambridge, 1978) and *The Theory of Social and Economic Organisation* (Free Press: New York, 1947) edited by Talcott Parsons are also good sources. Weber's influential discussion of 'The City' in *Economy and Society* is reproduced in a more user-friendly form in D. Martindale and G. Neuwrith (eds) *The City* (Heinemann: London, 1958), which also contains an excellent introduction. Weber's *General Economic History* (Allen and Unwin: London, 1923) was put together, after Weber's death, from his students' lecture notes from a wide-ranging series of lectures given in 1919–20 and contains a wealth of material from the 'evolution of the family' to the 'origin of modern capitalism'.

The classic biography of Weber is that of Marianne Weber, but weighing in at over 700 minutely detailed pages it is somewhat off-putting. The essay *'A Biographical View'* in the aforementioned collection edited by Gerth and Mills probably gives as much detail of Weber's life as one would require. Martin Albrow's *Max Weber's Construction of Social Theory* (Macmillan: London, 1990) also gives a good overview of his life and thought as does D. Kassler's *Max Weber: An Introduction to his Life and Work* (Polity: Oxford, 1988). A good short and critical introduction is *Max Weber* (Tavistock: London, 1982) by Frank Parkin. *Max Weber: An Intellectual Portrait* (Methuen: London, 1960) by Reinhard Bendix is also worth looking at and contains an extensive review of Weber's work on comparative religions. Wolfgang Mommsen's *The Age of Bureaucracy: Perspectives on the Political Sociology of Max Weber* (Blackwell: Oxford, 1978) is a nicely written account of Weber's views on power, politics and his pessimism over the fate of modern society. Derek Sayer's *Capitalism and Modernity: An Excursus on Marx and Weber* (Routledge: London, 1991) is a superb and fascinating comparison of a Marxist and Weberian account of modernity, and R. Brubaker's *The Limits of Rationality: An Essay on the Social and Moral Thought of Max Weber* (Allen and Unwin: London, 1984) takes a detailed look at Weber's notion of 'rationality'. Finally, Karl Lowith's *Max Weber and Karl Marx* (Allen and Unwin: London, 1982) is a classic and brilliant study (first published in 1932) which revolves around a comparison of Weber's concept of 'rationality' and Marx's discussion of 'alienation'. The 'Protestant ethic thesis' is dealt with in Gianfranco Poggi's *Calvinism and the Capitalist Spirit: Max Weber's Protestant Ethic* (Macmillan: London, 1983) and in *In Search of the Spirit of Capitalism: An Essay on Max Weber's Protestant Ethic Thesis* (Hutchinson: London, 1982) by Gordon Marshall.

SECTION THREE
EMILE DURKHEIM

EMILE DURKHEIM: A BRIEF BIOGRAPHY

David Emile Durkheim was born in 1858 in Epinal in France. His father, grandfather and great-grandfather were rabbis. His mother was the daughter of a trader. Durkheim grew up within the context of a tight-knit and traditional Jewish family of modest income, themselves part of a long-established Jewish community, and it seemed that he was destined to carry on the family tradition. However, for reasons never made clear, Durkheim decided not to proceed along this chosen path. In 1879, at the third attempt, he was finally admitted to the prestigious Ecole Normale Supérieure in Paris. Durkheim left Paris to take up a number of posts where he taught philosophy. During the mid-1880s he worked on his doctorates (the subsidiary thesis had to be written in Latin) – the principal thesis was to become *The Division of Labour* – and was awarded a scholarship to visit several German Universities, after which he wrote two reports that were well received and established his reputation as a social thinker of great potential. In 1887 he married Louise Dreyfus and took up a post, specially created for him, at the University of Bordeaux. Although Durkheim was appointed (as with his position at the Sorbonne) to lecture mainly on education, an area in which he produced a number of influential writings, he devoted much of his energies to establishing sociology as an academic discipline with its own object of study and distinctive perspective indeed Durkheim was probably the first professional, university based sociologist. In 1895 his efforts were rewarded when he was given the first French chair of social science. His time at Bordeaux (1887–1902) was incredibly productive. Apart from numerous articles, papers and other writings he also published *The Division of Labour* (1893), *The Rules of Sociological Method* (1895), and *Suicide* (1897). In 1896 with the help of some colleagues he founded a new journal, the influential *Année Sociologique*, believing that this would do more to establish sociology than any single work could ever do. Durkheim was also a popular public speaker and lecturer giving courses on, amongst other things, the family, criminology, education, the history of socialism and religion – the later course, first offered in 1894–5, being of particular importance to the development of Durkheim's thought – and he was involved in a number of the social and political issues of the day, most notably the Dreyfus affair.

In 1902 Durkheim moved back to Paris to take up a position at the Sorbonne and by this time he was the best known and most influential figure within French, if not European, sociology. In Paris he completed his most ambitious work, the monumental *The Elementary Forms of the Religious Life* (1912) which was both a brilliant sociological account of the origins and practice of religion and the social basis of our basic categories of thought.

Durkheim was a fervent French patriot and, at the outbreak of the First World War, threw himself into a wide range of activities for the French 'war effort'; writing numerous reports and pamphlets and working tirelessly on endless committees. During the war many of his students were killed and Durkheim lost much of his motivation for academic work. In 1916 his son André, one of his most brilliant students, was killed in action and Durkheim's already failing health never recovered. He died a year later at the age of fifty-nine.

3.1 *The Division of Labour in Society*: Introduction

First published in 1893, *The Division of Labour in Society* was Durkheim's first major work and identified a number of issues and themes that were to recur throughout many of his writings. In this extract Durkheim discusses the widespread growth of the division of labour across many areas of social life, not just economic life, and poses questions as to how we should respond to this tendency and what impact it will have on our 'moral constitution'.

From: E. Durkheim, *The Division of Labour in Society* (Macmillan: London, 1984) pp. 1–5.

The Problem

Although the division of labour is not of recent origin, it was only at the end of the last century that societies began to become aware of this law, to which up to then they had submitted almost unwittingly. Undoubtedly even from antiquity several thinkers had perceived its importance. Yet Adam Smith was the first to attempt to elaborate the theory of it. Moreover, it was he who first coined the term, which social science later lent to biology.

Nowadays the phenomenon has become so widespread that it catches everyone's attention. We can no longer be under any illusion about the trends in modern industry. It involves increasingly powerful mechanisms, large-scale groupings of power and capital, and consequently an extreme division of labour. Inside factories, not only are jobs demarcated, becoming extremely specialised, but each product is itself a speciality entailing the existence of others. Adam Smith and John Stuart Mill persisted in hoping that agriculture at least would prove an exception to the rule, seeing in it the last refuge of small-scale ownership. Although in such a matter we must guard against generalising unduly, nowadays it appears difficult to deny that the main branches of the agricultural industry are increasingly swept along in the general trend. Finally, commerce itself contrives ways to follow and reflect, in all their distinctive nuances, the boundless diversity of industrial undertakings. Although this evolution occurs spontaneously and unthinkingly, those economists who study its causes and evaluate its results, far from condemning such diversification or attacking it, proclaim its necessity. They perceive in it the higher law of human societies and the condition for progress.

Yet the division of labour is not peculiar to economic life. We can observe its increasing influence in the most diverse sectors of society. Functions, whether political, administrative or judicial, are becoming more and more specialised. The same is true in the arts and sciences. The time lies far behind us when philosophy constituted the sole science. It has become fragmented into a host of special disciplines, each having its purpose, method and ethos. 'From one half-century to another the men who have left their mark upon the sciences have become more specialized.'

Having to pinpoint the nature of the studies which for over two centuries had engaged the most celebrated scientists, de Candolle noted that in the age of Leibnitz and Newton he would have had to write down:

> two or three descriptions almost always for each scientist: for example, astronomer and physicist, or mathematician, astronomer and physicist, or alternatively, to use only such general terms as philosopher or naturalist. Even that would not have been enough. Mathematicians and naturalists were sometimes scholars or poets. Even at the end of the eighteenth century, a number of designations would have been needed to indicate precisely what was remarkable about men such as Wolff, Haller or Charles Bonnet in several different branches of science and letters. In the nineteenth century this difficulty no longer exists or at least occurs very infrequently.

Not only is the scientist no longer immersed in different sciences at the same time, but he can no longer encompass the whole field of one science. The range of his research is limited to a finite category of problems or even to a single one of them. Likewise, the functions of the scientist which formerly were almost always exercised alongside another more lucrative one, such as that of doctor, priest, magistrate or soldier, are increasingly sufficient by themselves. De Candolle even predicts that one day not too far distant the profession of scientist and that of teacher, at present still so closely linked, will be irrevocably separated.

The recent philosophical speculations in biology have finally caused us to realise that the division of labour is a fact of a generality that the economists, who were the first to speak of it, had been incapable of suspecting. Indeed, since the work of Wolff, von Baer and Milne-Edwards we know that the law of the division of labour applies to organisms as well as to societies. It may even be stated that an organism occupies the more exalted a place in the animal hierarchy the more specialised its functions are. This discovery has had the result of not only enlarging enormously the field of action of the division of labour, but also of setting its origins back into an infinitely distant past, since it becomes almost contemporaneous with the coming of life upon earth. It is no longer a mere social institution whose roots lie in the intelligence and the will of men, but a general biological phenomenon, the conditions for which must seemingly be sought in the essential properties of organised matter. The division of labour in society appears no more than a special form of this general development. In conforming to this law societies apparently yield to a movement that arose long before they existed and which sweeps along in the same direction the whole of the living world.

Such a fact clearly cannot manifest itself without affecting profoundly our moral constitution, for the evolution of mankind will develop in two utterly opposing directions, depending on whether we abandon ourselves to this tendency or whether we resist it. Yet, then, one question poses itself urgently: of these two directions, which one should we choose? Is it our duty to seek to become a rounded, complete creature, a whole sufficient unto itself or, on the contrary, to be only a part of the whole, the organ of an organism? In short, whilst the division of labour is a law of nature, is it also a moral rule for human conduct and, if it possesses this last characteristic, through what causes and to what extent? There is no need to demonstrate the serious nature of this practical problem: whatever assessment we make of the division of labour, we all sense that it is, and increasingly so, one of the fundamental bases of the social order.

The problem is one that the moral consciousness of nations has often posed, but in a muddled fashion, and without being able to resolve it. Two opposing tendencies confront one another, and neither has succeeded in gaining entirely the upper hand.

It seems undoubtedly clear that the view is gaining ground that the division of labour should become a categorical rule of behaviour, one that should be imposed as a duty. It is true that those who infringe it are not meted out any precise punishment laid down by law, but they do suffer rebuke. The time is past when the perfect man seemed to us the one who, capable of being interested in everything but attaching himself exclusively to nothing, able to savour everything and understand everything, found the means to combine and epitomise within himself the finest aspects of civilisation. Today that general culture, once so highly extolled, no longer impresses us save as a flabby, lax form of discipline. To struggle against nature we need to possess more vigorous faculties, deploy more productive energies. We desire our activity to be concentrated, instead of being scattered over a wide area, gaining in intensity what it has lost in breadth. We are wary of those too volatile men of talent, who, lending themselves equally to all forms of employment, refuse to choose for themselves a special role and to adhere to it. We feel a coolness towards those men whose sole preoccupation is to organise their faculties, limbering them up, but without putting them to any special use or sacrificing a single one, as if each man among them ought to be self-sufficient, constituting his own independent world. It appears to us that such a state of detachment and indeterminateness is somewhat antisocial. The man of parts, as he once was, is for us no more than a dilettante, and we accord no moral value to dilettantism. Rather, do we perceive perfection in the competent man, one who seeks not to be complete but to be productive, one who has a well-defined job to which he devotes himself, and carries out his task, ploughing his single furrow. 'To perfect oneself,' says Secrétant, 'is to learn one's role, to make oneself fit to fulfil one's function . . . The yardstick for our perfection is no longer to be found in satisfaction with ourselves, in the plaudits of the crowd or the approving smile of an affected dilettantism, but in the sum total of services rendered, and in our ability to continue to render them. Thus the moral ideal, from being the sole one, simple and impersonal, has become increasingly diversified. We no longer think that the exclusive duty of man is to realise within himself the qualities of man in general, but we believe that he is no less obliged to have those qualities that relate to his employment. One fact, among others, reflects this view: this is the increasingly specialist character assumed by education. More and more we deem it necessary not to subject all children to a uniform culture, as if all were destined to lead the same life, but to train them differently according to the varying functions they will be called upon to fulfil. In short, in one of its aspects the categorical imperative of the moral consciousness is coming to assume the following form: *Equip yourself to fulfil usefully a specific function.*

Yet, confronted with these facts, we can cite others that contradict them. If public opinion recognises the rule of the division of labour, it is not without some anxiety and hesitation. Whilst commanding men to specialise, it has always seemingly the fear that they will do so to excess. Side by side with maxims extolling intensive labour are others, no less widely current, which alert us to its dangers. 'It is,' declares Jean-Baptiste Say, 'sad to have to confess that one has never produced more than the eighteenth part of a pin; and do not let us imagine that it is solely the workman who all his life wields a file and hammer, who demeans the dignity of his nature in this way. It is also the man who, through his status, exercises the most subtle faculties of his mind.' At the very beginning of the century Lemontey, comparing the existence of the modern worker to the free and easy life of the savage, found the latter more favoured than the former. Nor is de Tocqueville any less severe. 'As the principle of the division of labour is ever increasingly applied,' he states, 'art makes progress but the artisan regresses.' Generally speaking, the maxim that decrees that we should specialise is as if refuted everywhere by its opposite, which bids us all realise the same ideal, one that is far from having lost all authority. In principle this conflict of ideas is certainly not surprising. Moral life, like that of body and mind, responds to different needs which may even be contradictory. Thus it is natural for it to be made up in part of opposing elements, which have a mutually limiting and balancing effect. Nevertheless, there is truly something about so marked an antimony which should trouble the moral consciousness of nations. It needs indeed to be able to explain how such a contradiction can arise.

3.2 Sanctions and Mechanical and Organic Solidarity

For Durkheim, simple societies with an undeveloped division of labour have strong and well-defined states of the 'conscience collective' and a 'mechanical' form of social solidarity. As the division of labour becomes more differentiated, societies become more complex and people more individualistic. The 'conscience collective' diminishes in its impact and the form of solidarity bonding individuals together changes to what Durkheim terms 'organic solidarity'.

The form of punishment meted out to those who undertake a 'criminal' act is seen by Durkheim to be a visible indicator of the strength of the 'conscience collective'. 'Repressive' sanctions are evidence of a society with a well-defined 'conscience collective' and 'restitutive' sanctions are more typical of social forms of the organic type. Durkheim's discussion of solidarity and sanctions is one of his most influential and original, particularly when set against the individualistic perspective of utilitarianism prevalent at the time. In particular, 'Durkheim's assertion that there is no such thing as an inherently criminal act, as it is the social reaction to the act which defines it as such, has been of lasting influence within fields of criminology and the sociology of deviance.

From: A. Giddens, *Emile Durkheim: Selected Writings* (Cambridge University Press, 1972 pp. 123–8, 135–40.

The link of social solidarity to which repressive law corresponds is one whose break constitutes a crime; we give this name to every act which, in any degree whatever, evokes against its author the characteristic reaction which we term 'punishment'. To seek the nature of this link is thus to ask what is the cause of punishment, or, more precisely what crime essentially consists in . . .

. . .an act is criminal when it offends strong and defined states of the *conscience collective.* The statement of this proposition is rarely disputed, but it is ordinarily given a sense very different from that which it ought to have. We take it as if it expressed, not the essential property of crime, but one of its repercussions. We well know that crime violates very general and intense sentiments; but we believe that this generality and intensity derive from the criminal character of the act, which consequently remains to be defined. We do not deny that every delict is universally condemned, but we take as agreed that the condemnation to which it is subjected results from its delinquent character. Then, however, we are hard put to say in what its delinquent character consists. Is it to be found in an especially serious transgression? Perhaps so; but that is simply to restate the question by putting one word in place of another, for it is precisely the problem to understand what this transgression is, and particularly this specific transgression which society reproves by means of organised punishment and which constitutes eriminality. It can evidently come only from one or several characteristics common to all criminological types. The only one which satisfies this condition is the very opposition between a crime, whatever it may be, and certain collective sentiments. It is, accordingly, this opposition which forms the crime, rather than being a derivation of crime. In other words, we must not say that an action shocks the *conscience collective* because it is criminal, but rather that it is criminal because it shocks the *conscience collective*. We do not condemn it because it is a crime, but it is a crime because we condemn it. As for the intrinsic nature of these sentiments, it is impossible to specify them; they have the most diverse objects and cannot be encompassed in a single formula. We cannot say that they relate to the vital interests of society, or to a minimum of justice: all such definitions are inadequate. By this alone can we recognise it: a sentiment, whatever its origin and end, is found in all minds with a certain degree of strength and clarity, and every action which violates it is a crime [. . .]

Punishment is, first and foremost, an emotional reaction. This character is especially apparent in less developed societies. Primitive peoples punish for the sake of punishing, making the guilty party suffer solely for the sake of making him suffer and without seeking any advantage for themselves from the suffering which they impose. The proof of this is that they seek neither to strike back justly nor to strike back usefully, but merely to strike back. Thus they punish animals which have committed a wrong-doing and even inanimate objects which were its passive instrument. When punishment is applied only to people, it often extends further than the guilty party and reaches the innocent, his wife, his children, his neighbours, etc. That is because the passion which is the spirit of punishment ceases only when it is exhausted. If, therefore, after it has destroyed the one who immediately called it forth, it still remains strong, it expands in a quite mechanical fashion. Even when it is fairly mild, and relates only to the guilty party, it makes its presence felt by the tendency to surpass in severity the action against which it is reacting. That is the origin of the refinements of suffering added to capital punishment. Even in Rome the thief not only had to return the stolen object, but also pay retribution of double and quadruple the amount. Moreover, is not the very common punishment of the *lex talionis* a mode of satisfying the passion for vengeance?

But today, it is said, punishment has changed its character; it is no longer to avenge itself that society punishes, it is to defend itself. The suffering which it inflicts is in its hands no longer anything but a methodical means of protection. It punishes, not because chastisement offers it any intrinsic satisfaction, but so that the fear of punishment may paralyse those who contemplate evil. It is no longer anger, but a well thought-out precaution which determines repression. The preceding observations could not then be generalised; they would refer only to the primitive form of punishment and would not extend to the modern form.

But to justify such a radical distinction between these two sorts of punishment, it is not enough to state that they are employed with different ends in view. The nature of a practice does not necessarily change because the conscious intentions of those who apply it are modified. It might, in fact, still play the same role as before, but without this being perceived. In this case, why should it only become changed in that we are more aware of the effects which it produces? It adapts itself to new conditions of existence without any essential changes. This is the case with punishment. In fact, it is a mistake to believe that vengeance is simply useless cruelty. It is very possible that, in itself, it consists of a mechanical and aimless reaction, an emotional and unthinking action, an irrational need to destroy; but, in reality, it does tend to destroy that which is a threat to us. It consists, then, in a true act of defence, although an instinctive and unreflective one. We avenge ourselves only upon what has harmed us, and what has harmed us is always a threat. The instinct of vengeance is, in sum, only the instinct of conservation heightened by peril. Thus, vengeance is far from having had the negative and sterile role in the history of mankind which is attributed to it. It is a defensive weapon which has a definite value, although it is a crude weapon. Since it is not informed with an awareness of the end it serves, but functions automatically, it cannot, consequently, regulate itself, but responds rather haphazardly to the blind causes which urge it on, without anything moderating its responses. Today, as we understand more clearly the end to be attained, we know better how to utilise the means at our disposal; we protect ourselves more systematically and, accordingly, more efficiently. But this result was also obtained previously, although in a rather imperfect manner. There is no radical division between the punishment of today and yesterday, and consequently it was not necessary for the latter to change its nature in order to accommodate itself to the role that it plays in our civilised societies. The whole difference derives from the fact that it now produces its effects with a heightened awareness of what it does. But, although the individual or social consciousness may not be without influence upon the reality that it clarifies, it has not the power to change its nature. The internal structure of the phenomenon remains the same, whether men be conscious of it or not. We may thus conclude that the essential elements of punishment are the same as of old.

And in fact, punishment has remained, at least in part, a work of vengeance. It is said that we do not make the guilty party suffer for the sake of suffering; it is nonetheless true that we find it right that he should suffer. Perhaps we are wrong, but that is not the question. We seek, at the moment, to define punishment as it is or has been, not as it ought to be. It is certain that this expression of public prosecution which finds its way again and again into the language of the courts is not a mere expression. In supposing that punishment can really serve to protect us in the future, we think that it must be above all an *expiation* of the past. This is shown by the minute precautions we take to allot punishment as exactly as possible in relation to the severity of the crime; this would be inexplicable if we did not believe that the guilty party ought to suffer because of his wrongdoing, and in the same degree. This gradation is not necessary if punishment is only a means of defence. No doubt, there would be danger for society if the most serious offences were treated as simple transgressions; but it would be greater, in the majority of cases, if the latter were treated in the same way as the former. Against an enemy, we cannot take too much precaution. Shall we say that the authors of the smallest misdeeds have less perverse natures, and that to neutralise their criminal instincts less stringent punishments will suffice? But if their inclinations are less vicious they are not on that account less intense. Robbers are as strongly inclined to rob as murderers are to murder; the resistance offered by the former is not less than that of the latter, and consequently, to control it, we would have recourse to the same means. If, as has been said, it was solely a question of putting down a noxious force by an opposing force, the intensity of the second would be measured solely by the intensity of the first, without the quality of the latter entering into the consideration.

The penal scale would then encompass only a small number of gradations. Punishment would vary only as the criminal is more or less hardened, and not according to the nature of the criminal act. An incorrigible robber would be treated in the same way as an incorrigible murderer. But, in fact, if it were shown that a misdoer was completely incurable, we would still not feel bound to punish him excessively. This is proof that we are faithful to the talion principle, although we apply it in a more refined sense than previously. We no longer measure in so material and gross a manner either the extent of the deed or of the punishment; but we still think that there ought to be an equation between the two terms, whether or not we benefit from this balance. Punishment thus remains for us what it was for our forefathers. It is still an act of vengeance since it is an expiation. What we avenge, what the criminal expiates, is the outrage to morality [. . .]

As for the social character of this reaction, it comes from the social nature of the offended sentiments. Because they are found in the consciousness of every individual, the infraction which has been committed arouses the same indignation in those who witness it or who learn of its existence. Everybody is attacked; consequently, everybody opposes the attack. Not only is the reaction general, but it is collective, which is not the same thing. It is not produced in an isolated manner in each individual, but is a total, unified response, even if this varies according to the case. In fact, in the same way as contrary sentiments repel each other, similar sentiments attract each other, and they attract as strongly as they themselves are intense. As contradiction is a threat which stirs them, it adds to their force of attraction. Never do we feel the need of the company of our compatriots so greatly as when we are in a foreign country; never does the believer feel so strongly attracted to his fellow believers as during periods of persecution. Of course, we always love the company of those who feel and think as we do, but it is with passion, and no longer solely with pleasure, that we seek it immediately after discussions where our common beliefs have been directly attacked. Crime brings together honest men and concentrates them. We have only to notice what happens, particularly in a small town, when some moral scandal has just occurred. Men stop each other on te street, they visit each other , they seek to come together to talk of the event and to wax indignant in common. From all the similar impressions which are exchanged, and the anger that is expressed, there emerges a unique emotion, more or less determinate according to the circumstances, which emanates from no specific person, but from everyone. This is the public wrath.

Moreover, this is what gives it its functions: the sentiments in question derive all their force from the fact that they are common to everyone. They are strong because they are unquestioned. It is the fact that they are universally respected which gives them the specific respect which they are accorded. Now, crime is possible only if this respect is not truly universal; consequently, it implies that they are not absolutely collective, and thus damages this unanimity which is the source of their authority. If, then, when a crime takes place, the individuals whom it offends do not unite to manifest what they share in common, and to affirm that the case is anomalous, they would be permanently shaken. They must fortify themselves by the mutual assurance that they are still in unison. The only means for this is action in common. In short, since it is the *conscience collective* which is attacked, it must be that which resists, and accordingly the resistance must be collective [. . .]

Thus, the analysis of punishment has confirmed our definition of crime. We began by establishing inductively that crime consisted essentially in an act contrary to strong and defined states of the *conscience collective*. We have just seen that all the qualities of punishment ultimately derive from this nature of crime. That is because the rules that it sanctions express the most essential social likenesses.

Thus we see what type of solidarity penal law symbolises. It is well known, indeed, that there is a form of social cohesion whose cause lies in a certain conformity of all specific individuals to a common type which is none other than the mental type of the society. In these conditions, not only are all the members of the group individually attracted to one-another because they resemble one-another, but also because they are joined to that which is the condition of existence of this collective type: that is to say; to the society that they form by their union. Not only do citizens love each other and seek each other out in preference to strangers but they love their country. They want for it what they want for themselves, and wish it to prosper and endure, because without it, a great part of their psychological life would be hampered in its functioning. Conversely, society demands that they present these fundamental resemblances, because that is a condition of its cohesion. There are in us two forms of consciousness: one contains states which are personal to the character of each of us, while the states which comprise the other are common to the whole society. The first represent only our individual personality and constitute it; the second represent the collective type and, consequently, society, without which it would not exist. When it is one of the elements of this latter which determines our conduct, we do not act in our personal interest; we pursue collective ends. Although distinct, these two forms of consciousness are linked one to the other, since in the end they are only one, having one and the same organic substratum. They are thus interdependent. From this results a solidarity *sui generis*, based upon mutual resemblance, and directly linking individual to society [. . .]

What distinguishes [the restitutive] sanction is that it is not expiatory but consists of a simple return in state. The person who violates or disregards the law is not made to suffer in relation to his wrongdoing; he is simply sentenced to comply. If certain things have already been done, the judge reinstates them as they should have been. He speaks of law; he says nothing of punishment. Damage payments have no penal character; they are only a means of reviewing the past in order to reinstate it, as far as possible, in its normal form [. . .]

Neglect of these rules is not even punished diffusely. The defendant who has lost in litigation is not disgraced, his honour is not smirched. We can even imagine these rules differing from how they are now without any feeling of distaste. The idea of tolerating murder makes us indignant, but we quite easily accept modification of the law of inheritance, and can even conceive of its possible abolition. It is at least a question which we do not refuse to discuss. In the same way, we readily accept that the law of easements or that of usufructs may be organised differently, that the obligations of vendor and purchaser may be determined in another way, or that administrative functions may be distributed according to different principles. As these prescriptions do not correspond to any sentiment in us, and as we generally do not know scientifically the reasons for their existence, since this science does not exist, they have no roots in the majority of us. Of course, there are exceptions. We do not tolerate the idea that a contract, contrary to custom or obtained either through force or fraud, can bind the contracting parties. Thus, when public opinion finds itself in the presence of a case of this sort, it shows itself less indifferent than we have previously said, and it increases the legal sanction by its censure. The different domains of moral life are not radically separated one from another; on the contrary, they are continuous, and accordingly they contain marginal regions where these different characteristics are found at the same time. However, the preceding proposition remains true in the great majority of cases. It is proof that rules with a restitutive sanction either do not at all derive from the *conscience collective*, or are only feeble states of it. Repressive law corresponds to the heart, the centre of the common conscience; purely moral rules are already a less central part; finally, restitutive law originates in very marginal regions, spreading well beyond. The more it becomes truly itself, the more removed it becomes.

This characteristic is, moreover, manifest in the manner of its functioning. While repressive law tends to remain diffuse within society, restitutive law creates organs which are increasingly specialised: commercial courts, councils of arbitration, administrative courts of many kinds. Even in its most general part, that which pertains to civil law, it is exercised only through particular functionaries: magistrates, lawyers, etc., who are able to fill this role in virtue of very specialised training.

But, although these rules are to some degree outside the *conscience collective*, they do not refer only to individuals. If this were so, restitutive law would have nothing in common with social solidarity, for the relations that it regulates would bind individuals to one-another without binding them to society. These would simply be happenings in private life, as friendly relations are. But it is necessarily the case that society is far from being absent in this sphere of legal life. It is true that, generally, it does not intervene directly and actively; it must be solicited by the interested parties. But in being called forth, its intervention is nonetheless the essential cog in the machine, since it alone makes it function. It propounds the law through the organ of its representatives.

It has been contended, however, that this role has nothing properly social about it, but reduces itself to that of a conciliator of private interests; that, consequently, any individual can fill it, and that, if society is in charge of it, it is only for reasons of convenience. But nothing is more incorrect than to consider society as a sort of third-party arbitrator. When it is led to intervene, it is not to rectify individual interests. It does not seek to discover what may be the most advantageous solution for the adversaries and does not propose a compromise for them. Rather it applies to the particular case which is submitted to its general and traditional rules of law. Now law is, above all, a social thing, the objective of which is something other than the interest of the litigants. The judge who examines a request for divorce is not concerned with knowing whether this separation is truly desirable for the married parties, but rather whether the causes which are adduced come under one of the categories embodied in the law [. . .]

Since rules with restitutive sanctions are foreign to the *conscience collective*, the ties that they determine are not those which relate indiscriminately to everyone. That is to say, they are established, not between the individual and society, but between restricted, specific parts of soicety{??? m/s p. 245}, whom they link to one-another. But, on the other hand, since society is not absent, it must be more or less directly interested, and it must feel the repercussions. Thus, according to the force with which society feels them, it intervenes more or less directly and actively, through the intermediary of special organs charged with representing it. These relations are, then, quite different from those which repressive law regulates, for the latter attach the particular individual to the *conscience collective* directly and without mediation: that is, the individual to society [. . .]

To sum up: the relations governed by co-operative law with restitutive sanctions, and the solidarity which they express, result from the division of social labour. We have explained, moreover, that, in general, co-operative relations do not convey other sanctions. In fact, it is in the nature of specialised tasks to escape the action of the *conscience collective*, for, in order for a thing to be the object of common sentiments, it must necessarily be shared: that is to say, it must be present in all minds such that everyone can represent it in one and the same manner. To be sure, in so far as functions have a certain generality, everybody can have some idea of them. But the more specialised they are, the more restricted the number of individuals who know each of them; consequently, the more marginal they are to the *conscience collective*. The rules which determine them cannot have that dominating force and transcendent authority which, when offended, demands expiation. It is also from public opinion that their authority derives, as with penal rules, but from such opinion localised in restricted regions of society.

Moreover, even in the special circles where they apply and where, consequently, they are represented in men's minds, they do not correspond to very active sentiments, nor even very often to any type of emotional state. For, as they fix the manner in which the different functions ought to concur in diverse combinations of circumstances which can arise, the objects to which they are connected are not always present in consciousness. We are not constantly called upon to administer guardianship, trusteeship, or exercise the rights of creditor or buyer, etc., or, more important, to exercise them in such and such a situation. Now, states of consciousness are strong only in so far as they are permanent. The violation of these rules reaches neither the common spirit of society, nor even, generally speaking, that of special groups, and consequently it can stimulate only a very moderate reaction. All that is necessary is that the functions concur in a regular manner. If this regularity is disrupted, it is sufficient for us to re-establish it. Assuredly, this is not to say that the development of the division of labour cannot influence penal law. There are, as we already know, administrative and governmental functions in which certain relations are regulated by repressive law, because of the particular character of this agency of the *conscience collective* and everything connected with it. In still other cases, the links of solidarity which unite certain social functions can be such that their breach stimulates repercussions which are sufficiently extensive to provoke a penal reaction. But, for the reason we have given, these reactions are exceptional[. . .][thus] we recognise only two kinds of positive solidarity, which are distinguishable by the following qualities:

1. The first ties the individual directly to society without any intermediary. In the second, he depends upon society, because he depends upon the parts which compose it.
2. Society is not seen in the same aspect in the two cases. In the first, what we call 'society' is a more or less closely organised totality of beliefs and sentiments common to all the members of the group: it is the collective type. By contrast, the society to which we are bound in the second instance is a system of differentiated and specialised functions which are united in definite relationships. These two societies really make up only one. They are two aspects of one and the same reality, but nonetheless they must be distinguished.
3. From this second difference there arises another which helps us to characterise and name the two kinds of solidarity.

The first can be strong only to the degree that the ideas and tendencies common to all the members of the society are greater in number and intensity than those which pertain to each individual member. Its strength is determined by the degree to which this is the case. But what makes our personality is how many particular characteristics we possess which distinguish us from others. This solidarity thus can grow only in inverse ratio to personality. There are in each of us, as we have said, two forms of consciousness: one which is common to our group as a whole, which, consequently, is not ourself, but society living and acting within us; the other, on the other hand, represents that in us which is personal and distinct, that which makes us an individual. Solidarity which comes from resemblance is at its *maximum* when the *conscience collective* completely envelops our whole consciousness and coincides in all points with it. But, at that moment, our individuality is nil. It can develop only if the community takes a lesser part of us. There are, here, two contrary forces, one centripetal, the other centrifugal, which cannot flourish at the same time. We cannot, at one and the same time, develop ourselves in two opposite senses. If we have a strong inclination to think and act for ourselves, we cannot be as strongly inclined to think and act as others do. If our ideal is to present a unique and personal appearance, we cannot resemble everybody else. Moreover, at the moment when this latter solidarity exercises its force, our personality vanishes, by definition, one might say, for we are no longer ourselves, but the collective being.

The social molecules which cohere in this way can act together only in so far as they have no action of their own, as with the molecules of inorganic bodies. That is why we propose to call this form of solidarity 'mechanical'. The term does not signify that it is produced by mechanical and artificial means. We call it that only by analogy to the cohesion which unites the elements of an inorganic body, as contrasted to that which forms a unity out of the elements of a living body. What finally justifies this term is that the link which thus unites the individual to society is wholly comparable to that which attaches a thing to a person. The individual consciousness, considered in this light, is a simple appendage of the collective type and follows all of its actions, as the possessed object follows those of its owner. In societies where this type of solidarity is highly developed, the individual is not his own master, as we shall see later; solidarity is, literally something which the society possesses. Thus, in these types of society, personal rights are not yet distinguished from real rights.

It is quite different with the solidarity which the division of labour produces. Whereas the previous type implies that individuals resemble each other, this latter presumes that they differ. The former is possible only in so far as the individual personality is absorbed into the collective personality; the latter is possible only if each one has a sphere of action which is peculiar to him – that is, if he possesses a personality. It is necessary, then, that the *conscience collective* leave open a part of the individual consciousness in order that special functions may be established there, functions which it cannot regulate. The more this region is extended, the stronger is the cohesion which results from this solidarity. In fact, on the one hand, every individual depends more directly on society as labour becomes more divided; and, on the other, the activity of every individual becomes more personalised to the degree that it is more specialised. No doubt, as circumscribed as it is, it is never completely original; even in the exercise of our occupation, we conform to conventions and practices which are common to our whole occupational group. But, in this instance, the yoke that we submit to is much less heavy than when society completely controls us, and it leaves much more place open for the free play of our initiative. Here, then, the individuality of all grows at the same time as that of its parts. Society becomes more capable of collective action, at the same time that each of its elements has more freedom of action. This solidarity resembles that which we observe among the higher animals. Each organ, in effect, has its special character and autonomy; and yet the unity of the organism is as great as the individuation of the parts is more marked. Because of this analogy, we propose to call the solidarity which is due to the division of labour, 'organic'.

3.3 The Division of Labour: Causes and Abnormal Forms

This section starts out by posing an apparent paradox: how can the division of labour unite at the same time as it differentiates. Durkheim dismisses the solution offered by British sociologist Herbert Spencer and the Utilitarians (and we might add much political economy) that society is maintained through co-operation and exchange. Durkheim argues brilliantly that this presupposes an already existing moral framework within which these transactions can take place, be understood and adhered to.

In the rest of this selection Durkheim deals with 'pathological' or 'abnormal' forms of the division of labour. Generally industrial capitalist societies had developed a range of inequalities along fault-lines of wealth, power and class which would have to be removed, along with other 'external inequalities' such as inherited wealth (which makes the claim that Durkheim was an arch-conservative somewhat ludicrous) in order for a balanced organic solidarity to develop spontaneously. Otherwise an 'anomic' (the concept of 'anomie' is given a fuller treatment in *Suicide*, see below) or 'forced division of labour' will be the inevitable result.

The selection ends with Durkheim at his most interesting and provocative, pondering the problems facing modern complex industrial societies and contemplating the role of sociology for the task ahead. Durkheim here urges us not to look to the past for old remedies and inappropriate traditions but to look forward to find new ways of achieving 'harmonious co-operation'.

From: E. Durkheim, *The Division of Labour in Society* (Macmillan: London, 1984) pp. 217–21, 291–3, 306–8, 312–14, 323–4, 326–8, 337–40.

A corollary of everything that has gone before is that the division of labour cannot be carried out save between the members of a society already constituted.

Indeed when competition opposes isolated individuals not known to one another, it can only separate them still more. If they have ample space at their disposal, they will flee from one another. If they cannot go beyond set limits, they will begin to differentiate, but in a way so that they become still more independent of one another. We can cite no case where relationships of open hostility have been transformed into social relationships, without the intervention of any other factor. Thus, as there is generally no bond between individuals or creatures of the same vegetable or animal species, the war they wage upon one another serves only to diversify them, to give rise to dissimilar varieties that increasingly grow further apart. It is this progressive disjunction that Darwin has called the law of the divergence of characteristics. Yet the division of labour unites at the same time as it sets at odds; it causes the activities that it differentiates to converge; it brings closer those that it separates. Since competition cannot have determined their coming together, it must indeed have already pre-existed. The individuals between whom the conflict is joined must already be solidly linked to one another and feel so, that is, they belong to the same society. This is why, where this sentiment of solidarity is too weak to resist the centrifugal influence of competition, the latter produces completely different effects from the division of labour. In countries where existence is too difficult because of the extreme density of the population, the inhabitants, instead of specialising, withdraw permanently or provisionally from society by emigrating to other areas.

Moreover, it is enough to represent to ourselves what the division of labour is to make us understand that things cannot be otherwise. It consists in the sharing out of functions that up till then were common to all. But such an allocation cannot be effected according to any preconceived plan. We cannot say beforehand where the line of demarcation is drawn between tasks, once they have been separated. In the nature of things that line is not marked out so self-evidently, but on the contrary depends upon a great number of circumstances. The division must therefore come about of itself, and progressively. Consequently, in these conditions for a function to be capable of being shared out in two exactly complementary fractions, as the nature of the division of labour requires, it is indispensable that the two parties specialising should be in constant communication over the whole period that this dissociation is occurring. There is no other way for one part to take over from the other the whole operation that the latter is surrendering, and for them to adapt to each other. Now, just as an animal colony, the tissue of whose members is a continuum, constitutes an individual, so every aggregate of individuals in continuous contact forms a society. The division of labour can therefore only occur within the framework of an already existing society. By this we do not just simply mean that individuals must cling materially to one another, but moral ties must also exist between them. Firstly, material continuity alone gives rise to links of this kind, provided that it is lasting. Moreover, they are directly necessary. If the relationships beginning to be established during the period of uncertainty were not subject to any rule, if no power moderated the clash of individual interests, chaos would ensue from which no new order could emerge. It is true that we imagine that everything occurs by means of private agreements freely argued over. All social action therefore seems to be absent. But we forget that contracts are only possible where a legal form of regulation, and consequently a society, already exists.

Thus it has been wrong sometimes to see in the division of labour the basic fact of all social life. Work is not shared out between independent individuals who are already differentiated from one another, who meet and associate together in order to pool their different abilities. It would be a miracle if these differences, arising from chance circumstances, could be so accurately harmonised as to form a coherent whole. Far from their preceding collective life, they derive from it. They can only occur within a society, under the pressure of social sentiments and needs. This is what makes them essentially capable of being harmonised. Thus there is a social life outside of any division of labour, but one that the latter assumes. This is in fact what we have directly established by demonstrating that there are societies whose cohesion is due essentially to a community of beliefs and sentiments, and that it is from these societies that others have emerged whose unity is ensured by the division of labour. The conclusions of the preceding book and those at which we have just arrived can therefore serve as a check, mutually confirming each other. In physiology the division of labour is itself subject to this law: it never occurs save with polycellular masses that are already endowed with a certain cohesion.

For a number of theorists, it is a self-evident truth that any society consists essentially in co-operation. Spencer states that 'a society, in the sociological sense, is formed only when, beside juxtaposition there is co-operation'. We have just seen that this alleged axiom is the opposite of the truth. On the contrary, it is evident, as Auguste Comte says, 'that co-operation, far from being able to produce a society, supposes necessarily its spontaneous establishment beforehand'. What draws men together are mechanical forces and instinctive forces such as the affinity of blood, attachment to the same soil, the cult of their ancestors, a commonality of habits, etc. It is only when the group has been formed on these bases that co-operation becomes organised.

Even so, the sole co-operation possible in the beginning is so intermittent and weak that social life, if it lacked any other source, would itself lack strength or continuity. *A fortiori*, the complex co-operation that results from the division of labour is a later, derived phenomenon. It results from the internal movements that develop within the mass of people, when this mass has been constituted. It is true that once co-operation has made its appearance, it tightens social bonds and imparts to society a more complete individuality. But this integration supposes another sort that it replaces. For social units to be able to differentiate from one another, they must first be attracted or grouped together through the similarities that they display. This process of formation is observed, not only at the origins, but at every stage of evolution. We know in fact that higher societies are the result of the coming together of lower societies of the same type. First of all, these latter must be blended together in the sense of a single and identical common consciousness so that the process of differentiation can begin or begin again. It is in this way that more complex organisms are formed by the replication of more simple organisms, similar to one another, which only differentiate after they have been associated together. In short, association and co-operation are two distinct events, and if the second, once it has been developed, reacts upon the first and transforms, if human societies consist increasingly of groups co-operating together, the dual nature of the two phenomena does not in consequence disappear.

If this important truth failed to be realised by the Utilitarians, it is an error springing from the manner in which they conceived the genesis of society. They supposed that originally there were isolated and independent individuals who thus could only enter into relationships with one another in order to co-operate, for they had no other reason to bridge the empty gap separating them, and to associate together. But this theory, which is so widely held, postulates a veritable creation *ex nihilo*.

It consists, in fact, of deducing society from the individual. But we possess no knowledge that gives grounds for believing in the possibility of such a spontaneous generation. On Spencer's admission, for society to be able to be formed on such an hypothesis, 'the units [must] pass from the state of perfect independence to that of mutual dependence'. But what can have determined them to make so complete a transformation? The prospect of the advantages that social life offers? But these are balanced, and even unduly so, by the loss of independence, because for creatures destined by nature for a free and solitary life, such a sacrifice is the most intolerable of all. In addition, in the first social types, the sacrifice was as absolute as possible, because nowhere is the individual more completely absorbed within the group. How could man, if he were born an individualist, as we suppose, have resigned himself to an existence that goes so violently against his most fundamental inclination? How very pallid the problematic utility of co-operation must have appeared to him in comparison with such a surrender! From autonomous individualities, like those we imagine, nothing can therefore emerge save what is individual; consequently co-operation itself, which is a social fact, subject to social rules, cannot arise. It is in this way that the psychologist who begins to shut himself up within his own self can no longer emerge from it, to find again the non-self.

Collective life did not arise from individual life; on the contrary, it is the latter that emerged from the former. On this condition alone can we explain how the personal individuality of social units was able to form and grow without causing society to disintegrate. Indeed, since in this case it developed from within a pre-existing social environment, it necessarily bears its stamp. It is constituted in such a way as not to ruin that collective order to which it is solidly linked. It remains adapted to it, whilst detaching itself from it. There is nothing antisocial about it, because it is a product of society. It is not the absolute personality of the monad, sufficient unto itself, and able to do without the rest of the world, but that of an organ or part of an organ that has its own definite function, but that cannot, without running a mortal risk, separate itself from the rest of the organism. In these conditions co-operation not only becomes possible, but necessary. The Utilitarians therefore reverse the natural order of events, and there is nothing less surprising than this reversal. It is a particular illustration of the general truth that what is first to be known is last in reality. Precisely because co-operation is the most recent fact, this it is that strikes one's gaze first. If therefore we look only to appearances, as does common sense, inevitably we see it as the primary fact of moral and social life. [. . .]

The Anomic Division of Labour

Up to now we have studied the division of labour only as a normal phenomenon. Yet, like all social facts, and more generally, like all biological ones, it manifests pathological forms that we must analyse. If normally the division of labour produces social solidarity, it can happen, however, that it has entirely different or even opposite results. It is important that we should investigate what makes it deviate in this way from its natural course, for so long as it has not been established that these cases are exceptional, the division of labour might be suspected of logically implying them. Moreover, the study of deviant forms will allow us to determine better the conditions for the existence of the normal state. When we know the circumstances in which the division of labour ceases to engender solidarity, we shall know better what is necessary for it to have its full effect. Here as elsewhere pathology is a precious ancillary to physiology.

We might be tempted to range among the irregular forms of the division of labour the criminal profession and other harmful professions. They are the very negation of solidarity and yet they are made up of just as many specialised activities. But, precisely speaking, here there is no division of labour, but differentiation pure and simple, and the two terms should not be confused. In the same way cancer and tuberculosis increase the diversity of the organic tissues without it being possible to see in this a fresh specialisation of the biological functions. In all these cases there is no allocation of a common function, but within the organism, whether it is individual or social is formed another one that seeks to live at the expense of the first one. There is even no function at all, for a way of acting does not deserve that term unless it concerts with others to maintain life generally. This question does not therefore enter into the scope of our investigation.

We shall reduce to three types the exceptional forms of the phenomenon that we are studying. This is not because there cannot be others, but those that we shall discuss are the most general and the most serious.

A first case of this nature is provided for us by industrial or commercial crises, and by the bankruptcies that are so many partial breaks in organic solidarity. They demonstrate in fact that at certain points of the organism certain social functions are not adjusted to one another. As labour becomes increasingly divided up these phenomena seem to become more frequent, at least in certain cases. From 1845 to 1869 bankruptcies increased by 70 per cent. However, this fact cannot be ascribed to the growth of economic life, for business undertakings have become more concentrated rather than increasing in number.

Hostility between labour and capital is another example, a more striking one, of the same phenomenon. As industrial functions specialise more the struggle becomes more fierce, far from solidarity increasing. In the Middle Ages the workman everywhere lived side by side with his master, sharing in his work 'in the same shop, on the same bench'. Both formed part of the same corporation and led the same existence. 'Both were almost equal to each other; he who had completed his apprenticeship could, at least in many trades, set up on his own, if he had the wherewithal.' Thus conflicts were completely exceptional. From the fifteenth century onwards things began to change. 'The trade guild is no longer a common refuge for all; it is the exclusive possession of the masters who decide everything on their own [. . .] From then onwards a deep gulf was established between masters and journeymen. The latter formed, so to speak, a separate order; they had their habits, their rules, their independent associations.' Once this separation had been carried out quarrels became frequent. 'As soon as the journeymen thought they had something to complain about, they went on strike or boycotted a town or an employer, and all were forced to obey the call [. . .] The power of association gave the workers the means to struggle with equal weapons against their employers.' However, matters were far from having reached then the 'point where we see them at present. The journeymen rebelled in order to obtain a higher salary or some change in working conditions, but they did not consider their employer to be a perpetual enemy to be obeyed under constraint. They wanted him to give way on one point and they applied themselves to this energetically, but the struggle did not last for ever. The workshops did not contain two enemy races; our socialist doctrines were unknown.' Finally, in the seventeenth century there began the third phase of this history of the working classes: the coming of large-scale industry. The workman became even more separated from his boss. 'To some extent he is regimented. Each individual has his function, and the system of the division of labour makes some progress. In the factory of the Van Robais, which employed 1,692 workmen, there were special workshops for the cartwright's craft, for cutlery, washing, dyeing, and warping cloth, and the weaving mills themselves included several kinds of workers whose work was completely distinct.' At the same time as specialisation becomes greater, revolts become more frequent. 'The slightest cause of discontent was enough to cause a firm to be boycotted, and woe to the journeyman who did not respect the decision of his community.' We know well enough that since then the war has become increasingly more violent

We shall certainly see in the following chapter that this tension in social relationships is due in part to the fact that the working classes do not really desire the status assigned to them and too often accept it only under constraint and force, not having any means of gaining any other status. Yet this constraint alone would not by itself account for the phenomenon. Indeed it weighs down no less heavily upon all who are generally bereft of fortune, and yet this state of permanent hostility is absolutely peculiar to the industrial world. Then, within that world, it is the same for all workers without exception. Now small-scale industry, where work is less divided up, affords the spectacle of a relative harmony existing between employer and worker; it is only within large-scale industry that these upheavals are acute. It is therefore because they depend in part upon a different cause. [. . .]

The foregoing removes all grounds for one of the gravest reproaches that have been made against the division of labour.

It has often been accused of diminishing the individual by reducing him to the role of a machine. And indeed, if he is not aware of where the operations required of him are leading, if he does not link them to any aim, he can no longer perform them save out of routine. Every day he repeats the same movements with monotonous regularity, but without having any interest or understanding of them. He is no longer the living cell of a living organism, moved continually by contact with neighbouring cells, which acts upon them and responds in turn to their action, extends itself, contracts, yields and is transformed according to the needs and circumstances. He is no more than a lifeless cog, which an external force sets in motion and impels always in the same direction and in the same fashion. Plainly, no matter how one represents the moral ideal, one cannot remain indifferent to such a debasement of human nature. If the aim of morality is individual perfection, it cannot allow the individual to be so utterly ruined, and if it has society as its end, it cannot let the very source of social life dry up. The evil not only threatens economic functions, but all the social functions, no matter how elevated these may be. 'If,' says Comte, 'we have often rightly deplored on the material plane the fact of the worker exclusively occupied throughout his life in making knife handles or pinheads, a healthy philosophy must not, all in all, cause us to regret any the less on the intellectual plane the exclusive and continual use of the human brain to resolve a few equations or classify a few insects: the moral effect, in both cases, is unfortunately very similar.'

Occasionally the remedy has been proposed for workers, that besides their technical and special knowledge, they should receive a general education. But even assuming that in this way some of the bad effects attributed to the division of labour can be redeemed, it is still not a means of preventing them. The division of labour does not change its nature because it has been preceded by a liberal education. It is undoubtedly good for the worker to be able to interest himself in artistic and literary matters, etc. But it remains none the less wrong that throughout the day he should be treated like a machine. Moreover, who can fail to see that these two types of existence are too opposing to be reconciled or to be able to be lived by the same man! If one acquires the habit of contemplating vast horizons, overall views, and fine generalisations, one can no longer without impatience allow oneself to be confined within the narrow limits of a special task. Such a remedy would therefore only make specialisation inoffensive by making it intolerable, and in consequence more or less impossible.

What resolves this contradiction is the fact that, contrary to what has been said, the division of labour does not produce these consequences through some imperative of its own nature, but only in exceptional and abnormal circumstances. For it to be able to develop without having so disastrous an influence on the human consciousness, there is no need to mitigate it by means of its opposite. It is necessary and sufficient for it to be itself, for nothing to come from outside to deform its nature. For normally the operation of each special function demands that the individual should not be too closely shut up in it, but should keep in constant contact with neighbouring functions, becoming aware of their needs and the changes that take place in them, etc. The division of labour supposes that the worker, far from remaining bent over his task, does not lose sight of those co-operating with him, but acts upon them and is acted upon by them. He is not therefore a machine who repeats movements the sense of which he does not perceive, but he knows that they are tending in a certain direction, towards a goal that he can conceive of more or less distinctly. He feels that he is of some use. For this he has no need to take in very vast areas of the social horizon; it is enough for him to perceive enough of it to understand that his actions have a goal beyond themselves. Thenceforth, however specialised, however uniform his activity may be, it is that of an intelligent being, for he knows that his activity has a meaning. The economists would not have left this essential characteristic of the division of labour unclarified and as a result would not have lain it open to this undeserved reproach, if they had not reduced it to being only a way of increasing the efficiency of the social forces, but had seen it above all as a source of solidarity. [. . .]

The forced division of labour is thus a second morbid type that we can distinguish. But we must not mistake the meaning of the term. What causes constraint is not any kind of regulation, since on the contrary the division of labour, as we have just seen, cannot do without this. Even when functions are allocated in accordance with set rules, the distribution is not necessarily the result of constraint. This is what takes place even under a caste regime, so long as it is based upon the nature of society. Indeed the institution of caste is not at all times and places an arbitrary one. When it functions regularly in a society, meeting with no opposition, it is because it at least approximately expresses the immutable way in which professional abilities are distributed throughout society. This is why, although tasks are to a certain extent allocated by law, each organ performs its own spontaneously. Constraint begins only when regulation, no longer corresponding to the true state of affairs and consequently without any moral foundation, is only maintained by force.

Conversely, we may therefore state that the division of labour only produces solidarity if it is spontaneous, and to the degree that it *is* spontaneous. But spontaneity must mean not simply the absence of any deliberate, formal type of violence, but of anything that may hamper, even indirectly, the free unfolding of the social force each individual contains within himself. It not only supposes that individuals are not consigned forcibly to performing certain determined functions, but also that no obstacle whatsoever prevents them from occupying within the ranks of society a position commensurate to their abilities. In short, labour only divides up spontaneously if society is constituted in such a way that social inequalities express precisely natural inequalities. It is a necessary and sufficient condition for these inequalities neither to be emphasised nor played down through some external cause. Perfect spontaneity is therefore only a sequel to, and another form of, this further fact: absolute equality in the external conditions of the struggle. It does not consist of a state of anarchy which would allow men to satisfy freely every inclination they have, good or bad. It rather comprises a finely articulated organisation in which each social value, neither distorted in one direction or the other by anything outside it, is appreciated at its true worth. It will be objected that even under these conditions, struggle still occurs, because of the fact that there must be victors and vanquished, with the latter accepting their defeat only under constraint. But this constraint does not resemble the other form; it has nothing in common with it save the term. What constitutes real constraint is when even struggle becomes impossible, and one is not even allowed to fight.

It is true that this perfect spontaneity is nowhere encountered as a fact realised in practice. There is no society where it exists in an unalloyed form. If the institution of castes corresponds to the natural distribution of abilities, it nevertheless does so only approximately – in short, in a rough and ready way. Indeed, heredity never acts with such precise accuracy that even where it meets with conditions most favourable for its influence, children are the exact replicas of their parents. There are always exceptions to the rule. Consequently cases occur where the individual is not attuned to the functions that are attributed to him. Such disharmonies become more frequent as society develops, until the time when the bounds burst, having become too constricting. When the caste regime has disappeared by law, it survives in morality. Thanks to the persistence of certain prejudices, a certain favouritism is attached to some individuals, and the converse, unrelated to their merits, obtains for others. Finally, even when, so to speak, no trace of all these past vestiges remains, the hereditary transmission of wealth suffices to render very unequal the external conditions for the struggle, since it gives to some the benefit of advantages that do not necessarily correspond to their personal value. Even today, among the most cultured peoples, careers exist that are totally closed, or more difficult to enter for those ill-blessed by fortune. It might then appear that we have no right to consider as normal a characteristic that the division of labour never manifests in its pure state, if on the other hand, we did not observe that the higher the elevation in the social scale, the more the segmentary type of society is submerged beneath the organised type, and the more also these inequalities tend to be evened out completely. [. . .]

Another Abnormal Form

There remains one last abnormal form to describe.

It often happens in a commercial, industrial or any other kind of undertaking that functions are distributed in such a way that they fail to afford sufficient scope for individual activity. It is plain that there is a regrettable waste of effort, although we need not deal with the economic aspect of the phenomenon here. What should be of interest to us is another fact that always accompanies this wastage, that is, a more or less lack of co-ordination of these functions. We know that in a business where every employee has not enough work to occupy himself activities are badly co-ordinated and operations are carried out without concertation; in short, solidarity relaxes its hold, and incoherency and disorder appear. At the court of the Eastern Roman Empire functions were infinitely specialised, and yet the outcome was veritably a state of anarchy. Thus there are cases where the division of labour, although very highly developed, result in a very imperfect integration. From where does this arise? It would be tempting to reply that what is lacking is some kind of regulatory organ, a managing body. Such an explanation is hardly satisfying, for very often this state of sickness is the work of the controlling management itself. For the evil to vanish it does not therefore suffice to have some kind of regulatory mechanism; it needs to be exercised in a certain way. Consequently we must know how it will be exercised. The prime task of an intelligent and experienced leader will be to abolish useless jobs and distribute work in such a way that each individual will be kept sufficiently busy, thus increasing the functional activity of every worker. Then order will spontaneously arise once more, at the same time as the work is more economically arranged. How is this to be brought about? At first sight this is very difficult to envisage. For if every operator has a clearly determined task and performs it with precision, he will necessarily require the co-operation of his neighbours and cannot fail to feel solidly linked to them. What does it matter whether this task is great or small, provided that it is specialised? What does it matter whether it absorbs his time and energy fully or not? [. . .]

Thus if the work provided is not only not of a large amount, but is even insufficient, that solidarity is itself naturally not only less than perfect, but may even be more or less completely missing. This is what happens in business enterprises where the tasks are distributed in such a way that each worker's activity is lower than what it should normally be. The different functions are therefore too discontinuous to be adjusted precisely to one another or to work harmoniously together. This is where their lack of cohesion is noticeable.

But exceptional circumstances must prevail for the division of labour to occur in this way. Normally it does not develop without functional activity increasing at the same time and in the same proportion. Indeed the same causes that force us to specialise more also force us to work harder. When the number of competitors increases generally throughout society, it increases also in each individual profession. The struggle within them becomes more fierce, and consequently greater effort must be put forward to be able to sustain it. Furthermore, the division of labour itself tends of its own accord to render functions more active and sustained. For a long time the economists have set out reasons for this phenomenon, the main ones being as follows:

1. When tasks are not divided up one is constantly disturbed, passing from one occupation to another. The division of labour economises all this lost time; according to Karl Marx's expression, it causes the pores of the working-day to contract.
2. Functional activity increases with skill, the ability of the worker, which the division of labour develops. There is less time used up in vacillation and trial and error.

Carey, the American sociologist, has very clearly highlighted this characteristic of the division of labour. He states that there can be no continuity in the actions of the isolated settler. Depending for his subsistence upon his acquisitive ability and obliged to cover immense areas of ground, he is often in danger of perishing through lack of food. Even when he succeeds in obtaining it he is forced to suspend his operations and to think of how to accomplish the indispensable removal of his dwelling-place in order to transport at the same time his subsistence, his miserable home and himself. Once he has arrived, he is forced to become cook and tailor in turn. Deprived of the aid of artificial light, his nights are spent in complete idleness, and at the same time his ability to use the daylight in fruitful employment depends completely on the hazard of temperature. Finally, however, discovering he has a neighbour, exchanges take place between them. But since both occupy different parts of the island, they are forced to move closer together, just like the stones with the help of which they grind their corn. Moreover, when they meet, difficulties arise in fixing the terms on which they trade, because of the irregularity of the supply of the various foodstuffs they wish to barter. The fisherman has had good luck and has caught a vast quantity of fish, but by chance the hunter has been able to get fish already and at this moment needs only fruit, and the fisherman does not have any. Differentiation being, as we know, indispensable for association, the absence of this condition would set up an obstacle to association, one difficult to overcome.

Yet, continues Carey, with time, wealth and population grow and, with this development there appears an increase in movements within society. From then onwards the husband exchanges services with his wife, parents with those of their children, and the children with one another. The one provides fish, the second meat, a third corn, whilst a fourth converts wool into cloth. At every step we perceive a growth in the speed of the exchanges, at the same time as an increase in strength on the part of man.

Moreover, we can observe that work becomes more continuous the more it is divided up. Animals and savages work in most capricious a fashion, when they are compelled by necessity to satisfy some immediate need. In exclusively agricultural or pastoral societies work is almost entirely suspended during bad weather. At Rome it was interrupted by a whole host of feast days or unpropitious days. In the Middle Ages free time was still further increased. Yet, as time passes, work becomes a permanent occupation, a habit, and even a necessity, if this habit has been sufficiently reinforced.

But such a habit could not have grown up, and the corresponding need could not have arisen, if work had remained regular and intermittent, as once it was.

We are thus led to acknowledge another reason that makes the division of labour a source of social cohesion. Not only does it cause individuals to be solidly linked to one another, as we have maintained up to now, because it limits the activity of each one, but also because it increases that activity. It fosters the unity of the organism, by the very fact that it adds to its life. In the normal state, at least, it does not produce one effect without the other. [. . .]

Yet if the division of labour produces solidarity, it is not only because it makes each individual an agent of exchange, to use the language of the economists. It is because it creates between men a whole system of rights and duties joining them in a lasting way to one another. Just as social similarities give rise to a law and a morality that protect them, so the division of labour gives rise to rules ensuring peaceful and regular co-operation between the functions that have been divided up. If economists have believed that this would produce enough solidarity, however it came about, and in consequence have maintained that human societies could and should resolve themselves into purely economic associations, it is because they believed that only individual and temporary interests were at stake. Thus, in order to evaluate the interests that conflict and ascertain how they should be balanced, that is, to determine the conditions in which exchange should take place, individuals alone are competent. Moreover, since these interests are continually developing, there is no room for any permanent regulatory system. But from every viewpoint such a conception is inadequate and does not fit the facts. The division of labour does not present individuals to one another, but social functions. Society has an interest in the interplay of those functions: depending on whether they co-operate regularly or not, society will be healthy or sick. Its existence is therefore dependent upon them, all the more intimately bound up with them the more they are divided. This is why it cannot let them remain in an indeterminate state; moreover, they determine one another. It is like this that rules arise which increase in number the more labour is divide – rules whose absence makes organic solidarity either impossible or imperfect.

But the mere existence of rules is not sufficient: they must also be just. For this the external conditions of competition should be equal. If, on the other hand, we call to mind that the collective consciousness is increasingly reduced to the cult of the individual, we shall see that the characteristic of morality in organised societies, as compared to segmentary societies, is that it possesses something more human, and consequently more rational, about it. It does not cause our activity to depend upon ends that do not directly concern us. It does not make us the servants of some ideal powers completely different in nature from ourselves, powers who follow their own course without heeding the interests of men. It requires us only to be charitable and just towards our fellow-men, to fulfil our task well, to work towards a state where everyone is called to fulfil the function he performs best and will receive a just reward for his efforts. The rules constituting this morality have no constraining power preventing their being fully examined. Because they are better made for us and, in a certain sense, by us, we are freer in relation to them. We seek to understand them and are less afraid to change them. Moreover, we must be careful not to esteem such an ideal defective on the pretext that it is too down-to-earth, too easily within our grasp. An ideal is no more lofty because it is more transcendent, but because it opens up broader vistas to us. It is not important that such an ideal should soar high above us – to an extent that it becomes foreign to us. But it is important that it should open up for our activity a long-term perspective – and such an ideal is far from being on the point of realisation. We feel only too well how laborious a task it is to erect such a society, one in which each individual will have the place he merits and will be rewarded according to his deserts, where everyone will consequently cooperate spontaneously both for the common good and that of the individual. Likewise no morality is superior to all others because its imperatives are couched in a drier, more authoritarian manner, or because it is immune from reflective thinking. Doubtless it must be capable of linking us to something other than ourselves. But there is no need for it to fetter us to the point that it immobilises us.

It has been rightly stated that morality – and this must include both theory and the practice of ethics – is in the throes of an appalling crisis. What we have expounded can help us to understand the causes and nature of this sickness. Over a very short space of time very profound changes have occurred in the structure of our societies. They have liberated themselves from the segmentary model with a speed and in proportions without precedent in history. Thus the morality corresponding to this type of society has lost influence, but without its successor developing quickly enough to occupy the space left vacant in our consciousness. Our beliefs have been disturbed. Tradition has lost its sway. Individual judgement has thrown off the yoke of the collective judgement. On the other hand, the functions that have been disrupted in this period of trial have had no time to adjust to one another. The new life that all of a sudden has arisen has not been able to organise itself thoroughly. Above all, it has not been organised so as to satisfy the need for justice that has been aroused even more passionately in our hearts. If this is so, the remedy for the ill is nevertheless not to seek to revive traditions and practices that no longer correspond to present-day social conditions, and that could only subsist in a life that would be artificial, one only of appearance. We need to put a stop to this anomie, and to find ways of harmonious co-operation between those organs that still clash discordantly together. We need to introduce into their relationships a greater justice by diminishing those external inequalities that are the source of our ills. Our disease is therefore not, as occasionally we appear to believe, of an intellectual order, but linked to deeper causes. We are not suffering because we no longer know on what theoretical idea should be sustained the morality we have practised up to now. The cause is that certain elements of this morality have been irretrievably undermined, and the morality we require is only in the process of taking shape. Our anxiety does not arise because the criticism of scientists has demolished the traditional explanation handed down to us regarding our duties. Consequently it is not a new philosophical system that will ever be capable of dispelling that anxiety. Rather is it because certain of these duties no longer being grounded on reality, a loosening of ties has occurred that can only stop when a new discipline has become established and consolidated itself. In short, our first duty at the present time is to fashion a morality for ourselves. Such a task cannot be improvised in the silence of the study. It can arise only of its own volition, gradually, and under the pressure of internal causes that render it necessary. What reflection can and must do is to prescribe the goal that must be attained. That is what we have striven to accomplish.

3.4 The Rules of Sociological Method

Durkheim intended the *Rules* to be a 'manifesto' for the cause of sociology's scientific standing. The methodological rigour and objectivity of sociology revolved around his famous dictum that we should 'treat social facts as things'. This meant that we should approach 'facts' within the social world as if they are no less 'real' than facts from the natural world and the social scientist should adopt the same detached and inquiring stance that is characteristic of the natural scientist.

In the first part of this selection Durkheim discusses the nature of social facts. In the second part he summarises the 'distinctive characteristics' of the method outlined in the *Rules*.

From: E. Durkheim, *The Rules of Sociological Method* (The Free Press: New York, 1966) pp. 1–3, 13, 141–6.

What is a social fact?

Before inquiring into the method suited to the study of social facts, it is important to know which facts are commonly called 'social'. This information is all the more necessary since the designation 'social' is used with little precision. It is currently employed for practically all phenomena generally diffused within society, however small their social interest. But on that basis, there are, as it were, no human events that may not be called social. Each individual drinks, sleeps, eats, reasons; and it is to society's interest that these functions be exercised in an orderly manner. If, then, all these facts are counted as 'social' facts, sociology would have no subject matter exclusively its own, and its domain would be confused with that of biology and psychology.

But in reality there is in every society a certain group of phenomena which may be differentiated from those studied by the other natural sciences. When I fulfil my obligations as brother, husband, or citizen, when I execute my contracts, I perform duties which are defined, externally to myself and my acts, in law and in custom. Even if they conform to my own sentiments and I feel their reality subjectively, such reality is still objective, for I did not create them; I merely inherited them through my education. How many times it happens, moreover, that we are ignorant of the details of the obligations incumbent upon us, and that in order to acquaint ourselves with them we must consult the law and its authorized interpreters! Similarly, the church-member finds the beliefs and practices of his religious life ready-made at birth; their existence prior to his own implies their existence outside of himself. The system of signs I use to express my thought, the system of currency I employ to pay my debts, the instruments of credit I utilize in my commercial relations, the practices followed in my profession, etc., function independently of my own use of them. And these statements can be repeated for each member of society. Here, then, are ways of acting, thinking, and feeling that present the noteworthy property of existing outside the individual consciousness.

These types of conduct or thought are not only external to the individual but are, moreover, endowed with coercive power, by virtue of which they impose themselves upon him, independent of his individual will. Of course, when I fully consent and conform to them, this constraint is felt only slightly, if at all, and is therefore unnecessary. But it is, nonetheless, an intrinsic characteristic of these facts, the proof thereof being that it asserts itself as soon as I attempt to resist it. If I attempt to violate the law, it reacts against me so as to prevent my act before its accomplishment, or to nullify my violation by restoring the damage, if it is accomplished and reparable, or to make me expiate it if it cannot be compensated for otherwise.

In the case of purely moral maxims; the public conscience exercises a check on every act which offends it by means of the surveillance it exercises over the conduct of citizens, and the appropriate penalties at its disposal. In many cases the constraint is less violent, but nevertheless it always exists. If I do not submit to the conventions of society, if in my dress I do not conform to the customs observed in my country and in my class, the ridicule I provoke, the social isolation in which I am kept, produce, although in an attenuated form, the same effects as a punishment in the strict sense of the word. The constraint is nonetheless efficacious for being indirect. I am not obliged to speak French with my fellow-countrymen nor to use the legal currency, but I cannot possibly do otherwise. If I tried to escape this necessity, my attempt would fail miserably. As an industrialist, I am free to apply the technical methods of former centuries; but by doing so, I should invite certain ruin. Even when I free myself from these rules and violate them successfully, I am always compelled to struggle with them. When finally overcome, they make their constraining power sufficiently felt by the resistance they offer. The enterprises of all innovators, including successful ones, come up against resistance of this kind.

Here, then, is a category of facts with very distinctive characteristics: it consists of ways of acting, thinking, and feeling, external to the individual, and endowed with a power of coercion, by reason of which they control him. These ways of thinking could not be confused with biological phenomena, since they consist of representations and of actions; nor with psychological phenomena, which exist only in the individual consciousness and through it. They constitute, thus, a new variety of phenomena; and it is to them exclusively that the term 'social' ought to be applied. And this term fits them quite well, for it is clear that, since their source is not in the individual, their substratum can be no other than society, either the political society as a whole or some one of the partial groups it includes, such as religious denominations, political literary, and occupational associations [. . .]

Our definition will then include the whole relevant range of facts if we say: *A social fact is every way of acting, fixed or not, capable of exercising on the individual an external constraint;* or again, *every way of acting which is general throughout a given society, while at the same time existing in its own right independent of its individual manifestations* [. . .]

Conclusion

To sum up, the distinctive characteristics of our method are as follows: First, it is entirely independent of philosophy. Because sociology had its birth in the great philosophical doctrines, it has retained the habit of relying on some philosophical system and thus has been continuously overburdened with it. It has been successively positivistic, evolutionary, idealistic, when it should have been content to be simply sociology. We should even hesitate to describe it as naturalistic, unless the term indicates merely that the sociologist considers social facts as capable of being explained naturally, or that he is a scientist and not a mystic. We reject the term if it is given a doctrinal meaning concerning the essence of social objects – if, e.g., by it is meant that social objects are reducible to the other cosmic forces.

Sociology does not need to choose between the great hypotheses which divide metaphysicians. It needs to embrace free will no more than determinism. All that it asks is that the principle of causality be applied to social phenomena. Again, this principle is enunciated for sociology not as a rational necessity but only as an empirical postulate, produced by legitimate induction. Since the law of causality has been verified in the other realms of nature, and since it has progressively extended its authority from the physicochemical world to the biological, and from the latter to the psychological, we are justified in claiming that it is equally true of the social world; and it is possible to add today that the researches undertaken on the basis of this postulate tend to confirm it. However, the question as to whether the nature of the causal bond excludes all chance is not thereby settled.

This emancipation of sociology is decidedly to the advantage of philosophy. For, in so far as the sociologist has not sufficiently eliminated philosophy from social science, he considers social facts only from their most general aspect, the aspect from which they most resemble the other things in the universe. Now, if sociology, thus conceived, serves to illustrate philosophy with curious facts, it does not enrich it with new views, since it points out nothing new in the objects which it studies. But, if the fundamental facts of the other fields of knowledge actually recur in the social field, they do so under special forms, which clarify the nature of these facts since they are their highest expression. However, in order to treat them from this aspect, we must leave generalities behind and enter into the detail of facts. Thus, as sociology becomes specialized, it will furnish more original materials for philosophical reflection.

All this has already given us an idea of how the essential concepts, such as those of species, organ, function, health and morbidity, cause and effect, appear in sociology under entirely new aspects. Moreover, may not sociology feature an idea which might well be the basis not only of a psychology but of a whole philosophy – the idea of association?

With reference to practical social doctrines, our method permits and commands the same independence. Sociology thus understood will be neither individualistic, communistic, nor socialistic in the sense commonly given these words. On principle, it will ignore these theories, in which it could not recognize any scientific value, since they tend not to describe or interpret, but to reform, social organization. At least, if it takes an interest in them, it is in proportion as it sees in them social facts which can aid it both in understanding the social reality and in disclosing the needs that are the motivating power in society. We do not mean, however, that it ought to take no interest in practical questions. It has been evident, on the contrary, that our constant preoccupation has been to orient it so that it might have practical results. It necessarily meets these problems at the end of its researches. But, by the very fact that they present themselves to sociology only at this moment, and that, consequently, they are derived from facts and not from emotions, one can foresee that they must be formulated for the sociologist in quite other terms than for the masses, and that the tentative solutions it can give them could not coincide exactly with any of those which now satisfy various interest groups. But the role of sociology from this point of view must properly consist in emancipating us from all parties, not to the extent of negating all doctrine, but by persuading us to assume toward these questions a special attitude that science alone can give in its direct contact with things. Science alone can teach us to treat historic institutions, whatever they may be, with respect but without mystic awe, by making us appreciate both their permanent and their ephemeral aspects, their stability and their infinite variability.

In the second place, our method is objective. It is dominated entirely by the idea that social facts are things and must be treated as such. No doubt, this principle is found again, under a slightly different form, at the basis of the doctrines of Comte and Spencer. But these great thinkers gave it theoretic formulation without putting it into practice. In order that it might not remain a dead letter, it is not sufficient to promulgate it; it is necessary to make it the basis of an entire discipline which will take hold of the student at the very moment he approaches the subject of his researches, and which will accompany him, step by step, in all his proceedings. We have devoted ourselves to instituting this discipline.

We have shown how the sociologist has to disregard the preconceptions which he had of facts, in order to face the facts themselves; how he has to discriminate among them according to their most objective characteristics; how he must seek in the facts themselves the means of classifying them as normal and pathological; how, finally, he must be inspired by the same principle in the explanations he attempts as in the way in which he tests these explanations. For, as soon as he has the feeling that he is in the presence of things, he will no longer think of explaining them by utilitarian calculations or by syllogistic reasonings of any sort. He will understand too well the gap that exists between such causes and such effects.

A thing is a force which can be engendered only by another force. In rendering an account of social facts, we seek, then, energies capable of producing them. Not only do the explanations thus given differ from the preceding ones, but they are differently verified, or, rather, it is only with them that the need of verification is felt. If sociological phenomena are only systems of objectivized ideas, to explain them is to rethink them in their logical order, and this explanation is in itself its own proof; at the very most, it will require confirmation by a few examples. Only methodical experiments, on the contrary, can extract from things their real secrets.

If we consider social facts as things, we consider them as *social things*. The third trait that characterizes our method is that it is exclusively sociological. It has often appeared that these phenomena, because of their extreme complexity, were either inhospitable to science or could be subject to it only when reduced to their elemental conditions, either psychic or organic, that is, only when stripped of their proper nature. We have, on the contrary, undertaken to establish that it is possible to treat them scientifically without removing any of their distinctive characteristics. We have even refused to identify the immateriality which characterizes them with the complex immateriality of psychological phenomena; we have, furthermore, refused to reabsorb it, with the Italian school, into the general properties of organized matter. We have shown that a social fact can be explained only by another social fact; and, at the same time, we have shown how this sort of explanation is possible by pointing out, in the internal social milieu, the principal factor in collective evolution. Sociology is, then, not an auxiliary of any other science; it is itself a distinct and autonomous science, and the feeling of the specificity of social reality is indeed so necessary to the sociologist that only distinctly sociological training can prepare him to grasp social facts intelligently.

In our opinion this progress is the most important that sociology still has to make. No doubt, when a science is in the process of being born, one is obliged, in order to construct it, to refer to the only models that exist, namely, the sciences already formed. These contain a treasure of experiences which it would be foolish to ignore. A science can regard itself as definitely established, however, only when it has achieved independence for itself. For it can justify its existence only when it has for its subject matter an order of facts which the other sciences do not study. It is impossible that the same concepts can fit equally well things of different natures.

Such appear to us to be the principles of sociological method. This collection of rules will perhaps appear needlessly complicated if one compares it with the procedures in current use. All this apparatus of precautions may seem very laborious for a science which, up to this point, scarcely demanded from those who devoted themselves to it more than general and philosophical training. It is certain, indeed, that the practice of such a method cannot have for its effect the popularization of interest in sociological matters. When, as a condition of their acceptance into the sociological fraternity, we ask men to discard the concepts they are accustomed to apply to an order of facts, in order to reexamine the latter in a new way, we cannot expect to recruit a numerous clientele. But this is not the goal toward which we are heading. We believe, on the contrary, that the time has come for sociology to spurn popular success, so to speak, and to assume the exacting character befitting every science. It will then gain in dignity and authority what it will perhaps lose in popularity. For, so long as it remains involved in partisan struggles, is content to expound common ideas with more logic than the layman, and, consequently, presumes no special competence, it has no right to speak loudly enough to silence passions and prejudices. Assuredly, the time when it will be able to play this role successfully is still far off. However, we must begin to work now, in order to put it in condition to fill this role some day.

3.5 *Suicide: A Study in Sociology*

Suicide is arguably the most famous and celebrated of all sociology books. The choice of the subject matter was a bold one: could sociology have something distinctive to say about one of the most individual of all acts? Durkheim's analysis of the available data revealed that suicide rates displayed stability and consistency over time within different countries; thus suicide rates could be treated as 'social facts'. If various societies were predisposed to different rates of suicide then this would seem to require not a psychological explanation but a sociological one.

Durkheim goes on to argue that an imbalance of integrative and regulative forces at times leading to too much or too little individualism and/or social constraint affects the rate of suicide within a society. From this insight Durkheim develops his famous classification of suicide types.

From: E. Durkheim, *Suicide: A Study in Sociology* (The Free Press: New York, 1958) pp. 41–6, 51–2, 208–21, 246–54, 318–20

Since the word 'suicide' recurs constantly in the course of conversation, it might be thought that its sense is universally known and that definition is superfluous. Actually, the words of everyday language, like the concepts they express, are always susceptible of more than one meaning, and the scholar employing them in their accepted use without further definition would risk serious misunderstanding. Not only is their meaning so indefinite as to vary, from case to case, with the needs of argument, but, as the classification from which they derive is not analytic, but merely translates the confused impressions of the crowd, categories of very different sorts of fact are indistinctly combined under the same heading, or similar realities are differently named. So, if we follow common use, we risk distinguishing what should be combined, or combining what should be distinguished, thus mistaking the real affinities of things, and accordingly misapprehending their nature. Only comparison affords explanation. A scientific investigation can thus be achieved only if it deals with comparable facts, and it is the more likely to succeed the more certainly it has combined all those that can be usefully compared. But these natural affinities of entities cannot be made clear safely by such superficial examination as produces ordinary terminology; and so the scholar cannot take as the subject of his research roughly assembled groups of facts corresponding to words of common usage. He himself must establish the groups he wishes to study in order to give them the homogeneity and the specific meaning necessary for them to be susceptible of scientific treatment. Thus the botanist, speaking of flowers or fruits, the zoologist of fish or insects, employ these various terms in previously determined senses.

Our first task then must be to determine the order of facts to be studied under the name of suicides. Accordingly, we must inquire whether, among the different varieties of death, some have common qualities objective enough to be recognizable by all honest observers, specific enough not to be found elsewhere and also sufficiently kin to those commonly called suicides for us to retain the same term without breaking with common usage. If such are found, we shall combine under that name absolutely all the facts presenting these distinctive characteristics, regardless of whether the resulting class fails to include all cases ordinarily included under the name or includes others usually otherwise classified. The essential thing is not to express with some precision what the average intelligence terms suicide, but to establish a category of objects permitting this classification, which are objectively established, that is, correspond to a definite aspect of things.

Among the different species of death, some have the special quality of being the deed of the victim himself, resulting from an act whose author is also the sufferer; and this same characteristic, on the other hand, is certainly fundamental to the usual idea of suicide. The intrinsic nature of the acts so resulting is unimportant. Though suicide is commonly conceived as a positive, violent action involving some muscular energy, it may happen that a purely negative attitude or mere abstention will have the same consequence. Refusal to take food is as suicidal as self-destruction by a dagger or firearm. The subject's act need not even have been directly antecedent to death for death to be regarded as its effect; the causal relation may be indirect without that changing the nature of the phenomenon. The iconoclast, committing with the hope of a martyr's palm the crime of high treason known to be capital and dying by the executioner's hand, achieves his own death as truly as though he had dealt his own death-blow; there is, at least, no reason to classify differently these two sorts of voluntary death, since only material details of their execution differ. We come then to our first formula: the term suicide is applied to any death which is the direct or indirect result of a positive or negative act accomplished by the victim himself.

But this definition is incomplete; it fails to distinguish between two very different sorts of death. The same classification and treatment cannot be given the death of a victim of hallucination, who throws himself from an upper window thinking it on a level with the ground, and that of the sane person who strikes while knowing what he is doing. In one sense, indeed, few cases of death exist which are not immediately or distantly due to some act of the subject. The causes of death are outside rather than within us, and are effective only if we venture into their sphere of activity.

Shall suicide be considered to exist only if the act resulting in death was performed by the victim to achieve this result? Shall only he be thought truly to slay himself who has wished to do so, and suicide be intentional self-homicide? In the first place, this would define suicide by a characteristic which, whatever its interest and significance, would at least suffer from not being easily recognizable, since it is not easily observed. How discover the agent's motive and whether he desired death itself when he formed his resolve, or had some other purpose? Intent is too intimate a thing to be more than approximately interpreted by another. It even escapes self-observation. How often we mistake the true reasons for our acts! We constantly explain acts due to petty feelings or blind routine by generous passions or lofty considerations.

Besides, in general, an act cannot be defined by the end sought by the actor, for an identical system of behavior may be adjustable to too many different ends without altering its nature. Indeed, if the intention of self-destruction alone constituted suicide, the name suicide could not be given to facts which, despite apparent differences, are fundamentally identical with those always called suicide and which could not be otherwise described without discarding the term. The soldier facing certain death to save his regiment does not wish to die, and yet is he not as much the author of his own death as the manufacturer or merchant who kills himself to avoid bankruptcy? This holds true for the martyr dying for his faith, the mother sacrificing herself for her child, etc. Whether death is accepted merely as an unfortunate consequence, but inevitable given the purpose, or is actually itself sought and desired, in either case the person renounces existence, and the various methods of doing so can be only varieties of a single class. They possess too many essential similarities not to be combined in one generic expression, subject to distinction as the species of the genus thus established. Of course, in common terms, suicide is pre-eminently the desperate act of one who does not care to live. But actually life is none the less abandoned because one desires it at the moment of renouncing it; and there are common traits clearly essential to all acts by which a living being thus renounces the possession presumably most precious of all. Rather, the diversity of motives capable of actuating these resolves can give rise only to secondary differences. Thus, when resolution entails certain sacrifice of life, scientifically this is suicide; of what sort shall be seen later.

The common quality of all these possible forms of supreme renunciation is that the determining act is performed advisedly; that at the moment of acting the victim knows the certain result of his conduct, no matter what reason may have led him to act thus. All mortal facts thus characterized are clearly distinct from all others in which the victim is either not the author of his own end or else only its unconscious author. They differ by an easily recognizable feature, for it is not impossible to discover whether the individual did or did not know in advance the natural results of his action. Thus, they form a definite, homogeneous group, distinguishable from any other and therefore to be designated by a special term. Suicide is the one appropriate; there is no need to create another, for the vast majority of occurrences customarily so-called belong to this group. We may then say conclusively: the term *suicide is applied to all cases of death resulting directly or indirectly from a positive or negative act of the victim himself, which he knows will produce this result.* An attempt is an act thus defined but falling short of actual death.

This definition excludes from our study everything related to the suicide of animals. Our knowledge of animal intelligence does not really allow us to attribute to them an understanding anticipatory of their death nor, especially, of the means to accomplish it. Some, to be sure, are known to refuse to enter a spot where others have been killed; they seem to have a presentiment of death. Actually, however, the smell of blood sufficiently explains this instinctive reaction. All cases cited at all authentically which might appear true suicides may be quite differently explained. If the irritated scorpion pierces itself with its sting (which is not at all certain), it is probably from an automatic, unreflecting reaction. The motive energy aroused by his irritation is discharged by chance and at random; the creature happens to become its victim, though it cannot be said to have had a preconception of the result of its action. On the other hand, if some dogs refuse to take food on losing their masters, it is because the sadness into which they are thrown has automatically caused lack of hunger; death has resulted, but without having been foreseen. Neither fasting in this case nor the wound in the other have been used as means to a known effect. So the special characteristics of suicide as defined by us are lacking. Hence in the following we shall treat human suicide only.

But this definition not only forestalls erroneous combinations and arbitrary exclusions; it also gives us at once an idea of the place of suicide in moral life as a whole. It shows indeed that suicides do not form, as might be thought, a wholly distinct group, an isolated class of monstrous phenomena, unrelated to other forms of conduct, but rather are related to them by a continuous series of intermediate cases. They are merely the exaggerated form of common practices. Suicide, we say, exists indeed when the victim at the moment he commits the act destined to be fatal, knows the normal result of it with certainty. This certainty, however, may be greater or less. Introduce a few doubts, and you have a new fact, not suicide but closely akin to it, since only a difference of degree exists between them. Doubtless, a man exposing himself knowingly for another's sake but without the certainty of a fatal result is not a suicide, even if he should die, any more than the daredevil who intentionally toys with death while seeking to avoid it, or the man of apathetic temperament who, having no vital interest in anything, takes no care of health and so imperils it by neglect. Yet these different ways of acting are not radically distinct from true suicide. They result from similar states of mind, since they also entail mortal risks not unknown to the agent, and the prospect of these is no deterrent; the sole difference is a lesser chance of death. Thus the scholar who dies from excessive devotion to study is currently and not wholly unreasonably said to have killed himself by his labor. All such facts form a sort of embryonic suicide, and though it is not methodologically sound to confuse them with complete and full suicide, their close relation to it must not be neglected. For suicide appears quite another matter, once its unbroken connection is recognized with acts, on the one hand, of courage and devotion, on the other of imprudence and clear neglect. The lesson of these connections will be better understood in what follows [. . .]

The suicide-rate is therefore a factual order, unified and definite, as is shown by both its permanence and its variability. For this permanence would be inexplicable if it were not the result of a group of distinct characteristics, solidary one with another, and simultaneously effective in spite of different attendant circumstances; and this variability proves the concrete and individual quality of these same characteristics, since they vary with the individual character of society itself. In short, these statistical data express the suicidal tendency with which each society is collectively afflicted. We need not state the actual nature of this, tendency, whether it is a state *sui generis* of the collective mind, [1] with its own reality, or represents merely a sum of individual states. Although the preceding considerations are hard to reconcile with the second hypothesis, we reserve this problem for treatment in the course of this work. Whatever one's opinion on this subject, such a tendency certainly exists under one heading or another. Each society is predisposed to contribute a definite quota of voluntary deaths. This predisposition may therefore be the subject of a special study belonging to sociology. This is the study we are going to undertake.

We do not accordingly intend to make as nearly complete an inventory as possible of all the conditions affecting the origin of individual suicides, but merely to examine those on which the definite fact that we have called the social suicide-rate depends. The two questions are obviously quite distinct, whatever relation may nevertheless exist between them. Certainly many of the individual conditions are not general enough to affect the relation between the total number of voluntary deaths and the population. They may perhaps cause this or that separate individual to kill himself, but not give society as a whole a greater or lesser tendency to suicide. As they do not depend on a certain state of social organization, they have no social repercussions. Thus they concern the psychologist, not the sociologist. The latter studies the causes capable of affecting not separate individuals but the group. Therefore among the factors of suicide the only ones which concern him are those whose action is felt by society as a whole. The suicide-rate is the product of these factors. This is why we must limit our attention to them.

Such is the subject of the present work, to contain three parts.

The phenomenon to be explained can depend only on extra-social causes of broad generality or on causes expressly social. We shall search first for the influence of the former and shall find it non-existent or very inconsiderable.

Next we shall determine the nature of the social causes, how they produce their effects, and their relations to the individual states associated with the different sorts of suicide.

After that, we shall be better able to state precisely what the social element of suicide consists of; that is, the collective tendency just referred to, its relations to other social facts, and the means that can be used to counteract it [. . .]

We have thus successively set up the three following propositions:

Suicide varies inversely with the degree of integration of religious society.
Suicide varies inversely with the degree of integration of domestic society.
Suicide varies inversely with the degree of integration of political society.

This grouping shows that whereas these different societies have a moderating influence upon suicide, this is due not to special characteristics of each but to a characteristic common to all. Religion does not owe its efficacy to the special nature of religious sentiments, since domestic and political societies both produce the same effects when strongly integrated. This, moreover, we have already proved when studying directly the manner of action of different religions upon suicide. Inversely, it is not the specific nature of the domestic or political tie which can explain the immunity they confer, since religious society has the same advantage. The cause can only be found in a single quality possessed by all these social groups, though perhaps to varying degrees. The only quality satisfying this condition is that they are all strongly integrated social groups. So we reach the general conclusion: suicide varies inversely with the degree of integration of the social groups of which the individual forms a part.

But society cannot disintegrate without the individual simultaneously detaching himself from social life, without his own goals becoming preponderant over those of the community, in a word without his personality tending to surmount the collective personality. The more weakened the groups to which he belongs, the less he depends on them, the more he consequently depends only on himself and recognizes no other rules of conduct than what are founded on his private interests. If we agree to call this state egoism, in which the individual ego asserts itself to excess in the face of the social ego and at its expense, we may call egoistic the special type of suicide springing from excessive individualism.

But how can suicide have such an origin?

First of all, it can be said that, as collective force is one of the obstacles best calculated to restrain suicide, its weakening involves a development of suicide. When society is strongly integrated, it holds individuals under its control, considers them at its service and thus forbids them to dispose wilfully of themselves. Accordingly it opposes their evading their duties to it through death. But how could society impose its supremacy upon them when they refuse to accept this subordination as legitimate? It no longer then possesses the requisite authority to retain them in their duty if they wish to desert; and conscious of its own weakness, it even recognizes their right to do freely what it can no longer prevent. So far as they are the admitted masters of their destinies, it is their privilege to end their lives. They, on their part, have no reason to endure life's sufferings patiently. For they cling to life more resolutely when belonging to a group they love, so as not to betray interests they put before their own. The bond that unites them with the common cause attaches them to life and the lofty goal they envisage prevents their feeling personal troubles so deeply. There is, in short, in a cohesive and animated society a constant interchange of ideas and feelings from all to each and each to all, something like a mutual moral support, which instead of throwing the individual on his own resources, leads him to share in the collective energy and supports his own when exhausted.

But these reasons are purely secondary. Excessive individualism not only results in favoring the action of suicidogenic causes, but it is itself such a cause. It not only frees man's inclination to do away with himself from a protective obstacle, but creates this inclination out of whole cloth and thus gives birth to a special suicide which bears its mark. This must be clearly understood for this is what constitutes the special character of the type of suicide just distinguished and justifies the name we have given it. What is there then in individualism that explains this result?

It has been sometimes said that because of his psychological constitution, man cannot live without attachment to some object which transcends and survives him, and that the reason for this necessity is a need we must have not to perish entirely. Life is said to be intolerable unless some reason for existing is involved, some purpose justifying life's trials. The individual alone is not a sufficient end for his activity. He is too little. He is not only hemmed in spatially; he is also strictly limited temporally. When, therefore, we have no other object than ourselves we cannot avoid the thought that our efforts will finally end in nothingness, since we ourselves disappear. But annihilation terrifies us. Under these conditions one would lose courage to live, that is, to act and struggle, since nothing will remain of our exertions. The state of egoism, in other words, is supposed to be contradictory to human nature and, consequently, too uncertain to have chances of permanence.

In this absolute formulation the proposition is vulnerable. If the thought of the end of our personality were really so hateful, we could consent to live only by blinding ourselves voluntarily as to life's value. For if we may in a measure avoid the prospect of annihilation we cannot extirpate it; it is inevitable, whatever we do. We may push back the frontier for some generations, force our name to endure for some years or centuries longer than our body; a moment, too soon for most men, always comes when it will be nothing. For the groups we join in order to prolong our existence by their means are themselves mortal; they too must dissolve, carrying with them all our deposit of ourselves. Those are few whose memories are closely enough bound to the very history of humanity to be assured of living until its death. So, if we really thus thirsted after immortality, no such brief perspectives could ever appease us. Besides, what of us is it that lives? A word, a sound, an imperceptible trace, most often anonymous, therefore nothing comparable to the violence of our efforts or able to justify them to us. In actuality, though a child is naturally an egoist who feels not the slightest craving to survive himself, and the old man is very often a child in this and so many other respects, neither ceases to cling to life as much or more than the adult; indeed we have seen that suicide is very rare for the first fifteen years and tends to decrease at the other extreme of life. Such too is the case with animals, whose psychological constitution differs from that of men only in degree. It is therefore untrue that life is only possible by its possessing its rationale outside of itself.

Indeed, a whole range of functions concern only the individual; these are the ones indispensable for physical life. Since they are made for this purpose only, they are perfected by its attainment. In everything concerning them, therefore, man can act reasonably without thought of transcendental purposes. These functions serve by merely serving him. In so far as he has no other needs, he is therefore self-sufficient and can live happily with no other objective than living. This is not the case, however, with the civilized adult. He has many ideas, feelings and practices unrelated to organic needs. The roles of art, morality, religion, political faith, science itself are not to repair organic exhaustion nor to provide sound functioning of the organs. All this supra-physical life is built and expanded not because of the demands of the cosmic environment but because of the demands of the social environment. The influence of society is what has aroused in us the sentiments of sympathy and solidarity drawing us toward others; it is society which, fashioning us in its image, fills us with religious, political and moral beliefs that control our actions. To play our social role we have striven to extend our intelligence and it is still society that has supplied us with tools for this development by transmitting to us its trust fund of knowledge.

Through the very fact that these superior forms of human activity have a collective origin, they have a collective purpose. As they derive from society they have reference to it; rather they are society itself incarnated and individualized in each one of us. But for them to have a raison d'être in our eyes, the purpose they envisage must be one not indifferent to us. We can cling to these forms of human activity only to the degree that we cling to society itself. Contrariwise, in the same measure as we feel detached from society we become detached from that life whose source and aim is society. For what purpose do these rules of morality, these precepts of law binding us to all sorts of sacrifices, these restrictive dogmas exist, if there is no being outside us whom they serve and in whom we participate? What is the purpose of science itself? If its only use is to increase our chances for survival, it does not deserve the trouble it entails. Instinct acquits itself better of this role; animals prove this. Why substitute for it a more hesitant and uncertain reflection? What is the end of suffering, above all? If the value of things can only be estimated by their relation to this positive evil for the individual, it is without reward and incomprehensible. This problem does not exist for the believer firm in his faith or the man strongly bound by ties of domestic or political society. Instinctively and unreflectively they ascribe all that they are and do, the one to his Church or his God, the living symbol of the Church, the other to his family, the third to his country or party. Even in their sufferings they see only a means of glorifying the group to which they belong and thus do homage to it. So, the Christian ultimately desires and seeks suffering to testify more fully to his contempt for the flesh and more fully resemble his divine model. But the more the believer doubts, that is, the less he feels himself a real participant in the religious faith to which he belongs, and from which he is freeing himself; the more the family and community become foreign to the individual, so much the more does he become a mystery to himself, unable to escape the exasperating and agonizing question: to what purpose?

If, in other words, as has often been said, man is double, that is because social man superimposes himself upon physical man. Social man necessarily presupposes a society which he expresses and services. If this dissolves, if we no longer feel it in existence and action about and above us, whatever is social in us is deprived of all objective foundation. All that remains is an artificial combination of illusory images, a phantasmagoria vanishing at the least reflection; that is, nothing which can be a goal for our action. Yet this social man is the essence of civilized man; he is the masterpiece of existence. Thus we are bereft of reasons for existence; for the only life to which we could cling no longer corresponds to anything actual; the only existence still based upon reality no longer meets our needs. Because we have been initiated into a higher existence, the one which satisfies an animal or a child can satisfy us no more and the other itself fades and leaves us helpless. So there is nothing more for our efforts to lay hold of, and we feel them lose themselves in emptiness. In this sense it is true to say that our activity needs an object transcending it. We do not need it to maintain ourselves in the illusion of an impossible immortality; it is implicit in our moral constitution and cannot be even partially lost without this losing its raison d'être in the same degree. No proof is needed that in such a state of confusion the least cause of discouragement may easily give birth to desperate resolutions. If life is not worth the trouble of being lived, everything becomes a pretext to rid ourselves of it.

But this is not all. This detachment occurs not only in single individuals. One of the constitutive elements of every national temperament consists of a certain way of estimating the value of existence. There is a collective as well as an individual humor inclining peoples to sadness or cheerfulness, making them see things in bright or sombre lights. In fact, only society can pass a collective opinion on the value of human life; for this the individual is incompetent. The latter knows nothing but himself and his own little horizon; thus his experience is too limited to serve as a basis for a general appraisal. He may indeed consider his own life to be aimless; he can say nothing applicable to others. On the contrary, without sophistry, society may generalize its own feeling as to itself, its state of health or lack of health. For individuals share too deeply in the life of society for it to be diseased without their suffering infection. What it suffers they necessarily suffer. Because it is the whole, its ills are communicated to its parts. Hence it cannot disintegrate without awareness that the regular conditions of general existence are equally disturbed. Because society is the end on which our better selves depend, it cannot feel us escaping it without a simultaneous realization that our activity is purposeless. Since we are its handiwork, society cannot be conscious of its own decadence without the feeling that henceforth this work is of no value. Thence are formed currents of depression and disillusionment emanating from no particular individual but expressing society's state of disintegration. They reflect the relaxation of social bonds, a sort of collective asthenia, or social malaise, just as individual sadness, when chronic, in its way reflects the poor organic state of the individual. Then metaphysical and religious systems spring up which, by reducing these obscure sentiments to formulae, attempt to prove to men the senselessness of life and that it is self-deception to believe that it has purpose. Then new moralities originate which, by elevating facts to ethics, commend suicide or at least tend in that direction by suggesting a minimal existence. On their appearance they seem to have been created out of whole cloth by their makers who are sometimes blamed for the pessimism of their doctrines. In reality they are an effect rather than a cause; they merely symbolize in abstract language and systematic form the physiological distress of the body social. As these currents are collective, they have, by virtue of their origin, an authority which they impose upon the individual and they drive him more vigorously on the way to which he is already inclined by the state of moral distress directly aroused in him by the disintegration of society. Thus, at the very moment that, with excessive zeal, he frees himself from the social environment, he still submits to its influence. However individualized a man may be, there is always something collective remaining – the very depression and melancholy resulting from this same exaggerated individualism. He effects communion through sadness when he no longer has anything else with which to achieve it.

Hence this type of suicide well deserves the name we have given it. Egoism is not merely a contributing factor in it; it is its generating cause. In this case the bond attaching man to life relaxes because that attaching him to society is itself slack. The incidents of private life which seem the direct inspiration of suicide and are considered its determining causes are in reality only incidental causes. The individual yields to the slightest shock of circumstance because the state of society has made him a ready prey to suicide.

Several facts confirm this explanation. Suicide is known to be rare among children and to diminish among the aged at the last confines of life; physical man, in both, tends to become the whole of man. Society is still lacking in the former, for it has not had the time to form him in its image; it begins to retreat from the latter or, what amounts to the same thing, he retreats from it. Thus both are more self-sufficient. Feeling a lesser need for self-completion through something not themselves, they are also less exposed to feel the lack of what is necessary for living. The immunity of an animal has the same causes. We shall likewise see in the next chapter that, though lower societies practice a form of suicide of their own, the one we have just discussed is almost unknown to them. Since their social life is very simple, the social inclinations of individuals are simple also and thus they need little for satisfaction. They readily find external objectives to which they become attached. If he can carry with him his gods and his family, primitive man, everywhere that he goes, has all that his social nature demands.

This is also why woman can endure life in isolation more easily than man. When a widow is seen to endure her condition much better than a widower and desires marriage less passionately, one is led to consider this ease in dispensing with the family a mark of superiority; it is said that woman's affective faculties, being very intense, are easily employed outside the domestic circle, while her devotion is indispensable to man to help him endure life. Actually, if this is her privilege it is because her sensibility is rudimentary rather than highly developed. As she lives outside of community existence more than man, she is less penetrated by it; society is less necessary to her because she is less impregnated with sociability. She has few needs in this direction and satisfies them easily. With a few devotional practices and some animals to care for, the old unmarried woman's life is full. If she remains faithfully attached to religious traditions and thus finds ready protection against suicide, it is because these very simple social forms satisfy all her needs. Man, on the contrary, is hard beset in this respect. As his thought and activity develop, they increasingly overflow these antiquated forms. But then he needs others. Because he is a more complex social being, he can maintain his equilibrium only by finding more points of support outside himself, and it is because his moral balance depends on a larger number of conditions that it is more easily disturbed [. . .]

Altruistic suicide

In the order of existence, no good is measureless. A biological quality can only fulfill the purposes it is meant to serve on condition that it does not transgress certain limits. So with social phenomena. If, as we have just seen, excessive individuation leads to suicide, insufficient individuation has the same effects. When man has become detached from society, he encounters less resistance to suicide in himself, and he does so likewise when social integration is too strong.

I

It has sometimes been said that suicide was unknown among lower societies. Thus expressed, the assertion is inexact. To be sure, egoistic suicide, constituted as has just been shown, seems not to be frequent there. But another form exists among them in an endemic state.

Bartholin, in his book, *De Causis contemptae mortis a Danis*, reports that Danish warriors considered it a disgrace to die in bed of old age or sickness, and killed themselves to escape this ignominy. The Goths likewise believed that those who die a natural death are destined to languish forever in caverns full of venomous creatures. On the frontier of the Visigoths' territory was a high pinnacle called *The Rock of the Forefathers*, from the top of which old men would throw themselves when weary of life. The same custom was found among the Thracians, the Heruli, etc. Silvius Italicus says of the Spanish Celts: 'They are a nation lavish of their blood and eager to face death. As soon as the Celt has passed the age of mature strength, he endures the flight of time impatiently and scorns to await old age; the term of his existence depends upon himself.' Accordingly they assigned a delightful abode to those who committed suicide and a horrible subterranean one to those who died of sickness or decrepitude. The same custom has long been maintained in India. Perhaps this favorable attitude toward suicide did not appear in the Vedas, but it was certainly very ancient. Plutarch says concerning the suicide of the brahmin Calanus: 'He sacrificed himself with his own hands as was customary with sages of this country.' And Quintus Curtius: 'Among them exists a sort of wild and bestial men to whom they give the name of sages. The anticipation of the time of death is a glory in their eyes, and they have themselves burned alive as soon as age or sickness begins to trouble them. According to them, death, passively awaited, is a dishonor to life; thus no honors are rendered those bodies which old age has destroyed. Fire would be contaminated did it not receive the human sacrifice still breathing.' Similar facts are recorded at Fiji, in the New Hebrides, Manga, etc. At Ceos, men who had outlived a certain age used to unite in a solemn festival where with heads crowned with flowers they joyfully drank the hemlock. Like practices were found among the Troglodytes and the Seri, who were nevertheless renowned for their morality.

Besides the old men, women are often required among the same peoples to kill themselves on their husbands' death. This barbarous practice is so ingrained in Hindu customs that the efforts of the English are futile against it. In 1817, 706 widows killed themselves in the one province of Bengal and in 1821, 2,366 were found in all India. Moreover, when a prince or chief dies, his followers are forced not to survive him. Such was the case in Gaul. The funerals of chiefs, Henri Martin declares, were bloody hecatombs where their garments, weapons, horses and favorite slaves were solemnly burned, together with the personal followers who had not died in the chief's last battle. Such a follower was never to survive his chief. Among the Ashantis, on the king's death his officers must die. Observers have found the same custom in Hawaii.

Suicide, accordingly, is surely very common among primitive peoples. But it displays peculiar characteristics. All the facts above reported fall into one of the following three categories:

1. Suicides of men on the threshold of old age or stricken with sickness.
2. Suicides of women on their husbands' death.
3. Suicides of followers or servants on the death of their chiefs.

Now, when a person kills himself, in all these cases, it is not because he assumes the right to do so but, on the contrary, *because it is his duty*. If he fails in this obligation, he is dishonored and also punished, usually, by religious sanctions. Of course, when we hear of aged men killing themselves we are tempted at first to believe that the cause is weariness or the sufferings common to age. But if these suicides really had no other source, if the individual made away with himself merely to be rid of an unendurable existence, he would not be required to do so; one is never obliged to take advantage of a privilege. Now, we have seen that if such a person insists on living he loses public respect; in one case the usual funeral honors are denied, in another a life of horror is supposed to await him beyond the grave. The weight of society is thus brought to bear on him to lead him to destroy himself. To be sure, society intervenes in egoistic suicide, as well; but its intervention differs in the two cases. In one case, it speaks the sentence of death; in the other it forbids the choice of death. In the case of egoistic suicide it suggests or counsels at most; in the other case it compels and is the author of conditions and circumstances making this obligation coercive.

This sacrifice then is imposed by society for social ends. If the follower must not survive his chief or the servant his prince, this is because so strict an interdependence between followers and chiefs, officers and king, is involved in the constitution of the society that any thought of separation is out of the question. The destiny of one must be that of the others. Subjects as well as clothing and armor must follow their master wherever he goes, even beyond the tomb; if another possibility were to be admitted social subordination would be inadequate. Such is the relation of the woman to her husband. As for the aged, if they are not allowed to await death, it is probably, at least in many instances, for religious reasons. The protecting spirit of a family is supposed to reside in its chief. It is further thought that a god inhabiting the body of another shares in his life, enduring the same phases of health and sickness and aging with him. Age cannot therefore reduce the strength of one without the other being similarly weakened and consequently without the group existence being threatened, since a strengthless divinity would be its only remaining protector. For this reason, in the common interest, a father is required not to await the furthest limit of life before transferring to his successors the precious trust that is in his keeping.

This description sufficiently defines the cause of these suicides. For society to be able thus to compel some of its members to kill themselves, the individual personality can have little value. For as soon as the latter begins to form, the right to existence is the first conceded it; or is at least suspended only in such unusual circumstances as war. But there can be only one cause for this feeble individuation itself. For the individual to occupy so little place in collective life he must be almost completely absorbed in the group and the latter, accordingly, very highly integrated. For the parts to have so little life of their own, the whole must indeed be a compact, continuous mass. And we have shown elsewhere that such massive cohesion is indeed that of societies where the above practices obtain. As they consist of few elements, everyone leads the same life; everything is common to all, ideas, feelings, occupations. Also, because of the small size of the group it is close to everyone and loses no one from sight; consequently collective supervision is constant, extending to everything, and thus more readily prevents divergences. The individual thus has no way to set up an environment of his own in the shelter of which he may develop his own nature and form a physiognomy that is his exclusively. To all intents and purposes indistinct from his companions, he is only an inseparable part of the whole without personal value. His person has so little value that attacks upon it by individuals receive only relatively weak restraint. It is thus natural for him to be yet less protected against collective necessities and that society should not hesitate, for the very slightest reason, to bid him end a life it values so little.

We thus confront a type of suicide differing by incisive qualities from the preceding one. Whereas the latter is due to excessive individuation, the former is caused by too rudimentary individuation. One occurs because society allows the individual to escape it, being insufficiently aggregated in some parts or even in the whole; the other, because society holds him in too strict tutelage. Having given the name of *egoism* to the state of the ego living its own life and obeying itself alone, that of *altruism* adequately expresses the opposite state, where the ego is not its own property, where it is blended with something not itself, where the goal of conduct is exterior to itself, that is, in one of the groups in which it participates. So we call the suicide caused by intense altruism *altruistic suicide*. But since it is also characteristically performed as a duty, the terminology adopted should express this fact. So we will call such a type *obligatory altruistic suicide* [. . .]

II

No living being can be happy or even exist unless his needs are sufficiently proportioned to his means. In other words, if his needs require more than can be granted, or even merely something of a different sort, they will be under continual friction and can only function painfully. Movements incapable of production without pain tend not to be reproduced. Unsatisfied tendencies atrophy, and as the impulse to live is merely the result of all the rest, it is bound to weaken as the others relax.

In the animal, at least in a normal condition, this equilibrium is established with automatic spontaneity because the animal depends on purely material conditions. All the organism needs is that the supplies of substance and energy constantly employed in the vital process should be periodically renewed by equivalent quantities; that replacement be equivalent to use. When the void created by existence in its own resources is filled, the animal, satisfied, asks nothing further. Its power of reflection is not sufficiently developed to imagine other ends than those implicit in its physical nature. On the other hand, as the work demanded of each organ itself depends on the general state of vital energy and the needs of organic equilibrium, use is regulated in turn by replacement and the balance is automatic. The limits of one are those of the other; both are fundamental to the constitution of the existence in question, which cannot exceed them.

This is not the case with man, because most of his needs are not dependent on his body or not to the same degree. Strictly speaking, we may consider that the quantity of material supplies necessary to the physical maintenance of a human life is subject to computation, though this be less exact than in the preceding case and a wider margin left for the free combinations of the will; for beyond the indispensable minimum which satisfies nature when instinctive, a more awakened reflection suggests better conditions, seemingly desirable ends craving fulfillment. Such appetites, however, admittedly sooner or later reach a limit which they cannot pass. But how determine the quantity of well-being, comfort or luxury legitimately to be craved by a human being? Nothing appears in man's organic nor in his psychological constitution which sets a limit to such tendencies. The functioning of individual life does not require them to cease at one point rather than at another; the proof being that they have constantly increased since the beginnings of history, receiving more and more complete satisfaction, yet with no weakening of average health. Above all, how establish their proper variation with different conditions of life, occupations, relative importance of services, etc.? In no society are they equally satisfied in the different stages of the social hierarchy. Yet human nature is substantially the same among all men, in its essential qualities. It is not human nature which can assign the variable limits necessary to our needs. They are thus unlimited so far as they depend on the individual alone. Irrespective of any external regulatory force, our capacity for feeling is in itself an insatiable and bottomless abyss.

But if nothing external can restrain this capacity, it can only be a source of torment to itself. Unlimited desires are insatiable by definition and insatiability is rightly considered a sign of morbidity. Being unlimited, they constantly and infinitely surpass the means at their command; they cannot be quenched. Inextinguishable thirst is constantly renewed torture. It has been claimed, indeed, that human activity naturally aspires beyond assignable limits and sets itself unattainable goals. But how can such an undetermined state be any more reconciled with the conditions of mental life than with the demands of physical life? All man's pleasure in acting, moving and exerting himself implies the sense that his efforts are not in vain and that by walking he has advanced. However, one does not advance when one walks toward no goal, or – which is the same thing – when his goal is infinity. Since the distance between us and it is always the same, whatever road we take, we might as well have made the motions without progress from the spot. Even our glances behind and our feeling of pride at the distance covered can cause only deceptive satisfaction, since the remaining distance is not proportionately reduced. To pursue a goal which is by definition unattainable is to condemn oneself to a state of perpetual unhappiness. Of course, man may hope contrary to all reason, and hope has its pleasures even when unreasonable. It may sustain him for a time; but it cannot survive the repeated disappointments of experience indefinitely. What more can the future offer him than the past, since he can never reach a tenable condition nor even approach the glimpsed ideal? Thus, the more one has, the more one wants, since satisfactions received only stimulate instead of filling needs. Shall action as such be considered agreeable? First, only on condition of blindness to its uselessness. Secondly, for this pleasure to be felt and to temper and half veil the accompanying painful unrest, such unending motion must at least always be easy and unhampered. If it is interfered with only restlessness is left, with the lack of ease which it, itself, entails. But it would be a miracle if no insurmountable obstacle were ever encountered. Our thread of life on these conditions is pretty thin, breakable at any instant.

To achieve any other result, the passions first must be limited. Only then can they be harmonized with the faculties and satisfied. But since the individual has no way of limiting them, this must be done by some force exterior to him. A regulative force must play the same role for moral needs which the organism plays for physical needs. This means that the force can only be moral. The awakening of conscience interrupted the state of equilibrium of the animal's dormant existence; only conscience, therefore, can furnish the means to re-establish it. Physical restraint would be ineffective; hearts cannot be touched by physio-chemical forces. So far as the appetites are not automatically restrained by physiological mechanisms, they can be halted only by a limit that they recognize as just. Men would never consent to restrict their desires if they felt justified in passing the assigned limit. But, for reasons given above, they cannot assign themselves this law of justice. So they must receive it from an authority which they respect, to which they yield spontaneously. Either directly and as a whole, or through the agency of one of its organs, society alone can play this moderating role; for it is the only moral power superior to the individual, the authority of which he accepts. It alone has the power necessary to stipulate law and to set the point beyond which the passions must not go. Finally, it alone can estimate the reward to be prospectively offered to every class of human functionary, in the name of the common interest.

As a matter of fact, at every moment of history there is a dim perception, in the moral consciousness of societies, of the respective value of different social services, the relative reward due to each, and the consequent degree of comfort appropriate on the average to workers in each occupation. The different functions are graded in public opinion and a certain coefficient of well-being assigned to each, according to its place in the hierarchy. According to accepted ideas, for example, a certain way of living is considered the upper limit to which a workman may aspire in his efforts to improve his existence, and there is another limit below which he is not willingly permitted to fall unless he has seriously bemeaned himself. Both differ for city and country workers, for the domestic servant and the day-laborer, for the business clerk and the official, etc. Likewise the man of wealth is reproved if he lives the life of a poor man, but also if he seeks the refinements of luxury overmuch. Economists may protest in vain; public feeling will always be scandalized if an individual spends too much wealth for wholly superfluous use, and it even seems that this severity relaxes only in times of moral disturbance. A genuine regime exists, therefore, although not always legally formulated, which fixes with relative precision the maximum degree of ease of living to which each social class may legitimately aspire. However, there is nothing immutable about such a scale. It changes with the increase or decrease of collective revenue and the changes occurring in the moral ideas of society. Thus what appears luxury to one period no longer does so to another; and the well-being which for long periods was granted to a class only by exception and supererogation, finally appears strictly necessary and equitable.

Under this pressure, each in his sphere vaguely realizes the extreme limit set to his ambitions and aspires to nothing beyond. At least if he respects regulations and is docile to collective authority, that is, has a wholesome moral constitution, he feels that it is not well to ask more. Thus, an end and goal are set to the passions. Truly, there is nothing rigid nor absolute about such determination. The economic ideal assigned each class of citizens is itself confined to certain limits, within which the desires have free range. But it is not infinite. This relative limitation and the moderation it involves, make men contented with their lot while stimulating them moderately to improve it; and this average contentment causes the feeling of calm, active happiness, the pleasure in existing and living which characterizes health for societies as well as for individuals. Each person is then at least, generally speaking, in harmony with his condition, and desires only what he may legitimately hope for as the normal reward of his activity. Besides, this does not condemn man to a sort of immobility. He may seek to give beauty to his life; but his attempts in this direction may fail without causing him to despair. For, loving what he has and not fixing his desire solely on what he lacks, his wishes and hopes may fail of what he has happened to aspire to, without his being wholly destitute. He has the essentials. The equilibrium of his happiness is secure because it is defined, and a few mishaps cannot disconcert him.

But it would be of little use for everyone to recognize the justice of the hierarchy of functions established by public opinion, if he did not also consider the distribution of these functions just. The workman is not in harmony with his social position if he is not convinced that he has his deserts. If he feels justified in occupying another, what he has would not satisfy him. So it is not enough for the average level of needs for each social condition to be regulated by public opinion, but another, more precise rule, must fix the way in which these conditions are open to individuals. There is no society in which such regulation does not exist. It varies with times and places. Once it regarded birth as the almost exclusive principle of social classification; today it recognizes no other inherent inequality than hereditary fortune and merit. But in all these various forms its object is unchanged. It is also only possible, everywhere, as a restriction upon individuals imposed by superior authority, that is, by collective authority. For it can be established only by requiring of one or another group of men, usually of all, sacrifices and concessions in the name of the public interest.

Some, to be sure, have thought that this moral pressure would become unnecessary if men's economic circumstances were only no longer determined by heredity. If inheritance were abolished, the argument runs, if everyone began life with equal resources and if the competitive struggle were fought out on a basis of perfect equality, no one could think its results unjust. Each would instinctively feel that things are as they should be.

Truly, the nearer this ideal equality were approached, the less social restraint will be necessary. But it is only a matter of degree. One sort of heredity will always exist, that of natural talent. Intelligence, taste, scientific, artistic, literary or industrial ability, courage and manual dexterity are gifts received by each of us at birth, as the heir to wealth receives his capital or as the nobleman formerly received his title and function. A moral discipline will therefore still be required to make those less favored by nature accept the lesser advantages which they owe to the chance of birth. Shall it be demanded that all have an equal share and that no advantage be given those more useful and deserving? But then there would have to be a discipline far stronger to make these accept a treatment merely equal to that of the mediocre and incapable.

But like the one first mentioned, this discipline can be useful only if considered just by the peoples subject to it. When it is maintained only by custom and force, peace and harmony are illusory; the spirit of unrest and discontent are latent; appetites superficially restrained are ready to revolt. This happened in Rome and Greece when the faiths underlying the old organization of the patricians and plebeians were shaken, and in our modern societies when aristocratic prejudices began to lose their old ascendancy. But this state of upheaval is exceptional; it occurs only when society is passing through some abnormal crisis. In normal conditions the collective order is regarded as just by the great majority of persons. Therefore, when we say that an authority is necessary to impose this order on individuals, we certainly do not mean that violence is the only means of establishing it. Since this regulation is meant to restrain individual passions, it must come from a power which dominates individuals; but this power must also be obeyed through respect, not fear.

It is not true, then, that human activity can be released from all restraint. Nothing in the world can enjoy such a privilege. All existence being a part of the universe is relative to the remainder; its nature and method of manifestation accordingly depend not only on itself but on other beings, who consequently restrain and regulate it. Here there are only differences of degree and form between the mineral realm and the thinking person. Man's characteristic privilege is that the bond he accepts is not physical but moral; that is, social. He is governed not by a material environment brutally imposed on him, but by a conscience superior to his own, the superiority of which he feels. Because the greater, better part of his existence transcends the body, he escapes the body's yoke, but is subject to that of society.

But when society is disturbed by some painful crisis or by beneficent but abrupt transitions, it is momentarily incapable of exercising this influence; thence come the sudden rises in the curve of suicides which we have pointed out above.

In the case of economic disasters, indeed, something like a declassification occurs which suddenly casts certain individuals into a lower state than their previous one. Then they must reduce their requirements, restrain their needs, learn greater self-control. All the advantages of social influence are lost so far as they are concerned; their moral education has to be recommenced. But society cannot adjust them instantaneously to this new life and teach them to practice the increased self-repression to which they are unaccustomed. So they are not adjusted to the condition forced on them, and its very prospect is intolerable; hence the suffering which detaches them from a reduced existence even before they have made trial of it.

It is the same if the source of the crisis is an abrupt growth of power and wealth. Then, truly, as the conditions of life are changed, the standard according to which needs were regulated can no longer remain the same; for it varies with social resources, since it largely determines the share of each class of producers. The scale is upset; but a new scale cannot be immediately improvised. Time is required for the public conscience to reclassify men and things. So long as the social forces thus freed have not regained equilibrium, their respective values are unknown and so all regulation is lacking for a time. The limits are unknown between the possible and the impossible, what is just and what is unjust, legitimate claims and hopes and those which are immoderate. Consequently, there is no restraint upon aspirations. If the disturbance is profound, it affects even the principles controlling the distribution of men among various occupations. Since the relations between various parts of society are necessarily modified, the ideas expressing these relations must change. Some particular class especially favored by the crisis is no longer resigned to its former lot, and, on the other hand, the example of its greater good fortune arouses all sorts of jealousy below and about it. Appetites, not being controlled by a public opinion become disoriented, no longer recognize the limits proper to them. Besides, they are at the same time seized by a sort of natural erethism simply by the greater intensity of public life. With increased prosperity desires increase. At the very moment when traditional rules have lost their authority, the richer prize offered these appetites stimulates them and makes them more exigent and impatient of control. The state of de-regulation or anomy is thus further heightened by passions being less disciplined, precisely when they need more disciplining.

But then their very demands make fulfillment impossible. Overweening ambition always exceeds the results obtained, great as they may be, since there is no warning to pause here. Nothing gives satisfaction and all this agitation is uninterruptedly maintained without appeasement. Above all, since this race for an unattainable goal can give no other pleasure but that of the race itself, if it is one, once it is interrupted the participants are left empty-handed. At the same time the struggle grows more violent and painful, both from being less controlled and because competition is greater. All classes contend among themselves because no established classification any longer exists. Effort grows, just when it becomes less productive. How could the desire to live not be weakened under such conditions?

This explanation is confirmed by the remarkable immunity of poor countries. Poverty protects against suicide because it is a restraint in itself. No matter how one acts, desires have to depend upon resources to some extent; actual possessions are partly the criterion of those aspired to. So the less one has the less he is tempted to extend the range of his needs indefinitely. Lack of power, compelling moderation, accustoms men to it, while nothing excites envy if no one has superfluity. Wealth, on the other hand, by the power it bestows, deceives us into believing that we depend on ourselves only. Reducing the resistance we encounter from objects, it suggests the possibility of unlimited success against them. The less limited one feels, the more intolerable all limitation appears. Not without reason, therefore, have so many religions dwelt on the advantages and moral value of poverty. It is actually the best school for teaching self-restraint. Forcing us to constant self-discipline, it prepares us to accept collective discipline with equanimity, while wealth, exalting the individual, may always arouse the spirit of rebellion which is the very source of immorality. This, of course, is no reason why humanity should not improve its material condition. But though the moral danger involved in every growth of prosperity is not irremediable, it should not be forgotten [. . .]

Observation thus confirms our hypothesis. The regularity of statistical data, on the one hand, implies the existence of collective tendencies exterior to the individual, and on the other, we can directly establish this exterior character in a considerable number of important cases. Besides, this exteriority is not in the least surprising for anyone who knows the difference between individual and social states of consciousness. By definition, indeed, the latter can reach none of us except from without, since they do not flow from our personal predispositions. Since they consist of elements foreign to us they express something other than ourselves. To be sure in so far as we are solidary with the group and share its life, we are exposed to their influence; but so far as we have a distinct personality of our own we rebel against and try to escape them. Since everyone leads this sort of double existence simultaneously, each of us has a double impulse. We are drawn in a social direction and tend to follow the inclinations of our own natures. So the rest of society weighs upon us as a restraint to our centrifugal tendencies, and we for our part share in this weight upon others for the purpose of neutralizing theirs. We ourselves undergo the pressure we help to exert upon others. Two antagonistic forces confront each other. One, the collective force, tries to take possession of the individual; the other, the individual force, repulses it. To be sure, the former is much stronger than the latter, since it is made of a combination of all the individual forces; but as it also encounters as many resistances as there are separate persons, it is partially exhausted in these multifarious contests and reaches us disfigured and enfeebled. When it is very strong, when the circumstances activating it are of frequent recurrence, it may still leave a deep impression on individuals; it arouses in them mental states of some vivacity which, once formed, function with the spontaneity of instinct; this happens in the case of the most essential moral ideas. But most social currents are either too weak or too intermittently in contact with us to strike deep roots in us; their action is superficial. Consequently, they remain almost completely external. Hence, the proper way to measure any element of a collective type is not to measure its magnitude within individual consciences and to take the average of them all. Rather, it is their sum that must be taken. Even this method of evaluation would be much below reality, for this would give us only the social sentiment reduced by all its losses through individuation.

So there is some superficiality about attacking our conception as scholasticism and reproaching it for assigning to social phenomena a foundation in some vital principle or other of a new sort. We refuse to accept that these phenomena have as a substratum the conscience of the individual, we assign them another; that formed by all the individual consciences in union and combination. There is nothing substantival or ontological about this substratum, since it is merely a whole composed of parts. But it is just as real, nevertheless, as the elements that make it up; for they are constituted in this very way. They are compounds, too. It is known today that the ego is the resultant of a multitude of conscious states outside the ego; that each of these elementary states, in turn, is the product of unconscious vital units, just as each vital unit is itself due to an association of inanimate particles. Therefore if the psychologist and the biologist correctly regard the phenomena of their study as well founded, merely through the fact of their connection with a combination of elements of the next lower order, why should it not be the same in sociology? Only those have the right to consider such a basis inadequate who have not renounced the hypothesis of a vital force and of a substantive soul. Nothing is more reasonable, then, than this proposition at which such offense has been taken; that a belief or social practice may exist independently of its individual expressions. We clearly did not imply by this that society can exist without individuals, an obvious absurdity we might have been spared having attributed to us. But we did mean: 1. that the group formed by associated individuals has a reality of a different sort from each individual considered singly; 2. that collective states exist in the group from whose nature they spring, before they affect the individual as such and establish in him in a new form a purely inner existence.

Such a way of considering the individual's relations to society also recalls the idea assigned the individual's relations with the species or the race by contemporary zoologists. The very simple theory has been increasingly abandoned that the species is only an individual perpetuated chronologically and generalized spacially. Indeed it conflicts with the fact that the variations produced in a single instance become specific only in very rare and possibly doubtful cases. The distinctive characteristics of the race change in the individual only as they change in the race in general. The latter has therefore some reality whence come the various shapes it assumes among individual beings, far from its consisting simply of a generalization of these beings. We naturally cannot regard these doctrines as finally demonstrated. But it is enough for us to show that our sociological conceptions, without being borrowed from another order of research, are indeed not without analogies to the most positive sciences.

Note

1. By the use of this expression we of course do not at all intend to hypostasize the collective conscience. We do not recognize any more substantial a soul in society than in the individual.

3.6 Religion and Society

The Elementary Forms of the Religious Life is probably Durkheim's greatest work. *The Elementary Forms* is an inquiry into the manner in which religion acts both as a source of moral authority and, via its practices and rituals, social solidarity. In the *Elementary Forms* Durkheim also argues that our basic categories of thought are social in origin. In this book Durkheim displays his tendency towards evolutionary thinking as he uses an in-depth case-study of a 'simple' clan-based society (Australian Aborigines) with a totemic religion to provide an understanding of the relations between religion and society in more complex societies.

In this extract Durkheim, in typical fashion, works up to a definition of religion. He then goes on to discuss the notion of the 'totemic principle' whereby very often mundane, ordinary and profane objects can be imbued with a sacredness that serves as a symbol and a source of collective identity for the group – think of the power of a national flag for example. This division between the sacred and the profane is, Durkheim believes, common to all religions. The source of the sacred nature of the totem and the awe and feelings of 'collective effervescence' it can engender is, for Durkheim, nothing other than the clan or society itself. Given this we can see that religious ceremonies and acts of worship can serve the purpose of increasing and reaffirming collective sentiments and social solidarity as well as the moral authority of 'society'.

From: E. Durkheim, *The Elementary Forms of the Religious Life* (Allen and Unwin: London, 1971) pp. 1–2, 10, 43–7, 188–90, 206–9, 219–21, 315, 317–21, 427.

In this book we propose to study the most primitive and simple religion which is actually known, to make an analysis of it, and to attempt an explanation of it. A religious system may be said to be the most primitive which we can observe when it fulfils the two following conditions: in the first place, when it is found in a society whose organization is surpassed by no others in simplicity;[1] and secondly, when it is possible to explain it without making use of any element borrowed from a previous religion.

We shall set ourselves to describe the organization of this system with all the exactness and fidelity that an ethnographer or an historian could give it. But our task will not be limited to that: sociology raises other problems than history or ethnography. It does not seek to know the passed forms of civilization with the sole end of knowing them and reconstructing them. But rather, like every positive science, it has as its object the explanation of some actual reality which is near to us, and which consequently is capable of affecting our ideas and our acts: this reality is man, and more precisely, the man of to-day, for there is nothing which we are more interested in knowing. Then we are not going to study a very archaic religion simply for the pleasure of telling its peculiarities and its singularities. If we have taken it as the subject of our research, it is because it has seemed to us better adapted than any other to lead to an understanding of the religious nature of man, that is to say, to show us an essential and permanent aspect of humanity.

But this proposition is not accepted before the raising of strong objections. It seems very strange that one must turn back, and be transported to the very beginnings of history, in order to arrive at an understanding of humanity as it is at present. This manner of procedure seems particularly paradoxical in the question which concerns us. In fact, the various religions generally pass as being quite unequal in value and dignity; it is said that they do not all contain the same quota of truth. Then it seems as though one could not compare the highest forms of religious thought with the lowest, without reducing the first to the level of the second. If we admit that the crude cults of the Australian tribes can help us to understand Christianity, for example, is that not supposing that this latter religion proceeds from the same mentality as the former, that it is made up of the same superstitions and rests upon the same errors? This is how the theoretical importance which has sometimes been attributed to primitive religions has come to pass as a sign of a systematic hostility to all religion, which, by prejudging the results of the study, vitiates them in advance.

There is no occasion for asking here whether or not there are scholars who have merited this reproach, and who have made religious history and ethnology a weapon against religion. In any case, a sociologist cannot hold such a point of view. In fact, it is an essential postulate of sociology that a human institution cannot rest upon an error and a lie, without which it could not exist. If it were not founded in the nature of things, it would have encountered in the facts a resistance over which it could never have triumphed. So when we commence the study of primitive religions, it is with the assurance that they hold to reality and express it; this principle will be seen to re-enter again and again in the course of the analyses and discussions which follow, and the reproach which we make against the schools from which we have separated ourselves is that they have ignored it. When only the letter of the formulæ is considered, these religious beliefs and practices undoubtedly seem disconcerting at times, and one is tempted to attribute them to some sort of a deep-rooted error. But one must know how to go underneath the symbol to the reality which it represents and which gives it its meaning. The most barbarous and the most fantastic rites and the strangest myths translate some human need, some aspect of life, either individual or social. The reasons with which the faithful justify them may be, and generally are, erroneous; but the true reasons do not cease to exist, and it is the duty of science to discover them.

In reality, then, there are no religions which are false. All are true in their own fashion; all answer, though in different ways, to the given conditions of human existence. It is undeniably possible to arrange them in a hierarchy. Some can be called superior to others, in the sense that they call into play higher mental functions, that they are richer in ideas and sentiments, that they contain more concepts with fewer sensations and images, and that their arrangement is wiser. But howsoever real this greater complexity and this higher ideality may be, they are not sufficient to place the corresponding religions in different classes. All are religions equally, just as all living beings are equally alive, from the most humble plastids up to man. So when we turn to primitive religions it is not with the idea of depreciating religion in general, for these religions are no less respectable than the others. They respond to the same needs, they play the same rôle, they depend upon the same causes; they can also well serve to show the nature of the religious life, and consequently to resolve the problem which we wish to study.

But why give them a sort of prerogative? Why choose them in preference to all others as the subject of our study? – It is merely for reasons of method.

In the first place, we cannot arrive at an understanding of the most recent religions except by following the manner in which they have been progressively composed in history. In fact, historical analysis is the only means of explanation which it is possible to apply to them. It alone enables us to resolve an institution into its constituent elements, for it shows them to us as they are born in time, one after another. On the other hand, by placing every one of them in the condition where it was born, it puts into our hands the only means we have of determining the causes which gave rise to it. Every time that we undertake to explain something human, taken at a given moment in history – be it a religious belief, a moral precept, a legal principle, an æsthetic style or an economic system – it is necessary to commence by going back to its most primitive and simple form, to try to account for the characteristics by which it was marked at that time, and then to show how it developed and became complicated little by little, and how it became that which it is at the moment in question. One readily understands the importance which the determination of the point of departure has for this series of progressive explanations, for all the others are attached to it [. . .]

The general conclusion of the book which the reader has before him is that religion is something eminently social. Religious representations are collective representations which express collective realities; the rites are a manner of acting which take rise in the midst of the assembled groups and which are destined to excite, maintain or recreate certain mental states in these groups. So if the categories are of religious origin, they ought to participate in this nature common to all religious facts; they too should be social affairs and the product of collective thought. At least – for in the actual condition of our knowledge of these matters, one should be careful to avoid all radical and exclusive statements – it is allowable to suppose that they are rich in social elements [. . .]

The really religious beliefs are always common to a determined group, which makes profession of adhering to them and of practising the rites connected with them. They are not merely received individually by all the members of this group; they are something belonging to the group, and they make its unity. The individuals which compose it feel themselves united to each other by the simple fact that they have a common faith. A society whose members are united by the fact that they think in the same way in regard to the sacred world and its relations with the profane world, and by the fact that they translate these common ideas into common practices, is what is called a Church. In all history, we do not find a single religion without a Church. Sometimes the Church is strictly national, sometimes it passes the frontiers; sometimes it embraces an entire people (Rome, Athens, the Hebrews), sometimes it embraces only a part of them (the Christian societies since the advent of Protestantism); sometimes it is directed by a corps of priests, sometimes it is almost completely devoid of any official directing body.[2] But wherever we observe the religious life, we find that it has a definite group as its foundation. Even the so-called private cults, such as the domestic cult or the cult of a corporation, satisfy this condition; for they are always celebrated by a group, the family or the corporation. Moreover, even these particular religions are ordinarily only special forms of a more general religion which embraces all;[3] these restricted Churches are in reality only chapels of a vaster Church which, by reason of this very extent, merits this name still more.[4]

It is quite another matter with magic. To be sure, the belief in magic is always more or less general; it is very frequently diffused in large masses of the population, and there are even peoples where it has as many adherents as the real religion. But it does not result in binding together those who adhere to it, nor in uniting them into a group leading a common life. *There is no Church of magic.* Between the magician and the individuals, who consult him, as between these individuals themselves, there are no lasting bonds which make them members of the same moral community, comparable to that formed by the believers in the same god or the observers of the same cult. The magician has a clientele and not a Church, and it is very possible that his clients have no other relations between each other, or even do not know each other; even the relations which they have with him are generally accidental and transient; they are just like those of a sick man with his physician. The official and public character with which he is sometimes invested changes nothing in this situation; the fact that he works openly does not unite him more regularly or more durably to those who have recourse to his services.

It is true that in certain cases, magicians form societies among themselves: it happens that they assemble more or less periodically to celebrate certain rites in common; it is well known what a place these assemblies of witches hold in European folk-lore. But it is to be remarked that these associations are in no way indispensable to the working of the magic; they are even rare and rather exceptional. The magician has no need of uniting himself to his fellows to practise his art. More frequently, he is a recluse; in general, far from seeking society, he flees it. 'Even in regard to his colleagues, he always keeps his personal independence.' Religion, on the other hand, is inseparable from the idea of a Church. From this point of view, there is an essential difference between magic and religion. But what is especially important is that when these societies of magic are formed, they do not include all the adherents to magic, but only the magicians, the laymen, if they may be so called, that is to say, those for whose profit the rites are celebrated, in fine, those who represent the worshippers in the regular cults, are excluded. Now the magician is for magic what the priest is for religion, but a college of priests is not a Church, any more than a religious congregation which should devote itself to some particular saint in the shadow of a cloister, would be a particular cult. A Church is not a fraternity of priests; it is a moral community formed by all the believers in a single faith, laymen as well as priests. But magic lacks any such community.

But if the idea of a Church is made to enter into the definition of religion, does that not exclude the private religions which the individual establishes for himself and celebrates by himself? There is scarcely a society where these are not found. Every Ojibway, as we shall see below, has his own personal *manitou*, which he chooses himself and to which he renders special religious services; the Melanesian of the Banks Islands has his *tamaniu*; the Roman, his *genius*; the Christian, his patron saint and guardian angel, etc. By definition all these cults seem to be independent of all idea of the group. Not only are these individual religions very frequent in history, but nowadays many are asking if they are not destined to be the pre-eminent form of the religious life, and if the day will not come when there will be no other cult than that which each man will freely perform within himself.

But if we leave these speculations in regard to the future aside for the moment, and confine ourselves to religions such as they are at present or have been in the past, it becomes clearly evident that these individual cults are not distinct and autonomous religious systems, but merely aspects of the common religion of the whole Church, of which the individuals are members. The patron saint of the Christian is chosen from the official list of saints recognized by the Catholic Church; there are even canonical rules prescribing how each Catholic should perform this private cult. In the same way, the idea that each man necessarily has a protecting genius is found, under different forms, at the basis of a great number of American religions, as well as of the Roman religion (to cite only these two examples); for, as will be seen later, it is very closely connected with the idea of the soul, and this idea of the soul is not one of those which can be left entirely to individual choice. In a word, it is the Church of which he is a member which teaches the individual what these personal gods are, what their function is, how he should enter into relations with them and how he should honour them. When a methodical analysis is made of the doctrines of any Church whatsoever, sooner or later we come upon those concerning private cults. So these are not two religions of different types, and turned in opposite directions; both are made up of the same ideas and the same principles, here applied to circumstances which are of interest to the group as a whole, there to the life of the individual. This solidarity is even so close that among certain peoples, the ceremonies by which the faithful first enter into communication with their protecting geniuses are mixed with rites whose public character is incontestable, namely the rites of initiation.

There still remain those contemporary aspirations towards a religion which would consist entirely in internal and subjective states, and which would be constructed freely by each of us. But howsoever real these aspirations may be, they cannot affect our definition, for this is to be applied only to facts already realized, and not to uncertain possibilities. One can define religions such as they are, or such as they have been, but not such as they more or less vaguely tend to become. It is possible that this religious individualism is destined to be realized in facts; but before we can say just how far this may be the case, we must first know what religion is, of what elements it is made up, from what causes it results, and what function it fulfils – all questions whose solution cannot be foreseen before the threshold of our study has been passed. It is only at the close of this study that we can attempt to anticipate the future.

Thus we arrive at the following definition: *A religion is a unified system of beliefs and practices relative to sacred things, that is to say, things set apart and forbidden – beliefs and practices which unite into one single moral community called a Church, all those who adhere to them.* The second element which thus finds a place in our definition is no less essential than the first; for by showing that the idea of religion is inseparable from that of the Church, it makes it clear that religion should be an eminently collective thing.[5] [. . .]

Since individual totemism is later than the totemism of the clan, and even seems to be derived from it, it is to this latter form that we must turn first of all. But as the analysis which we have just made of it has resolved it into a multiplicity of beliefs which may appear quite heterogeneous, before going farther, we must seek to learn what makes its unity.

We have seen that totemism places the figured representations of the totem in the first rank of the things it considers sacred; next come the animals or vegetables whose name the clan bears, and finally the members of the clan. Since all these things are sacred in the same way, though to different degrees, their religious character can be due to none of the special attributes distinguishing them from each other. If a certain species of animal or vegetable is the object of a reverential fear, this is not because of its special properties, for the human members of the clan enjoy this same privilege, though to a slightly inferior degree, while the mere image of this same plant or animal inspires an even more pronounced respect. The similar sentiments inspired by these different sorts of things in the mind of the believer, which give them their sacred character, can evidently come only from some common principle partaken of alike by the totemic emblems, the men of the clan and the individuals of the species serving as totem. In reality, it is to this common principle that the cult is addressed. In other words, totemism is the religion, not of such and such animals or men or images, but of an anonymous and impersonal force, found in each of these beings but not to be confounded with any of them. No one possesses it entirely and all participate in it. It is so completely independent of the particular subjects in whom it incarnates itself, that it precedes them and survives them. Individuals die, generations pass and are replaced by others; but this force always remains actual, living and the same. It animates the generations of today as it animated those of yesterday and as it will animate those of to-morrow. Taking the words in a large sense, we may say that it is the god adored by each totemic cult. Yet it is an impersonal god, without name or history, immanent in the world and diffused in an innumerable multitude of things.

But even now we have only an imperfect idea of the real ubiquity of this quasi-divine entity. It is not merely found in the whole totemic species, the whole clan and all the objects symbolizing the totem: the circle of its action extends beyond that. In fact, we have seen that in addition to the eminently holy things, all those attributed to the clan as dependencies of the principal totem have this same character to a certain degree. They also have something religious about them, for some are protected by interdictions, while others have determined functions in the ceremonies of the cult. Their religiousness does not differ in kind from that of the totem under which they are classified; it must therefore be derived from the same source. So it is because the totemic god – to use again the metaphorical expression which we have just employed – is in them, just as it is in the species serving as totem and in the men of the clan. We may see how much it differs from the beings in which it resides from the fact that it is the soul of so many different beings.

But the Australian does not represent this impersonal force in an abstract form. Under the influence of causes which we must seek, he has been led to conceive it under the form of an animal or vegetable species, or, in a word, of a visible object. This is what the totem really consists in: it is only the material form under which the imagination represents this immaterial substance, this energy diffused through all sorts of heterogeneous things, which alone is the real object of the cult. We are now in a better condition for understanding what the native means when he says that the men of the Crow phratry, for example, are crows. He does not exactly mean to say that they are crows in the vulgar and empiric sense of the term, but that the same principle is found in all of them, which is their most essential characteristic, which they have in common with the animals of the same name and which is thought of under the external form of a crow. Thus the universe, as totemism conceives it, is filled and animated by a certain number of forces which the imagination represents in forms taken, with only a few exceptions, from the animal or vegetable kingdoms: there are as many of them as there are clans in the tribe and each of them is also found in certain categories of things, of which it is the essence and vital principle.

When we say that these principles are forces, we do not take the word in a metaphorical sense; they act just like veritable forces. In one sense, they are even material forces which mechanically engender physical effects. Does an individual come in contact with them without having taken proper precautions? He receives a shock which might be compared to the effect of an electric discharge. Sometimes they seem to conceive of these as a sort of fluid escaping by points. If they are introduced into an organism not made to receive them, they produce sickness and death by a wholly automatic action. Outside of men, they play the rôle of vital principle; it is by acting on them, we shall see, that the reproduction of the species is assured. It is upon them that the universal life reposes.

But in addition to this physical aspect they also have a moral character. When someone asks a native why he observes his rites, he replies that his ancestors always have observed them, and he ought to follow their example. So if he acts in a certain way towards the totemic beings, it is not only because the forces resident in them are physically redoubtable, but because he feels himself morally obliged to act thus, he has the feeling that he is obeying an imperative, that he is fulfilling a duty. For these sacred beings, he has not merely fear, but also respect. Moreover, the totem is the source of the moral life of the clan. All the beings partaking of the same totemic principle consider that owing to this very fact, they are morally bound to one another; they have definite duties of assistance, vendetta, etc., towards each other; and it is these duties which constitute kinship. So while the totemic principle is a totemic force, it is also a moral power; so we shall see how it easily transforms itself into a divinity properly so-called.

Moreover, there is nothing here which is special to totemism. Even in the most advanced religions, there is scarcely a god who has not kept something of this ambiguity and whose functions are not at once cosmic and moral. At the same time that it is a spiritual discipline, every religion is also a means enabling men to face the world with greater confidence. Even for the Christian, is not God the Father the guardian of the physical order as well as the legislator and the judge of human conduct? [. . .]

It is the figurative representations of this plant or animal and the totemic emblems and symbols of every sort, which have the greatest sanctity; so it is in them that is found the source of that religious nature, of which the real objects represented by these emblems receive only a reflection.

Thus the totem is before all a symbol, a material expression of something else. But of what?

From the analysis to which we have been giving our attention, it is evident that it expresses and symbolizes two different sorts of things. In the first place, it is the outward and visible form of what we have called the totemic principle or god. But it is also the symbol of the determined society called the clan. It is its flag; it is the sign by which each clan distinguishes itself from the others, the visible mark of its personality, a mark borne by everything which is a part of the clan under any title whatsoever, men, beasts or things. So if it is at once the symbol of the god and of the society, is that not because the god and the society are only one? How could the emblem of the group have been able to become the figure of this quasi-divinity, if the group and the divinity were two distinct realities? The god of the clan, the totemic principle, can therefore be nothing else than the clan itself, personified and represented to the imagination under the visible form of the animal or vegetable which serves as totem.

But how has this apotheosis been possible, and how did it happen to take place in this fashion?

In a general way, it is unquestionable that a society has all that is necessary to arouse the sensation of the divine in minds, merely by the power that it has over them; for to its members it is what a god is to his worshippers. In fact, a god is, first of all, a being whom men think of as superior to themselves, and upon whom they feel that they depend. Whether it be a conscious personality, such as Zeus or Jahveh, or merely abstract forces such as those in play in totemism, the worshipper, in the one case as in the other, believes himself held to certain manners of acting which are imposed upon him by the nature of the sacred principle with which he feels that he is in communion. Now society also gives us the sensation of a perpetual dependence. Since it has a nature which is peculiar to itself and different from our individual nature, it pursues ends which are likewise special to it; but, as it cannot attain them except through our intermediacy, it imperiously demands our aid. It requires that, forgetful of our own interests, we make ourselves its servitors, and it submits us to every sort of inconvenience, privation and sacrifice, without which social life would be impossible. It is because of this that at every instant we are obliged to submit ourselves to rules of conduct and of thought which we have neither made nor desired, and which are sometimes even contrary to our most fundamental inclinations and instincts.

Even if society were unable to obtain these concessions and sacrifices from us except by a material constraint, it might awaken in us only the idea of a physical force to which we must give way of necessity, instead of that of a moral power such as religions adore. But as a matter of fact, the empire which it holds over consciences is due much less to the physical supremacy of which it has the privilege than to the moral authority with which it is invested. If we yield to its orders, it is not merely because it is strong enough to triumph over our resistance; it is primarily because it is the object of a venerable respect.

We say that an object, whether individual or collective, inspires respect when the representation expressing it in the mind is gifted with such a force that it automatically causes or inhibits actions, *without regard for any consideration relative to their useful or injurious effects.* When we obey somebody because of the moral authority which we recognize in him, we follow out his opinions, not because they seem wise, but because a certain sort of physical energy is imminent in the idea that we form of this person, which conquers our will and inclines it in the indicated direction. Respect is the emotion which we experience when we feel this interior and wholly spiritual pressure operating upon us. Then we are not determined by the advantages or inconveniences of the attitude which is prescribed or recommended to us; it is by the way in which we represent to ourselves the person recommending or prescribing it. This is why commands generally take a short, peremptory form leaving no place for hesitation; it is because, in so far as it is a command and goes by its own force, it excludes all idea of deliberation or calculation; it gets its efficacy from the intensity of the mental state in which it is placed. It is this intensity which creates what is called a moral ascendancy.

Now the ways of action to which society is strongly enough attached to impose them upon its members, are, by that very fact, marked with a distinctive sign provocative of respect. Since they are elaborated in common, the vigour with which they have been thought of by each particular mind is retained in all the other minds, and reciprocally. The representations which express them within each of us have an intensity which no purely private states of consciousness could ever attain; for they have the strength of the innumerable individual representations which have served to form each of them. It is society who speaks through the mouths of those who affirm them in our presence; it is society whom we hear in hearing them; and the voice of all has an accent which that of one alone could never have. The very violence with which society reacts, by way of blame or material suppression, against every attempted dissidence, contributes to strengthening its empire by manifesting the common conviction through this burst of ardour. In a word, when something is the object of such a state of opinion, the representation which each individual has of it gains a power of action from its origins and the conditions in which it was born, which even those feel who do not submit themselves to it. It tends to repel the representations which contradict it, and it keeps them at a distance; on the other hand, it commands those acts which will realize it, and it does so, not by a material coercion or by the perspective of something of this sort, but by the simple radiation of the mental energy which it contains. It has an efficacy coming solely from its psychical properties, and it is by just this sign that moral authority is recognized. So opinion, primarily a social thing, is a source of authority, and it might even be asked whether all authority is not the daughter of opinion.[6] It may be objected that science is often the antagonist of opinion, whose errors it combats and rectifies. But it cannot succeed in this task if it does not have sufficient authority, and it can obtain this authority only from opinion itself. If a people did not have faith in science, all the scientific demonstrations in the world would be without any influence whatsoever over their minds. Even to-day, if science happened to resist a very strong current of public opinion, it would risk losing its credit there.[7]

Since it is in spiritual ways that social pressure exercises itself, it could not fail to give men the idea that outside themselves there exist one or several powers, both moral and, at the same time, efficacious, upon which they depend. They must think of these powers, at least in part, as outside themselves, for these address them in a tone of command and sometimes even order them to do violence to their most natural inclinations. It is undoubtedly true that if they were able to see that these influences which they feel emanate from society, then the mythological system of interpretations would never be born. But social action follows ways that are too circuitous and obscure, and employs psychical mechanisms that are too complex to allow the ordinary observer to see whence it comes. As long as scientific analysis does not come to teach it to them, men know well that they are acted upon, but they do not know by whom. So they must invent by themselves the idea of these powers with which they feel themselves in connection, and from that, we are able to catch a glimpse of the way by which they were led to represent them under forms that are really foreign to their nature and to transfigure them by thought.

But a god is not merely an authority upon whom we depend; it is a force upon which our strength relies. The man who has obeyed his god and who, for this reason, believes the god is with him, approaches the world with confidence and with the feeling of an increased energy. Likewise, social action does not confine itself to demanding sacrifices, privations and efforts from us. For the collective force is not entirely outside of us; it does not act upon us wholly from without; but rather, since society cannot exist except in and through individual consciousnesses,[8] this force must also penetrate us and organize itself within us; it thus becomes an integral part of our being and by that very fact this is elevated and magnified [. . .]

We have shown how the clan, by the manner in which it acts upon its members, awakens within them the idea of external forces which dominate them and exalt them; but we must still demand how it happens that these forces are thought of under the form of totems, that is to say, in the shape of an animal or plant.

It is because this animal or plant has given its name to the clan and serves it as emblem. In fact, it is a well-known law that the sentiments aroused in us by something spontaneously attach themselves to the symbol which represents them. For us, black is a sign of mourning; it also suggests sad impressions and ideas. This transference of sentiments comes simply from the fact that the idea of a thing and the idea of its symbol are closely united in our minds; the result is that the emotions provoked by the one extend contagiously to the other. But this contagion, which takes place in every case to a certain degree, is much more complete and more marked when the symbol is something simple, definite and easily representable, while the thing itself, owing to its dimensions, the number of its parts and the complexity of their arrangement, is difficult to hold in the mind. For we are unable to consider an abstract entity, which we can represent only laboriously and confusedly, the source of the strong sentiments which we feel. We cannot explain them to ourselves except by connecting them to some concrete object of whose reality we are vividly aware. Then if the thing itself does not fulfil this condition, it cannot serve as the accepted basis of the sentiments felt, even though it may be what really aroused them. Then some sign takes its place; it is to this that we connect the emotions it excites. It is this which is loved, feared, respected; it is to this that we are grateful; it is for this that we sacrifice ourselves. The soldier who dies for his flag, dies for his country; but as a matter of fact, in his own consciousness, it is the flag that has the first place. It sometimes happens that this even directly determines action. Whether one isolated standard remains in the hands of the enemy or not does not determine the fate of the country, yet the soldier allows himself to be killed to regain it. He loses sight of the fact that the flag is only a sign, and that it has no value in itself, but only brings to mind the reality that it represents; it is treated as if it were this reality itself.

Now the totem is the flag of the clan. It is therefore natural that the impressions aroused by the clan in individual minds – impressions of dependence and of increased vitality – should fix themselves to the idea of the totem rather than that of the clan: for the clan is too complex a reality to be represented clearly in all its complex unity by such rudimentary intelligences. More than that, the primitive does not even see that these impressions come to him from the group. He does not know that the coming together of a number of men associated in the same life results in disengaging new energies, which transform each of them. All that he knows is that he is raised above himself and that he sees a different life from the one he ordinarily leads. However, he must connect these sensations to some external object as their cause. Now what does he see about him? On every side those things which appeal to his senses and strike his imagination are the numerous images of the totem. They are the waninga and the nurtunja, which are symbols of the sacred being. They are churinga and bull-roarers, upon which are generally carved combinations of lines having the same significance. They are the decorations covering the different parts of his body, which are totemic marks. How could this image, repeated everywhere and in all sorts of forms, fail to stand out with exceptional relief in his mind? Placed thus in the centre of the scene, it becomes representative. The sentiments experienced fix themselves upon it, for it is the only concrete object upon which they can fix themselves. It continues to bring them to mind and to evoke them even after the assembly has dissolved, for it survives the assembly, being carved upon the instruments of the cult, upon the sides of rocks, upon bucklers, etc. By it, the emotions experienced are perpetually sustained and revived. Everything happens just as if they inspired them directly. It is still more natural to attribute them to it for, since they are common to the group, they can be associated only with something that is equally common to all. Now the totemic emblem is the only thing satisfying this condition. By definition, it is common to all. During the ceremony, it is the centre of all regards. While generations change, it remains the same; it is the permanent element of the social life. So it is from it that those mysterious forces seem to emanate with which men feel that they are related, and thus they have been led to represent these forces under the form of the animate or inanimate being whose name the clan bears.

When this point is once established, we are in a position to understand all that is essential in the totemic beliefs.

Since religious force is nothing other than the collective and anonymous force of the clan, and since this can be represented in the mind only in the form of the totem, the totemic emblem is like the visible body of the god. Therefore, it is from it that those kindly or dreadful actions seem to emanate, which the cult seeks to provoke or prevent; consequently, it is to it that the cult is addressed. This is the explanation of why it holds the first place in the series of sacred things.

But the clan, like every other sort of society, can live only in and through the individual consciousnesses that compose it. So if religious force, in so far as it is conceived as incorporated in the totemic emblem, appears to be outside of the individuals and to be endowed with a sort of transcendence over them, it, like the clan of which it is the symbol, can be realized only in and through them; in this sense, it is imminent in them and they necessarily represent it as such. They feel it present and active within them, for it is this which raises them to a superior life. This is why men have believed that they contain within them a principle comparable to the one residing in the totem, and consequently, why they have attributed a sacred character to themselves, but one less marked than that of the emblem [. . .]

At the beginning of this work, we said that all the essential elements of religious thought and life ought to be found, at least in germ, in the most primitive religions: the preceding facts confirm this assertion. If there is any one belief which is believed to be peculiar to the most recent and idealistic religions, it is the one attributing a sanctifying power to sorrow. Now this same belief is at the basis of the rites which have just been observed. Of course, it is understood differently at the different moments of history when it is studied. For the Christian, it acts especially upon the soul: it purges it, ennobles it, spiritualizes it. For the Australian, it is the body over which it is efficient: it increases its vital energies; it makes its beard and hair grow; it toughens its members. But in both cases the principle is the same. In both it is admitted that suffering creates exceptional strength. And this belief is not without foundation. In fact, it is by the way in which he braves suffering that the greatness of a man is best manifested. He never rises above himself with more brilliancy than when he subdues his own nature to the point of making it follow a way contrary to the one it would spontaneously take. By this, he distinguishes himself from all the other creatures who follow blindly wherever pleasure calls them; by this, he makes a place apart for himself in the world. Suffering is the sign that certain of the bonds attaching him to his profane environment are broken; so it testifies that he is partially freed from this environment, and, consequently, it is justly considered the instrument of deliverance. So he who is thus delivered is not the victim of a pure illusion when he believes himself invested with a sort of mastery over things: he really has raised himself above them, by the very act of renouncing them; he is stronger than nature, because he makes it subside [. . .]

Having determined what the system of interdicts consists in and what its positive and negative functions are, we must now seek the causes which have given it birth.

In one sense, it is logically implied in the very notion of sacredness. All that is sacred is the object of respect, and every sentiment of respect is translated, in him who feels it, by movements of inhibition. In fact, a respected being is always expressed in the consciousness by a representation which, owing to the emotion it inspires, is charged with a high mental energy; consequently, it is armed in such a way as to reject to a distance every other representation which denies it in whole or in part. Now the sacred world and the profane world are antagonistic to each other. They correspond to two forms of life which mutually exclude one another, or which at least cannot be lived at the same time with the same intensity. We cannot give ourselves up entirely to the ideal beings to whom the cult is addressed and also to ourselves and our own interests at the same time; we cannot devote ourselves entirely to the group and entirely to our own egoism at once. Here there are two systems of conscious states which are directed and which direct our conduct towards opposite poles. So the one having the greater power of action should tend to exclude the other from the consciousness. When we think of holy things, the idea of a profane object cannot enter the mind without encountering grave resistance; something within us opposes itself to its installation. This is because the representation of a sacred thing does not tolerate neighbours. But this psychic antagonism and this mutual exclusion of ideas should naturally result in the exclusion of the corresponding things. If the ideas are not to coexist, the things must not touch each other or have any sort of relations. This is the very principle of the interdict.

Moreover, the world of sacred things is, by definition, a world apart. Since it is opposed to the profane world by all the characteristics we have mentioned, it must be treated in its own peculiar way: it would be a misunderstanding of its nature and a confusion of it with something that it is not, to make use of the gestures, language and attitudes which we employ in our relations with ordinary things, when we have to do with the things that compose it. We may handle the former freely; we speak freely to vulgar beings; so we do not touch the sacred beings, or we touch them only with reserve; we do not speak in their presence, or we do not speak the common language there. All that is used in our commerce with the one must be excluded from our commerce with the other.

But if this explanation is not inexact, it is, nevertheless, insufficient. In fact, there are many beings which are the objects of respect without being protected by systems of rigorous interdictions such as those we have just described. Of course there is a general tendency of the mind to localize different things in different places, especially when they are incompatible with each other. But the profane environment and the sacred one are not merely distinct, but they are also closed to one another; between them there is an abyss. So there ought to be some particular reason in the nature of sacred things, which causes this exceptional isolation and mutual exclusion. And, in fact, by a sort of contradiction, the sacred world is inclined, as it were, to spread itself into this same profane world which it excludes elsewhere: at the same time that it repels it, it tends to flow into it as soon as it approaches. This is why it is necessary to keep them at a distance from one another and to create a sort of vacuum between them.

What makes these precautions necessary is the extraordinary contagiousness of a sacred character. Far from being attached to the things which are marked with it, it is endowed with a sort of elusiveness. Even the most superficial or roundabout contact is sufficient to enable it to spread from one object to another. Religious forces are represented in the mind in such a way that they always seem ready to escape from the points where they reside and to enter everything passing within their range. The nanja tree where the spirit of an ancestor lives is sacred for the individual who considers himself the reincarnation of this ancestor. But every bird which alights upon this tree participates in this same nature: it is also forbidden to touch it. We have already had occasion to show how simple contact with a churinga is enough to sanctify men and things; it is also upon this principle of the contagiousness of sacredness that all the rites of consecration repose. The sanctity of the churinga is so great that its action is even felt at a distance. It will be remembered how this extends not only to the cave where they are kept, but also to the whole surrounding district, to the animals who take refuge there, whom it is forbidden to kill, and to the plants which grow there, which must not be touched. A snake totem has its centre at a place where there is a water-hole. The sacred character of the totem is communicated to this place, to the water-hole and even to the water itself, which is forbidden to all the members of the totemic group. The initiate lives in an atmosphere charged with religiousness, and it is as though he were impregnated with it himself. Consequently all that he possesses and all that he touches is forbidden to the women, and withdrawn from their contact, even down to the bird he has struck with his stick, the kangaroo he has pierced with his lance or the fish which has bit on his hook. But, on the other hand, the rites to which he is submitted and the things which have a part in them have a sanctity superior to his own: this sanctity is contagiously transmitted to everything which evokes the idea of one or the other. The tooth which has been knocked out of him is considered very holy. For this reason, he may not eat animals with prominent teeth, because they make him think of his own lost tooth. The ceremonies of the Kuringal terminate with a ritual washing; aquatic birds are forbidden to the neophyte because they make him think of this rite. Animals that climb to the tops of trees are equally sacred for him, because they are too near to Daramulun, the god of the initiation, who lives in heaven. The soul of a dead man is a sacred thing: we have already seen how this same property passes to the corpse in which the soul resided, to the spot where this is buried, to the camp in which he lived when alive, and which is either destroyed or quitted, to the name he bore, to his wife and to his relations. They, too, are invested, as it were, with a sacred character; consequently, men keep at a distance from them; they do not treat them as mere profane beings. In the societies observed by Dawson, their names, like that of the dead man, cannot be pronounced during the period of mourning. Certain animals which he ate may also be prohibited.

This contagiousness of sacredness is too well known a phenomenon to require any proof of its existence from numerous examples; we only wish to show that it is as true in totemism as in the more advanced religions. When once established, it quickly explains the extreme rigour of the interdicts separating the sacred from the profane. Since, in virtue of this extraordinary power of expansion, the slightest contact, the least proximity, either material or simply moral, suffices to draw religious forces out of their domain, and since, on the other hand, they cannot leave it without contradicting their nature, a whole system of measures is indispensable for maintaining the two worlds at a respectful distance from one another. This is why it is forbidden to the profane, not only to touch, but even to see or hear that which is sacred, and why these two sorts of life cannot be mixed in their consciousnesses. Precautions are necessary to keep them apart because, though opposing one another, they tend to confuse themselves into one another.

When we understand the multiplicity of these interdicts we also understand the way in which they operate and the sanctions which are attached to them. Owing to the contagiousness inherent in all that is sacred, a profane being cannot violate an interdict without having the religious force, to which he has unduly approached, extend itself over him and establish its empire over him. But as there is an antagonism between them, he becomes dependent upon a hostile power, whose hostility cannot fail to manifest itself in the form of violent reactions which tend to destroy him. This is why sickness or death are considered the natural consequences of every transgression of this sort; and they are consequences which are believed to come by themselves, with a sort of physical necessity. The guilty man feels himself attacked by a force which dominates him and against which he is powerless. Has he eaten the totemic animal? Then he feels it penetrating him and gnawing at his vitals; he lies down on the ground and awaits death. Every profanation implies a consecration, but one which is dreadful, both for the subject consecrated and for those who approach him. It is the consequences of this consecration which sanction, in part, the interdict.

It should be noticed that this explanation of the interdicts does not depend upon the variable symbols by the aid of which religious forces are conceived. It matters little whether these are conceived as anonymous and impersonal energies or figured as personalities endowed with consciousness and feeling. In the former case, of course, they are believed to react against profaning transgressions in an automatic and unconscious manner, while in the latter case, they are thought to obey passionate movements determined by the offence resented. But at bottom, these two conceptions, which, moreover, have the same practical effect, only express one and the same psychic mechanism in two different languages. The basis of both is the antagonism of the sacred and the profane, combined with the remarkable aptitude of the former for spreading over to the latter; now this antagonism and this contagiousness act in the same way, whether the sacred character is attributed to blind forces or to conscious ones. Thus, so far is it from being true that the real religious life commences only where there are mythical personalities, that we see that in this case the rite remains the same, whether the religious beings are personified or not. This is a statement which we shall have occasion to repeat in each of the chapters which follow [. . .]

Thus there is something eternal in religion which is destined to survive all the particular symbols in which religious thought has successively enveloped itself. There can be no society which does not feel the need of upholding and reaffirming at regular intervals the collective sentiments and the collective ideas which make its unity and its personality. Now this moral remaking cannot be achieved except by the means of reunions, assemblies and meetings where the individuals, being closely united to one another, reaffirm in common their common sentiments; hence come ceremonies which do not differ from regular religious ceremonies, either in their object, the results which they produce, or the processes employed to attain these results. What essential difference is there between an assembly of Christians celebrating the principal dates of the life of Christ, or of Jews remembering the exodus from Egypt or the promulgation of the decalogue, and a reunion of citizens commemorating the promulgation of a new moral or legal system or some great event in the national life?

Notes

1. In the same way, we shall say of these societies that they are primitive, and we shall call the men of these societies primitives. Undoubtedly the expression lacks precision, but that is hardly evitable, and besides, when we have taken pains to fix the meaning, it is not inconvenient.
2. Undoubtedly it is rare that a ceremony does not have some director at the moment when it is celebrated; even in the most crudely organized societies, there are generally certain men whom the importance of their social position points out to exercise a directing influence over the religious life (for example, the chiefs of the local groups of certain Australian societies). But this attribution of functions is still very uncertain.
3. At Athens, the gods to whom the domestic cult was addressed were only specialized forms of the gods of the city (Ζεύς κτήδιος, Ζεύς ἐρκεὶος). In the same way, in the Middle Ages, the patrons of the guilds were saints of the calendar.
4. For the name Church is ordinarily applied only to a group whose common beliefs refer to a circle of more special affairs.
5. It is by this that our present definition is connected to the one we have already proposed in the *Année Sociologique*. In this other work, we defined religious beliefs exclusively by their obligatory character; but, as we shall show, this obligation evidently comes from the fact that these beliefs are the possession of a group which imposes them upon its members. The two definitions are thus in a large part the same. If we have thought it best to propose a new one, it is because the first was too formal, and neglected the contents of the religious representations too much. It will be seen, in the discussions which follow, how important it is to put this characteristic into evidence at once. Moreover, if their imperative character is really a distinctive trait of religious beliefs, it allows of an infinite number of degrees; consequently there are even cases where it is not easily perceptible. Hence come difficulties and embarrassments which are avoided by substituting for this criterium the one we now employ.
6. This is the case at least with all moral authority recognized as such by the group as a whole.
7. We hope that this analysis and those which follow will put an end to an inexact interpretation of our thought, from which more than one misunderstanding has resulted. Since we have made constraint the *outward sign* by which social facts can be the most easily recognized and distinguished from the fact of individual psychology, it has been assumed that according to our opinion, physical constraint is the essential thing for social life. As a matter of fact, we have never considered it more than the material and apparent expression of an interior and profound fact which is wholly ideal: this is *moral authority*. The problem of sociology – if we can speak of *a* sociological problem – consists in seeking, among the different forms of external constraint, the different sorts of moral authority corresponding to them and in discovering the causes which have determined these latter. The particular question which we are treating in this present work has as its principal object, the discovery of the form under which that particular variety of moral authority which is inherent in all that is religious has been born, and out of what elements it is made. It will be seen presently that even if we do make social pressure one of the distinctive characteristics of sociological phenomena, we do not mean to say that it is the only one. We shall show another aspect of the collective life, nearly opposite to the preceding one, but none the less real.
8. Of course this does not mean to say that the collective consciousness does not have distinctive characteristics of its own.

Guide To Further Reading

[The original date of publication is given in brackets where appropriate]

The Division of Labour in Society (Macmillan: London, 1984) [1893]

The Rules of Sociological Method (The Free Press: New York, 1966) [1895]

Suicide: A Study in Sociology (The Free Press: New York, 1958) [1897]

'On Totemism', *The History of Sociology* 5 (Spring) 1985 91–122 [1902]

(with M. Mauss) *Primitive Classification* (University of Chicago Press: Chicago, 1963) [1903]

The Elementary Forms of the Religious Life (Allen and Unwin: London, 1971) [1912]

Emile Durkheim: Selected Writings (A. Giddens ed., Cambridge University Press: Cambridge, 1972)

Durkheim's main books *The Division of Labour* (the 1984 Macmillan edition with an introduction by Lewis Coser is recommended), *The Rules of Sociological Method* (especially the 1982 Macmillan edition which contains additional writings on sociology and method and a good introductory essay by Steven Lukes), *Suicide* and *The Elementary Forms of the Religious Life* – probably in that order – are all essential reading and more accessible than might be imagined, with the possible exception of the latter. If going straight to Durkheim's texts is too daunting a prospect then there are a host of works about Durkheim – most of them, confusingly, called *Emile Durkheim*! Steven Lukes' *Emile Durkheim: His Life and Work* (Penguin: London, 1973) is probably the classic work on Durkheim and is at the same time a fascinating biography and a brilliant critical analysis of his work and thought. Far shorter and worth reading are Kenneth Thompson's excellent *Emile Durkheim* (Tavistock: London, 1982); R. A. Jones' *Emile Durkheim: An Introduction to Four Major Works* (Sage: London, 1986) and Anthony Giddens' *Durkheim* (Fontana: London, 1978). Giddens' *Emile Durkheim: Selected writings* (Cambridge University Press, 1972) is a useful collection and the editor's introductory essay is excellent. *The Foundation of Sociological Theory* (Random House: New York, 1970) by Theodore Abel is useful and also contains discussions of Weber. W. S. F. Pickering's *Durkheim's Sociology of Religion* (Routledge: London, 1984) is a comprehensive treatment of Durkheim on religion which unfortunately actually manages to be longer than *The Elementary Forms of the Religious Life*!

COPYRIGHT ACKNOWLEDGEMENTS

Grateful acknowledgement is made to the following sources for permission to reproduce material in this book previously published elsewhere. Every effort has been made to trace copyright holders, but if any have been inadvertently overlooked the publisher will be pleased to make the necessary acknowledgement at the first opportunity.

Section One: Karl Marx

'Alienated Labour', from *Karl Marx: Selected Writings*, ed. D. McLellan, Oxford University Press, 1977. © David McLellan 1977. Reprinted with the permission of Oxford University Press.

'Theses on Feuerbach', from *Karl Marx: Selected Writings*, ed. D. McLellan, Oxford University Press, 1977. © David McLellan 1977. Reprinted with the permission of Oxford University Press.

The German Ideology, from *The German Ideology: Students Edition*, ed. C. J. Arthur, Lawrence and Wishart, 1970. Reprinted with the permission of Lawrence and Wishart.

The Communist Manifesto, from *Karl Marx: Selected Writings*, ed. D. McLellan, Oxford University Press, 1977. © David McLellan 1977. Reprinted with the permission of Oxford University Press.

'Wage Labour and Capital', from *Selected Works*, by K. Marx and F. Engels, Lawrence and Wishart, 1968. Reprinted with the permission of Lawrence and Wishart.

Preface to *A Critique of Political Economy*, from *Karl Marx: Selected Writings*, ed. D. McLellan, Oxford University Press, 1977. © David McLellan 1977. Reprinted with the permission of Oxford University Press.

'The Fetishism of Commodities', from *Karl Marx: Selected Writings*, ed. D. McLellan, Oxford University Press, 1977. © David McLellan 1977. Reprinted with the permission of Oxford University Press.

'The So-called Primitive Accumulation', from *Capital, Volume One*, by K. Marx, Lawrence and Wishart, 1954. Reprinted with the permission of Lawrence and Wishart.

'Letter to Annenkov', from *Selected Works*, by K. Marx and F. Engels, Lawrence and Wishart, 1968. Reprinted with the permission of Lawrence and Wishart.

'Letter to Weydemyer', from *Selected Works*, by K. Marx and F. Engels, Lawrence and Wishart, 1968. Reprinted with the permission of Lawrence and Wishart.

'Letter to Mikhailovski', from *Karl Marx: Selected Writings*, ed. D. McLellan, Oxford University Press, 1977. © David McLellan 1977. Reprinted with the permission of Oxford University Press.

Section Two: Max Weber

The Protestant Ethic and the Spirit of Capitalism, from *The Protestant Ethic and the Spirit of Capitalism*, by M. Weber, translated by T. Parsons, Allen and Unwin, 1978. Reprinted with the permission of Routledge, Chapman and Hall Ltd.

'Class, Status and Party', from *From Max Weber: Essays in Sociology*, ed. H. H. Gerth and C. Wright Mills, Routledge, 1991. © Reprinted with the permission of Oxford University Press.

'Bureaucracy', from *From Max Weber: Essays in Sociology*, ed. H. H. Gerth and C. Wright Mills, Routledge, 1991. © Reprinted with the permission of Oxford University Press.

'Science as a Vocation', from *From Max Weber: Essays in Sociology*, ed. H. H. Gerth and C. Wright Mills, Routledge, 1991. © Reprinted with the permission of Oxford University Press.

'Definitions of Sociology and Social Action', from *Max Weber: The Theory of Social and Economic Organisation*, by M. Weber, translated by A. M. Henderson and T. Parsons, ed. T. Parsons, The

Free Press, 1964. Reprinted with the permission of The Free Press, an imprint of Simon & Schuster Inc. Copyright © 1947, renewed 1975 by T. Parsons.

'Legitimacy and Authority', from *From Max Weber: Essays in Sociology*, ed. H. H. Gerth and C. Wright Mills, Routledge, 1970 and *Max Weber: The Theory of Social and Economic Organisation*, by M. Weber, translated by A. M. Henderson and T. Parsons, ed. T. Parsons, The Free Press, 1964. © Reprinted with the permission of Oxford University Press a:.d The Free Press, an imprint of Simon & Schuster Inc. Copyright © 1947, renewed 1975 by T. Parsons.

Section Three: Emile Durkheim

Introduction to *The Division of Labour in Society*, from *The Division of Labour in Society* by E. Durkheim, translated by W. D. Halls, introduced by L. A. Coser, Macmillan, 1984. Reprinted with the permission of Macmillan Press Ltd and The Free Press, an imprint of Simon & Schuster Inc. Copyright © 1984 by Higher and Further Education Division, Macmillan Publishers Ltd. Introduction copyright © 1984 by L. A. Coser. Copyright © by The Free Press.

'Sanctions and Mechanical and Organic Solidarity', from *Emile Durkheim: Selected Writings*, ed. Anthony Giddens, Cambridge University Press, 1972. Reprinted with the permission of Cambridge University Press.

'The Division of Labour: Causes and Abnormal Forms', from *The Division of Labour in Society* by E. Durkheim, translated by W. D. Halls, introduced by L. A. Coser, Macmillan, 1984. Reprinted with the permission of Macmillan Press Ltd and The Free Press, an imprint of Simon & Schuster Inc. Copyright © 1984 by Higher and Further Education Division, Macmillan Publishers Ltd. Introduction copyright © 1984 by L. A. Coser. Copyright © by The Free Press.

The Rules of Sociological Method, from *The Rules of Sociological Method*, by E. Durkheim, translated by S. A. Solovay and J. H. Mueller, ed. G. E. G. Catlin, The Free Press, 1966. Reprinted with the permission of The Free Press, an imprint of Simon & Schuster Inc. Copyright © 1938 by G. E. G. Catlin; copyright renewed 1966 by S. A. Solovay, J. H. Mueller and G. E. G. Catlin.

Suicide: A Study in Sociology, from *Suicide: A Study in Sociology*, by E. Durkheim, translated by J. A. Spalding and G. Simpson, The Free Press, 1958. Reprinted with the permission of Routledge, Chapman and Hall Ltd and The Free Press, an imprint of Simon & Schuster Inc. Copyright © 1950, 1978 by The Free Press.

'Religion and Society', from *The Elementary Forms of Religious Life*, by E. Durkheim, translated by J. Ward Swain, Allen and Unwin, 1971. Reprinted with the permission of Routledge, Chapman and Hall Ltd and The Free Press, an imprint of Simon & Schuster Inc. Copyright © 1965 by the Free Press.

INDEX